D1599770

NEOAVANGUARDIA:
ITALIAN EXPERIMENTAL LITERATURE AND ARTS IN THE 1960S

EDITED BY PAOLO CHIRUMBOLO,
MARIO MORONI, AND LUCA SOMIGLI

NEOAVANGUARDIA

Italian Experimental Literature and Arts in the 1960s

UNIVERSITY OF TORONTO PRESS
Toronto Buffalo London

Toronto Buffalo London
www.utppublishing.com
Printed in Canada

ISBN 978-0-8020-9998-3

Printed on acid-free, 100% post-consumer recycled paper with vegetable-based inks.

Toronto Italian Studies

Library and Archives Canada Cataloguing in Publication

Neoavanguardia : Italian experimental literature and arts in the 1960s / edited by Paolo Chirumbolo, Mario Moroni, and Luca Somigli.

(Toronto Italian Studies)
Includes bibliographical references.
ISBN 978-0-8020-9998-3

1. Italian literature – 20th century – History and criticism. 2. Literature, Experimental – History and criticism. 3. Gruppo 63. 4. Arts – Experimental methods. I. Chirumbolo, Paolo II. Moroni, Mario, 1955– III. Somigli, Luca IV. Series: Toronto Italian Studies.

PQ4088.N452 2010 850.9′0091 C2010-902178-9

This book has been published with the aid of a grant from Victoria University, University of Toronto.

University of Toronto Press acknowledges the financial assistance to its publishing program of the Canada Council for the Arts and the Ontario Arts Council.

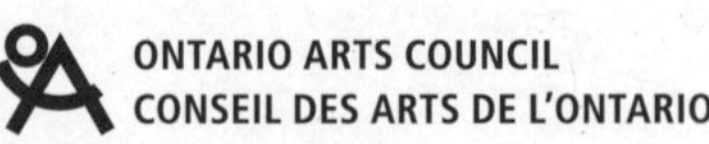

University of Toronto Press acknowledges the financial support for its publishing activities of the Government of Canada through the Canada Book Fund.

Contents

NEOAVANGUARDIA:
ITALIAN EXPERIMENTAL LITERATURE AND ARTS IN THE 1960S

Literature and the Arts in the 1960s: An Introduction

PAOLO CHIRUMBOLO AND MARIO MORONI

In October 1963, thirty-four Italian writers, poets, critics, artists, and composers gathered in Palermo and founded the Gruppo 63. This meeting was the official birth of the Italian *neoavanguardia*, a literary and artistic movement that provoked a cultural turmoil at the time, and contributed to stir the Italian intellectual scene from the stagnant condition that had characterized the cultural discourses and creative practices of the 1950s. There were four subsequent meetings of the group: in Reggio Emilia, 1–3 November 1964; in Palermo, 3–6 September 1965, where discussion was devoted entirely to the experimental novel; in La Spezia, 10–12 June 1966; and lastly in Fano, 26–28 May 1967. Although these five *incontri* [meetings] remain among the most celebrated and exciting cultural events of the 1960s, any historicizing of the *neoavanguardia* cannot be limited to those four years (1963–7). On the contrary, to speak of the *neoavanguardia* phenomenon in general is to take into consideration (as Barilli does in his monographic study) a period extending from the publication of Sanguineti's *Laborintus* and the foundation of *Il verri* in 1956 to the last issue of *Quindici*, the journal seen as the 'official' voice of the group, in July 1969.

Neoavanguardia in/and North America

The main scope of our endeavour is to enhance and promote in the Anglo-American context the critical debate about the controversial literary experience of the *neoavanguardia*. In fact, as far as scholarship in the English-speaking world is concerned very little has been produced. Furthermore, the focus has always been on literature, and particularly on poetry. Whereas in Italy the literary production of the *neoavanguardia* has received a great deal of critical consideration, the same cannot be said of the Anglo-American academic world.[1] As John Picchione maintains in *The New Avant-garde in Italy,* the theoretical positions of its main protagonists are 'virtually unknown beyond a restricted circle of Italianists' (vii). In this regard, it should be noted that the first translation of *I novissimi* (1961), the historical anthology of neo-avant-garde poets, was not published in the United States until 1995, and that both the translation of *I novissimi* and Picchione's study (the only two significant, book-length contributions on the *neoavanguardia* in English) are limited to what we have already defined as the literary side of the movement.

To explain the belated translation of this seminal text of the Italian *neoavanguardia,* it is necessary to provide a brief historical and theoretical account, beginning with a telling anecdote. In 1987 critic and translator Lawrence R. Smith met Geoffrey Hartman in Bologna and mentioned the existence of the *neoavanguardia.* Smith recalls this episode:

> In the summer of 1987, I attended a pair of lectures delivered by Geoffrey Hartman at the University of Bologna. Just before the second lecture, I chatted with him, and suggested that some of the statements he made in his first lecture might have to be modified in the light of what is now being called the 'New Modern.' When I spoke of the Italian avant-garde, he seemed surprised, and said he wasn't aware that there was one. [...] Then Hartman said, why don't people tell me these things? (Smith 169–70)

The fact that Hartman acknowledged being totally unaware of this movement and of its importance in the Italian and European scene of the 1960s is extremely significant since he and the other Yale critics, were, ironically, quite interested in the works of the 1960s French group *Tel Quel.* This latter group was indebted to *I novissimi* in terms of linguistic experimentation and theoretical formulations.

We believe that the reception of the Italian *neoavanguardia* in the United States is only one aspect of a more complex issue. First, in the past, various trends of American literary criticism, following the New Criticism, were reluctant to grant credit to any avant-garde movement after the Second World War, including not only those originating in Europe but also those that developed within the United States. As far as Europe was concerned, the New Critics granted credit only to French modernism (from Rimbaud to surrealism). This preference was due to the fact that French was for a long time the most studied foreign language in the

American academia. It was in this context that the Yale school developed an interest in *Tel Quel*.

The other problem concerning the reception of the *neoavanguardia* in the United States is more theoretical. Historically, American literary criticism seems to have created a view of modernism that we would define as 'neutralized,' in which literary and artistic phenomena are emptied of any cultural, political, and historical tension and implications. It becomes clear that on the basis of this 'neutralization,' American criticism in the 1950s and later looked with diffidence to European forms of avant-garde (including the Italian *neoavanguardia*) whose cultural projects were, in fact, characterized by a high level of political commitment, which took the form of critique of the very linguistic structures that lay behind the circulation of discourses of power. Furthermore, because these European movements tended to associate themselves with leftist politics, it was difficult for liberal but still anticommunist American critics to accept politicized forms of avant-garde. As Smith argues:

> North Americans have suffered, and obviously continue to suffer, under the power of that old New Criticism, even though few would openly profess its obsolete aesthetics today. This conservative force in criticism, from the thirties until now, has kept from the readers at large, and to some extent writers as well, the necessary connection between political radicalism, cultural revolution, and the avant-garde. What better antidote to this misunderstanding than an examination of texts from the *novissimi* discussed in their historical context? (171)

In the case of the *neoavanguardia*, a very good example of the abovementioned implications of these movements vis-a-vis the American critical approach, remains the notion of a 'poetica schizomorfa' [poetics of schizomorphism], as theorized by the poet Alfredo Giuliani in the anthology *I novissimi*. This notion represented a radical departure from the notion of schizophrenia developed within the American modern poetic tradition. American readers of poetry have usually identified mental illness as a symptom of individual creative pathologies, as in the cases of such prominent poets as Robert Lowell, Silvia Plath, and Anne Sexton. Giuliani and *I novissimi* proposed instead a notion of schizophrenia understood as a historical category, the aim of which was to emphasize the drastic break of the relationship between the individual/historic subject and reality in its political, ideological, and linguistic spheres. In the case of language, schizomorphism was practiced by the *novissimi* in the form of an actual 'schizofasia linguistica' [linguistic schizophasia]. In this scenario, the schizoid condition theorized by Giuliani appears for what it really is: a programmatic choice, a deliberate cultural strategy for a critique of the ideological and linguistic institutions of those times.

An Interdisciplinary Perspective

Deeply affected by Luciano Anceschi's phenomenological and interdisciplinary outlook, and by the foundation of the influential journal *Il verri*, the young *neoavanguardisti* were from the outset encouraged to pursue a 'nuova idea di letteratura' [new idea of literature], and to experiment and dialogue with different art forms, including music, visual arts, cinema, and theatre. We are certainly aware of the fact that the Italian *neoavanguardia* was predominantly literary. However, because of the widespread effect of such fundamental notions as '*opera aperta*' [open work], as theorized by Umberto Eco, and of the phenomenological 'riduzione dell'io' [reduction of the self] on all artistic languages of the 1960s, it is our intention to investigate the *neoavanguardia* as an overall interdisciplinary cultural phenomenon.

During the celebration of the fortieth anniversary of Gruppo 63, for instance, one panel in the conference, significantly titled 'Il Gruppo 63 e le arti' [Group 63 and the Arts], was devoted to the interdisciplinary aspect of the movement.[2] Those present at this session, which aimed at underlining the theoretical and formal 'vicinanza' [proximity] between literature and other forms of expression, included art critic Gillo Dorfles, architect Vittorio Gregotti, and playwright Luigi Gozzi. One goal of our collection is to take this significant feature of the *neoavanguardia* into account. Thus we devote the final section of the book – 'Beyond Literature' – to discussion of this topic. To date, there is almost nothing written in Italy or elsewhere about this interaction among the arts during the 1960s. Our volume is an attempt to offer a broader discussion of this movement as a complex cultural and epistemological formation that involved a series of disciplines. Our endeavour is only the first step in this direction, an effort that could, in the future, lead to more in-depth discussions of the interdisciplinary aspects of the *neoavanguardia.*

The 1960s

The 1960s – a decade of great change, during which Italy radically transformed its social and economic structure, were also characterized by deep cultural turmoil. Important literary movements such as neorealism and hermetism had come to an end, and Italian intellectuals were thus obliged to redefine their position and update their poetics. In order to understand the new Italy arising after the so-called 'economic boom,' they had to renovate their *Weltanschaung*. The old-fashioned cultural categories were no longer useful to describe the neocapitalistic context that emerged from the ruins of the Second World War and had to be replaced by new and more dynamic modes of representation. In the years following the immediate postwar period, during which the nation had experienced extreme poverty and misery, Italy underwent the first major industrial development in its history. Between 1958 and 1963 it became one of the most powerful industrial countries in Europe and in the world. Suddenly, the country was able to compete, politically and economically, with the rest of the world; the production – and consumption – of permanent goods such as cars, refrigerators, and televisions, dramatically changed the cultural landscape of contemporary Italy. As English historian Paul Ginsborg put it: 'The years of the Miracle were the key period of an extraordinary process of transformation that was taking place in the everyday life of the Italians – in their culture, family life, leisure-time activities, consumption habits, even the language they spoke and their sexual mores' (239).

Ginsborg's remark about the linguistic habits of Italians is a crucial one. Far from being a frozen and immutable entity, everyday language – like art in general – is a living organism that adapts itself to many different social and cultural situations. Thus, if one conceives of art as a dynamic 'system' (Corti 23) and not just as a 'luogo asettico' [aseptic space] (22), immune from any change, it is easy to understand how aesthetic codes maintain a dialogic relationship with reality, and how every transformation in the world is reflected within their structure.[3] As Eco argues in 'Del modo di formare come impegno sulla realtà' [Form as social commitment], one of the most significant essays in *Opera aperta* [Open work], the moment the avant-garde artist realizes that the system of communication in use is alienated from the historical condition s/he must understand that the only way to re-establish a meaningful relationship with the world is through the invention of 'strutture formali che si facciano il *modello* di questa situazione' [new formal structures that will embody this situation and become its *model*]' (269). To further quote Eco:

> Il vero contenuto dell'opera diventa il suo modo di vedere il mondo e di

giudicarlo, risolto in modo di formare, e a questo livello andrà condotto il discorso sui rapporti tra l'arte e il proprio mondo. L'arte conosce il mondo attraverso le proprie strutture formative (che quindi non sono il suo momento formalistico ma il suo vero momento di contenuto): la letteratura organizza parole che significano aspetti del mondo, ma l'opera letteraria significa in proprio il mondo attraverso il modo in cui queste parole sono disposte.

[The real content of a work is the vision of the world expressed in its manner of formation. Any analysis of the relationship between art and the world will have to take place at this level. Art knows the world through its formal structures (which, therefore, can no longer be considered from a purely formalistic point of view but must be seen as its true content). Literature organizes words that signify different aspects of the world, but the literary work itself signifies the world in the way its words are organized.] (270)

The dramatic metamorphosis of Italian society in the 1960s had such a remarkable impact on literature and the arts that the rise and success of new aesthetic phenomena (experimental music, *Nuova figurazione*, Action Poetry) have to be related to the renewal of Italian society in all its different facets. As Italo Calvino acutely observed, the 1960s forced Italian intellectuals to reorganize their 'bookshelf' and, as a consequence, 'mettere in discussione la scala dei valori e il codice dei significati stabiliti' [question the established scale of values and code of meanings] (*Una pietra sopra* 159). Whereas in the immediate aftermath of the Second World War it was sufficient to write political novels directed towards 'un lettore interessato principalmente alla cultura politica e alla storia contemporanea' [a reader principally interested in political culture and contemporary history] (160), in a very different social and cultural context, the writer realizes that from then on 'si scriveranno romanzi per un lettore che avrà finalmente capito che non deve più leggere romanzi' [we will write novels for a reader who has finally understood that he does not have to read novels anymore] (161). Thus, by presupposing the existence of a reader/receiver 'che ne sa più di lui' [who knows more than the writer does] (162), Calvino emphasizes on one hand, the necessity of looking for new aesthetic codes able to take into account the achievements of new disciplines (linguistics, information theory, anthropology, sociology), and on the other, the importance of challenging readers with more experimental works.

Epistemological Issues

Literary critic Niva Lorenzini has described the situation of literary practices of the 1960s in Italy as situated between 'subject and object.' In fact, in any creative practice there is no such thing as a linear, or plain, relationship between its creative code and reality/the world (*Il presente* 61). According to Lorenzini, in the 1960s the question became even more complex because of the radicalization of the discrepancy between words and things. The complexity reached by literary and artistic languages in the 1960s was the result of the questioning of such notions as 'real' and 'reality' (61). The consequence was to complicate the degrees of linguistic representation of the world and the self, and to open unprecedented possibilities for experimentation. If we look at the process of complication that the notion of the 'object' and its representation underwent in the 1960s, we begin to understand that the radical questioning of the epistemological status of the external 'object' had enormous consequences for all artistic practices. In fact, that very 'object' had been functioning as a screen upon which the traditional creative self had been projecting its own desires, memories, and the confirmation of its own existence. Once such practices as that of the *neoavanguardia* questioned the status of the 'object,' the text itself – as well as the artwork or the musical composition – stopped representing the semantic space where a preorganized meaning could be conveyed.

More specifically, the phenomenological notion of the 'riduzione dell'io' (reduction of the self) played a fundamental role in the development of the experimentation of the 1960s. This notion meant primarily a suspension of subjectivity – and of the 'subject' as a cognitive agency – in order to establish a more authentic approach to the world. It is in this context that the idea of an anti-solipsistic cognitive subject open to the sphere of intersubjectivity, theorized by Luciano Anceschi and Enzo Paci in the early 1960s, can be better understood.[4] Why and how the idea of 'riduzione dell'io' moved effectively from the realm of philosophy to that of literature also becomes clear: once the subject – understood as both grammatical element and cognitive agency – was put in a state of suspension, the possibilities for language to approach reality multiplied. It may be added that the state of suspension of the subject did not mean the total rejection of subjectivity, but, rather, the questioning of a preconstituted form of subjectivity, one that exists prior to the actual experience, in order to leave room for a subject understood as 'being-in-the-world.'

Along with the reduction of the self, a fundamental role was also played by Umberto Eco's *Opera aperta.* In fact, no meaningful discussion and reconsideration of the *neoavanguardia* is possible without looking back at Eco's seminal book, which was published in 1962, just a year before the foundation of the Gruppo 63 in Palermo. It is no coincidence that a number of essays in our volume make reference to *Opera aperta* from different angles. For instance, Mario Moroni's essay deals with, among other issues. Eco's own articulation of the relationship between technique and worldview in artistic practice. Eco focused in particular on the notion of alienation, which he considered as a constitutive element of the contemporary world. For Eco, however, the awareness of the constitutive nature of alienation did not imply its passive acceptance. On the contrary, the task was to denounce and demystify the consequences of alienation in people's relationships. In terms of artistic languages, the task was to elaborate new formal structures that could respond actively to the alienating situation. It is not an overstatement to say that *Opera aperta* provided the fundamental theoretical background to the questioning by artists and writers of both traditional ideas of knowledge, which are based on an immutable idea of order, and traditional notions of artistic communication. The aim of an *opera aperta* was to provoke a sense of uneasiness in the audience with respect to the traditional view of the world, and to initiate a new relationship between the audience itself and the text or the artwork.[5]

The fundamental and inevitable consequence of the notion of *opera aperta* on literary and artistic practices was the development of self-referential expressive codes. However, within the *neoavanguardia* this self-referentiality, accomplished through experimentation across the artistic disciplines, was not meant to provide just an autonomous and self-sufficient set of creative tools. As Francesco Muzzioli clearly demonstrates in his essay, the self-referentiality of the *neoavanguardia* represented a conscious effort to produce a new approach to cultural-political engagement. The long-term goal of such an effort was to generate a dramatic impact on the discursive production of official institutions, and ultimately to provoke an explosion of their ideological contradictions.[6] However, according to the intellectuals of the *neoavanguardia,* an oppositional cultural-political project could best be practised within the structural elements of art and literature, rather than within their immediate social and political contents.

Another novelty of the present volume is its discussion of issues pertaining to women's studies. For the first time in the scholarship on this movement the discussion focuses, in Lucia Re's essay, on the complex relationship between the *neoavanguardia* as a male-dominated phenomenon and the feminist movement of the 1960s and 1970s in Italy. Powerful tools initially used in the context of the *neoavanguardia* – strategies of demystification (which, not coincidentally, had been proposed by Eco) and demythization, along with working within the institutions – later influenced the practices of the feminist movement.

Neoavanguardia and Postmodernism

Another theme we would like to discuss briefly is the relation between *neoavanguardia* and postmodernism. Although this issue is thoroughly analysed by Monica Jansen in her essay, it is worth making a few preliminary remarks here. John Picchione investigates the diverse theoretical components of the *neoavanguardia* in an engaging fashion. Instead of following the usual and accepted division between the three different 'anime' [souls] of the group – the ideological, the a-ideological, and the phenomenological (Gambaro 77) – Picchione prefers to distinguish between two major camps:

> The first, still loyal to the project of modernity, assigned to literature and to the arts a role of emancipation and social antagonism by adopting an iconoclastic language as the expression of a subversive ideology [...] The second, anticipating a postmodern aesthetics, saw literature as completely impotent when confronted by sociopolitical realities. (47–8)

What is interesting about Picchione's statement is the way he outlines the different theoretical trends of Gruppo 63, redefining them using much broader categories. In other words, Picchione sees the *neoavanguardia* as a sort of *trait d'union* between two different artistic and cultural experiences. In fact, his intention, in speaking of modernist and postmodernist camps, is to emphasize the role of the *neoavanguardia* as that crucial moment during which, as a result of economic and social changes in Italian society, the traditional canons of Italian culture were put into question. The contradiction, one of many concerning the *neoavanguardia*, lies in the fact that, despite a common goal (to create a new language and renew the Italian cultural landscape), the proposals were utterly different. Thus, on one hand we find writers such as Sanguineti who, belonging to the 'modernist' camp, 'perceived language as a constant projection of something other than itself on the ground of the dialectical relationship it establishes with social, political, and any other extra literary aspect of life' (48). On the other hand are intellectuals such as Guglielmi who, contrary to any kind of politicization of art, 'saw poetry and literature strictly as an exploration of language' (48) and paved the way for the new postmodern aesthetics.

Whatever conclusion one might draw from this analysis, it is important to stress that the *neoavanguardia* provided the first formulation of postmodernist theoretical discourse in Italy, and brought to the fore the complex relationship between the arts and the world. We would like our volume to contribute to a critical discussion of the issues outlined in this introduction and to promote other scholarly contributions on the *neoavanguardia* as a whole. Furthermore, it is important to emphasize that our purpose is not to commemorate, but rather to interrogate the experience of the *neoavanguardia* so as to verify what this cultural movement of the 1960s can offer to readers and scholars of the twenty-first century in the fields of literary studies, gender studies, and epistemological and aesthetic theories. What we envision is a comparative cultural scenario in which the study of such groups as Gruppo 63, *Tel Quel*, the German Gruppe 47, and similar groups in Spain and in South and North America (such as the L=A=N=G=U=A=G=E poets) will finally enter current cultural debates and course curricula in colleges and universities.

The Essays

Because of the interdisciplinary purpose of this volume, we invited contributions of scholars from a variety of disciplines and countries: the United States, Canada, Italy, France, England, and the Netherlands. The first section, entitled 'The Cultural Debate,' opens with Francesco Muzzioli's essay on the critical and theoretical discourses developed within the *neoavanguardia*. Muzzioli focuses on the notion of *critica militante* [militant criticism], understood as a form of critical practice that is articulated concurrently with creative practices, rather than *a posteriori*. Muzzioli deals with such *neoavanguardisti* as Alfredo Giuliani, Angelo Guglielmi, and Edoardo Sanguineti.

Another aspect is the fundamental function of criticism as a tool by means of which the *neoavanguardia* was able to introduce its creative principles and cultural-political position to the rest of the literary world, and in the international cultural scene of the 1960s. Muzzioli's essay offers an important reconstruction of the debate of those years up to the transition from literature to politics that marked the explosion of the contradictions in the *neoavanguardia*, the crisis of the journal *Quindici* in 1969, and the end of the experience.

The second essay, by Mario Moroni, relates to and expands a specific point made by Muzzioli: that the *neoavanguardia* needed to go beyond national tradition and to reflect on their relationship with historical avant-gardes such as futurism (in particular futurism as it was practiced by such authors as Aldo Palazzeschi and Gianpiero Lucini), and more importantly, surrealism. In fact, surrealism constituted a major source of the works of such *neoavanguardisti* as Adriano Spatola, Corrado Costa, Giorgio Celli, and Antonio Porta. Moroni deals with this important aspect of the movement by looking at the journal *Malebolge,* published between 1964 and 1967. Examining the articles and creative works in various issues, Moroni analyses the formulation of two essential cultural-political discourses – *parasurrealismo* and technological utopia – as they became part of international and interdisciplinary artistic experimental practices whose influence became more visible in the areas of concrete, visual, and sound poetry, and multimedia and performance art.

Monica Jansen's essay closes the first section of the volume with a detailed reconstruction of the complex relationship between *neoavanguardia* and postmodernism. This relationship surfaced over and over again through the 1970s, 1980s, 1990s, and up to 2003. In each decade Jansen identifies and analyses the implications of crucial moments when, even long after the end of the movement in 1969, the debate on *neoavanguardia* and postmodernism continued to take on new shapes and new directions within the Italian literary and cultural scene.

The second group of essays, collected under the title of 'Revisiting Literature,' concentrates on the different ways in which the idea of literature changed as a result of the new critical discourses of *neoavanguardia.* Silvia Contarini considers the effects of the above-mentioned discourses in the realm of fiction in a study of the idea of a *nuovo romanzo* [new novel], developed within the *neoavanguardia,* beginning with the evolution of literary models and linguistic experimentations in the 1960s. In light of her own introductory discussion, Contarini offers illuminating readings of *nuovi romanzi* by Paolo Volponi, Raffaele La Capria, Edoardo Sanguineti, and others.

Florian Mussgnug focuses on the works of Giorgio Manganelli, outlining his peculiar position within the history of the *neoavanguardia.* More than forty years after the foundation of the Gruppo 63 Manganelli's name remains as intrinsically linked to the group's history as is the assumption that this author never entirely committed himself to its aims and beliefs. In light of this apparent contradiction Mussgnug looks back to Manganelli's status as an avant-garde author who was also a critic of the avant-garde, arguing that while the originality of Manganelli's work within the *neoavanguardia* is evident, his debts to the Gruppo 63 and his influence on the radical rethinking of the novel that took place in Italy during the 1960s are less obvious.

John Picchione deals with the poets of the anthology *I novissimi* (1961), the best known editorial product of the *neoavanguardia*. Picchione demonstrates that theoretical and aesthetic orientation of these poets led them to explore the materiality of the word, and that their ambition was to force life to rewrite itself. He argues that by reducing language to a material entity the poets attempted to break off the traditional ties to referentiality and to allowed syntactic and semantic constructions. For the *novissimi*, it was the text itself that could recover the inventiveness of poetry and challenge the readers' habitual linguistic and mental grids.

The last two essays of the second section, by Lucia Re and by Rebecca West, deal with the complex relationship between the *neoavanguardia* on one side and women writers and the issue of gender on the other. Re gives a brief overview of the development of mass culture in Italy in the 1960s, commenting on such crucial topics as the connection between *neoavanguardia* and neorealism, futurism, and semiotics. She establishes a parallel between the women's movement and the *neoavanguardia*. As Re points put, the issues tackled by both movements were similar: both called into question the repressive power of bourgeois ideology and culture. Re discusses the ways in which the women's movement questioned the hegemonic (and phallogocentric) use of language, and demonstrates how critical the quest for an alternative and more democratic voice was. The problematic relationship between the *neoavanguardia* and the feminine and the paradoxical marginalization of women writers is explored through references to writers such as Carla Lonzi, Carla Accardi, and Amelia Rosselli, and male authors such as Pagliarani, Balestrini, and Sanguineti.

Rebecca West's article concentrates on Giulia Niccolai and her newest avant-garde works. The analysis of Niccolai's first novel, *Il grande angolo* [Wide angle] (1966) centres on Niccolai's background as a photojournalist, an experience that deeply affected the structure of her text. Conceived as a story narrated through the camera lens, *Il grande angolo* presents many similarities with Michelangelo Antonioni's *Blow Up* (1966) and the director's unique cinematic vision, which influenced several avant-garde artists. West also explores Niccolai's transition from prose to visual and experimental poetry in the collection *Harry's Bar e altre poesie* [Harry's Bar and Other Poems] and in *Poema e oggetto* [Poetry and Object], and underlines the continual exploration of the magical and mysterious power of language in Niccolai's latest work, *Prima e dopo la Stein* [Before and after Stein], which is still characterized by a relentless avant-garde thrust.

The third section of the volume explores the interdisciplinary aspects of the *neoavanguardia*, focusing on the relationship between literature and the visual arts, on music, and finally on radical and experimental architecture. Chirumbolo's article proposes a comparison between Edoardo Sanguineti's literary and Enrico Baj's visual experimentation. With references to both the nuclear movement of the 1950s and the Pop Art phenomenon of the 1960s, Chirumbolo investigates the reciprocal influence of literature and the visual arts, and demonstrates how Sanguineti innovatively took up Baj's avant-gardist stands in order to explore new linguistic and literary territories.

The problematic relationship between Gruppo 63 and music is analysed in Paolo Somigli's essay. In addition to providing an overview of the experimental musical scenario of the 1950s and 1960s (which includes the journal *Incontri musicali*, the cultural association Vita musicale contemporanea, and the conference Arte e comunicazione) and underlining the multi-disciplinary *zeitgeist* of that period, Somigli points out that the relationship between the *neoavanguardia* and music was never really one of osmosis and integration. Despite the enthusiasm of intellectuals such as Umberto Eco and Edoardo Sanguineti (who actively collaborated with composer Luciano Berio), and in spite of a common experimental agenda, many members of the Gruppo 63 remained extremely cautious and never fully embraced either the musical innovations of such composers as Stockhausen, Pousser, and Berio and of *musica aleatoria* [chance music].

In the final essay of the volume, Laura Chiesa addresses the link between radical architecture and the *neoavanguardia*, focusing her attention particularly on the works of Superstudio, an architecture firm founded in Florence in 1966 by Adolfo Natalini and Cristiano Toraldo di Francia, whose innovative and provocative research was carried out until 1978. The original blend of architecture and poetry, rationalism and functionalism, along with the interplay of space, word, and video images in Superstudios's works epitomize and embody the dialogical atmosphere of the 1960s, where contamination of styles, genres, and art forms was frequent. Chiesa's essay provides an appropriate conclusion, in that she demonstrates the pervasive interdisciplinarity of the *neoavanguardia* and, more importantly, an opening toward similar investigations in the future.

NOTES

1 The most important critical studies published in Italy about the *Neoavanguardia* are Roberto Esposito, *Le ideologie della neoavanguardia* (1976); Francesco Muzzioli, *Teoria e critica della letteratura nelle avanguardie degli anni sessanta* (1982); Lucio Vetri, *Letteratura e caos* (1986); Fabio Gambaro, *Invito a conoscere la neoavanguardia* (1993); and Renato Barilli, *La neoavanguardia italiana* (1995). Of the anthologies edited and published by members of the *neoavanguardia*, we should mention: *Gruppo 63: la nuova letteratura*, edited by Nanni Balestrini and Alfredo Giuliani (1964); *Gruppo 63: il romanzo sperimentale*, edited by Nanni Balestrini (1966); *Gruppo 63: critica e teoria*, edited by Renato Barilli and Angelo Guglielmi (1976, republished 2003); *Gruppo 63: l'antologia*, edited by Nanni Balestrini and Alfredo Giuliani (2002); and *Il Gruppo 63 quarant'anni dopo*, edited by Renato Barilli, Fausto Curi, and Niva Lorenzini (2005).

2 See Barilli, Curi, and Lorenzini, eds., 119–50.

3 In her semiological analysis of literary communication Maria Corti dwells at length on this notion and writes: 'La letteratura non è un acropolis, nemmeno una città cinta da mura. Già i formalisti russi degli anni Trenta, sulla loro scia i semiologi della scuola di Praga (Mukarovsky) e gli odierni della scuola di Tartu hanno messo in luce come la società, nel suo rapporto con la letteratura, appaia un ricco fascio di direzioni socio-culturali, economiche, ideologiche che più o meno intensamente agiscono sul sistema letterario in quanto fanno parte della coscienza collettiva' [Literature is not an acropolis, nor even a walled city. The Russian formalists of the thirties and, in their wake, the semiologists of the Prague School (Mukarovsky) and the current School of Tartu, have all shown how society, in its relation to literature, seems like a rich cluster of sociocultural, economic and ideological directions that, with more or less intensity, influence the literary system because they form part of the collective consciousness] (23). This and all subsequent translations are ours.

4 See Luciano Anceschi, 'Orizzonte della poesia,' and Enzo Paci, 'Qualche osservazione filosofica sulla critica e sulla poesia.'

5 See Eco 2, 62–3.

6 For examples of this critical position among the *neoavanguardisti*, see Adriano Spatola, 'Poesia a tutti i costi,' and Nanni Balestrini, 'Linguaggio e opposizione,' 196–8.

WORKS CITED

Anceschi, Luciano. 'Orizzone della poesia.' *Il verri* 1 (1962): 6–21.

Balestrini, Nanni, 'Linguaggio e opposizione.' In Alfredo Giuliani, ed., *I novissimi: poesie per gli anni sessanta.* Turin: Einaudi, 1972. 196–8.

Balestrini, Nanni, ed. *Gruppo 63: il romanzo sperimentale, Palermo 1965.* Milan: Feltrinelli, 1966.

Balestrini, Nanni, and Alfredo Giuliani, eds. *Gruppo 63: la nuova letteratura, 34 scrittori, Palermo ottobre 1963.* Milan: Feltrinelli, 1964.

– *Gruppo 63: l'antologia.* Turin: Testo & Immagine, 2002.

Barilli, Renato. *La neoavanguardia italiana: dalla nascita del Verri alla fine di Quindici.* Bologna: Il Mulino, 1995.

Barilli, Renato, Fausto Curi, and Niva Lorenzini, eds. *Il Gruppo 63 quarant'anni dopo.* Bologna: Pendragon, 2005.

Barilli, Renato, and Angelo Guglielmi, eds. *Gruppo 63: critica e teoria.* Milano: Feltrinelli, 1976; Turin: Testo & Immagine, 2003.

Calvino, Italo. *Una pietra sopra.* Turin: Einaudi, 1980.

Corti, Maria. *Principi della comunicazione letteraria.* Milan: Bompiani, 1976.

Eco, Umberto. *Opera aperta.* Milan: Bompiani, 1962.

Esposito, Roberto. *Le ideologie della neoavanguardia.* Naples: Liguori, 1976.

Gambaro, Fabio. *Invito a conoscere la Neoavanguardia.* Milan: Mursia, 1993.

Ginsborg, Paul. *A History of Contemporary Italy.* London: Penguin Books, 1990.

Giuliani, Alfredo, ed. *I novissimi: poesie per gli anni sessanta.* Turin: Einaudi 1972. English translation. *I Novissimi: Poems for the Sixties.* Prose and notes trans. David Jakobson, poetry trans. Luigi Ballerini, Bradley Dick, Michael Moore, Stephen Sartarelli, and Paul Vangelisti. Los Angeles: Sun and Moon Press, 1995.

Lorenzini, Niva. *Il presente della poesia.* Bologna: Il Mulino, 1991.

Luperini, Romano. *Controtempo.* Naples: Liguori, 1999.

Muzzioli, Francesco. *Teoria e critica della letteratura nelle avanguardie degli anni sessanta.* Rome: Istituto della Enciclopedia Italiana, 1982.

Paci, Enzo. 'Qualche osservazione filosofica sulla critica e sulla poesia.' *Aut Aut,* 61–2 (1961): 1–21.

Picchione, John. *The New Avant-garde in Italy: Theoretical Debate and Poetic Practices.* Toronto: University of Toronto Press, 2004.
Smith, Lawrence R. 'Avant-garde Italian Poetry in Translation.' In John Picchione and Laura Pietropaolo, eds., *Italian Literature in North America: Pedagogical Strategies.* Toronto: Biblioteca di Quaderni d'italianistica, 1990. 169–77.
Spatola, Adriano. 'Poesia a tutti i costi.' *Malebolge* 1.2 (1964): 51–2.
Vetri, Lucio. *Letteratura e caos: poetiche della neo-avaguardia italiana degli anni sessanta.* Mantova: Edizioni del Verri, 1986.

PART ONE

The Cultural Debate

1 Subverting Literature: Literary Theory and Critical Discourse in the Italian *Neoavanguardia*

FRANCESCO MUZZIOLI

Literary Practice and Critical Discourse

Critical practice is one of the founding aspects of avant-garde. By refusing the coeval literary modes, avant-garde implicitly questions the validity of these models and assesses them negatively. The historical avant-gardes expressed their criticism of the past in extremely polemical and provocative terms (*pars destruens*). However, the constructive aspect of their discourse (*pars construes*) was conveyed through the use of manifestos, the language of which was more creative and poetic rather than rigorously critical. This is hardly mere coincidence. Criticism, understood as an opinion based upon ascertained aesthetical parameters, was not part of the cultural background of the historical avant-gardes. They saw literary criticism as one element of the academic institutions they meant to challenge and oppose. To escape from professors and their canons it was necessary to dodge this problem. As the surrealist René Crevel proposed: 'La critique d'art se fait par l'absurde' [art criticism is done through the absurd].

In the 1960s the situation changes. The new avant-gardes realize that they do not have the power and strength for a revolutionary act, and undertake a more complex journey within the academic and literary institutions. It is not an overt war but a guerrilla campaign, a 'semiotic guerrilla.' The new avant-gardes advertise themselves not with outrageous self-promoting manifestos but through experiments typical of a scientific laboratory. In this new context, the use of criticism becomes an indispensable means of control and verification and an essential guidebook for understanding writing models otherwise incomprehensible. It is hardly a surprise that one of the most important activities of Gruppo

63 was to organize conferences and debates during which several texts were read, discussed, and criticized not only by poets and writers, but also by professional critics who were themselves part of the movement. Although I have previously written on this subject[1] I return to it now to outline some of the theoretical questions and to re-examine, after a few years, the close relationship between literary practice and critical discourse.

Neoavanguardia and Critical Practice

Avant-garde criticism cannot be made *a posteriori*: it has to be concurrent with creative writing. It has to be *critica militante* [militant criticism], always in movement and connected with the works in progress. We can identify three types of critical discourse: militant criticism, the recognition and mapping of different 'souls' of the movement, and the theoretical outline of the *neoavanguardia*.

Militant Criticism

This refers, first and foremost, to the ruthless discussions that followed the reading of texts, a sort of legendary critical practice of which, unfortunately, we have only a few testimonies.[2] Militant criticism also refers to the articles and essays written by two professional critics: Alfredo Giuliani and Angelo Guglielmi. Besides writing the preface to the anthology *I Novissimi* (1961), which is considered the first theoretical elaboration of Gruppo 63, Giuliani was also able to use his sharp sarcasm and uncompromised judgment to foster the *neoavanguardia*'s aggressive outlook. A good case in point is his review of *Il Menabò* 2 published in *Il verri* (April 1960).[3] In order to clearly emphasize the differences between the experimental positions of the avant-garde and the lyrical and engaged attitude of the national poetical tradition, Giuliani sarcastically asserts that the rival journal 'fa un effetto patetico' [has a pathetic effect] (*Immagini* 100). He also describes Roversi's poems as 'scialbe lasse floreali' [weak flowery laisses] (100), Volponi's poetry as 'stucchevole pascolismo' [tedious *pascolismo*] (100), and Fortini's poetical lines as 'speciosi computi' [specious computations] (102).[4]

In like manner, in his essays on the 'ancestors' of the *neoavanguardia* and the new experimental authors, Angelo Guglielmi makes ample and clever use of figurative language (metaphors, comparisons, and other tropes). To reject and challenge the idea of ideology as a preordered and prepackaged view of the world, Guglielmi is inclined to employ images that allow him to aptly discuss texts that transcend the accepted literary canons. When speaking of Gadda, for instance, Guglielmi highlights the pure *cosalità* [objectification] of his writing by describing an outlandish landscape: 'non rimangono che alcune forme lucidissime, alcuni potentissimi blocchi, statici e inespressivi, come vecchi sassi di un mondo non ancora abitato' [one is left with some extremely lucid forms, some powerful, static, and inexpressive blocks, like ancient stones of a world not yet inhabited] (*Vero* 54–5). Similarly, the dynamism and movement of Gadda's *plurilinguismo* is exemplified through a culinary metaphor:

> Gadda dimostra una grande curiosità per il linguaggio, per il mescolamento degli stili, per le più raffinate combinazioni verbali, che costituiscono un valido strumento per operare alcune fondamentali distorsioni nella materia assunta a oggetto della narrazione, e portarla ad un certo bollore, all'intensità voluta. [...] Si tratta piuttosto di un fuoco che brucia sotto una pentola, nella quale c'è qualcosa che ha così poco a che fare con quel fuoco, come un pezzo di carne con il gas che lo cuoce.
>
> [Gadda displays a great curiosity for the language, the assortment of styles, the most refined verbal combinations, which compose the instrument through which he deforms the narration and takes it to its boiling point ... It is like a fire burning beneath a pot in which there is something that has little to do with that fire, like a piece of meat has nothing to do with the gas that cooks it.] (55)

Although the independence of form from content (reduced to mere 'matter') could be reminiscent of the formalist and structuralistic point of view, Guglielmi's analysis is very different. He positively judges both the breaking of the code and the voluntary production of disorder, and is able to convey a similar energy not with a rational critical discourse but, as has been said, through a discourse that is highly expressive and figurative. The same thing happens when he writes about new authors such as Nanni Balestrini. Although Guglielmi talks of Balestrini's literary techniques in terms of 'strutturazione di segni' [structures of signs] (*Vero* 141), 'organizzazione narrativa' [narrative organization] and 'tecnica combinatorial' [combinatory technique], the deep meaning of his writing is, once again, expressed by a 'metafora energetica' [energetic metaphor], referring in this case to the process of ignition and extinction.[5]

Such 'dinamica ermeneutica' [dynamic hermeneutics] does not neglect the polemical and often tactical aspects of criticism. In this light Guglielmi's essays on Pasolini, at that time considered both a travelling companion and a competitor, are significant. I would like to discuss not Sanguineti's frontal attacks on Pasolini,[6] but rather the more diplomatic and less explicit articles by Giuliani and Guglielmi. Giuliani, for instance, reviewed *Le ceneri di Gramsci* [The ashes of Gramsci] in 1957. Despite some ironical comments ('Vien voglia di soffiare su queste *Ceneri* per vedere che cosa resta di tanto illusorio fuoco' [One feels like blowing on these ashes, to see what's left of such illusory fire], *Immagini* 90), Giuliani holds Pasolini's text in great consideration, and acknowledges the consonance and validity of some of the poetical devices that Pasolini employs (for example, the 'endecasillabo degenere' [degenerate hendecasyllable] that allows the poet a 'completa libertà tematica' [complete thematic freedom], 89). In his final assessment Giuliani is not negative, but rather limitative, as he condemns the ideological and aesthetic limits of Pasolini's work: '*Le ceneri di Gramsci* è un'opera di crisi, metà confessione metà protesta sociale, con tratti di suggestiva bellezza e molto narcisismo letterario; un'opera un po' troppo matura e un po' troppo acerba' [*The ashes of Gramsci* is a work of crisis, half confession and half social protest, with some parts of impressive beauty and a lot of literary narcissism; it is a work a little too mature and a little too unripe] (93).

Guglielmi, on his part, rejects neither Pasolini's adherence to reality nor his irrationalism, but criticizes the conventional treatment of the characters and their outrageous stories that, in the end, are portrayed in a very 'edible' and conventional fashion. According to Guglielmi, Pasolini's main attribute – and fault – is ambiguity, both ethical and ideological. Thus, in his 1960 review he questions Pasolini's 'cheap' representation of crucial social themes: 'Per salvare Pier Paolo Pasolini, non ci rimane che pensare che egli rappresenta il miglior risultato cui, nell'ordine di un impegno di "eleganza," una cultura sottosviluppata come la nostra è capace di pervenire' [In order to save and justify Pasolini we can only think that he represents the best outcome that an underdeveloped culture like ours is able to produce] (*Vero* 84).

Reconstructing the Map

The *neoavanguardisti* of the 1960s are well aware that everything has already been done and that they were not born out of nowhere. Their main problem is then to identify the opponents and, at the same time, position the movement both ideologically and historically. In order to be truly alternative it is necessary to rewrite history, to outline a different 'tradizione del nuovo' [tradition of the new], and to carefully consider the legacies to embrace and reject. Needless to say, the heavy use of criticism is but a consequence of this attitude toward history and tradition, and Sanguineti's attempt to re-interpret and reconsider the literary history of the twentieth century is one of the most important endeavours in this direction. His anthology *Poesia del Novecento*[7] is polemically directed toward not only Pasolini's own reconstruction of contemporary Italian poetry, but also, in order to consider a wider perspective, toward the common and widespread notion of the Italian lyrical tradition imbued with mysticism.

It was also necessary to go beyond the national tradition and to reflect on the relationship with historical avant-gardes such as futurism[8] (in particular the futurism of Palazzeschi and Lucini, whose positions were more distant from the official poetics of the historical avant-garde) and more importantly, surrealism. In fact, as the literary production of writers such as Spatola, Costa, Celli, Porta, and Sanguineti himself clearly shows, surrealism was still a very fruitful and essential point of reference for the *neoavanguardia*, both from the technical point of view (for example, the casual literary juxtapositions that produced linguistic compositions of great intensity) as well as the ideological (for example, the relationship between aesthetics and politics). It should also be noted that the links with surrealism become stronger toward 1968, when the increasing politicization of the avant-garde forced the *neoavanguardisti* to leave the experimental laboratory, join the battle, and embrace the surrealist revolution. The journal *Quindici*, in this context, is extremely important. In its pages Sanguineti proposed what he defined, with reference to Artaud, as a *letteratura della crudeltà* [literature of cruelty]. Sanguineti's intention, in stating the need to 'uscire dalla letteratura' [leave literature] (*Ideologia e linguaggio* 110) and 'mettere la letteratura al servizio della rivoluzione' [make literature work for the revolution] (110) was to acknowledge the magnitude of surrealism: 'come ultima tra le grandi avanguardie storiche (e non in senso semplicemente cronologico, ma quasi in forza di un provocante simbolo), il surrealismo è il fantasma che giustamente perseguita ogni avanguardia ulteriore, e le nega pacifico sonno' [as the last of the great historical avant-gardes (not only chronologically but also symbolically) surrealism is the ghost that rightly persecutes any possible future avant-garde, and denies its peaceful sleep] (110).[9]

As far as fiction (a genre neglected by the historical avant-gardes) is concerned it is worth remembering Barilli's proposition to compare different writers in order to underscore their innovative and original literary techniques.[10] Barilli chooses a European perspective and identifies three pairs of authors: Joyce and Robbe Grillet; Kafka and Sanguineti; Musil and Grass. The first pairing alludes to the transition from the 'interior monologue' to the 'exterior monologue' and the consequent enhanced adherence to matter and objects; the second pairing, characterized by oneiric atmospheres, marks the transition from tragedy to comedy; the third pairing emphasizes the shift from rationality to corporeality. It is through these genealogies that the avant-garde attempts to investigate the realm of fiction and create a *romanzo sperimentale* [experimental novel] or *anti-romanzo* [anti-novel].

Another crucial role of this critical practice was the identification of the different and diverse areas of the *neoavanguardia*. A good case in point is Sanguineti's essay 'Il trattamento del materiale verbale nei testi della nuova avanguardia' [The treatment of verbal material in the works of the new avant-garde], particularly the section entitled 'Situazioni narrative' [Narrative situations]. Besides using Auerbach's method of sampling, Sanguineti compares his work with the texts of two other fellow writers, Filippini and Di Marco, discussing both similarities (the novel that challenges itself) and differences (embodiment of classical genres such as the tragic, the elegiac, and the comic). Filippini dissolves the world of words through the introduction of 'pure' reality; Di Marco privileges the uncertain and liminal space of the 'libro che si fa il verso da solo' [book that imitates itself] (*Ideologia* 85); Sanguineti recuperates the comic dimension of fiction produced by a 'fabula onirica' [oneiric discourse] (91), which is 'vera e falsa insieme' [true and false at the same time] (91). Sanguineti's goal is not to distinguish and isolate himself from the other two writers but rather to validate his poetics in the name of a common literary and intellectual research. This is, in my opinion, one of the crucial elements of the *neoavanguardia*: to place the emphasis on the act of creation.

The Theory of the Avant-garde

Another function of avant-garde criticism is to provide the movement with a series of theoretical formulas whose purpose is to introduce the group to the rest of the literary world. As noted above, the new avant-gardes are very much aware of the impossibility of using overly radical manifestos. It is now necessary to employ less explicit ways of communication capable of stressing the 'scientific' mindset of the new writers. Giuliani's above-mentioned preface to the anthology *I Novissimi* is, in this light, the first attempt to draw attention to the *neoavanaguardia*'s research on language and literary structures and to the relationship between poetry and contemporary world. As Giuliani states, poetry is 'mimesi critica della schizofrenia universale, rispecchiamento e contestazione di uno stato sociale e immaginativo disgregato' [the critical mimesis of the universal schizophrenia, the reflection and objection of a social and imaginative fragmented state] (*I novissimi* 9).

Linguistic research is justified by Angelo Guglielmi as the only possible choice of experimentalism in a situation where a direct provocative act is no longer possible. In a highly ambiguous and flexible system every move must be carefully planned and prepared. The semantic field employed by the critic to illustrate this new scenario is that of a war where the conflict is now indirect – 'La situazione della cultura contemporanea è simile a quella di una città dalla quale il nemico, dopo averla cosparsa di mine, è fuggito' [The situation of contemporary culture is similar to that of a city from which the enemy, after having mined it, has flown] ('Avanguardia' 18) – and therefore, one needs 'i reparti specializzati che avanzeranno nella città abbandonata non con le mitragliatrici ma con gli apparecchi Geiger' [the special troops that will advance into the abandoned city not with machine guns but with Geiger guns] (18). According to Barilli, whose password 'normalizzazione' [normalization] follows the same line, it is indispensable to make avant-garde art something ordinary and part of an every day life that can be experienced and practiced by everyone. This entails the rejection of the shocking protest and the consequent devolution to language (the textual avant-garde) and theoretical investigations.

Sanguineti, in 'Sopra l'avanguardia' [On avant-garde], questions the myth of avant-garde art as the last product of romanticism, an art capable of instantly changing the world and creating an alternative reality miraculously free from alienation and ideology. According to Sanguineti, who builds his theory on the ideology/language equation, it is impossible to stand outside ideology, and even the simplest use of language has an ideological implication. This notion does not hinder the polemical charge of avant-garde art, but rather forces it to be aware of the dialectic between the 'eroico-patetico' [heroic-pathetic] element (the transgression of common sense and its cultural codes) and the 'cinico' [cynical] one, according to which the avant-garde is 'nella circolazione del consumo artistico una merce capace di vincere, con un gesto sorprendente e audace, la concorrenza indebolita e stagnante di produttori meno avvertiti e meno spregiudicati' [within the arena of artistic consumption, a product capable of beating, with a brave and startling gesture, the weakened and stagnant competition of less aware and aggressive producers] (*Ideologia* 55). In other words, the writer must be aware that his/her subversive act is performed within the market and will end up in the museum. By experiencing and showing the conflict between authentic and false, or in Benjamin's terms, between expression and convention, the literary text allegorically criticizes the mechanisms of capitalist and bourgeois society. Deprived of its mysticism, the avant-garde achieves a contradictory position and openly exhibits its historical limits.

The role of avant-garde criticism is thus clear. An aesthetic discourse that intends to call into question established literary codes needs a theoretical apparatus that legitimizes its accomplishments, explains its modus operandi, and, at the same time, avoids any pretentious claim by practicing both self-irony and self-awareness. As Fausto Curi aptly states, there was a need for 'un'avanguardia che operasse nella forma della razionalità e della coscienza storica; un'avanguardia lucidamente consapevole del proprio rapporto col tempo vivente, dei propri limiti categoriali e situazionali' [an avant-garde that worked at the level of rationality and historical consciousness; an avant-garde cogently aware of its relation with the coeval society, of its own categorical and situational limits] ('Sulla giovane poesia' 54) – in short, a theoretical and practical avant-garde.

Theoretical Criticism within Literary Practice

In Sanguineti's observations on the *trattamento del materiale verbale* [treatment of the verbal material], the idea of a literature able to design for itself its own criticism (its own deconstruction) is already present. The great quantity of essays, reviews, and theoretical discussions produced by the *neoavanguardia* has been thoroughly analysed by both advocates and opponents of the movement, although less critical attention has been given to the critical elements implicitly introduced within the literary texts. This is hardly a surprise. The 'internal' critical component is, in fact, the unmistakable signal of a literary practice that does not want to sanctify and mystify itself but, on the contrary, plans to challenge its own privileged status and subvert its established rules and values. I would like to discuss how criticism is expressed through fiction, or more precisely, through the essay-novel, the metanovel, and the interruption/dyscrasia procedure.

The Essay-Novel

In this case the theoretical and critical discussion permeates the thematic dimension of the text. The most prominent example is Arbasino's *Fratelli d'Italia* [Brothers of Italy] (1963), a text that has been repeatedly rewritten, augmented, and adapted according to different historical contexts. Arbasino's humorous language, characterized by a mixture of cultural quotations and intellectual jargon, aims at mimicking the promiscuous, polyglot, and rambling contemporary literary society. What really matters is no longer the events and characters represented in a plausible and possible world, but rather, the ideas that originate from the dense dialogues between the characters (concerning, for example, a novel or a film to be made that 'finisce a non farsi' [cannot be finished]). It is not mere coincidence, then, that *Fratelli d'Italia* embeds in itself a theory of the waning and crisis of narrative content in favour of what Arbasino calls 'immagini poetiche dominanti' [dominant poetic images] (256). Furthermore, the introduction of references to international places and characters in the plot[11] challenges trivial provincialism and the essay form is intentionally used to widen the boundaries of the genre. The multiplicity of materials is amalgamated by an ironic *pastiche* that sometimes transforms the text into an accumulation of aphorisms. The endeavour, closely controlled by the narrator-intellectual, is conducted with a sharp satirical attitude that allows the estranged re-employment of bad taste. The pastiche is appreciated as an 'atto creativo-critico' [creative and critical act]: Arbasino's text is thus not just pure mimesis but an effort that creates a mixed and ambiguous genre, something similar to the tragicomic. As Arbasino, referring to the 'Mago di Berlino' [Wizard of Berlin], a character that recalls Brecht and his theories on alienation, writes:

> Risolvere il dramma in commedia... Deve far ridere, dev'essere un po' urtante, deve nutrirsi di una profonda verità morale. Anche se i riflessi sono tenebrosi, e alla fine si piange. Il Mago di Berlino non lo amo poi moltissimo: però qui ha capito tutto. La rappresentazione che nasce già come giudizio critico.
>
> [To unravel the tragedy into comedy ... It has to be funny, it has to be annoying, it has to possess a deep moral truth. Even if the reflexes are tenebrous and you cry at the end. I don't love the Wizard of Berlin that much: but here, he understood everything. The representation is already created as a moral judgment.] (256)

While this is a character speaking about one of the works quoted within the text, the passage also sounds like Arbasino's own declaration of poetics about the novel he is writing.

The Metanovel

Although metanarrative theories are already present in Arbasino's work, the author who, in the 1960s, primarily develops this particular theoretical aspect is Giorgio Manganelli. Manganelli is representative of that peculiar kind of avant-garde that does not disdain the past but challenges literature with a sort of hyper-rhetoric mannerism rife with parody. Manganelli pushes the 'fictionality' of literature to its furthest limits: if 'normal' fiction is based on the as-if principle, according to which what one reads is the equivalent of real life (or, following Aristotle, verisimilar), then fiction must be a representation without referents, a representation of nothing. Accordingly, fiction is always oscillating between a state of exaltation (because it creates a virtual reality that does not really exist) and one of depression (because what is created cannot be real). Furthermore, in his first work, *Hilarotragoedia* (1964), Manganelli uses the form of the treatise (a classical genre of critical discourse) in order to subvert it from within through the utilization of ceremonial and satirical themes that undermine the narrative plot. The plot is on one hand replaced by notes, hypotheses, insertions, and glosses, and, on the other, put aside and reduced to mere anecdote. The use of the critical form is even more obvious in Manganelli's *Nuovo commento* [New commentary] (1969), where the commentary takes over the entire text (the text is always somewhere else and is 'un nulla sceltosi sotto forma di testo' [a nothing that actualizes itself in the form of a text]) and multiplies itself in an infinite semiotic series of 'chiose di chiose' [glosses of glosses], therefore generating a baroque and disproportionate book. It is an explanation that endlessly explains itself, a metacommentary more than a metanovel. In other words, Manganelli intends to defy traditional forms through stylistic excesses. The questionability of the commentary (why is the author commenting this passage and not another one?) is also the consequence of its implicit potential infinite ability to create numerous textual digressions. By replacing the story of a character with the story of forms and their inordinate montage[12] Manganelli intends to highlight three conflicts. First, the propagation of interpretation denies its care *a latere*, and the comment is seen both as a poison inoculated in the text and as a defect (the failure of creation). Second, the 'false' critical discourse emphasizes the impersonality of writing and sanctions the death of the Author. Third, this grotesque and self-sufficient[13] piece of criticism simultaneously underlines the concrete reality of every piece of writing and the *scritturazione* [writing] of the whole world, including the body (which is, according to the author, 'rilegato in pelle' [bound in leather]). Manganelli, after all, brings the paradoxical relationship between avant-garde and commentary to its most extreme consequences. The commentary is, in fact, the critical discourse devoted to classical authors and it can only be practiced 'after,' whereas for the avant-garde all writings are at the same level. In order to be used in a contemporary context this philological form must be completely transformed by parody, radicalize its textual proliferation, and replace the usual narrative forms. The linearity of fiction is thus finally destroyed and fragmented. This is my next point.

The Interruption/Dyscrasia Procedure

The interruption device is characteristic of the *poesia novissima* [new poetry]. From Giuliani's non-sense to Sanguineti's catalogue poetry, from Pagliarani's montage to Balestrinis's 'cut' lines and Porta's poetical lists, the composition of texts with heterogeneous material implies the *décalage* of poetical elements. Interruption and interference: it is like putting a displacing charge between two different levels of the text that are reciprocally critical. This also happens in the experimental narrative, as, for example, in novels written in fragmented and disconnected laisses, in Sanguineti's *Capriccio italiano* (where the characters play cards and eventually spread them incoherently), or in Malerba's comical fiction that leads to a *salto mortale* [deadly jump] of a narrative that erases its own data.

Here, however, I would like to focus on Roberto Di Marco's fiction, with particular reference to his *Telemachia* (1968), a clear allusion to one of the most ancient and famous myths. The mythical text is reinstated in the present (the Vietnam War is the equivalent of the Trojan War) and reduced to a series of static relationships among characters, unaccomplished movements (is Telemachus chasing one woman or two? will he leave, will he not? etc.), and a list of juxtaposed and anonymous lines. The myth, thus interpreted, becomes the foundation of a sort of self-reflexive writing that questions its own form and meaning to emphasize, at the same time, its stationary status. However, in Di Marco's text one does not find only the ironic procedure of parabasis according to which the readers are told not to trust what they are reading.[14] The text cannot be divided into two different levels – one about the characters and the other about the relationship between narrator and receivers. There is only one hypothetical level in which the text establishes itself as a sort of permanent parabasis, in the middle of a discussion between 'io' [I], 'noi' [we], the actants, and their rambling 'atti' [acts]. It should also be noted that the critical drive of Di Marco's text is not exclusively literary but also political. Let us consider a short passage:

> Telemaco, invece, ha probabilmente in mente che questo cammino non consente ancora molto circa le possibilità di superare l'ostacolo di fondo che rimane politico oltre ogni apparenza mitologica e letteraria, soprattutto in vista di una effettiva partecipazione dal basso che liberi le attuali istituzioni dal loro carattere tecnocratico nonostante l'incantata cornice che le circonda.
>
> [Telemachus, on the other hand, probably thinks that this journey does not allow much in terms of the possibility of overcoming political obstacles, especially in light of an actual participation from below that frees the institutions from their technocratic character despite the enchanted frame that surrounds them.] (*Telemachia* 71)

One of the legacies of the *neoavanguardia* is the consciousness that it is no longer possible to represent reality: it is only possible to stage the crisis of representation itself (the allegory of failure). The loss of this consciousness in the following decades produced a return to more traditional forms of narrative that reject any type of literary research.

Neoavanguardia and the Critique of Practice

I would like to state this point a second time: the critical magnitude of the Italian *neoavanguardia* is at its best when it is not simply literary criticism. This is especially clear in Sanguineti's remarks. During the first conference of the Gruppo 63, in fact, he talks about the cultural, ideological, and political significance of the avant-garde, illustrating at the same time its 'anormalità' [abnormality], 'rispetto a una ideologia data, l'ideologia borghese, che si è concretata in determinate operazioni linguistiche e presumenti a una stabile normalità, e più largamente, quindi, rispetto alle norme estetiche borghesi, e, in quelle, rispetto alle norme sociali borghesi nel loro complesso' [with respect to a given ideology, the bourgeois ideology, that has actualized itself in certain linguistic, aesthetic, and social norms] (in Balestrini and Giuliani 383). The problem was that in many respects the new avant-garde was still an all-literary phenomenon, a new form of literature satisfied with the scandal provoked within the traditionalist camp. In many cases the most extreme possibility was to assume and suppose that the new literary forms could actually change not only the readers' perception of reality, but the world itself.[15] The attempt to push the text towards a 'critica della realtà' [critique of reality] was supported by left wingers of the group, such as Di Marco in his essay 'Ipotesi per una letteratura di contestazione' [Hypothesis for a literature of protest]. Literature, Di Marco argues, should not mirror and represent praxis, but activate it. What is necessary, therefore, is a 'progetto di Storia' [project of History] embedded in the text, and a quest for a meaning that does not end in itself but is 'istanza di socializzazione dei valori e dei significati [...] nella espansione delle forze produttive e nella contraddizione tra tale espansione e la *forma* (capitalistica) di tali rapporti di produzione' [an example of the socialization of values and meanings in the expansion of productive forces and in the contradiction of such expansion and the capitalistic form of the relations of production] (15). A similar view was shared by Fausto Curi, who in his article 'Presa politica della parola' [The word and the taking of politics] (1968), wrote:

> Quello che alcuni di noi stanno già compiendo [...] è un lavoro di *cultura politica* [...] ciò che conta veramente è la carica ideologica di ogni operazione, meglio ancora ciò che conta è il significato pratico di ogni operazione: la discriminante non è una discriminante di 'generi' (e comunque deve esser chiaro che i 'generi' hanno tutti pari dignità), ma una verifica nella prassi della parola letteraria.
>
> [What some of us are already doing ... is work of *political culture* ... What really matters is the ideological charge of every act or, better, the practical relevance of every act. The distinction does not concern the 'genres' (the 'genres' all have the same dignity), but the role of the literary word in the praxis.] (*Metodo* 224)

The transition from literature to politics is the event that marks the explosion of the contradictions of the *neoavanguardia*, the crisis of the journal *Quindici*, and the end of the experience. From that moment on we have what could be called the *blocco dell'avanguardia* [avant-garde block]. Several debates have been held about the impossibility of the avant-garde and its relationship with postmodernism and consumerism. Nevertheless, a return to the 1960s inevitably entails addressing the magnitude of the *neoavanguardia* and the relationship between literature and politics. The situation is nowadays much different because of contingent factors (the lack of brave publishers such as Feltrinelli) and global factors (we are surrounded by false, merely technical, revolutions), and because progressive culture is most of the time highly conservative. In this context, it is easy to see how Brecht's motto 'Nicht an das gute Alte anknüpfen, sondern an das schlechte Neue' [Don't hang on to the good old things but on to the bad new ones] is today impossible. And yet, in writing about that crucial literary season, as I have tried to do here, one element stands out: if today critical practice is necessary in order not to become victims of the ideology of confusion and consumerism, it is then useful to return to the literary tendencies that brought the critical discourse to the fore, embedding it in the text itself, and using it, at the same time, in the broad perspective of social 'reproduction.'

Translated by Paolo Chirumbolo

NOTES

1 See Muzzioli, *Teoria e critica della letteratura nelle nuove avanguardie degli anni sessanta* (1982).

2 As Eco wrote: 'Dato che c'erano fratture, ogni lettura fatta non riscuoteva il consenso generale. Così ciascuno esponeva il proprio punto di vista, e nel modo più impietoso. Non ci si dichiarava perplessi: ci si diceva contro. E si diceva il perché. Quali fossero i perché non conta. Conta che in questa società letteraria l'unità si stava realizzando a poco a poco attraverso due implicite assunzioni di metodo: (1) ogni autore sentiva necessario controllare la sua ricerca sottoponendola alle reazioni altrui; (2) la collaborazione si manifestava come assenza di pietà e di indulgenza. Correvano definizioni da levare la pelle agli animi troppo sensibili' [Due to the conflicts of the group, no reading ever received unanimous consensus. Thus, you would express your point of view mercilessly. You would not state your bewilderment: you would express your strong opposition. And you would explain your reasons, whatever they were. In this literary society unity was slowly reached through two implicit methodological assumptions: (1) every author felt it was essential to verify his/her research by submitting it to the rest of the group; (2)

collaboration was based on, and expressed through, the absence of piety and indulgence. The definitions employed could offend the most sensitive souls] ('Generazione' 410).

3 'Il Menabò 2: un contributo alla conservazione degli equivoci'; reprinted in Giuliani's *Immagini e maniere* (1965).

4 Giuliani's confrontational disposition goes well beyond the chronological boundaries of the *neoavanguardia*, as exemplified by his severe review of Elsa Morante's *La Storia* published in *La Repubblica* in 1986. The article, entitled 'Che brutta storia' [An ugly story] begins: 'Ho vissuto lunghe ore di abbrutimento: ho riletto per dovere d'ufficio, con scrupolosa angoscia, *La Storia* di Elsa Morante, seicentocinquanta pagine di noia e di ambizioni sbagliate' [I went through many hours of brutalization: out of duty, I have reread with scrupulous agony Elsa Morante's *La Storia*, six hundred and fifty pages of boredom and wrong ambitions].

5 Consider, for instance, the following passage: 'Tralasciando di spegnere alcune aree di tensione retorica, ha acceso in corrispondenza alcune isole semantiche ritornanti' [Not worried about switching off some areas of rhetoric tension, the author has turned on some reoccurring semantic islands] (*Vero* 141).

6 Sanguineti said of Pasolini: 'Eravamo due persone molto lontane e diverse, e sarebbe stato veramente difficile trovare dei punti d'intesa' [We were two extremely different persons, and it would be very hard to find something in common] (in Gambaro 36).

7 Edoardo Sanguineti, ed., *Poesia del Novecento* [Poetry in the Twentieth Century] (Turin: G. Einaudi 1969); a new two-volume edition of this anthology was published by Einaudi in 1993.

8 I am referring here to an article written by Sanguineti in 1995, 'Per una critica dell'avanguardia poetica in Italia' [For a citique of the poetical avant-garde in Italy] reprinted in the 2001 edition of *Ideologia e linguaggio* (115–27).

9 On the same subject, see also Fausto Curi's article 'Il sogno la crudeltà, il gioco,' *Il verri* 29 (1968): 18–30; reprinted in *Metodo, storia, strutture* (1971).

10 See, in particular, Barilli's essay, 'Le strutture del romanzo,' in the introductory section of the anthology *Gruppo 63: la nuova letteratura.*

11 Arbasino once spoke of a 'gita a Chiasso' [trip to Chiasso] in order to emphasize the necessity of crossing national frontiers to retrieve theoretical texts not yet translated into Italian.

12 'Non v'è eroe per il commentatore [...] in codesto processo sempre disfacendosi, dilatandosi come macchia, muffa, muschio, fradicia fungaia; rallentata esplosione, deflagrazione secolare, grazie alla quale le scheg-

ge dell'esploso toccano infiniti luoghi e forme, in nessuno quietandosi. Dunque, non v'è inizio, non conclusione' [There is no hero for the commentator ... in this process that is always undoing, expanding like a stain, like mould, a soaked mushroom bed; slackened explosion, secular deflagration, thanks to which the splinters touch infinite places and forms, not finding rest anywhere. Therefore, there's no beginning, no conclusion] (*Nuovo commento* 80).

13 'Continuare a commentare, nella persuasione che alla fin fine un testo si troverà cui questo commento si attagli' [To keep on commenting, strongly believing that eventually this commentary will find its own text] (*Nuovo commento* 143).

14 'È un problema di moralità professionale, infatti: l'autore deve sempre avvertire il lettore quando la lettura d'un suo libro nasconde dei rischi, quali che siano' [It is a moral problem: the author must always warn the reader when the reading of one of his books entails some risks, whatever they are] (*Telemachia* 41).

15 As Eco maintains in 'Del modo di formare come impegno sulla realtà [Form as social commitment], an article originally published in *Il menabò* (1962) also included in *Opera aperta.*

WORKS CITED

Arbasino, Alberto. *Fratelli d'Italia.* Milan: Feltrinelli, 1963.

– 'Gita a Chiasso.' In Renato Barilli and Angelo Guglielmi, eds. *Gruppo 63: critica e teoria.* 180–4.

Balestrini, Nanni, and Alfredo Giuliani, eds. *Gruppo 63: la nuova letteratura, 34 scrittori, Palermo ottobre 1963.* Milan: Feltrinelli, 1964.

Barilli, Renato. 'Le strutture del romanzo.' In Nanni Balestrini and Alfredo Giuliani, eds. *Gruppo 63: la nuova letteratura.* 25–47.

Barilli, Renato, and Angelo Guglielmi, eds. *Gruppo 63: critica e teoria.* Milan: Feltrinelli, 1976; Turin: Testo & Immagine, 2003.

Curi, Fausto. *Metodo, storia, strutture.* Turin: Paravia, 1971.

– 'Sulla giovane poesia.' In Nanni Balestrini and Alfredo Giuliani, eds. *Gruppo 63: la nuova letteratura.* 48–60.

Di Marco, Roberto. 'Ipotesi per una letteratura di contestazione (3).' *Marcatrè* 16–18 (1965).

– *Telemachia.* Turin: Einaudi, 1968.

Eco, Umberto. 'La generazione di Nettuno.' In Nanni Balestrini and Alfredo Giuliani, eds. *Gruppo 63: la nuova letteratura.* 407–16.

– *Opera aperta.* Milan: Bompiani, 1967.
Gambaro, Fabio. *Colloquio con Edoardo Sanguineti: quarant'anni di cultura italiana attraverso i ricordi di un poeta intellettuale.* Milan: Anabasi, 1993.
Giuliani, Alfredo. 'Che brutta storia.' *La repubblica,* 11 April 1986.
– 'Il Menabò 2: un contributo alla conservazione degli equivoci.' In his *Immagini e maniere.* Milan: Feltrinelli, 1965. 100–5.
Giuliani, Alfredo, ed. *I Novissimi: poesie per gli anni '60.* Turin: Einaudi, 1965.
Guglielmi, Angelo. "Avanguardia e sperimentalismo." In Nanni Balestrini and Alfredo Giuliani, eds. *Gruppo 63: la nuova letteratura.* 15–24.
– *Vero e falso.* Milan: Feltrinelli, 1968.
Manganelli, Giorgio. *Hilarotragoedia.* Milan: Feltrinelli, 1964.
– *Nuovo commento.* Turin: Einaudi, 1969.
Muzzioli, Francesco. *Teoria e critica della letteratura nelle nuove avanguardie degli anni sessanta.* Rome: Istituto della Enciclopedia Italiana, 1982.
Sanguineti, Edoardo. *Ideologia e linguaggio.* Milan: Feltrinelli, 2001.

2 *Neoavanguardia* and Postmodernism: Oscillations between Innovation and Tradition from 1963 to 2003

MONICA JANSEN

A volte i principî, a cui noi obbediamo, entrano in contrasto con se stessi.
– Francesco Biamonti, *Le parole la notte*

The question of whether postmodernism marks the end of any avant-garde transgression and thus the end of modernity is crucial within the context of contemporary Italian fiction, both for Marxist literary critics and for those with a hermeneutic or poststructuralist orientation. If postmodernism is to be intended as a rupture with modernism, the problem is how to deal with it. Does it mark a new epoch or rather a new phase within the history of modernity? The 'grand narrative' of the avant-garde, founded on the absolute value of the 'modern' and on a linear-progressive concept of history, enters into crisis when the concept of the 'end of history,' introduced by postmodernist thinkers, has problematized the utopian opposition between a revolutionary 'future' and a reactionary 'past.' The poet Lello Voce, one of the founding members of the 'post-avant-garde' Gruppo 93, has observed that the avant-garde in the end does nothing more than found a new tradition. Both 'avant-garde' and 'tradition' impose themselves as absolute norms and in this sense they are mutually exclusive. Voce's alternative consists in a paradox that situates tradition within the avant-garde, and no longer in opposition to it. In the trajectory of time that leads from the *neoavanguardia* of the Gruppo 63 to the 'critical postmodernism' of the Gruppo 93 it is indeed possible to detect an inversion of values: the so-called avant-garde 'tradition of the new' has become in the end the postmodern 'newness of tradition.'

That the relationship between modernism and postmodernism should be conceived in terms of 'oscillation' rather than in terms of rupture becomes clear in Umberto Eco's view on the normalization of the avant-garde, which implies the postmodern interpretation of the 'end of history.' In an interview with Rocco Capozzi he states:

> Il lavoro di invenzione e sovvertimento linguistico [...] oggi viene praticato dai cantanti rock, dagli autori di videoclips televisivi, dai comici di cabaret. Era normale che dovesse accadere così, ed è quello che si chiama normalizzazione dell'avanguardia.
>
> [Nowadays the work of linguistic invention and subversion [...] is practiced by rock singers, by the authors of music videos, by stand-up comedians. It was quite normal that this should have happened. It's what is called the normalization of the avant-garde.] (Capozzi 93)[1]

The combination of highbrow and lowbrow cultures is considered by Eco as an alternative to the 1960s avant-garde rebellion against 'consensus' culture, which in its ultimate consequences can bring about only the rejection of communication *tout court*.[2] However, the hypothesis of a normalization of the conflict between avant-garde art and tradition is rejected by those literary critics that defend Adorno's 'contradiction' thesis of the avant-gardes. The Marxist-oriented critic Romano Luperini, for example, states:

> Il postmoderno nasce dall'idea che sono finite le grandi contraddizioni. L'avanguardia, che nasce dalle contraddizioni [...] va respinta in quanto tale; si tratta di un rifiuto teorico, dovuto tanto alla perdita del senso della storia, quanto alla negazione della storia come contraddizione.
>
> [The postmodern originates from the notion that all great contradictions are over. The avant-garde, which is created by contradictions ... must be rejected as such. This theoretical rejection is due as much to the loss of a sense of history as to the negation of history as being a contradiction.] (*Lezioni sul postmoderno* 10)

The difference between the 'normalization' thesis and the 'contradiction' thesis is nevertheless not as rigid as it seems. The 'metahistoric' or normalized perspective does not necessarily lead to a position of cultural relativism. In fact, this perspective may still propose a new critical function for an art form that no longer coincides with the utopia of the final reconciliation between a historical and an aesthetic meaning. And vice versa: the antagonistic perspective on avant-garde art cannot be blind to a changing situation that calls for new forms of contradiction rather than historical-dialectical ones.

When situating the literary debate on the avant-garde within the philosophical debate on postmodernism, it is possible to identify three different interpretations of the end of the avant-gardes. Jürgen Habermas ('Moderno') considers the avant-garde to be an 'aporia' of the modern project that should be reintegrated in the sphere of the life world. Jean-François Lyotard ('Intervento italiano'), who identifies normalization with consumerism, contrasts the cultural industry with the postmodern sublime, a radicalization of the modernist revolt against representation. Finally, Gianni Vattimo (*La società trasparente*) considers the historical avant-garde to be a utopian discourse that, reread in the light of the normalization of aesthetic experience, can function as a pluralistic 'heterotopia,' as the anticipation of a postmodern art of contamination.

The complexities of the debate on the 'end of the avant-garde,' which in substance addressed the problem that art could no longer be legitimated either by the master narrative of unitary reason or by art's own autonomy, can be traced back to occasions between 1963 and 2003 on which the Italian avant-garde – or better the *neoavanguardia* – gathered in order to legitimize its existence and persistence or to argue for its death. There are four principal moments in which critics and artists of different disciplines and orientations felt the need to discuss new artistic forms in the light of a changed reality. The first meeting, held in Palermo in 1963, was opened by Luciano Anceschi, founder of the journal *Il verri*; Anceschi sensed a 'mutamento della situazione letteraria' [change in the literary situation] (in Barilli and Guglielmi 264) in need of a new generation able to break with dogmatisms and to promote, within a European context, the 'emergenza del nuovo' [emergence of the new] (cit. in Barilli, Curi, and Lorenzini 13). This occasion gave birth to the Gruppo 63, whose short but far-reaching life ended formally in 1967. The second meeting, organized in 1984 by the editorial board of the cultural review *Alfabeta* with the title 'Il senso della letteratura' [The meaning of literature], was also held in Palermo. This time the alarm was sounded to warn of a 'dispersion' in the production of criticism and literature, without the collective project brought forward by the Gruppo 63. The third gathering, held in Reggio Emilia in 1993, was intended to evaluate the project of a new avant-garde poetry represented by the Gruppo 93. The fourth gathering was the celebration of the fortieth anniversary of the

Gruppo 63 in 2003, held in Palermo and in Bologna. The proceedings of the Bologna conference, published by Pendragon in 2005, manifest a twofold objective: to illustrate historically the artistic course of the group in its different disciplines, and to map the cultural opportunities opened up by these experimental experiences for future generations.

According to Lucia Re's analysis of the 1984 debate on the 'meaning of literature,' the central issue in the discussion on the avant-garde legacy of the Gruppo 63 was the epistemological problem of the loss of certainties. In 1963 this loss of foundations was judged positively as the dissolution of bourgeois ideology and of Marxist hegemony.[3] In 1984, however, the avant-garde alternative of disorder is set against the 'weak' ontology of postmodernism that translates instability of meaning into a new way of being. In Reggio Emilia in 1993 a group of poets and critics tried to respond to the loss of ideological and aesthetical certainties in a more concrete fashion, with an avant-garde literary production and with theoretical alternatives that take into account a reconstruction (instead of deconstruction) of the 'meaning' of literature. The 'tradition of the new' formulated by Anceschi in the 1960s thus becomes the 'newness of tradition' of the 1990s. In the new millennium, the search for a new tradition continues, but it differs from both the antagonistic model represented by the neo-avant-garde and from the 'anti-model' identified with postmodernism. In 2003 the tension between opposed models is transformed into the notion of the 'end of models.' This notion turns the generation of 'uncertainty' of the 1980s into a generation of 'flexibility' that floats freely forwards and backwards between the waves of avant-garde and postmodernism.

1963: The Loss of Certainties as Rupture

The annals of the first meeting of the Gruppo 63 in Palermo on 3 October 1963 are collected in two volumes, both published by Feltrinelli: *Gruppo 63: la nuova letteratura* (1964), edited by Nanni Balestrini and Alfredo Giuliani, and *Gruppo 63: critica e teoria* (1976), edited by Renato Barilli and Angelo Guglielmi. As noted above, the 1963 conference was inaugurated by Luciano Anceschi, whose journal *Il verri* (founded in 1956) opposed northern 'Enlightenment' to the southern legacy of Benedetto Croce (Eco, in Barilli, Curi, and Lorenzini 27). According to Anceschi, the literary situation had certainly changed, but 'quale esso sia, come si manifesti, e con quali motivazioni, è proprio ciò di cui qui si deve ragionare' [what it is, how it manifests itself, and for what reasons, this is precisely what needs to be discussed here] (Barilli and Guglielmi 264). It is interesting to compare this statement with one made by Anceschi in his essay 'Metodologia del nuovo' (1964), where he tries to get hold of literary change in its unprecedented phenomenology:

> Pare veramente si dichiarino, nel nostro paese, una realtà di nuova poesia, una volontà di nuovo romanzo, una condizione di coerente convergenza tra le arti nella ricerca comune, e un orientamento di pensiero capace di intendere, di dominare, di sollecitare il tumulto del nuovo.
>
> [We truly seem to be witnessing in our country a reality of new poetry, a wish for a new novel, a condition of coherent convergence between the arts toward a common research, and an orientation of thought capable of understanding, dominating, and stimulating the uproar of the new.] (7–8)

Anceschi is asking which approach is most suitable to judge the value of the new *in statu nascendi*: do we have to accept it, to reject it, or rather suspend our judgment? When the 'new' is related to the work of art, the recycling of some motives of the historical avant-gardes, in Anceschi's view, should not be explained as an anachronistic repetition but as a 'recovery' of forms that assume other meanings in interaction with the new contexts in which they operate ('Metodologia' 10). The newness of the neo-avant-garde thus consists rather in a new, inclusive conception of the 'new,' different from the absolute and exclusive value of the 'new' adopted by the historical avant-gardes. The avant-garde's rupture with the past no longer seems valid when there is no monolithic order to resist. In 'Avanguardia e sperimentalismo' Angelo Guglielmi speaks of the disorder brought into existence by a cultural environment in which everything is permitted (17), a situation that renders any avant-garde crusade against canonical Art useless and out of date:

> Quali porte vuole aprire, se tutte sono aperte? Quali forzature provare, se la situazione è forzata su tutta la linea? Indubbiamente nessuna. Il vero è che oggi si può lavorare liberamente, in tutte le direzioni possibili, volgendosi verso le ricerche e gli esperimenti espressivi più spericolati. Nessuno ce lo impedisce. Non c'è nessun argine o ostacolo obiettivo da abbattere.
>
> [Which doors does it want to open, if they are all open? Which locks does it want to break, when they have all been broken? None, obviously. The truth is that today one can work freely, in all possible directions, turning to the

most daring expressive projects and experiments. No one gets in our way. There are no barriers or obstacles to take down.] (17)

Guglielmi considers the world to be a centre of unconquerable disorder. In consonance with the 'anything goes' slogan of international postmodernism in the 1960s and 1970s, he acknowledges, during the debate on the first meeting of the Gruppo 63, the complete loss of meaning of History in a space where every event is simultaneously meaningless and falsified (in Barilli and Guglielmi 268). The question is not how to represent the real or how to oppose its representation, but rather how to 'demystify' the real by underscoring its contradictory integrity. The ideal literary form to achieve this goal, according to Guglielmi, is pastiche, an art form that has a strong devaluating force because it combines contrasting levels of knowledge. For Guglielmi the only possible avant-garde is 'a-ideologica, disimpegnata, astorica, in una parola 'atemporale' [a-ideological, unengaged, ahistorical, in a word 'a-temporal'] (269).

Although for Guglielmi the main objective is no longer the 'contradiction' of a given situation, as had been the case for the historical avant-gardes, his proposal of 'demystification' of the real is still conceived within the binary logic of dialectics. Concepts such as 'ideology,' 'engagement,' and 'history' – the core of neorealism – are 'demystified' in order to form the alternative of a new avant-garde. According to Alfredo Giuliani, spearhead of the *novissimi* poets, the *neoavanguardia* actually sets up two fundamental oppositions: between tradition and avant-garde, and between language and ideology. Nevertheless, if we picture these oppositions in a space where 'anything goes' and where there are no obstacles to defeat, it becomes problematic to think of them in terms of contradiction.

The extreme confusion described by Guglielmi is also concerned with the coexistence within the Gruppo 63 of the various shapes of the two oppositions delineated by Giuliani. Renato Barilli, for example, places tradition and avant-garde within the perspective of historical integration, which implies the normalization of the avant-garde once it has become part of history. In *Postille a Il nome della rosa* Umberto Eco remarks that during the 1965 meeting of the Gruppo 63 Barilli asked for a revision of the equation 'consenso = disvalore' [consensus = non-value] and for a reconsideration of plot and action in the novel. Eco interprets this communicative turn as a sign that the avant-garde was already becoming tradition (36). However, those closer to the Marxist side, such as Edoardo Sanguineti, identified normalization with the ideology of 'museification,' and defended the 'unrepresentable' in art against the pressures of consensus. Sanguineti attacks Giuliani's opposition between ideology and language, which presumes the possibility of distinguishing between linguistic transparency and opacity:

> Non credo che ciò che caratterizza l'avanguardia sia questa assunzione privilegiata del linguaggio contro l'ideologia, ma la ferma consapevolezza che non si dà operazione ideologica che non sia, contemporaneamente e immediatamente, verificabile nel linguaggio.
>
> [I do not believe that the avant-garde is characterized by this privileged opposition of language and ideology, but by the certainty that any ideological operation can immediately and at the same time be verified in language.] (Barilli and Guglielmi 272)

Sanguineti thus introduces a third element into Giuliani's scheme – the avant-garde's consciousness of the relationship between language and ideology – and thus formulates a new metahistorical temporality as the starting point of an avant-garde conscious both of the historicity of the museum and of its own revolt (286). He accepts neither Barilli's historical relativism nor Guglielmi's a-historicism: while Barilli's view is flawed by dangerous neutrality, Guglielmi's view reduces itself to a complete paralysis of judgment. What should be emphasized is not the inevitable normalization of every avant-garde, nor the immediate and concrete meaning of the work of art, but rather its functioning (288).

Sanguineti's polemic against Barilli and Guglielmi thus highlights three kinds of temporality: the historical (Barilli), the a-historical (Guglielmi), and the metahistorical or dialectical (Sanguineti). This distinction is important in order to determine the relationship not only between *neoavanguardia* and postmodernism but also between *neoavanguardia* and the historical avant-gardes. In the positions analysed thus far one notices a rethinking of the absolute value of the 'new' in relation to the functioning of the work of art as well as to its 'historicity' – both elements that depend on the change of art's situation in time. The neo-avant-garde is thus no longer conceived as a movement that puts itself ahead of a revolution, in the literal sense of avant-garde. In *Pasolini contro Calvino* Carla Benedetti studies the 'death of art' phenomenon and distinguishes between the utopian interpretation of art proposed by the historical avant-gardes (to destroy art as a separate sphere from the life world) and its 'dystopic' version introduced by the neo-avant-garde, which considers the death of art in terms of commodification. Using Sanguineti as an example, Benedetti argues that the *neoavanguardia* 'non fu tanto una "nuova arte," quanto divulgazione militante della fine dell'arte, della sua degradazione a merce, di cui non si poteva più rimandare la consapevolezza' [the *neoavanguardia* was not so much a 'new art,' but rather the militant popularization of the end of art, of its degradation into commodity. The awareness of this situation could no longer be postponed] (192). This is also valid for Sanguineti's position on 'museification,' which Benedetti describes as a defence by identifying with the aggressor (192).

According to Benedetti, the neo-avant-garde's self-destructive attitude in facing the 'death of art' distinguishes it from postmodernism. In its consciousness of not being able to produce anything new, postmodernism on the contrary considers the death of art as a means to propel art beyond the crisis of modernism (193). What connects them is their relationship with tradition, which is no longer contrasted but reused through pastiche and through the (ironic) art of quotation. It is precisely the discourse on 'museification' initiated by Adorno that, set against the change in the 'meaning of literature' between 1984 and 1993, sheds light on the shift of emphasis from the 'self-consciousness of the avant-garde, which tended towards the future annihilation of the artistic revolt, to a proactive self-consciousness, which tends towards a revalorization of otherness within the past.[4]

1984: The Loss of Certainties as Dispersion

> Uno spazio di ricerca, di proposta, di selezione, di confronto intorno a tendenze per un'istituzione culturale e letteraria alternativa, è cosa che ciascuno rimpiange e dice valida e urgente, mentre denuncia la stagnazione e il vuoto esistenti.
>
> [A space for research, for new ideas, for selection, for the comparison of tendencies in order to create an alternative cultural and literary institution – everybody mourns the loss of all this and claims that it is important and urgent, while denouncing the existing stagnation and emptiness.] (Marcello Carlino 123)

This is Marcello Carlino's reading of the many newspaper articles that appeared in 1983 to commemorate the defunct Gruppo 63. It was precisely this need to form an intellectual community, not necessarily a 'group,' that brought many figures of the literary milieu back together in Palermo. During the 2003 gathering in Bologna, Renato Barilli recalled that in 1973 there had been no celebration because the Gruppo 63 had just fallen apart, while in 1983 the right atmosphere for celebrating was absent (*Il Gruppo 63 quarant'anni dopo* 274). In fact, the organizers of the 1984 conference – Francesco Leonetti, Gianni Sassi, and Antonio Porta – did not register a radical, and in many respects liberating, transformation in the literary situation, as Anceschi had done in 1963. Rather, they noticed a 'certain dispersion' that was probably due to the hegemony of other media, to the confusing multiplication of the ways of making and interpreting literature, and to the minor and marginalized circulation of literary and critical works.

What had gone astray was thus the 'senso della letteratura' [the meaning of literature], as a result of the different directions followed by authors with individual agendas, and of the electronic opportunities opened up by new techniques of communication. 'Transformation' indicates a direction 'beyond,' projected into the future; 'dispersion' seems rather to refer to a feeling of disorientation and of senselessness, a negative reading of the chaos that in 1963 was valued positively in contrast to bourgeois rationality.

The journal *Alfabeta* played an important role in the 1984 conference, publishing a series of preparatory articles (issues 57 and 58, 1984) as well as the contributions read during the conference, including the general discussion (issue 69, 1985). Lucia Re has offered a useful analysis of the debate on the meaning of literature based on the first series of papers. According to Re, it is necessary to specify the two contrasting tendencies pointed out by the organizers: the Marxist perspective of the 'espressionisti' [expressionists] or 'allegorici' [allegorists], and the 'neoromantic' perspective founded on a blend of poststructuralist and neo-hermeneutic elements. The first group is connected to the:

> istanze etico-politiche, spesso di orientamento marxista, già presenti in un'ala della neoavanguardia (Leonetti, Pagliarani, Sanguineti), opponendo polemicamente alle nozioni di intertestualità e di autoreferenzialità del discorso letterario il richiamo alla Storia da un lato (soprattutto da parte dei critici), e alla Vita dall'altro (soprattutto da parte dei poeti).
>
> [ethical-political demands, often of a Marxist stance, already present within one wing of the avant-garde (Leonetti, Pagliarani, Sanguineti), polemically countering the notions of intertextuality and self-referentiality of literary

> discourse with an appeal to History on one hand (especially by the critics), and to Life on the other (especially by the poets).] (Re 190)

The neoromantic position:

> Si richiama più o meno implicitamente al pensiero post-nietzscheano e post-heideggeriano 'al di là del soggetto,' alla problematica della decostruzione e a quella del pensiero debole. Per questa seconda linea il problema del 'senso della letteratura' si presenta o come un 'falso problema,' o come un problema che richiede una risposta paradossale [...] o comunque una problematizzazione del problema stesso.
>
> [relates more or less explicitly to post-Nietzschean and post-Heiddegerian thought 'beyond the subject,' to the question of deconstruction and of weak thought. For this approach, the problem of the 'meaning of literature' is either a 'false problem,' or a problem that calls for a paradoxical answer ... or, in any case, a problematizing of the problem itself.] (190)

The conference addressed three fundamental issues: the 'loss of certainties' as an epistemological problem; the effects of new technologies and mass media on literary production and reception; and finally, postmodernism as the creative and critical discourse of the 1980s. Re concludes, from the results of the conference, that the 'expressionists' tended to 'reconstruct' a meaning for literature and to purport an act of 'restoration,' while the 'neoromantics,' which Re associates with poststructuralism and with Vattimo's 'weak thought,' tried to a certain extent to 'deconstruct' the foundation of meaning.

At first sight, it may seem paradoxical to call the Marxist orientation 'restorative.' It is true that the concept of 'restoration' appears often in various statements but it rarely has a positive connotation. The meaning of this concept depends on what it is related to. If it is related to the literature of the 1970s the term is absolutely negative. According to many of the critics involved in the discussion, those years produced a 'void' of meaning. Angelo Guglielmi, for example, declared that the 1970s repeated the experiments of the 1960s, simply replacing revolt with communication to produce a literature of epigones ('Nuovo intervento' 22). In his view, the 1970s are responsible for the disastrous current situation described by Marxist literary critic Romano Luperini as a moment of opaque inertia ('Statuto' 15).

The option of restoration, however, can also open up positive alternatives when set in opposition to the meaninglessness produced by the restorative literature of the 1970s. Luperini reaches the paradoxical conclusion that it is precisely the restorative solution that can reopen dialectics:

> Non direi che poi in questo ritorno al fondo istituzionale o tradizionale o alle origini della letteratura si debba vedere soltanto l'aspetto predominante, che ovviamente è questo restaurativo. Direi che, paradossalmente, in una società che distrugge il passato e il futuro, questo aspetto restaurativo può risultare forse utile: può rinascere, voglio dire, una tradizione, si può riaprire una dialettica.
>
> [I would not say that one should only see the predominant aspect of this return to the institutional or traditional foundations or to the origins of literature, which is obviously a restorative one. I would say that, paradoxically, in a society that destroys both past and future, this restorative aspect can perhaps be useful in the end. What I mean is that from it a tradition can be reborn, a dialectics can be reestablished.] ('Un confronto' 18)

The return to tradition in this case has nothing in common with Barilli's historical relativism, but can be linked instead to Sanguineti's awareness that every tradition is a temporary construction that can be deconstructed and then reconstructed in a different way. It entails a kind of 'letteratura di secondo grado,' [second degree literature] – as Luperini argues in 'Un confronto tra posizioni diverse' – with a kind of 'letteratura-letteratura' that, by contesting itself, can reweave the threads of tradition. A comparison of his treatment of the problem of 'avant-garde vs. tradition' with Sanguineti's treatment reveals a number of significant parallels. Luperini declares, for instance, that against 'letteratura-consumo, subordinata all'immediatezza, si contrappone la letteratura-funzione, che punta al "ri-uso" e tende alla scuola e al museo anche quando intende combatterli' [literature-consumption, subordinated to immediacy, one can oppose literature-function, which aims at 're-using' and tends towards the school and the museum even when it intends to fight them] ('Statuto' 15). Luperini also argues that, at present, avant-garde art has become useless because the domination of multimedia has confined literature to a kind of Indian reserve, with the paradoxical consequence that those who in 1963 tried to conquer new territories are chased back to the separate autonomy of art. He concludes his paper by rather desperately exhorting, 'bisogna restaurare i musei per riaprire la lotta contro i loro recinti' [we must re-establish the museums in order to fight again against their fences] (15).

Re's distinction between a tendency aiming at reconstructing a meaning for literature and one aiming at its deconstruction becomes even more relevant when applied to the epistemological problem at the centre of the conference: the general 'loss of certainties.' How should artists react to this loss, and can postmodernism be blamed for it? Francesco Leonetti, listed among the expressionists, explores different philosophical territories, including that of 'weak thought.' Rather than following Adorno's disastrous conclusions on mass culture, he points out a partially positive outcome of the loss of meaning ('Stile e statuto' 3), envisaging a kind of expressionism that is double-headed, or has an oscillating spirit (5). Moreover, today's intellectuals, confronted with the homogenizing forces of mass communication, cannot choose the way of dialectical conflict but should work instead in the interstices, in order to poke a 'hole' in the hegemony of the media.

Leonetti's statement has been fruitful for the debate, offering many directions for research related to postmodernism. The image of postmodernism as a double-headed artistic practice that simultaneously rejects and re-embraces modernism can likewise be found in poet Antonio Porta's declaration that the crisis of finding historical definitions can be resolved 'considerando falsa l'antitesi moderno postmoderno e ipotizzando al suo posto una storica interazione, come se simbolo della nostra situazione fosse il Giano Bifronte' [by considering the antithesis modern-postmodern to be false, and postulating in its place a historical interaction, as if the two-faced Janus were the symbol of our situation] ('Sentimento e forma' 5). A 'postmodern' writer such as Antonio Tabucchi also associates himself with Porta,[5] asserting that literature no longer moves in one linear and progressive direction but instead, operates in two directions: 'influenza il futuro ma anche il passato, è una freccia geometrica con due punte e due direzioni' [it influences the future, but also the past, it is a geometrical arrow with two heads and two directions]. Modern and postmodern in the end have become (Siamese) twins (3).

Porta states furthermore that in the 1960s his energies had been devoted to the work of art itself, but now his poetical project can be called 'communicability.' The times have definitely changed for him as well. In the general discussion Porta concludes that in the 1980s nobody dreamed any longer of closing himself in the ancient tower of the avant-garde ('Contro il grande stile' 23).

The stress placed on communicability can be linked to the weakening of old oppositions, such as transgression against communication or innovation against convention. Not unlike Porta, who substitutes the notion of antithesis with that of interaction, critic Gian Carlo Ferretti uses the dialogical notion of 'copresences' instead of the dialectical notion of 'dichotomies' to underscore the point that certain binary oppositions tend to resolve in different contradictory pairs, or even in their opposites ('Ricerca e consumo' 7). As an example, he takes the phenomenon of postmodernism in literature that introduces an ironic use of intertextuality in order to bridge the distance between the reader and the experiments of the novel. Ferretti is thus echoing Eco, who declares that the ideal postmodern novel should overcome the diatribe between elite and popular literature, and that the ideal postmodern writer should have the intuition that today reaching a mass public and inhabiting its dreams may entail avant-garde work (*Postille* 41).

Eco's postmodernism is clearly inspired by American novelist John Barth and stimulated by critic Leslie Fiedler, but in the Italian debate in *Alfabeta* Ferretti detects a tendency to reconstruct oppositions through which experimental and postmodern literature are again separated, the latter being identified with the cultural logic of mass communication. In this way postmodernism, a creative and critical discourse of present times is, according to Re, confined to the flattening horizon of mass media, which should not be engaged with but resisted. Ferretti wonders whether the 'dispersion' – the starting point of the conference – represents only 'uno scenario *di fronte* al quale la situazione del lavoro letterario viene a trovarsi, o non piuttosto una condizione *dentro* la quale il lavoro letterario stesso è fatto ed opera' [a scenario the literary work must *confront*, or rather a condition *within* which the literary work itself is made and operates] ('Una replica'18).

From Porta's and Ferretti's arguments it would be legitimate to conclude that postmodern literature is to be understood as a 'democracy of forms,' while avant-garde literature belongs to the elite ivory tower, and furthermore, that this claim is supported not only by formal characteristics of postmodern literature but also by the changed structure of making art. However, from the point of view of Angelo Guglielmi, whose contributions to the conference reveal a growing hostility towards the category of postmodernism, the 'democracy of forms' belongs instead to avant-garde and trivial literature, both of which respond to the needs of a new mass society. Guglielmi thus argues that their common enemy is traditional literature – or better, the literary institution – and that the binary tradition–avant-garde opposition (demolished in Ferretti's view) remains intact ('Una democrazia' 6).

This could explain Guglielmi's strong polemical position against postmodernism in his second essay, 'Critica del post-moderno,' where he offers a number of reasons why postmodernism is unacceptable. It is thus not surprising that this contribution is included in *Gruppo 93: la recente avventura del dibattito teorico letterario in Italia* (1990), edited by Marxist critics Filippo Bettini and Francesco Muzzioli, a book of essays that could be called an anti-postmodern manifesto. 'Restorative' critics can find a confirmation of their choice to revalorize tradition in Guglielmi's statement that postmodernism is an ideology of the present, and that it designates not a historical phase but on the contrary a permanent and absolute 'after' – 'la stabile dimora in una sala in cui le luci sono già mezze spente' [the stable dwelling in a room in which half the lights have already been turned off] ('Critica del post-moderno' II). Against the a-historical discourse of postmodernism, Guglielmi positions the evidence of the 'past-museum' discourse that 'la realtà del mondo non esiste per se stessa ma per lo sforzo di azione e di pensiero che l'uomo vi sa profondere' [that the reality of the world exists not on its own account but thanks to the effort of action and thought that human beings can imprint on it] (2).

This belief that lived 'History' can confer meaning to narrated 'history' appears to contrast Guglielmi's standpoint in 1963, when the world seemed to him evidence of the impossibility of History and dialectics, a situation to which the avant-garde neither could nor would be able to respond. In yet another commentary, he explains that in the meantime the world seems to have changed from chaotic to incommensurable: today 'il mondo è ripugnantemente scoperto, è un mondo abitato da spie spiate e da spiati che spiano' [the world is horribly open, it is a world inhabited by spied spies and by spied people who spy] ('Nuovo intervento' 22). Instead of using art to discover and demystify reality, it is now necessary to 'reunite' and to 'reassemble' the scattered fragments of pastiche, to reinstall the world as enigma by revitalizing the truth of fable and myth.

In short, what is at stake here is the choice between the reconstruction of the 'antithesis' on new foundations and the 'interaction' between old and weakened contradictions. It becomes clear from this survey that the notions that characterize the historical avant-garde – 'transformation,' 'rupture' and 'contradiction' – have become too 'strong' within the horizon of the loss of certainties. Even some of the most engaged critics no longer propose the tactics of frontal attack, but prefer an explosion from within, working in the interstices (Leonetti). I would suggest that Ferretti really goes to the heart of the matter by asking himself if literature works *within* the postmodern situation or rather *faces* it. In the first case there is necessarily an interaction between experimentation and communication; in the second the result is a new contradiction between memory and postmodern amnesia, as suggested by Guglielmi.

1993: Loss and Reconstruction of Certainties

The debate in *Alfabeta* stimulated a reflection on a number of recurring topics in the discourses of those critics who continue to think within the dialectical tradition of the avant-gardes. In *Campo,* a journal born out of the 'allegoric' wing of *Alfabeta,* Luperini argues that the 1984 conference on the meaning of literature was also the zenith and nadir of the irrational tendencies identified with the 'neoromantic' wing. Triumphantly he exclaims that this has been the moment 'dove queste tendenze e i loro teorici hanno avuto la maggior forza ma nel medesimo tempo e per la prima volta sono stati combattuti apertamente, sia pure da una posizione di minoranza' [in which these tendencies and their theoreticians showed their greatest strength but at the same time and for the first time were fought openly, even if from a minority position] ('Romano Luperini' 39).

One hope of the organizers of the conference on the 'senso della letteratura' – the constitution of a platform composed of scholars as well as writers – seemed to be fulfilled in 1989 with the birth of the Gruppo 93. In the newspaper *L'unità* Filippo Bettini explained the genealogy of this anomalous group formed in 1989 and intended to last until 1993: 'nel 1993 la tendenza […] o si scioglierà […] o diventerà finalmente gruppo' [in 1993 the movement … will either be dissolved … or will finally become a group) ('La nostalgia' 20).[6] The name of the group is deliberately polemical and nostalgic because it recalls the example of the Gruppo 63, but it also aims to call attention to itself as an autonomous movement. Furthermore, its components are the result of the reconciliation of two formerly opposed lines within the *neoavanguardia:* the poets of the anthology *I novissimi* and the experimental poets of *Officina.* The 'old' generation is naturally joined by the 'younger,' which, according to Bettini, represents the soul of this emergent trend and its reason for existence.[7] This new generation is schematically subdivided into three collective groups gathered around three journals: *K.B.* (the poets Durante,

Frasca, Frixione, and Ottonieri); *Baldus* (Baino, Cepollaro, Voce); and *Altri Luoghi* (Berisso, Cademartori, Caserza, Gentiluomo, Jannantuono).

In 1993, when the various 'factions' came together in Reggio Emilia under the banner 63/93 – Trent'anni di ricerca letteraria' [63/93 – thirty years of literary research], it was time for a new assessment of results. What had happened along the trajectory leading from 1963 to 1993? In the search for an answer to this question, the participants of the conference encountered several difficulties: How can one write a history of the last thirty years? What can be considered the turning points, and are they to be seen in terms of continuity or of discontinuity? Does the notion of 'avant-garde' as a poetics of conflict and innovation remain intact, or does it need to be readjusted? And is postmodernism still an adequate concept to describe the present situation?

Romano Luperini's contribution to the volume *63/93 – Trent'anni di ricerca letteraria* (1995) can be considered an attempt to respond systematically to these questions. First of all, he tries to structure the contributions on the Gruppo 63 by dividing them into two groups: one characterized by a historicist approach, with an accent on continuity between past and present; the other characterized by a dialectical approach that highlights the necessity of rupture. Luperini's distinction recalls that of Sanguineti in 1963, in which he called into question Barilli's hypothesis of 'normalization' of the avant-garde. Thirty years later, according to Luperini, the historicist perspective seems to dominate and to reinterpret the poetics of the Gruppo 63 in terms of adaptation to the new situation, of innovation within the mainstream of tradition rather than in contrast to it. It seems that the avant-garde of the Gruppo 63 corresponds not to the dialectical definition of 'sabotage' but rather to that of 'compromise,' of 'rinnovamento culturale volto ad adeguare le strutture ideologiche e le poetiche letterarie al nuovo momento economico e sociale' [cultural renewal aimed at adapting ideological structures and literary poetics to a new socio-economic moment] ('Per la critica' 20). This for Luperini explains the fact that it is possible to draw a continuous line through the 1960s, 1970s, and 1980s, three decades during which were opened the breaches through which neo-hermeneutic and postmodern ideologies could enter (21). Habermas's modern project is not far away.

In Luperini's view, however, if one substitutes this historicist standpoint with a dialectical one, the contradictions within the Gruppo 63 regarding postmodernism are present also in the 1980s, with the 'postmodernists' (Barilli, Eco, Porta, Malerba) on one side and the team of the 'allegoricists' (Sanguineti, Pagliarani, Giuliani, Leonetti, Di Marco,

Balestrini, and Angelo Guglielmi)[8] on the other. In other words, Luperini criticizes the normalization of the avant-garde and argues for reopening a space for conflict. The question is how to create this space when avant-garde and postmodernism have changed places. The solution is found by making a distinction between 'postmodernism' and 'postmodernity.' Luperini draws on Fredric Jameson (*The Postmodern*) and Remo Ceserani ('A proposito di moderno e di postmoderno') who define 'postmodernity,' as a precise historical condition, and 'postmodernism,' as the ideology and cultural practices corresponding to that condition. Since these two categories do not necessarily overlap, 'nelle età della postmodernità accanto all'ideologia e alla pratica artistica del postmodernismo, possono darsi anche tendenze ideologiche e artistiche diverse, antipostmoderniste o estranee al postmodernismo' [in the age of postmodernity, next to the ideology and the artistic practice of postmodernism, there can also be room for different ideological and artistic trends that are anti-postmodernist or unrelated to postmodernism] ('Bilancio' 7).

In Luperini's view, while the trajectory of postmodernity contains possibilities for culture to escape from the postmodern condition, postmodernism can be only the consolidation of its cultural logic, and must therefore be rejected. The space of conflict seems to be exclusively the domain of the negative dialectics of the avant-garde, which however is obliged to reformulate its opposition against tradition. For this problem Luperini offers two solutions of a historicist nature in a dialectical sense. The first solution is related to the anti-postmodernist branch of the Gruppo 63, from which are taken stylistic features such as the use of polyphony and allegory. The second solution entails instead the formulation of 'new' inverted contradictions such as the binary oppositions 'centre-periphery' and 'past-present' ('I pesci rossi' 13). In place of the poststructuralist avant-garde opposition between language and ideology, Luperini proposes 'un ritorno alla materialità del significare [...], a un rapporto fra parole e cose' [a return to the materiality of signifying ... to a relationship between words and things] ('Per la critica' 25). He makes it clear, however, that his proposition is not to be intended as a reinstatement of the (neo) realist emphasis on content.

As we have seen in Luperini's attempts to schematize, Angelo Guglielmi's position remains problematic, hovering as it does between his ascendance to the 'postmodern' neo-avant-gardists and his affiliation with the 'anti-postmodernists.' After his polemical statement in 'Critica del post-moderno' (1985) Guglielmi surprised his readers again with his contribution to the 63/93 conference, in which he reopened the question of postmodernism in a new and even positive way. As with his previous contributions, Guglielmi starts with the idea that the world has changed radically since the 1970s. If the writer-intellectual first reacted to the 'mystification' of the world with a literature of demystification, the writer must now find objectifying filters, not in language, but in his own (auto)biographical experience or in the moral messages contained in fables. In Guglielmi's view, the phenomenon of the 'postmodern' consists in the return to the pleasure of storytelling:

> Gli scrittori del post-moderno dunque riprendono a raccontare; ripropongono una letteratura di rappresentazione che tuttavia non si risolve nel puro e automatico trasporto sulla pagina di brani della realtà dell'esperienza ma nel coglierli, quei brani, come fuori fase, anticipandoli o ritardandoli, dunque utilizzandoli come strumento di ricerca di tensioni ignorate e di significati inattesi.
>
> [Post-modern writers thus return to storytelling. They offer again a literature of representation that, however, does not coincide with the mere and automatic transposition onto the written page of fragments of experienced reality. Rather, they seek to grasp these fragments as if they were out of phase, anticipating or postponing them, and using them in this way as the tool to investigate ignored tensions and unexpected meanings.] ('Trent'anni' 78)

Under the banner of the postmodern Guglielmi returns to the proposition of the 'past-museum,' which should function as a kind of 'memento' that reminds you from afar not to give up ('Trent'anni,' 78). Guglielmi even turns his back on the avant-garde proposed by the Gruppo 93, accusing it of 'epigonism.' In spite of a change of labels Guglielmi does not really change his perspective or his game. What changes, in his view, is the game played by the real world, which urges art to continuously change its rules.

The same can be said of Renato Barilli who, according to Luperini, claims an uninterrupted consistency with his earlier statements ('Per la critica' 21). McLuhan's binary model, adopted by Barilli to demonstrate that there are always two conflicting artistic solutions to a technological revolution, indeed remains valid through time. In his statement for Reggio Emilia, Barilli even dares to present the results of the Gruppo 93 as a possible Hegelian 'synthesis' of cultural opposites. In the end, Luperini remains likewise faithful to his principles, since the world in all its facets is always contemplated through a (neo-)realist matrix. The relationship between art and the external world cannot function without the mediation of dialectical contradiction.

The picture of Italian literary criticism drawn on the occasion of the anniversaries of the Gruppo 63 seems to be that of theoretical immobility despite efforts to move with artistic innovations. One possible explanation for this theoretical inflexibility is generational conflict. Indeed, from the second half of the 1990s onwards, growing signs of intolerance are noticed on the part of a 'new tribe' of writers who refuse to be judged by 'pure' critics. According to Niva Lorenzini, this shows that at present the link between the critical moment and the moment of expression is in danger (Barilli, Curi, and Lorenzini 163). In *Romanzi di culto*, a pamphlet published in 1995, Renzo Paris defended a new generation of authors (Tamaro, Ballestra, Brizzi, Culicchia) against their 'wicked' reviewers, among whom he also counts Angelo Guglielmi. The often lamented divorce between critics and writers should be explained, Paris argues, as a growing distance between critics who grew up with the neo-avant-garde and the first economic miracle, and the younger generation whose way of life is rooted in the 'third wave' of consumerism:

> Chi è nato in epoca pretelevisiva ha qualche problema con la telematica e con la nuova idea di realtà con cui le nuove generazioni si confrontano o sono chiamate a creare. È l'immaginario, oltre al linguaggio, che è cambiato.
>
> [Those born in a pretelevision age have some problems with telematics and with the new idea of reality that new generations are confronted with or have to create. It is not only language that has changed: it is also the imagination.] (*Romanzi* 8)

Paris, however, also blames the 1968 generation for having broken the link with tradition. Dealing with the paradox of history he proposes curiously enough the 'neo-antico' [neo-ancient] novel best able to represent the end of the second millennium. The 'sacred' and the 'ancient' are pitted against any ideological or nostalgic use of historical materials.

Time seems to proceed in a zigzag movement from futuristic utopia to the eternal present of postmodernism and a revival of premodern origins. It becomes almost impossible to analyse and to value the literature of the new millennium strictly in terms of avant-garde and postmodernism. Perhaps more attention should be paid to what happens 'between' the waves.

2003 – 'After 1963': From the Generation of Uncertainty to the Generation of Flexibility

The events organized for the 2003 anniversary have added new fuel to the debate on the death of the avant-garde. The fortieth anniversary of the Gruppo 63 was celebrated in two symbolic places: during May in Bologna, the university town of the group's spiritual father Luciano Anceschi; and during November in Palermo, the place where it all started.

The Palermo conference, 'La questione dello sperimentalismo,' was organized around groups of papers and responses with the intention of combining past and future perspectives on the complex relationship between avant-garde and experimentalism. According to the report of a 'witness,' Lavinia Spalanca, the discussion was polarized to such an extent that two extreme positions – a 'maximalist' view represented by Edoardo Sanguineti, and a 'reformist' perspective headed by critic Alfonso Berardinelli – ended up fighting one another and the debate degenerated into an ideological confrontation. In order to stress the importance of experimentalism, Sanguineti went as far as to include Calvino's *Cosmicomiche* among the results of the Gruppo 63, while Berardinelli denied any innovative value of the *neoavanguardia*, arguing that its members only reclaimed, in a postmodern way, the achievements of the historical avant-gardes. According to Berardinelli, the only revolution was its organization into a group in order to guarantee legitimacy to its members beyond the quality of their single works.[9] Significantly, a review of the event in the newspaper *L'avvenire* was entitled 'L'avanguardia non c'è più' [The avant-garde no longer exists].

The proceedings of the Bologna conference collected in the volume *Il Gruppo 63 quarant'anni dopo* (2005) reveal a similar phenomenon of polarization that can be characterized as a growing self-consciousness on the part of the old guard of the Gruppo 63, and a growing intolerance on the part of the younger generation that had to come to terms with a complex and contradictory inheritance. The conference structure was conceived as an un-academic and open structure, with round tables moderated by the organizers: Fausto Curi, a neutral party interested in the objective and structural conditions that made the existence of the Gruppo 63 possible (Barilli, Curi, and Lorenzini 45); Niva Lorenzini, who as a participating outsider summarized and reflected critically on the different positions taken; and Renato Barilli, an interested party who sometimes became directly involved in rather strong polemics. The focus here will be on the actual debate and will not consider either the merits of the accompanying CD (which contains live recordings of neo-avant-garde literary texts)or the wider range of avant-garde movements and disciplines of the 1960s and 1970s that helped to differentiate and complete the picture of the Gruppo 63.

The round table discussion 'Le ragioni del gruppo (Come eravamo),' on the participation in the neo-avant-garde movement of different art forms, clarifies the concept of the group as an open space or laboratory. Furio Colombo, in his survey of the roles played by cinema, music, architecture, and theatre, concludes that, compared to other avant-garde movements he had observed in the United States, the Gruppo 63 was unique in the sense that it represented first of all a liberation from dogmas, a 'macchina della libertà perché, mentre creava condizioni incoraggianti per la libera attività di ciascuno, non immaginava alcuna azione collettiva, non ha mai definito alcuna linea di credenze, non ha mai ammesso o dismesso qualcuno per avere o non avere osservato qualcosa' [machine for freedom, because while it produced conditions that encouraged everyone's free initiative, it did not envision any collective action, it never established any guiding principles, it never admitted or dismissed anyone for complying or not complying with something] (Barilli, Curi, and Lorenzini 107). In the round table discussion 'Il Gruppo 63 e le arti,' architect Vittorio Gregotti noted the philosophical influence of Enzo Paci and the review *aut aut* and defined an interdisciplinary perspective in the search of truth, in which the process of discovery matters more than the results (Barilli, Curi, and Lorenzini 124).

This portrait of unbound, interdisciplinary, 'multimedial'[10] experiments aimed at liberating language from ideology, or at fostering a free exchange of experiences and an opening of boundaries, is a joyful one. In his opening speech Eco remarked that he considered himself to be part of a lucky generation: 'Noi siamo stati una generazione che ha iniziato a entrare nell'età adulta quando tutte le opportunità erano aperte, ed eravamo pronti a ogni rischio' [Ours was a generation that began to enter adulthood when all options were available and we were ready to take any risk] (Barilli, Curi, and Lorenzini 33). Likewise, Giuliani, borrowing an expression from Arbasino, speaks euphorically of a little 'jazz age':

> Nella nostra piccola Età del Jazz si mescolavano il piacere di scoprire il mondo e le idee in corso con il gusto e la necessità di sperimentare, un'etica della conoscenza con la pratica dei giochi linguistici; il pungolo della sfida con la continua riflessione sulle forme delle arti.

> [In our little Jazz Age, the pleasure of discovering the world and current ideas mixed with the taste and need for experimentation; an ethics of familiarity with the practice of linguistic games; the spur of a challenge with the continuous reflection on art forms.] (Barilli, Curi, and Lorenzini 103)

Giuliani concludes by saying that, unlike his friend Leonetti, he has never suffered from 'strazi ideologici' [ideological torments] (103).

Borrowing another expression from Arbasino, not only was Chiasso reached, but foreign countries also discovered Italy. Eco tells of his surprise and pride when, in 1963, the *Times Literary Supplement* asked him to contribute to a special issue dedicated to 'The Critical Moment' – that is to say, to new trends in criticism.[11] Likewise, Alfredo Giuliani recalled that his anthology *I novissimi* had aroused violent polemics in the Italian press while the *Times Literary Supplement* reviewed it very favourably in a detached and intelligent manner (Barilli, Curi, and Lorenzini 100). A neutral ground sometimes seemed necessary in the highly politicized landscape of Italy in the early 1960s. Eco stressed that in those years artistic innovation was considered 'communist' by the majority of the Italian public (Barilli, Curi, and Lorenzini 25).

This politicization of art forms does not apply only to the past. The two foreign 'observers' invited to the Bologna conference – Peter Carravetta from New York and Paolo Valesio from Yale University – both pointed out the limits of a party-bound approach. According to Carravetta, one of the editors of *Postmoderno e letteratura* (1984), Italian postmodernism never left behind linguistic contamination and never became the multicultural, emancipating hybridism produced by postmodernism in the United States, where criticism is not 'partitico, come lo è stato in Italia, ma è ideologico in un senso più ampio e più flessibile del termine' [party-bound, as it was in Italy, but ideological in a broader and more flexible sense of the word] (Barilli, Curi, and Lorenzini 170). Valesio commented that while it was extremely positive to see how combative the Gruppo 63 still was, this defensive attitude could also become a limit or even a form of determinism (Barilli, Curi, and Lorenzini 264, 267). Walter Pedullà, who, like Carravetta and Valesio, was not a member of the *neoavanguardia*, warns in similar terms against what he calls 'the syndrome of the cage':

> Siamo attenti alla sindrome della gabbia: non colpisce solo gli uccelli. Anche gli uomini dicono spesso di desiderare la libertà, ma, quando essa

> comporta il rischio di perdere il cibo e un ambiente comodo e caldo, si corre tutti dentro la vecchia gabbia. Insomma, finita la festa, tocca rimettersi in volo senza guardarsi indietro, senza nostalgia. Comincia sempre un'altra avventura.
>
> [Let us beware of the syndrome of the cage: it does not affect only birds. People too often profess their desire for freedom, but when it entails the danger of losing food and a warm and comfortable environment, we all run back into the old cage. In other words, when the party is over, it's time to be airborne again without looking back, without nostalgia. A new adventure is always about to begin.] (Barilli, Curi, and Lorenzini 195)

The conception of the Gruppo 63 is linked retrospectively to two different personalities, its spiritual 'father' Luciano Anceschi, who in the early 1960s felt the need for a rupture, and its executive 'son' Nanni Balestrini, whose organizational skills are celebrated throughout the conference with expressions such as 'nato manager culturale' (Inge Feltrinelli, in Barilli, Curi, and Lorenzini 17) and 'il cervello organizzativo del gruppo' (Fausto Curi, in Barilli, Curi, and Lorenzini 75). This suggests that the movement had two different souls, one of necessity and one of contiguity; or, to paraphrase Enzo Golino, the Gruppo 63 can be considered the result of the marriage between Mister Chance and Lady Necessity (Barilli, Curi, and Lorenzini 173). This marriage also explains why the group is perceived either as a fluid, mercurial, open-ended structure, or as a determinist cage. Among the old members, Balestrini is in fact the most pragmatic and the least nostalgic: 'Certo, noi tutti siamo targati ormai per sempre con questa etichetta, mentre in realtà per ognuno di noi è stata solo una delle tante cose che ha fatto nella vita – è come se uno che è stato alpino rimanesse poi alpino e basta per tutta la vita' [Of course, this label will stick on us forever, when in reality for all of us it was only one of the many things we did in our life – someone who served in the Alpine Troops remains nothing but an *alpino* throughout his life] (Barilli, Curi, and Lorenzini 77). Balestrini's nonchalance seems to contrast Angelo Guglielmi's fervent revelation that he experienced his membership in the Gruppo 63 as an almost anthropologic revolution (Barilli, Curi, and Lorenzini 93).

Niva Lorenzini lucidly summarizes four recurrent positions in the debate: those who envision the necessity of a new avant-garde; those who sanction the end of the avant-garde; those who are convinced that after that experience there is nothing left to hope for; and finally, those who see possible affiliations (Barilli, Curi, and Lorenzini 218). The diehard defenders of avant-garde antagonism against the ideology of postmodernism of the present are Filippo Bettini and Francesco Muzzioli, the creators of the so-called 'Terza ondata' (the third wave embodied by the Gruppo 93). Bettini argues that a re-foundation of the notion and practice of the avant-garde is needed in order to unmask the misunderstanding on which the concept of postmodernism is based: 'cioè la pretesa di dichiarare finito il futuro attraverso l'identificazione dell'ideologia, della forma della coscienza, con la realtà esistente' [namely, its claim that the future is finished, based on the identification of ideology and of the form of conscience, with existing reality] (Barilli, Curi, and Lorenzini 162). Muzzioli defends the thesis of an avant-garde that has become invisible because it has lost its grip on the situation, on the specific material and historical contradictions that formed the stronghold of the last visible avant-garde, that of the Gruppo 63. The antagonist practice has, however, survived under the surface of the cultural dominance of postmodernism, preserving the literature-politics tie and formulating the resistant alternative of a radical modernity: 'Ecco: non *commemorare* l'avanguardia, ma *ripensarla,* e proprio nel suo nucleo più contestativo, significa riaprire oggi, scontando il *clinamen* assai poco favorevole in cui si trova, la questione dell'antagonismo della scrittura' [That is the point: not to *commemorate* the avant-garde, but to *rethink* it, precisely in its most contentious core, means to reopen today the question of antagonistic writing, in spite of the rather unlucky star in which it finds itself) (Barilli, Curi, and Lorenzini 187). Muzzioli's statement that the Gruppo 63 was the last visible avant-garde could however be contrasted with Eco's contingent observation that Gruppo 63 became visible thanks to its adversaries: 'oserei dire che la fortuna del Gruppo, la sua visibilità massmediatica, è stata dovuta ai suoi avversari' [I daresay that the fortune of the Gruppo, its visibility in the media, was due to its opponents] (Barilli, Curi, and Lorenzini 38).

The thesis of the end of the avant-garde is argued by Sanguineti from a metahistorical standpoint and by Balestrini and Barilli from a historical point of view. Sanguineti, one of the leftist icons of the Gruppo 63, in 2003 seemed to keep his distance from the avant-garde experience, speaking about it in the past tense ('quello che volevamo denunciare era' [what we wanted to denounce was]) and using a first person narrative ('quando spiego come eravamo non posso non spiegare in qualche modo com'ero io prima di tutto' [when I explain what we were like, I first have to explain in some way how I was]) (Barilli, Curi, and Lorenzini

86). When Sanguinetti explains the etymology of *I novissimi*, with its double meaning of the latest and the last, and concludes his exercise with 'Dopo di noi il diluvio' [After us, the deluge] (Barilli, Curi, and Lorenzini 89), Lello Voce, one of the representatives of the younger generation, responds polemically: 'et moi, je suis le déluge' (Barilli, Curi, and Lorenzini 268). Sanguineti is referring of course to the 'deluge' of postmodernism that, culturally speaking, marked the end of a period of radical change, a period of which he considers himself to be a protagonist and of which he is absolutely satisfied (Barilli, Curi, and Lorenzini 90).

Renato Barilli remains faithful to his thesis of normalization and democratization of the avant-garde, a thesis that Sanguineti called 'barilliana.'[12] Barilli considers his position to be that of historical materialism, in a technological rather than a Marxist sense. He firmly believes in the existence of a third wave of avant-garde art that could be called neo-neo-avant-garde, postmodern, or simply 'wave.' Since he also believes profoundly in the concept of generation – a concept cast into doubt by Valesio, who considers it to be another form of determinism (Barilli, Curi, and Lorenzini 262) – Barilli proposes to dedicate the third wave of the new millennim to Aeolus, 'il dio dei venti, che ben si conviene a questa atmosfera impalpabile delle telecomunicazioni' [the god of winds, as is appropriate for the impalpable atmosphere of telecommunications] (Barilli, Curi, and Lorenzini 277).

Balestrini, it seems, is equally willing to 'follow the waves,' and it is therefore no coincidence that he and Barilli founded Ricercare in 1993 in Reggio Emilia. Ricercare is a laboratory of creative writing modeled on the public readings of the Gruppo 63; its first anthology, *Narrative Invaders*, was produced in 2000. In Balestrini's view the only real rupture with tradition occurred in the early 1960s; the years that followed were the beginning of a new period, initially called new avant-garde or experimentalism, and later labeled postmodern (Barilli, Curi, and Lorenzini 104). In an interview with Claudio Brancaleoni (published in *Allegoria*) Balestrini easily traces a continuity from the experimentalism of the neo-avant-garde to the so-called 'cannibali' writers of the 1990s, referring to 'una pratica della letteratura come continua ricerca attraverso quelli che sono gli strumenti dello scrittore, il linguaggio, la scrittura. E nel rifiuto di una funzione demiurgica, delle tentazioni del sublime, della dipendenza da modi tradizionali consunti' [a literary practice as a continuous research through the instruments of the writer, language, and writing, along with the rejection of any demiurgic function, of the temptations of the sublime, and of the dependence on worn-out traditional modes] (Brancaleoni 117). Brancaleoni seems shocked by this answer and asks Balestrini if he is aware of the fact that these 'young cannibals' describe the society in which they live in rather morbid and disengaged terms. While the neo-avant-garde entails contradiction and rupture with normality, postmodernism stands here for the end of contradictions and the impossibility of any avant-garde. Again Balestrini sees no problem with the substitution of the term avant-garde for postmodernism, 'termine vago e ambiguo che ha avuto molteplici e contrastanti definizioni, ma che in mancanza di meglio possiamo riferire alle nuove forme della creazione artistica e letteraria degli ultimi decenni' [a vague and ambiguous term that has had multiple and conflicting definitions, but that, for lack of anything better, can be related to the new forms of artistic and literary creation of the last decades] (Brancaleoni 117). The avant-garde, in Balestrini's view, is linked not historically with rupture, but metahistorically with the ability of art to repeatedly establish new connections between the formal materiality of a work and the historical moment in which it functions.

In his contribution to the 2003 debate Romano Luperini maintains that contradiction is central to the avant-garde and therefore dismisses the possibility of a continuity of literary practices between neo-avant-garde and postmodernism. This possibility is sustained by the 'postmodern' faction within the neo-avant-garde (Barilli, Curi, and Lorenzini 180–1). This time he certainly would have included Balestrini in Barilli's party, whom he accuses of having a chameleonic attitude (182). In Luperini's view postmodernism starts in 1972 and brings with it the idea that contradictions and the avant-garde have become outmoded and that there is nothing left to hope for (179). However, in his conclusion that both postmodernity and postmodernism came to an end with the tragedy of 11 September 2001, he creates a new space for the dialectic of oppositions: 'È finito con l'attentato alle torri gemelle, con la guerra in Iraq, con l'esplosione di nuove contraddizioni. Il postmoderno è finito. Perché rincorrere qualcosa che non esiste più?' [It ended with the attack on the twin towers, with the war in Iraq, with the explosion of new contradictions. The postmodern is over. Why chase after something that no longer exists?] (182). Even Carravetta, invited as an expert of postmodernism to explain the genealogy of the term, starts his talk with the announcement that he is writing a book entitled *Fine del postmoderno* (Barilli, Curi, and Lorenzini 164), thus turning his exercise into that of archivist and undermining the current value of his terminology. Apparently, the wait is for something new and radical to appear on the horizon, something strong enough to start a new era. Guglielmi concludes his contribution by stating: 'Il secolo appena passato ha consumato il tutto della sua potenzialità: un altro secolo è iniziato e siamo in attesa (non lo ha ancora fatto) che mostri le sue idee, i suoi obiettivi, il suo coraggio.' [The century that just came to an end has consumed all its potential; a new century has begun and we are waiting for it to show its ideas, its objectives, its courage (it hasn't done so yet).] (Barilli, Curi, and Lorenzini 99). The loss of a grip on reality is not only the result of a changed world order but also the consequence of the normalization of the avant-garde, which Valesio calls an aporia inherent to its project (Barilli, Curi, and Lorenzini 265). Gregotti argues that what seems to be necessary now is not a breaking but rather a restoration of rules. He is proud to belong to the so-called 'generazione dell'incertezza' [generation of uncertainty], a generation that has become aware of the complexity of the real and the difficulty of giving it a unitary meaning (Barilli, Curi, and Lorenzini 126). Niva Lorenzini, borrowing Gregotti's expression, designates the present generation as the 'generation of flexibility,' in accordance with a 'mediatized' reality less bound to historically defined categories. Yet Lorenzini is concerned by the loss of the meaning of history and stresses the importance of the transmission of the experience of the Gruppo 63 by its witnesses (Barilli, Curi, and Lorenzini 152).

However, the young representatives of critics and writers rise in revolt against the idea of an end and the attempt to fill in the gap by falling back on history and tradition. Critic Andrea Cortelessa clearly distinguishes between those who, like Sanguineti, consider the avant-garde as a final stage and those who, following Giuliani, consider the neo-avant-garde to be the beginning of a new phase. Cortelessa also distinguishes between the innovative force of the neo-avant-garde that resulted in the 'end of models' – an expression borrowed from Alberto Savinio and used by different participants in the debate – and the institutional value of the neo-avant-garde, having itself become a 'closed' model. This double-bind is the problem writers and critics of the 1980s had to confront:

> Questa oggettiva difficoltà nel proseguire l'esperienza del Gruppo 63 segna in profondità gli anni Ottanta. È qui – quando fra l'altro si prende definitivamente coscienza di aver oltrepassato da tempo una discontinuità storica che per comodità definiamo 'postmodernità' – che veramente s'interrompe un succedersi di generazioni che fino a quel momento era dato leggere nei termini bloomiani, di rapporto tra 'padri' e 'figli' (cioè di acquisizione di modelli, o loro disconoscimento, in termini genealogici).

> [This objective difficulty in continuing the experience of the Gruppo 63 marks the 1980s profoundly. It is at this point – when, among other things, there is a full awareness of having gone well beyond the historical discontinuity that we define, for the sake of simplicity, as 'postmodernity' – that we have a true rupture in the sequence of generations, which up to that point could be read in Bloomian terms as a father-son relationship (that is, of the acquisition or rejection of models in genealogical terms).] (Barilli, Curi, and Lorenzini 224–5)

With this statement Cortellessa puts an end to the logic of generations so dear to Barilli, and to the idea that the 'end of models' would be an exclusive and conclusive achievement of the Gruppo 63, as argued by Sanguineti. Only now, after the exhaustion of the Gruppo 93 experiment, do we experience the end of all models, both avant-garde and traditional. Thus, proponents of intermediate positions are most apt to react to this loss in a flexible way. Surprisingly enough, Cortellessa considers Antonio Porta to be an exemplary voice for the new flexible generation of the neo-avant-garde. As we have seen, in the 1984 debate Porta was one of the few voices in favour of the oscillatory value of a two-headed postmodernism. This could mean that Luperini's conclusion in 1990 that the neo-hermeneutic tendencies were defeated in favour of a reconstruction of the dialectic should be revised: on the contrary, the position of an 'interactive' kind of postmodernism seems to have won in the long run.

This is why, according to Lello Voce, the Gruppo 93 should not be considered an avant-garde 'nostro malgrado' [in spite of ourselves] (Barilli, Curi, and Lorenzini 270), but rather a form of critical postmodernism, reacting to the new 'global' context rather than the 'bi-polar' historical and cultural context of 1989, in which it began to live 'literarily': 'E allora, per favore, almeno questo lasciatecelo: il postmoderno è nostro … Giù le mani!' [So, please, at least leave this to us: the postmodern is ours … Hands off!) (Barilli, Curi, and Lorenzini 272). Inspired by Sanguineti's metaphor of the deluge, poet Tommaso Ottonieri, who was active in the Gruppo 93, comments that the historical condition of postmodernity is inherent to the deluge and thus not so much following as preceding the neo-avant-garde. It is therefore necessary to 'sempre pensarci nel diluvio' [always think of ourselves as part of the deluge] (Barilli, Curi, and Lorenzini 253). Furthermore, Ottonieri points out the existence of another, more recent avant-garde experience – the '77 movement – which in his case has been far more decisive: 'è stato forse l'unico istante di avanguardia in vita, di avanguardia incarnata in società' [it was perhaps the only instance of a live avant-garde, of an avant-garde embodied in society] (251). In Ottonieri's view the 'cannibali' writers of the 1990s could represent a kind of 'no-avant-garde,' in the sense that they represent an experience 'beyond' the avant-garde and therefore they cannot consider themselves as still part of an avant-garde movement (252).

Writer Enrico Palandri and critic Roberto Carnero finally comment on the schemata Barilli uses to trace genealogical lines of affiliation with the Gruppo 63. Palandri, described by Barilli as a 'midway' phenomenon, an island rising in the desert of the 1970s, denies any exceptional position and stresses the fact that his generation feels a certain coldness towards the Gruppo 63, responding to the same feeling of hostility that the Gruppo showed towards them (Barilli, Curi, and Lorenzini 282–3). Carnero disagrees with Barilli's view of a third wave in the 1990s because it strips the importance from writers of the 1980s who simply did not have a collective program (286). Carnero concludes that the importance of the work of rupture achieved by the neo-avant-garde manifests itself in the first place in the obstacles it has created for its successors: 'L'ostacolo è stato salutare, perché l'esperienza neoavanguardistica ha insegnato, per esempio, a non dare nulla per scontato' [it was a useful obstacle, because the experience of the neo-avant-garde has taught us, for example, not to take anything for granted] (289).

But there are not only voices of dissent. There are also young writers who recognize the mentoring function of the Gruppo 63. Silvia Ballestra considers Ricercare, the creative laboratory founded by Barilli and Balestrini, essential for her career as a non-mainstream writer (Barilli, Curi, and Lorenzini 292–3). Rossana Campo is similarly generous towards her 'fathers,' although with a greater attitude of rivalry (Barilli, Curi, and Lorenzini 297). The same can be said for Mauro Covacich, who himself feels consonant with the antagonist figure of the saboteur (Barilli, Curi, and Lorenzini 300). It seems paramount to all participants of the Bologna conference that, for better or worse, forty years later the neo-avant-garde represents a point of no return. What remains to be decided is how to interpret the so-called 'end of models' and whether it is still possible to distinguish the 'tradizione del nuovo' questioned by the generation of uncertainty from the 'novità della tradizione,' manipulated by the generation of flexibility. In a word – what could be the meaning of the term 'after'?

Osmotic Membrane or Traumatic Rupture: To Be Continued

What has become problematic is how to interpret literary production after 1963. In Italian literary criticism there is an increasing attempt to retrodate the beginnings of literary postmodernism in Italy to the 1970s or even the mid-1960s. Carla Benedetti, in *Pasolini contro Calvino* (1998), demonstrates that in the early 1970s Calvino and Pasolini experienced the collapse of ideologies in the form of a collapse of poetics: Calvino by choosing the way of self-reflexive metafiction, and Pasolini by choosing the open alternative of a poetics of 'impureness.' In *Il tradimento dei critici* (2002) Benedetti translates her academic argument into a kind of manifesto against a certain 'made in Italy' postmodernism identified with Calvino's defence of the literary institution. Here she glorifies the only example of an Italian author who, for her, really dares to defy the labyrinth: Antonio Moresco. Benedetti's position can also be traced in recent contributions on postmodernism in Italy – for example an article by Antonio Tricomi, who analyses the 'caso Moresco' in Benedetti's terms (59). Similarly Raffaele Donnarumma shows affinities with Benedetti's polemical standpoint, declaring that: 'paragonato ai corrispettivi americani e ai modelli, il postmoderno italiano mostra di avere i caratteri dell'esaustione, dell'impallidimento, della contemplazione malinconica o scettica' [compared to its American counterparts and to its models, Italian postmodernism shows the characteristics of exhaustion, of paleness, of melancholic or skeptical contemplation] ('Postmoderno italiano' 73).

While these accusations of a lack of engagement risk closing the debate on Italian postmodern literature, the opposition between Calvino and Pasolini also functions as an invitation to young critics to look for other seeds of postmodernism in Italy's literary tradition. This new perspective can be seen as the result of Marco Belpoliti's *Settanta* (2001), which presents a meticulous contextualization of literary practices in the 1970s. For instance, Tricomi transposes Belpoliti's exploration of the *Ali Babà* project created by Calvino and Celati to the realm of postmodernism, declaring that Celati can be seen as the outpost of Italian postmodernism. In this light Calvino and Eco only tried to follow his pioneering results in a nostalgic, reactionary way. Thus Celati takes the same position as Pasolini in Benedetti's essay, representing a postmodernist alternative to those postmodern writers who, like Calvino and Eco, seem to have capitulated in favour of 'una più pacifica e arrendevole integrazione acritica al sistema culturale, editoriale e, in certi casi, accademico' [a more peaceful and compliant a-critical integration into the cultural system, the publishing industry, and, in some cases, the academy] ('Crisi della testualità' 56).

In his ambitious essay 'Postmoderno italiano: qualche ipotesi,' Donnarumma goes back to the mid-1960s, arguing that this backdating 'esalta la contraddittorietà della cultura postmoderna' (brings into relief the contradictoriness of postmodern culture) (59). He chooses Manganelli and Arbasino as the spiritual fathers of Italian postmodernism showing how their metaliterary dilemmas have become its norm. For him, Italian postmodernism continues the 'postmodern' wing of the neo-avant-garde, an assumption borrowed from Luperini. Donnarumma analyses Italian postmodernism in terms of a 'trauma' that results in a multiplicity of contradictory reactions.

The most elaborate effort to establish an Italian tradition of postmodernism was made by Matteo Di Gesù in *La tradizione del postmoderno* (2003). Di Gesù is not so much looking for models of postmodernism to be contrasted with others, but rather wants to show that there exists a continuity of ideas and literary practice between the Gruppo 63 and postmodernism. Donnarumma observes: 'Che nella neoavanguardia ci sia qualche germe del postmoderno, lo credo anch'io; ma l'appiattimento mi pare indebito. La neoavanguardia è al contrario l'ultimo sussulto del modernismo' [I also believe that there are seeds of the postmodern in the neo-avant-garde, but their identification seems to me unwarranted. On the contrary, the neo-avant-garde is the last gasp of modernism] ('Postmoderno italiano' 63). This statement can be read as a reaction against Di Gesù's plea for a return to the theoretical debate of the Gruppo 63 as a starting point to discuss 'del romanzo italiano contemporaneo [...] per collocarlo in quella che per convenzione ci siamo ormai abituati a chiamare postmodernità' [the contemporary Italian novel ... to place it into what we have now become accustomed to calling, conventionally, postmodernism] (*La tradizione* 48). According to Di Gesù, instead of a traumatic rupture between avant-garde and postmodernism, these two literary movements can be closely linked to each other. The divide between them would be just a 'membrana osmotica' (an osmotic membrane) (33). Voce boldly attributes the bi-polar world to the Gruppo 63, his own being postmodern. However, the remaining question is how flexible the flexible generation can be, trapped between the waves of the neo-avant-garde and the deluge of postmodernism.

Translated by the author

NOTES

This essay is an extended English version of my chapter 'Tradizione del nuovo o novità della tradizione?' in *Il dibattito sul postmoderno in Italia.*

1 All translations, unless indicated otherwise, are mine.
2 Eco's point of view, expressed for the first time in 1983 in 'Postille to *Il nome della rosa*,' has provoked polemical reactions not only in Italy but also abroad. For instance, on the 'Postille' Antoine Compagnon writes: 'Quelle caricature! Eco recourt paradoxalement au récit le plus orthodoxe de la tradition moderne afin de légitimer la postmodernité. La confusion du postmoderne et de l'avantgarde y est typique. La vision de l'histoire est toujours linéaire et progressive, alors même que Eco propose une approche méta-historique. Ce n'est sûrement pas ainsi qu'on réussira à penser les relations du postmoderne et du moderne, du postmoderne et l'histoire' [What a caricature! Paradoxically, Eco resorts to the most orthodox narrative of the modern tradition in order to legitimize postmodernity. The confusion between postmodernism and avant-garde is typical. His vision of history is always linear and progressive, even though Eco proposes a metahistorical approach. Surely, this cannot be the way to think of the relationship between the postmodern and the modern, and between the postmodern and history] (Compagnon 168–9).
3 Cf. Eco; 'rispetto al mondo della cultura marxista, i nuovi scrittori, che ritenevano che l'impegno stesse nel linguaggio e non nella tematica politicizzata, erano visti come mosche cocchiere del neocapitalismo' [with respect to the world of Marxist culture, the new writers, who considered engagement as part of language rather than of a political thematic, were seen as the heralds of neocapitalism] (in Barilli, Curi, and Lorenzini, *Il gruppo 63* 29).
4 We can perhaps consider this development as a confirmation of Andreas Huyssen's hypothesis in *Twilight Memories*: 'Against the anti-museum discourse still dominant among intellectuals, one might even see the museum as our own memento mori, and as such, a life-enhancing rather than mummifying institution in an age bent on the destructive denial of death: the museum thus as a site and testing ground for reflections on temporality and subjectivity, identity and alterity' (16).
5 In *Il Gruppo 63 quarant'anni dopo* Niva Lorenzini remembers Porta's awareness of the responsibility and contribution of poetry to a collective meaning of existence. This explains, according to Lorenzini, Porta's generosity as a cultural organizer during the years of *Alfabeta* and his proximity to younger generations of writers (56–7).
6 The movement was in fact dissolved in 1993.
7 Cf. Eco, who in his essay 'Il Gruppo 63, lo sperimentalismo e l'avanguardia,' drawing on Renato Poggioli's observations, includes the cult of youth among the characteristics of avant-garde movements (97).
8 Apparently Guglielmi changed position.
9 Cf. Berardinelli: 'Il gruppo d'avanguardia offre agli autori anzitutto

garanzie. Il caso di fallimento artistico personale nelle avanguardie non è contemplato. Qualunque prodotto d'avanguardia è visto come critica dell'istituzione artistica, come sabotaggio dell'Arte. È quindi interpretato e valorizzato a priori come momento necessario della dialettica storica.' [First of all, an avant-garde group provides assurances to its authors. Avant-gardes do not contemplate the possibility of a personal artistic failure. Any avant-garde product is seen as a critique of art as an institution, as sabotage of Art. It is therefore interpreted and assessed as a necessary moment in the historical dialectic] ('Postmodernità e avanguardia' 331).

10 Here it is possible to see a link with Alessandro Baricco's observation on the 'multimedial' spectacle invented by Laurie Anderson, which was absolutely avant-garde in the 1960s and already mainstream in the 1990s: 'una parola che allora era nuova, multimediale, sapeva un po' di farmacia, ma poi era meraviglia, e ti faceva sentire scemo, tu che il futuro l'avevi immaginato, sì, ma non era tutta quella roba lì. È impressionante come siamo veloci ad andare ad abitare i pianeti nuovi che certi avventurieri scoprono per noi' ['multimedial' was a new word then, it smacked of pharmacy, but it was a wonder, it stunned you, because, sure, you had imagined the future, but not that kind of stuff. It's remarkable how quickly we can settle on the new planets that some adventurers discover for us] (*Barnum 2* 12).

11 'Credo di averlo detto a mia moglie, per mostrarle che non aveva sposato proprio l'ultimo degli imbecilli, e poi ho taciuto' [I think I told my wife about it to show her that she hadn't married a complete idiot, then I kept my mouth shut] (Barilli, Curi, and Lorenzini 32).

12 'Potevo non essere d'accordo con l'idea che chiamerei social-democratica, in mancanza di meglio, scusate la metafora, soprattutto mi scusi il destinatario, barilliana di una normalizzazione e democratizzazione delle avanguardie' [It was impossibile for me to agree with the idea that I might call social-democratic, for lack of a better word, 'barillian,' with apologies for my metaphor, and in particular apologies to its addressee, of a normalization and democratization of the avant-gardes] (Barilli, Curi, and Lorenzini 87).

WORKS CITED

Anceschi, Luciano. 'Metodologia del nuovo.' In Balestrini and Giuliani, eds. *Gruppo 63: la nuova letteratura.* 7–14.

'L'avanguardia non c'è più.' *L'avvenire* 27 Nov. 2003: 26.

Balestrini, Nanni, Renato Barilli, et.al. *Narrative Invaders: Narratori di 'Ricercare' 1993–1999.* Turin: Testo & Immagine, 2000.

Balestrini, Nanni, and Alfredo Giuliani, eds. *Gruppo 63: la nuova letteratura, 34 scrittori, Palermo ottobre 1963*. Milan: Feltrinelli, 1964.

Baricco, Alessandro. *Barnum 2: altre cronache dal Grande Show*. Milan: Feltrinelli, 1998.

Barilli, Renato. *È arrivata la terza ondata: dalla neo alla neo-neoavanguardia'*. Turin: Testo & Immagine, 2000.

Barilli, Renato, Fausto Curi, and Niva Lorenzini, eds. *Il Gruppo 63 quarant'anni dopo*. Bologna: Pendragon, 2005.

Barilli, Renato, and Angelo Guglielmi, eds. *Gruppo 63: critica e teoria*. Milan: Feltrinelli, 1976.

Benedetti, Carla. *Pasolini contro Calvino: per una letteratura impura*. Turin: Bollati Boringhieri, 1998.

– *Il tradimento dei critici*. Turin: Bollati Boringhieri, 2002.

Berardinelli, Alfonso. 'Postmodernità e avanguardia.' *Nuovi argomenti* 25 (2004): 329–37.

Bettini, Filippo. 'La nostalgia dell'avanguardia.' *L'unità*, 29 April 1991.

Bettini, Filippo, and Francesco Muzzioli, eds. *Gruppo 93: la recente avventura del dibattito teorico letterario in Italia*. Lecce: Manni, 1990.

Biamonte, Francesco. *Le parole la notte*. Turin: Einaudi, 1998.

Brancaleoni, Claudio. 'Dalla neoavanguardia al postmoderno: Intervista a Nanni Balestrini.' *Allegoria* 45 (2003): 107–17.

Capozzi, Rocco. *Scrittori critici e industria culturale dagli anni '60 ad oggi*. Lecce: Manni, 1991.

Carlino, Marcello. 'Le "commemorazioni" del Gruppo 63.' *L'ombra d'Argo* 3 (1983): 117–24.

Carravetta, Peter, and Paolo Spedicato, eds. *Postmoderno e letteratura*. Milan: Bompiani, 1984.

Ceserani, Remo. 'A proposito di moderno e di postmoderno.' *Allegoria* 10 (1992): 121–31.

Compagnon, Antoine. *Les cinq paradoxes de la modernité*. Paris: Seuil, 1990.

Di Gesù, Matteo. *La tradizione del postmoderno: studi di letteratura italiana*. Milan: Francoangeli, 2003.

Donnarumma, Raffaele. 'Postmoderno italiano: qualche ipotesi.' *Allegoria* 43 (2003): 56–85.

Eco, Umberto. 'Il Gruppo 63: lo sperimentalismo e l'avanguardia.' In *Sugli specchi e altri saggi*. Milan: Bompiani, 1985. 93–104.

– 'Postille a *Il nome della rosa*.' *Alfabeta* 49 (1983): 19–22; Milan: Bompiani, 1984.

Ferretti, Gian Carlo. 'Ricerca e consumo.' *Alfabeta* 57 (1984): 7.

– 'Una replica e una postilla.' *Alfabeta* 69 (1985): 23.

Guglielmi, Angelo. 'Avanguardia e sperimentalismo.' In Nanni Balestrini and Alfredo Giuliani, eds. *Gruppo 63: la nuova letteratura*. 15–24.

– 'Critica del post-moderno.' *Alfabeta* 69 (1985a): 2–3.
– 'Una democrazia delle forme.' *Alfabeta* 59 (1984): 6.
– 'Nuovo intervento.' *Alfabeta* 69 (1985b): 22.
– 'Trent'anni di ricerca letteraria.' In *63/93: Trent'anni di ricerca letteraria*. Reggio Emilia: Elytra, 1995. 73–80.

Habermas, Jurgen. 'Moderno, postmoderno e neoconservatorismo.' *Alfabeta* 22 (1981): 15–17.

Huyssen, Andreas. *Twilight Memories: Marking Time in a Culture of Amnesia*. New York: Routledge, 1995.

Jameson, Fredric. *Il postmoderno o la logica culturale del tardo capitalismo*. Milan: Garzanti, 1989. 'Postmodernism, or the Cultural Logic of Late Capitalism.' *New Left Review* 146 (1984): 86–95.

Jansen, Monica. 'Tradizione del nuovo o novità della tradizione? Avanguardia e postmoderno messi a confronto.' In *Il dibattito sul postmoderno in Italia: In bilico tra dialettica e ambiguità*. Florence: Cesati, 2002. 143–63.

Leonetti, Francesco. 'Stile e statuto (ieri, oggi).' *Alfabeta* 57 (1984): 3–5.

Luperini, Romano. 'Bilancio di un trentennio letterario (1960–1990) e ipotesi sul presente.' In *Scrittori, tendenze letterarie e conflitto delle poetiche in Italia (1960–1990)*. Ed. Rocco Capozzi and Massimo Ciavolella. Ravenna: Longo, 1993. 7–16.
– 'Un confronto tra posizioni diverse.' *Alfabeta* 69 (1985): 18.
– *Lezioni sul postmoderno*. Ed. Franco Marchese. Palermo: Palumbo, 1997.
– 'Per la critica della retorica: continuità e rotture nel 63 e nel 93.' In *63/93. Trent'anni di ricerca letteraria. Convegno di dibattito e di proposta*. Reggio Emilia: Elytra, 1995. 19–26.
– 'I pesci rossi, l'acquario e una letteratura della lateralità.' In Grazia D'Oria, ed. *Gruppo 93: le tendenze attuali della poesia e della narrativa. Antologia di testi teorici e letterari*. Lecce: Manni, 1992. 11–20.
– 'Romano Luperini.' *Campo* (numero progetto) (1990): 39–40.
– 'Statuto del "letterario scritto."' *Alfabeta* 60 (1984): 15.

Lyotard, Jean-François. 'Intervento italiano.' *Alfabeta* 32 (1982): 9–11.

Paris, Renzo. *Romanzi di culto: sulla nuova tribù dei narratori e sui loro biechi recensori*. Rome: Castelvecchi, 1995.

Porta, Antonio. 'Contro il grande stile.' *Alfabeta* 69 (1985): 23.
– 'Sentimento e forma, appunti.' *Alfabeta* 57 (1984): 5.

Portoghesi, Paolo. 'Introduzione.' In Claudio Aldegheri and Maurizio Sabini, eds. *Immagini del post-moderno: il dibattito sulla società post-industriale e l'architettura*. Venice: Cluva, 1983. 7–20.

Re, Lucia. 'Il dibattito sul senso della letteratura oggi in Italia.' *Rivista di estetica* 19–20 (1985): 189–98.

63/93, Trent'anni di ricerca letteraria: convegno di dibattito e di proposta. Reggio Emilia: Elytra, 1995.

Spalanca, Lavinia. 'In occasione della XXIX edizione del Premio Mondello, il convegno sullo sperimentalismo.' *Prometheus* 66 (2003). http://www.rivista-prometheus.it/rivista/iii66/mondello.htm (accessed 2003).

Tabucchi, Antonio. 'Doppio senso.' *Alfabeta* 69 (1985): 3–4.

Tricomi, Antonio. 'Crisi delle testualità, esplosione della biblioteca: la nascita del postmoderno in Italia.' *Allegoria* 44 (2003): 35–60.

Valesio, Paolo. 'La domanda lapidaria.' Cited in Barilli, Curi, and Lorenzini, eds. *Il Gruppo 63 quarant'anni dopo.* 260–67.

Vattimo, Gianni. *La società trasparente.* Milan: Garzanti, 1989.

Voce, Lello. 'Avant-garde and Tradition: A Critique.' *Avant Garde Critical Studies* 10 (1996): 117–20.

3 Parasurrealism and Technological Utopia: The Project of *Malebolge*

MARIO MORONI

In this essay I will discuss *Malebolge*, a quarterly journal published in Reggio Emilia from 1964 to 1967. Along with such journals as *Il verri*, *Grammatica*, and *Quindici*, *Malebolge* was an essential means for the circulation of texts and ideas of the Italian *neoavanguardia*.[1] Before dealing directly with specific issues addressed in the magazine, however, I would like to discuss 'parasurrealism,' a notion that represented a constitutive critical and theoretical aspect of the project of *Malebolge*.

Literary critic Angelo Guglielmi delineated parasurrealism, although indirectly, in his *Vero e falso* with reference to *L'oblò* (1964), an experimental novel by Adriano Spatola (1941–88), one of the founders of *Malebolge*.[2] Guglielmi discussed Spatola's novel in terms of an experimental project that originated with the author's realization that contemporary society, influenced by the persuasive strategies of the mass media, had dispersed its values. The result of such dispersion was the standardization of culture and of aesthetic taste, along with contemporary society's ability to neutralize the intellectuals' capacity to express a critique of the status quo (*Vero e falso* 154). According to Guglielmi, on the basis of these assumptions Spatola had developed a peculiar language based on a sort of degradation, in which the narrator:

> entra in contatto con i materiali più avariati e sospetti. Con i contenuti più ributtanti che la società di massa propone e li manipola allegramente. La manipolazione avviene con l'ausilio di una macchina impastatrice (il meccanismo del romanzo) la cui caratteristica è di essere capace tanto di assorbire quei contenuti, di alimentarsene, quanto di digerirli, di sputarli.

[assimilates the most degraded and compromised linguistic materials. The

> most repulsive contents that mass society proposes, he merrily manipulates. The manipulation takes place with the help of a mixer machine (the mechanism of the novel) which has the ability to absorb those contents, to feed on them, as well as to digest and to expel them.][3] (*Vero e falso* 154)

These materials were, in fact, those produced by popular culture – that is, the product of the same standardization produced by the mass media. However, before focusing on the use of materials taken from popular culture, one must note the motif of metamorphosis that was to characterize Spatola's own cultural project in the pages of *Malebolge.* The metamorphosis motif appears at the beginning of the novel, in the accounts of the grotesque circumstances in which Guglielmo, the surreal protagonist of *L'oblò,* was born:

> Una notte più fonda, durante un allarme più lungo, Guglielmo-padre sbagliò buco. Suo figlio nacque dall'accoppiamento di un uomo e di una vacca. E nacque che la guerra era appena finita, nella confusione di quei giorni, per puro caso evitando uno statico destino in formalina ... E suo padre, allora guardiano di oche, fu fecondato da un corvo e depose un uovo contraffatto e deforme che un rospo covò. Dall'uovo, in primavera, dentro il fango del fosso fiorito, nacque Guglielmo, durante l'altra guerra, in tempo per vedere Caporetto.
>
> [On a dark night, during a longer alarm than usual, Guglielmo's father got the wrong hole. His son was born from the coupling of a man and a cow. He was born when the war had just ended, in the confusion of those days, by pure chance, avoiding a static destiny in formaldehyde ... And his father, then a keeper of geese, was impregnated by a crow and laid a deformed and counterfeit egg that was hatched by a toad. Guglielmo was born from the egg in the spring, inside the mud of the ditch full of flowers, during the other war, just in time to witness Caporetto.] (*L'oblo* 8)

In addition to elaborating a narrative based on metamorphosis, Spatola also placed the birth of the protagonist within a specific historical context, represented by the reference to the First and Second World Wars. It is within this historic scenario that he provides yet another alternate account of Guglielmo's birth, one that relates to Italy's postwar economic reconstruction, in which a shocking version of references to a new consumerist society are presented:

E a sua madre piacevano le automobili, aveva una vera passione per le automobili. Fin da piccola. 'Finirai per sposare un automobile e mettere al mondo un motoscooter,' le aveva diceva sempre sua madre ... Degenerata in vizio, la passione fece sì che a centosessanta all'ora sua madre si facesse fecondare da un camion che sorpassava. E Guglielmo nacque così, casualmente, sul margine dell'autostrada.

[And his mother liked cars, had a true passion for cars. Ever since she was a child. 'You will end up marrying a car and give birth to a motor scooter,' her mother always told her ... The passion degenerated into a vice and a truck passing at one hundred miles an hour impregnated his mother. And Guglielmo was born like that, by chance, on the side of the highway.] (*L'oblo* 9)

Ultimately, the title of Spatola's novel can be seen as referring to an enormous pothole or leak through which references to historical events, contemporary society, cartoons, war stories, movies, romance fiction, advertisements, and other things were expelled and judged.[4] Spatola confirms this structural feature of his novel in a note on the back page of the book:

E infatti *L'oblò* è una carta geografica priva di uno dei lati, cosicché da una falla che si apre nella diga dell'ordinata rete di meridiani e paralleli (una rete, fra l'altro, che imprigiona il mondo) fuoriescono violentemente i materiali eterogenei che il fiume della storia ha raccolto e ingerito durante il suo corso.

[In fact, *L'oblò* is a geographical map missing one side, so that the heterogeneous materials that the river of history collected and consumed are violently discharged through a leak that opens in the dam of the orderly network of meridians and parallels (a network that traps the world, among other things).][5]

An in-depth reading of *L'oblò* is beyond the purpose of this essay.[6] What interests me here, in relation to *Malebolge*, is that Guglielmi discusses surrealism with direct reference to the hallucinatory degradation of language in *L'oblò.* He interprets the bizarre imagery produced by Spatola's narrative journey as a way to produce a form of psychic automatism, which had characterized the language of the surrealist movement of the 1920s and 1930s. However, Guglielmi sees Spatola's version of the surrealist's automatism as a decontextualized practice with respect to the original. According to Guglielmi, this recovery of surrealism was limited to the scenographic aspect of the original movement and, ultimately, lacked the virulence conveyed by the surrealists' imagery (*Vero e falso* 155).

I believe that Guglielmi's reading of Spatola's postsurrealist stance was limited, and will elaborate several objections to such a reading as I approach a closer examination of *Malebolge.* First of all, Guglielmi missed the motif of metamorphosis, on which Spatola had constructed his narrative, and which would later constitute an essential aspect of parasurrealism. However, Guglielmi grasped the fundamental aspect that differentiates the historic French surrealism movement from parasurrealism as theorized by Spatola and others in *Malebolge,* beginning in 1964. In fact, the parasurrealist project consisted in elaborating a new linguistic and cultural approach, adequate to the culture and society of the 1960s. It was a project that directly confronted the phenomena of standardization and neutralization that Guglielmi had spoken of with reference to *L'oblò.* Because of this programmatic confrontation, the parasurrealist project would become a more critical and self-conscious creative practice than the original surrealist movement. An examination of several theoretical writings in *Malebolge* can clarify the difference between these two stages of surrealism and help us to come to terms with some of the cultural dynamics that characterized the Italian *neoavanguardia* around the mid-1960s.

In a programmatic article entitled 'Poesia a tutti i costi' [Poetry at all costs] (in *Malebolge* 1.2, 1964) Spatola articulates the crucial confrontation between poetic writing and the social and institutional context in which literature existed in the mid-1960s. He rejects the notion of political engagement in the traditional sense of the term:

> In poesia, la dimensione dell'engagement volgare è stata quella del patetico, e la sua rilevanza estetica, cioè per assurdo: la sua aspirazione al sublime, era garantita, ancora una volta, da un assoluto, la Storia. D'altra parte il patetico è la dimensione usuale dei mass media, che utilizzano il contenuto emotivo del linguaggio per soddisfare un'equazione standard del rapporto stimolo-risposta, e non è certo un caso che anche la rilevanza estetica dei mass media sia garantita da un assoluto, il Conformismo. Nessun dubbio sulla sterilità di questa dimensione, il patetico appare quindi come la sfera del disimpegno totale, rischia anzi di essere accuratemente utilizzato dalle classi al potere attraverso le élites tecnologiche.

> [In poetry, the usual dimension of engagement has been that of pathos,

> and its relevance aesthetic, that is, paradoxical: its aspiration to the sublime has been guaranteed, yet again, by an absolute category, History. On the other hand, pathos is the typical dimension of mass media, which utilizes the emotional content of language to satisfy a standard equation based on the relationship between stimulus and response, and it is certainly not a coincidence that the aesthetic relevance of the mass media is guaranteed by an absolute category as well, Conformism. There is no doubt about the sterility of this dimension; pathos appears, therefore, as the realm of total disengagement. Actually, it runs the risk of being effectively utilized by the ruling classes through technological elites.] (51)

Here Spatola summarizes his scepticism toward the notion of engagement – understood as just a representation of the social and political issues of the times – because, in his view, contemporary power had developed subtle ways to neutralize the attempts of poets and writers to criticize the status quo. Spatola's polemical statements were particularly directed to cultural and editorial projects of the 1950s such as the magazines *Officina* and *Il Menabò*. Both publications were born in the wake of Italian neorealism, after the fundamental postwar cultural project of *Il Politecnico*.[7] The editors of *Officina* and *Il Menabò* were fully aware of the objective decline of the neorealist approach to both language and reality. Furthermore, they were responding to another objective decline, that of *ermetismo*, whose poetic style had characterized the 1930s in Italy. It could be said that their response was in line with that of the *neoavanguadia*. However, unlike the neoavanguardists, the editors of *Officina* and *Il Menabò* – particularly Elio Vittorini and Pier Paolo Pasolini – still advocated a principle of political engagement based on representation. These intellectuals held that artists and writers should produce a language that would include new techniques but could still portray the social and political contradictions of their times. This principle was indebted to – although also critical of – Georg Lukács's theory of literature as a mirror of reality.[8] The result of this epistemological approach to reality, in Spatola's terms, was pathos. Because pathos was an emotional response, it could therefore be easily assimilated as just one among the many consumerist values of contemporary capitalist society.[9]

What Spatola instead had in mind was a textual project in which the use of grotesque language would stress what he considered the tragic nature of contemporary civilization, especially since that civilization was characterized by such global historical circumstances as the Cold War, the threat of nuclear war, political protest, and the Vietnam War. Spatola's project consisted of an expansion of experimental, alternative, and creative devices and textual solutions for poets and writers:

> Il grottesco, come ironia del patetico, e categoria del tragico, è la dimensione entro la quale deve lavorare oggi il poeta. L'attività a più voci, l'ampliamento ad libitum della tastiera, l'esplosione dei grumi ideologici, la stratificazione culturale come conpresenza, ecc., sono immagini di una disarmonia radicale, di una ambiguità critica in atto, e, al limite, di una condizione schizofrenica calcolata e coltivata, come condizio sine qua non del fare poesia. Lo scopo della poesia è oggi quello di provocare nel lettore una inquietudine ideologica, e di mettere in crisi la geometria euclidea della sua visione del mondo.
>
> [The grotesque style, as a way to be ironic about pathos, and as a category of tragedy, is the dimension in which today's poet must operate. The plurality of voices, the expansion ad libitum of the keyboard, the explosion of ideological formations, cultural stratification as interaction, etc., these are images of a radical disharmony, of an active critical ambiguity and even of a calculated and cultivated schizophrenic condition, understood as the *conditio sine qua non* of writing poetry. The goal of today's poetry is to provoke in the reader an ideological uneasiness and to put into crisis the Euclidean geometry of his conception of the world.] (52)

Spatola's article was both a theorization of experimental language and an invitation to embrace a new notion of cultural-political engagement, the long term goal of which was to produce a disruptive effect on the discursive production of official institutions, and ultimately to provoke an explosion of their ideological contradictions.[10] This explosion was inevitably linked to a notion of language understood as an oppositional political tool. It was, however, an opposition that could be best practiced within the structural elements of art and literature rather than within their immediate social and political contents. This principle unavoidably generated what to the general public of the time appeared to be the 'obscurity' of experimental art and literature.

Here it is important to remember that Umberto Eco's seminal work *Opera aperta* [Open work] was published in 1962. Although he was never actively involved with *Malebolge,* this book stresses the relationship existing, in artistic practice, between technique and worldview. Eco focuses in particular on the notion of alienation, and considers the worldview as a constitutive element of the contemporary world, in terms of both economic structures and cultural and ideological superstructures:

> La categoria dell'alienazione non definisce più soltanto una forma di relazione tra individui basata su una certa struttura della società, ma tutta una serie di rapporti intrattenuti tra uomo e uomo, uomo e oggetti, uomo e istituzioni, uomo e convenzioni sociali, uomo e universo mitico, uomo e linguaggio.
>
> [The category of alienation no longer defines just a kind of relationship among individuals based on a certain structure of society, but, rather, a whole series of relationships between individual and individual, the individual and objects, the individual and institutions, the individual and social conventions, the individual and the mythical universe, the individual and language.] (*Opera aperta* 242–3)

For Eco, however, the awareness of the constitutive nature of alienation does not imply its passive acceptance. On the contrary, the task would be to denounce and demystify the consequences of alienation in personal relationships. In terms of artistic languages, this task could be pursued by elaborating new formal structures that could respond actively to the alienating situation. From this perspective, the true content of contemporary artwork would consist in the way in which the artwork worked out, at the formal level, a view and a judgment of the world (*Opera aperta,* 269–70).

More in general, it can be said that *Opera aperta* provided the fundamental theoretical background for the new interest on the part of artists and writers in the notion of disorder, for their questioning of traditional ideas of knowledge based on an immutable idea of order, and of traditional notions of artistic communication. The aim of an *opera aperta* was precisely that of provoking in the audience a sense of uneasiness with respect to the traditional view of the world, and to initiate a new relationship between the audience and the text or the artwork (*Opera aperta* 2, 62–3).

For his part, in *L'oblò* Spatola purposefully recovered the macabre and ironic dimension of the original surrealism. He departed from the notion of André Breton and others of the unconscious, however. In fact, the surrealists believed that the unconscious represented an actual 'reality' and could function as an authentic and uncontaminated revolutionary force. The parasurrealists took a rather different direction, as seen in a statement made in 1992 by Giorgio Celli (one of the founders of *Malebolge*) commemorating Spatola, with reference to the meeting at which the magazine was originally conceived:

> Ma il punto cruciale, per noi, era un altro: come proporre alla nostra comunità letteraria una rivisitazione accelerata del surrealismo che non risultasse una esibizione di fossili, o una operazione da epigoni degli epigoni? ... decretammo che il parasurrealismo sarebbe stato una sorta di manierismo del surrealismo, un surrealismo freddo, alla seconda potenza, rivisitato sopra tutto nelle sue tecniche, con un uso intenzionale e retorico della scrittura automatica, e della psicoanalisi. Trattando insomma l'inconscio come metafora, in accordo, lo capimmo più tardi, con un certo Lacan e con la sua scuola.
>
> [But the crucial point, for us, was another: how to propose to our literary community an accelerated revisitation of surrealism that would not seem an exhibition of fossils, or an operation by imitators of imitators? ... we decreed that parasurrealism would be a sort of mannerism of surrealism, a cold surrealism, raised to a higher power, reconceived above all in terms of its techniques, with an intentional and rhetorical use of automatic writing and psychoanalysis. In other words, we wanted to treat the unconscious as a metaphor, in line with Lacan and his school, as we understood later.] ('Prefazione' 7)

This is an effective account of the decisive choice made by the parasurrealists – namely to accept and constructively use the unavoidable artificiality involved in their project. The editors' awareness of such artificiality constituted the essential ground for the differentiation between the two stages of surrealism. It was the need for a different approach to the unconscious in the context of a new and challenging social-historical reality that intellectuals and writers had to confront in the 1960s.[11]

It must be pointed out that in elaborating their own ideas the surrealists had, in turn, departed from Freud's theory of the unconscious. Freud considered the unconscious as the repository of all psychic energy and the source of instincts, desires, and impulses that are repressed because of rules and requirements imposed by culture and society. According to Freud, however, under certain circumstances (that is, in dreams or under hypnosis) the censuring mechanisms imposed upon the human mind could be relaxed in order for the subject to vocalize the energies hidden in the unconscious. It was in this linguistic aspect of the Freudian theory that the surrealists could best find the rationale for their technique of automatic writing. For Freud, however, the voice of the unconscious had to be interpreted in order to decrease the tension of the subject. Breton and the surrealists considered that same voice, instead, as a powerful tool for a more profound picture of the subject, one which could work toward its liberation from the inhibitions and constraints created by society. Thus the surrealists proceeded to politicize the unconscious by emphasizing the dramatic clash between two opposing forces: on one hand, reason and its moral and social values; on the other, the unconscious, now charged with unlimited revolutionary potential.[12]

For the surrealists the unconscious was both a psychological and a cosmological element, to the point that for Breton, poetry was a form of expression given a prori and language itself is a pre-existing entity. It can be argued, therefore, that in a peculiar way Breton's notion corresponded to an idea of 'pure' poetry, not far removed from the *poesia pura* [pure poetry] theorized by Benedetto Croce in Italy. In light of these reflections, one may also argue that, for Breton, poetic writing was an act of recovery of that pre-existing language, so that the poet represents a sort of prophet speaking through a voice coming from the depth of the psyche. However, the revolutionary aspect of surrealism was, and remains, the envisioning of the possibility that poetry becomes accessible to everybody through an appropriate method, and therefore that everybody may be able to practice it.

Spatola brought the problematic of the unconscious a step further with respect to both the surrealists and Freud. He had, in fact, started from the radical and provocative idea that contemporary civilization and its technologies made it increasingly more difficult to determine with certainty whether an event belonged to the realm of dream or of waking. He articulates this view first in *L'oblò* and even more effectively in his volume of poems *L'ebreo negro* (1966) and in his articles in *Malebolge.*[13]

In theorizing this view, Spatola was supported by Giorgio Celli. An article by Celli on *L'ebreo negro* describes a profound shift that occurred in the contemporary reality of the 1960s: traditionally, dreams are concerned with events that are extremely unlikely in the real experience of individuals. For instance, Celli argues, the apocalypse and the total destruction of humankind are always configured as unlikely events or paranoid ideas. However, if we consider the nuclear explosion at Alamogordo, New Mexico, in 1945, which demonstrated the concrete possibility of nuclear war, we are confronted with the irruption of the dream

– or nightmare – in the realm of everyday life, an event that can affect everybody's experience. Thus a paranoid idea becomes a constitutive element of human existence.[14]

From this perspective, and from an understanding of the project of *Malebolge*, it becomes apparent that from the onset, the magazine's editors were undertaking the crucial task of re-articulating the entire issue of the role of artists and writers in the social and political reality on the 1960s. How can today's reader identify the features of such a task, along with the so-called signs of the times, by looking at the pages of *Malebolge*? Certainly these signs are not available in the form of direct representations of the historic climate of those times; rather more subtly, they begin precisely with the idea of 'parasurrealism.' According to this idea, the notion that intellectuals should engage in a direct commitment to change reality must be rejected.

As far as the *Malebolge* editors' notion of political engagement is concerned, one of the most significant documents remains Spatola's article 'Gruppo 70, apocalittico e integrato,' which was published in the second issue of 1964.[15] In his discussion of the works of this emergent Florentine group of visual poets Spatola points out the risks of contamination between art and technology, as theorized at that time by the members of the Gruppo 70. There was the possibility that the use of technological means of expression would be severed from any significant purpose, to the point of creating an objective fetishization of the technique itself. Furthermore, this separation could ultimately lead to the fetishization and assimilation of the 'apocalyptic' ideas of technological art by the institutions of power (see especially 61–3). Spatola suggests that art's true 'apocalyptic' practice was not the representation, no matter how 'technological,' of a reality that already contains in it the potential for a nuclear apocalypse, but rather the elaboration of a language that might constitute an objective metamorphosis, and therefore an alternative discourse to the language circulated by the institutions of contemporary society.

On the basis of this principle of metamorphosis, *Malebolge* established itself from the beginning as a laboratory for the articulation of an idea of text understood as an objective metamorphosis of reality. The consequences of this principle in the magazine's pages were enormous, on a level of linguistic and structural experimentation. A comprehensive discussion of the creative and theoretical texts published in *Malebolge* is outside the scope of this essay.[16] I will therefore consider several examples of textual experimentation: 'Poesie a schema multiplo' [Poems with

Poesie a schema multiplo
di
Renato Pedio

coglieva una

stella la fine del mondo

piovendo nell'invaso un filtro

casto nel pugno del

cielo, punta d'astro

vigile sulla diga

le strade, i bar, nei pleniluni disperati

gli assassinii

terra che smotta. Non

è altro che un demone

scivolante di fianco,

mostro festoso, che al

balzo sciaqua le cosce

contro i tasti dei monti

assestandosi le ossa in petto

in preghiera

membrana crepitante, dondolante

lacerata argilla serica

pendolo di marea

bilico, schianto, sulle scarpe fradicie

tempo è fido e chi vola lo conta

nelle tane rancide, e tra buffe membra

sgorbi atleti che

rimediano

Fatto di cronaca, la nota diga. Le tre voci, cielo, frana, acqua. Orizzontale, e varie soluzioni oblique, molto più mondo che la vallata del Vajont. La poesia, sia scambiando prima e terza colonna, sia facendo scivolare in alto o in basso, insieme o una per volta, le due colonne periferiche rispetto a quella centrale, può essere letta in una ventina di modi diversi, molti dei quali però quasi identici. Calcolo che esistano, però, cinque o sei buone letture valide.

12

multiple patterns] by Renato Pedio (*Malebolge* 1.2, 1964); 'coin VOLT' [in VOLVED] by Patrizia Vicinelli (*Malebolge* 3–4, 1966); and 'Perimetri' [Perimeters] by Nanni Balestrini (*Malebolge* 1, 1967).

In 'Poesia a schema multiplo' Pedio deals with the text as if it were a score for a verbal performance. Three parallel texts are laid out in three columns whose lines are interchangeable from one column to the other. In terms of the idea of objective metamorphosis of reality, it must be noted that the source of this text was an actual event: a catastrophe resulting from a broken dam in the Vajont valley, as Pedio indicates in the note to the text ('Poesia' 12).

Pedio created a generative mechanism as an attempt to provoke a shift from a traditional literary format to that of a verbal composition. Spatola himself pursued such a format for texts such as 'Aviazione/Aviatore' [Aviation/aviator] (*Malebolge* 1, 1967), developing a text destined to become an essential model for the experiments with phonetic poetry of the 1970s and 1980s, which Spatola himself was to perform in public on many occasions.

Over the four years in which it was published, *Malebolge* documented the radical reconsideration that the notion of 'text' was undergoing among a number of authors of the *neoavanguardia*. The results of this reconsideration concerned not only the phonetic and the performatory dimensions but also the visual dimension, as in the case of Vincinelli's 'coin VOLT.' Here the linguistic material on the page is subdivided into horizontal, vertical, and oblique blocks and is printed in a combination of lower and upper case characters in order to create a dynamic effect intended to call into question both the semantic dimension of the text, traditionally understood, and its linear structure.

Balestrini's 'Perimetri' is constructed with similar blocks of verbal material, organized in an apparently more regular structure (rectangular and squared). At first glance, the blocks of text seem to create the effect of a verbal cage, and are even readable according to a principle of linearity. However, the syntactic and semantic sequences completely undermine the structure of the text from within, because of the syntagms that are combined, repeated, and interrupted at the end of each line.

This 'building block' method of verbal composition placed 'Perimetri' in the specific context of permutational and combinatorial experiments with language that represented another aspect of the *Malebolge* laboratory. In the first issue of 1967 the magazine confirmed the international aspect of its project by publishing the 'Manifesto dell'arte permutazionale' [Manifesto of permutational art] written by Abraham Moles and translated by Giovanni Anceschi.[17] Moles defines permutation as the combination of simple elements produced on the basis of a limited differentiation. The goal of the combinatorial method is to allow the perception of the incommensurability pertaining to the realm of the infinite possibilities of combination ('Manifesto' 69). Moles places permutation at the centre of the process of artistic creation, to the extent that permutation gives the artist the opportunity to experiment with differentiation within uniformity:

> l'arte permutazionale sarà estremamente sperimentale e si pone come

Aviazione/Aviatore

di

Adriano Spatola

A.	B.	C.	D.	E.	F.
vi	iol	ol	lat	ne	re
ol	viol	tol	tat	ne	re
tol	tot	tiot	tiol	lot	re
z	oz	lo	ol	tat	ol
az	iol	viol	lat	re	er
a	a	—	ar	tor	tor
rot	lot	tot	tat	ol	tiol
—	ol	laz	lat	or	or
ro	—	lio	lior	lazior	—
tro	trion	riol	tiol	er	or
ar	to	tu	ti	tra	ter
en	er	e	ol	toll	tel
tal	tar	zar	sar	ser	ur
ar	tor	—	er	an	ur
sur	sor	sol	loss	res	tess
tut	ot	at	—	tiss	is
sil	arl	orl	os	sot	is
sill	silk	klis	os	os	silt
laz	lai	lay	loi	laz	y
ax	tax	lay	toi	lor	lorn
lis	vis	vi	—	vial	vial
viol	vial	ol	ols	loss	lose
lost	lot	tol	too	oo	oos
—	t	tak	kat	el	eel

18

scopo di circoscrivere ed esaurire il campo delle possibilità raggiungibili attraverso un 'set' di regole; essa materializza la libertà, tutto questo corrisponde ad uno stesso processo spirituale e ad una stessa capacità creativa ... tutte le opere permutazionali, che sono comprese nel campo delle pos-

coin VOLT

di
Patrizia Vicinelli

condotto
condotto
condotto perma
nocondottomor
condotto
ma
ma respintoma condotto mor
che condotto mor
chelato mor
che condottelato mor
m o r (pen)
mortechelatoin sus sione,

coinVOLT ehmm! sìssi coinVOLT hahha la.
pappinapappetta hahha volto di sotto voin
pappinalapappetta hahhàcoin
il riCCon volgimento beurr! beurre di astiacappe
mamma
zerò
intro
alla zero versata
em
intro alla zero riversa m
mamma , di omio , mamma alla
!
zerò e finita , dimio mamma
restio
mamma . mamma mamma.
intro:
per ma
nocon
mammor
(che-ri
come r
illuce
che pensiero gentile
gridi
e que
li pi
ccoli
mammor
luce anche
oggi. GRI
di dolinie fuocore. mae eMen ! restio

Introdotto nella stanza nota, lo avvicinarono alla bala ustra, e così tanto legatolo, lo spinse; che non poté accorgersene, crediamo. Così, introdotto nella stanza nota nota, lo avvicinarono alla balla ustra, e così tanto legatolo, lo spinse; che non è possibile accorgersene, crediamo. Intanto, introdotto nella stanza nota, lo avvicinarono, e così da legato, non poteva la spinta. Già. Se introdotto.

ho vinto la pappina pappetta della attention de la
maison neuve em ! zia la Mariuccia l'incostante : sono fregato l'
imprevu : Q.I. inferieur 60. mi farà hahhà, dire ancora hahha la pappina pappet
ta del imprevu riCCon volgimento beurr. sono fregato
mank a.
em ! restio ; bisogna intro à la moins zerò;

) Il catarofrangente. Il cataplegico. Neuroconsulto Votatore di insetti. Il catato-plegico avanzato, L. 5.000. Puah, l' onirico suadente.

: ri (riCCon volgimento , (anche.

Perimetri
di
Nanni Balestrini

1.

e intanto che si muove sulla spiaggia che si alza
sulla spiaggia seduta sulla spiaggia ritagliata e
che cammina col gomito sulla pelle sollevata alza
ndolo e la spalla intanto la testa girata dall'al
tra parte sulla spiaggia bianca che si ferma e mu
ovendosi intorno sulla pelle bianca e guardandola
mentre seduta il gomito sollevato sulla spiaggia
in questo modo si creano delle ombre, e sulla bian

intorno ci sono le ragazze che guardano
il sole che filtrava col gomito alzato co
n gli occhiali che guardano muovendosi a destra
verso la spiaggia occorre osservare la differ
enza che si muovono intorno e guardano col go
mito alzato la pelle bianca poi che riabb
assano la spiaggia e intanto si solleva giung
endo oltre l' angolo dell' occhio ritagliandola
dove guarda mentre si solleva e i capelli sci
olti sulle spalle occorre osservare la differ-
enza fra e allora le ragazze che restavano fe

sibilità, che viene scelto a priori, hanno per ciò origini dello stesso valore e ci portano lo stesso grado di novità; realizzano tutte diversamente e tutte analogamente questo rinnovamento del prevedibile, che è completamente all'opposto della copia.

[permutational art will be extremely experimental and its goal is to circumscribe and exhaust the realm of possibilities that are attainable within a set of rules; it materializes freedom, all this corresponds to the same spiritual process and to the same creative ability ... all permutational artworks, which are included in the realm of possibilities, which is chosen a priori, therefore have origins of the same worth and convey the same degree of novelty; they all achieve in different ways but, at the same time, analogously, this renewal of what is predictable, which is the opposite of the copy.] (70)

Permutational art appeared to be the most natural creative practice for any project of experimental art or poetry. Furthermore, Moles indicated a spiritual and anthropological rationale for permutation:

lo spirito umano è sempre stato sottomesso al sogno della permutazione, ma nel secolo passato vi è quasi sempre rimasto soffocato dentro, poiché la potenza dell'algoritmo combinatorio supera sempre la possibilità di colui che gli si consegna ... ma noi uomini del XX secolo abbiamo scoperto il segreto cabalistico del controllo: i calcolatori digitali come ordinatori, senza fatica esauriscono la molteplicità delle combinazioni.

[the human spirit has always submitted to the dream of permutation, but in the past century it has almost always suffocated inside that dream, since the power of combinatorial algorithm always exceeds the possibilities of the one who hands himself over to it ... but we, as men of the twentieth century, have found the cabalistic secret of control: digital calculators such as computers, effortlessly exhaust the multiplicity of the combinations.] (70)

As far as artistic experimentation is concerned, one cannot but see the utopian implications of these experimental projects and artistic manifestos. The infinite possibilities that were implicit in the permutational principle suggested that its innovative results might produce forms of mental and, in the longer term, cultural liberation.

The same first issue of 1967 of *Malebolge* also introduced the artistic movement of concrete poetry with 'Poesia concreta brasiliana' [Brazilian concrete poetry] written and translated by Brazilian poet and theorist

Haroldo de Campos, the historic leader of the movement. De Campos delineates the history of concrete poetry, beginning with the experience of the group Noigandres, founded in São Paulo, Brazil, in 1952. These poets based their creative practice on such literary models as Mallarmé, Pound, Joyce, Cummings, and the Brazilian Osvaldo de Andrade, and identified themselves with the Poundian definition of poets as 'inventors' who had found a new process of poetic creation. By developing both verbal and visual ideograms, de Campos and the others made their texts into a model of specific possibilities inherent in a combinatorial process, the features of which had been delineated by Moles.[18] In Italy, Eco, starting from Moles's theory, had argued that contemporary artistic products appeared to convey a message rich with information precisely because such a message was ambiguous and was therefore difficult to decode. According to Eco, in this condition of relative obscurity, the highest level of unpredictability was directly proportional to the highest level of disorder, in which all possible meanings are difficult to organize (*Opera aperta* 114–17).

De Campos also refers to Moles's theory as it relates to the issue of the antiromantic stance of contemporary artists. This stance is characterized by an attempt to reduce the distance between the work of the artist and that of the scientist. However, the antiromantic approach also implies a further utopian aspect: the future possibility of creating collective artwork. According to de Campos, a contemporary feature of language is its ability to respond to a predominantly technological civilization. For de Campos, art's ability to develop means of expression that could be adequate to the dynamics of production in the contemporary world meant that art could not and should not leave technology exclusively in the hands of technocrats who would use it to generate alienating conditions for humankind. It is therefore a question of elaborating a true technological humanism through which art would not fear or be threatened by technology. Art would, instead, incorporate technology in the creative process.

In an article entitled 'The Informational Temperature of the Text,' de Campos stresses the link between concrete poetry and technological processes, identifying Mallarmé's *crise de verse* as the originating point of this link:

> Concrete poetry is included in a different historical and cultural dimension. Its point of departure is the 'crisis of verse' generated at the end of

> the last century by Mallarmé's 'Un Coup de Dès.' It responds to a notion of literature, not as a craftsmanship but, so to speak, as an industrial process. Its product is a prototype, not the typical handiwork of individual artistry. It tends toward a minimal, simplified language, increasingly objectified, and for that reason, easily and quickly communicated ... Its [concrete poetry's] program is 'the least common denominator' of language ... In this way it coincides with the sense of a progressively technical civilization within which it is postulated. (179–80)

In formulating the creative process behind concrete poetry, de Campos found support in the work of Max Bense, another major representative of aesthetic theory in the 1950s, whose work was also circulating among the editors of *Malebolge.* Bense had formulated an aesthetic of technology that, unlike the classical metaphysical one, was oriented toward the notion of a product belonging to the realm of *techne.*[19] The consequences of Bense's approach can be summarized in two points: the importance of the so-called 'signifier' as an essential part of the artistic message, and the principle that the work of art is primarily an act of expression, rather than communication. Therefore, Bense focused on the first phase of the communicative processes, constituted by the sender and the channel, and paid little or no attention to the recipient of the message.

The final question, then, in light of the creative and theoretical writings published in *Malebolge,* is what message can we receive today from the cultural experience produced by this magazine? Certainly, we are no longer confronted with the cultural and historical issues that generated a need on the part of Spatola and other writers for a formulation of a parasurrealist poetics and an aesthetics of technology. And yet, one basic reason behind the experiments of the *Malebolge* laboratory is still extant: it is the need for poets and artists to generate constant metamorphoses of their own creative tools, in order to produce a language that is not merely mimetic of their times but is able to acquire a conscience of these times, and consequently to elaborate an effective alternative to them, an alternative understood as a utopian project to be developed at the level of both the artistic creation and the cognitive sphere. I will close with a quotation from Spatola's editorial to the second issue of *Tam Tam* (1972),[20] in which he defines poetry in terms of a self-sufficient creation that 'si costruisca come metamorfosi oggettiva, non come parafrasi metaforica della realtà' [constructs itself as an objective metamorphosis, not as a metaphorical paraphrase of reality] (2).

NOTES

1 *Il verri,* founded by Luciano Anceschi in Milan in 1956 is still in publiation. Over the years this journal has had several series and has devoted special issues to the major topics of contemporary culture. *Grammatica* was an art and literature magazine edited by Alfredo Giuliani, Giorgio Manganelli, and visual artists Gastone Novelli and Achille Perilli. Five issues were published irregularly in Rome beginning in 1968. *Quindici* was published monthly in Rome from 1967 to 1969; its editors included all the major representatives of the *neoavanguardia.* In addition to these official magazines there was also the quarterly journal *Marcatré* (founded by art critic Eugenio Battisti and published from 1962 to 1970), an interdisciplinary journal that documented the debate within the various disciplines constituting the *neoavanguardia.*

2 *Malebolge* was founded after the 1964 conference of the Gruppo 63 held in Palermo; the other co-founders were Corrado Costa (1929–91) and Giorgio Celli. Vincenzo Accame, Giovanni Anceschi, Luigi Gozzi, and Antonio Porta were members of the editorial board. After Spatola's death, some of the most significant studies on his work were collected in *Adriano Spatola poeta totale* and issue 12 of the journal *Testuale.*

3 Unless otherwise indicated, all translations are mine.

4 The critic Ennio Scolari was one of the first to link this use of cultural collage to parasurrealism; see 'Progetto di lavoro,' 74.

5 Spatola confirmed this characterization of *L'oblò* many years later in an interview with Luigi Fontanella; see 'Conversazione con Adriano Spatola,' 45–6.

6 For a more recent and exhaustive reading of *L'oblò,* see Beppe Cavatorta, 'Rinnegato tra i rinnegati: l'iper-romanzo di Adriano Spatola.' Cavorta identifies a series of literary sources of the novel and provides the first in-depth study of its cultural and structural significance. Also important is the reading by Mario Lunetta ('La schizofrenia calcolata dell'Oblò di Spatola'), which focuses on the political significance of Spatola's writing, and that by Giorgio Terrone (Oblò del rappresentare). For a reading of the novel within the cultural climate of *Malebolge,* see Giorgio Celli, 'Il romanzo di Spatola.'

7 *Officina* was founded in 1955 by poets Pier Paolo Pasolini, Franco Fortini, and Roberto Roversi; it ceased publication in 1959. *Il Menabò* was founded by Elio Vittorini and Italo Calvino and was published between 1959 and 1967. *Il Politecnico* was founded by Elio Vittorini and published from 1945 to 1947.

8 For a synthesis of the debate among the intellectuals of *Officina, Il Menabò,*

and the *neoavanguardia*, see Fabio Gambaro, *Per conoscere la Neoavanguardia*, 27–32, 55–65; and Renato Barilli, *La Neoavanguardia italiana*, 16–30. For the influence of *Il Politecnico* on the cultural debate of the 1950s, see Lucio Vetri, *Letteratura e caos*, 17–34.

9 It is not a coincidence that Spatola's article entitled 'Inutilità di Lukács' [The uselessness of Lukács], devoted to a critique of the Hungarian philosopher, was published in 1961.

10 In the same article, Spatola identifies three volumes of poetry, all published in 1964, as emblematic of the new approach to cultural-political engagement: Elio Pagliarani's *Lezione di fisica*, Edoardo Sanguineti's *Triperuno*, and Corrado Costa's *Pseudobaudelaire*.

11 In 1966 *Marcatré* hosted a special issue of *Malebolge* devoted to the new surrealist poetry. For an account of *Malebolge*'s approach to surrealism and the unconscious, see Muzzioli, *Teoria e critica della letteratura nelle avanguardie italiane degli anni sessanta*, 190–96.

12 See André Breton, 'First Manifesto of Surrealism,' especially 10 and 26.

13 For an account of the differences between surrealism and parasurrealism, see Celli, '*L'ebreo negro* di Adriano Spatola,' especially 53; Corrado Costa, 'A proposito del surrealismo'; and Celli 'Intervento,' 131.

14 See Celli '*L'ebreo negro* di Adriano Spatola,' 53–4. From this perspective, it is important to remember that in 1966 Spatola had published his seminal poem, 'Alamogordo 45,' in his volume *L'ebreo negro*.

15 For the relationship between the *neoavanguardia* and Gruppo 70, see Renato Barilli, *La neoavanguardia italiana*, 268–78; Vetri, *Letteratura e caos*, 88–90.

16 I must, however, mention, in particular, Pierre Garnier's 'Théatre spatialiste.' For Garnier's spatialist poetics, see also his 'Manifeste.'

17 Moles's most significant contribution to aesthetic theory, however, is his *Théorie de l'information et perception esthétique* (1958).

18 For an exhaustive study of the composition techniques used by the Noigandres poets, see Claus Clüver, 'Reflections on Verbivocovisual Ideograms'; Dècio Pignatari, 'Concrete Poetry'; and Haroldo de Campos, 'The Concrete Coin of Speech.'

19 For an Italian translation of Bense's theory, see *Estetica*.

20 Spatola founded the magazine *Tam Tam* in 1971.

WORKS CITED

Balestrini, Nanni. 'Perimetri.' *Malebolge* 1 (1967): 3–9.

Barilli, Renato. *La neoavanguardia italiana*. Bologna: Il Mulino, 1995.

Bense, Max. *Estetica.* Trans. Giovanni Anceschi. Milan: Bompiani, 1974.
Breton, André. 'First Manifesto of Surrealism.' In *Manifestos of Surrealism.* Trans. R. Seaver and H. Lane. Ann Arbor: University of Michigan Press, 1969.
Campos, Haroldo de. 'The Concrete Coin of Speech.' 1957. Trans. Jon Tolman. *Poetics Today* 3.3 (1982): 167–76.
– 'The Informational Temperature of the Text.' Trans. Jon Tolman. *Poetics Today* 3.3 (1982): 177–87.
– 'Poesia concreta brasiliana.' Trans. Haroldo de Campos. *Malebolge* 1 (1967): 80–2.
Cavatorta, Beppe. 'Rinnegato tra i rinnegati: l'iper-romanzo di Adriano Spatola.' *Il verri* 25 (2004): 21–48.
Celli, Giorgio. '*L'ebreo negro* di Adriano Spatola.' *Malebolge* 1 (1967): 53–6.
– 'Intervento.' In *Gruppo 63: il romanzo sperimentale.* Ed. Nanni Balestrini. Milan: Feltrinelli, 1966. 129–32.
– 'Prefazione.' *Adriano Spatola poeta totale.* Ed. Pier Luigi Ferro. Genoa: Costa & Nolan, 1992. 5–10.
– 'Il romanzo di Spatola.' *Malebolge* 1.2 (1964): 70–2.
Clüver, Claus. 'Reflections on Verbivocovisual Ideograms.' *Poetics Today* 3.3 (1982): 137–48.
Costa, Corrado. 'A proposito del surrealismo.' *Malebolge* 1.2 (1964): 54–7.
– *Pseudobaudelaire.* Milan: Scheiwiller, 1964.
Eco, Umberto. *Opera aperta.* Milan: Bompiani, 1962.
Ferro, Pier Luigi, ed. *Adriano Spatola poeta totale.* Genoa: Costa & Nolan, 1992.
Fontanella, Luigi. 'Conversazione con Adriano Spatola.' In *Adriano Spatola poeta totale.* Ed. Pier Luigi Ferro. 41–9.
Gambaro, Fabio. *Per conoscere la Neoavanguardia.* Milan: Mursia, 1993.
Garnier, Pierre. 'Manifeste.' *Lettres* 8.29 (1963): 1–8.
– 'Théâtre spatialiste.' *Malebolge* 1 (1967): 22–8.
Guglielmi, Angelo. *Vero e falso.* Milan: Feltrinelli, 1964.
Lunetta, Mario. 'La schizofrenia calcolata dell'Oblò di Spatola.' In *Adriano Spatola poeta totale.* Ed. Pier Luigi Ferro. 75–86.
Moles, Abraham. 'Manifesto dell'arte permutazionale.' Trans. Giovanni Anceschi. *Malebolge* 1 (1967): 69–75.
– *Théorie de l'information et perception esthétique.* Paris: Flammarion, 1958.
Muzzioli, Francesco. *Teoria e critica della letteratura nelle avanguardie italiane degli anni sessanta.* Rome: Istituto dell'Enciclopedia Italiana, 1982.
Pagliarani, Elio. *Lezione di fisica.* Milan: Scheiwiller, 1964.
Pedio, Renato. 'Poesie a schema multiplo.' *Malebolge* 1.2 (1964): 12–14.
Pignatari, Dècio. 'Concrete Poetry: A Brief Structural-Historical Guideline.' 1957. Trans. Jon Tolman. *Poetics Today* 3.3 (1982): 189–95.

Sanguineti Edoardo. *Triperuno.* Milan: Feltrinelli, 1964.
Scolari, Ennio. 'Progetto di lavoro.' *Malebolge* 1.2 (1964): 73–4.
Spatola, Adriano. 'Aviazione/Aviatore.' *Malebolge* 1 (1967): 18–21.
– *L'ebreo negro.* Milan: Scheiwiller, 1966.
– 'Editoriale.' *Tam Tam* 2 (1972): 2–3.
– 'Gruppo 70: apocalittico e integrato.' *Malebolge* 1.2 (1964): 60–3.
– 'Inutilità di Lukacs.' *Il verri* 6 (1961): 157–68.
– *L'oblò.* Milan: Feltrinelli, 1964.
– 'Poesia a tutti i costi.' *Malebolge* 1.2 (1964): 51–3.
'Surrealismo e parasurrealismo. Malebolge.' *Marcatré* 26.9 (1966): 224–52.
Terrone, Giorgio. 'Oblò del rappresentare ('Idealità' e 'Morale' nel romanzo di Adriano Spatola).' In *Adriano Spatola poeta totale.* Ed. Pier Luigi Ferro. 87–101.
Testuale 12 (1991).
Vetri, Lucio. *Letteratura e caos: poetiche della neo-avaguardia italiana degli anni sessanta.* Milan: Mursia, 1992.
Vicinelli, Patrizia. 'CoinVOLT.' *Malebolge* 3–4 (1966): 24–5.

PART TWO

Revisiting Literature

4 The 'New' Novel of the *Neoavanguardia*

SILVIA CONTARINI

The Avant-garde Tradition

As is well known, the establishment of the Gruppo 63, which occurred in 1963, is the formal act that acknowledges the existence of an avant-garde and experimental movement whose origins date back to the times of *Il verri*, a journal founded in 1956 by Luciano Anceschi but that found identity and unity in 1961 with the publication of the poetry anthology *I novissimi*. The Gruppo 63 began to show signs of disintegration in 1965, but it was only between 1968 and 1969 – coinciding with the explosion of political movements and the reappraisal of the role and the social involvement ('impegno') of the intellectual – that the worsening internal fracture in the Gruppo 63 resulted in its final dissolution. The journal *Quindici*, more a political than a literary periodical, was the last incomplete expression of the avant-garde movement.[1]

Introducing a study about the neo-avant-garde narrative production with this brief chronology serves to emphasize two points. The first is the term 'neo-avant-garde,' which, depending on one's perspective, can range from few years to more than a decade, and thus include only the official members of the Gruppo 63 or a much larger number of affiliates. Indeed, only a wide-ranging view makes it possible to understand how, at the 1965 conference in Palermo, just two years after the group was founded, Umberto Eco could already speak of a 'tradition' of the neo-avant-garde novel, arguing that new and original characteristics of the narrative experiments of the group already belonged to a system of conventions, and that in any case 'ogni avanguardia aspira alla tradizione' [every avant-garde aspires to tradition] (in Balestrini 74). We will return to this idea. The second point concerns the political and ideological dimension, negated by some and claimed by others: an element of conflict, sometimes concealed, but other times so open and profound that is led to the disintegration of the group. Although it was presented as a theoretical and literary movement, the Italian neo-avant-garde always had to deal with political and ideological questions that became the subject of heated debate both within and outside the group. Such questions were far from unimportant regarding the group's critical reflection and the literary production, and its narrative in particular. The most emblematic example, to which we will return, is the evolution of Nanni Balestrini, who moved from works of great formal complexity, including electronic poetry developed on a computer, to manifesto texts of extreme lexical and syntactic simplicity in response to the double requirement of being accessible to the masses and of reflecting their language.

One immediately notes that the literary experimentalism and the pure linguistic research that characterized the beginning of the neo-avant-garde gave way to the demand of a close relationship with the socio-political reality and its language.

Theory and Criticism

The numerous and complex literary theories expressed by the neo-avant-garde must be understood in this context, although theoretical and critical discussions were at the centre of interest at every moment of its evolution. The creative production, in particular that which was presented at conferences, consists for the most part of a mere illustration of formal research, a sort of application of previously developed theories. In other words, the theory precedes, accompanies, and follows the creation, framing it, and taking on equal if not greater importance than the literary text. Roland Barthes would say that it is normal, since the value of avant-garde texts results precisely from the intentional elements (*Le plaisir* 15; *Roland Barthes* 58). It is therefore not surprising that one of the most active critics of the group, Angelo Guglielmi, for whom the 'new' novel in Italy was not producing satisfactory results on the literary level (we are in 1965), valued such texts only as objective critical analysis. Indeed, their poetic value lies precisely in this: 'La rilevanza che presentano dal punto di vista del discorso critico, si pone tout court come valore poético' [Their importance from the point of view of critical discourse is their poetic value tout court] (in Balestrini 36).

Umberto Eco's *Opera aperta* (1962) provided a remarkable stimulus to this theoretical debate and had a considerable influence on the narrative production. This volume, a collection of essays published in previous years, can be considered a sort of manifesto of the group. In addition to the typically avant-garde opposition between 'traditional order' and 'fruitful disorder,' Eco develops the concepts of indeterminacy, ambiguity, casualness, and multiplicity of meaning in a work. Artistic research must concentrate on the form that creates the greatest openness for the work. In the preface to the fourth edition of *Opera aperta* (published in 1968), Eco writes:

> 'L'opera d'arte è un messaggio fondamentalmente ambiguo, una pluralità di significati che convivono in un solo significante [...] Tale ambiguità diventa – nella poetiche contemporanee – una delle finalità esplicite dell'opera, un valore da realizzare di preferenza ad altri.'
>
> [The work of art is a fundamentally ambiguous message, a plurality of meanings, that coexist in one signifier ... Such ambiguity becomes – in contemporary poetics – an explicit aim of the work, a value to be produced in preference to any other.] (6)

Eco also distinguishes between poetics and poiesis, stressing that the intentional moment allows one to understand what an artist wanted to do, but not necessarily what he did (275). Nevertheless, for the critics of the group, Eco's theorized 'openness' becomes a criterion for the evaluation of works according to their level of polysemy and multiplicity of meaning.

Language is another fundamental element, not only for critics but also for experimental writers. Alfredo Giuliani, another well-known member of the Gruppo 63, tried to define the characteristics of avant-garde literature as follows.

> Il tipo di letteratura che chiamiamo tradizionale accetta l'esistenza della lingua colta nelle sue strutture semantiche e sintattiche, e ne accetta l'esistenza come una garanzia. Al contrario il tipo di letteratura che chiamiamo d'avanguardia non accetta l'esistenza della lingua colta corrente come una garanzia e non considera le sue strutture come razionali ma semplicemente come storiche.
>
> [The type of literature that we call traditional accepts the existence of a cultured language with its semantic and syntactic structures, and it accepts its existence as a guarantee. On the contrary, the type of literature that we call avant-garde does not accept the existence of a present cultured language

as a guarantee and does not consider its structures as rational but simply as historical.] (Balestrini and Giuliani 372)

Giuliani's pertinent suggestions are extremely useful because, as we will see in analysing the narrative production, the question of literary language is absolutely central to the 'new novel.'

New Novel?

We could discuss other valid theoretical variants on avant-garde work, all of which are applicable to the novel although not limited to it alone. Here, however, we will focus our study on specific characteristics of the novel. While it would indeed be impossible to completely develop a specific reflection on all aspects of the novel, it is sufficient to point out that if the term 'novel' is itself complex, and the term 'avant-garde novel' is almost an oxymoron and is even more complex insofar as the historical avant-garde in the early twentieth century – in Italy, futurism – had already destroyed conventional narrativity by transgressing rules and codes and eliminating barriers between disciplines, genres, and styles. Ranging form manifestos to 'words-in-freedom,' the historical avant-garde blended and invented without concern, demolishing the syntax. It may seem incongruous to consider outmoded codes in a discussion of the neo-avant-garde novel. And yet, it is necessary to do so, because the negative reference for the neo-avant-garde, the enemy that must be destroyed, is the traditional novel, which regained popularity in the post-war period, and particularly the neorealist novel. Thus, the Gruppo 63 writers refuse the novelist canon and experiment with 'transgenre' texts: examples include *Fratelli d'Italia* by Alberto Arbasino, *Hilarotragoedia* by Giorgio Manganelli, and *Vogliamo tutto* by Nanni Balestrini. In order to understand the structural and formal modernity of this narrative production, which is difficult to classify as a genre, one must keep in mind the significant turmoil that it provoked in 1960s Italy.

For all these reasons, in this study the term 'novel' must be broadly defined as a work in prose (thus excluding poetry), not originally intended for performance (thus excluding theatrical texts and scripts), and not written to argue an idea or to persuade (thus excluding essays). In parallel, the adjective 'new' indicates that we will examine experimental texts, written for the most part by authors of the neo-avant-garde. Finally, regarding the criteria of analysis and evaluation, the intention of the text is more important its actual results.

Evolution and Characteristics of the New Novel

In the late 1950s and early 1960s the Italian literary scene was dominated by a rather conformist realism, even though experimental writers such as Antonio Pizzuto, Giovanni Testori, Stefano D'Arrigo, and of course Carlo Emilio Gadda are already attracting attention on the sideline. Members of the Gruppo 63 rarely make reference to these isolated – Italian and contemporary – cases. In their search for models, on the theoretical level, of the neo-avant-garde novel, the group favours the foreign triad of Joyce, Kafka, and Musil; the Italian forefathers Pirandello and Svevo are mentioned with some reservation.

In this initial phase preceding the constitution of the Gruppo 63 the neo-avant-garde writers produce poetry but not yet fiction. In 1961 there is a precursor: the novel *Ferito a morte* by Raffaele La Capria, who participated in the activities of the Gruppo 63 but never became an integral part of the neo-avant-garde movement. In 1962 the journal *Il Menabò* published several experimental fragments by writers who, on the contrary, were to be full members of the group: Leonetti, Colombo, Filippini, and most importantly Edoardo Sanguineti, who contributed selections from *Capriccio italiano*, which was published the following year. The year 1962 also saw the release of Paolo Volponi's *Memoriale*, which is considered the first experimental Italian novel.

The most important novels by authors of the Gruppo 63 were published during a second phase, extending from 1962 to 1966. Moreover, numerous passages from works in progress were read in public at the meetings in Palermo in 1963 and 1965. Nevertheless, the production is not extensive and suffers from the aforementioned excess of intentionality. Critics even within the group blamed the new novels for being too demonstrative. Barbato observes:

> Pagine spesso difficili, di ardua lettura, ricche di prestiti tecnici da altre parti, composte in un linguaggio oscuro e qualche volta (ma solo raramente) davvero innovatore [...] Davanti al tribunale critico collettivo, le assoluzioni erano molto minori delle condanne, e sembravano dare ragione a chi rimproverava allo sperimentalismo italiano di essere scarso nella produzione letteraria in contrasto con il notevole accumulo di intenzioni critiche.

> [Pages that are often difficult, hard to read, full of technical borrowings from other sources, composed in a dark and sometimes (but only rarely) innovative language ... Before the critical collective tribunal, there were

> a lot fewer acquittals than guilty verdicts, and they seemed to prove right those who reproached Italian experimentalism for being scarce in literary production in contrast with the considerable accumulation of critical intentions.] (173)

Among the novels that follow *Memoriale* are a number of well-known works: Sanguineti's *Capriccio italiano, Fratelli d'Italia* (1963) by Alberto Arbasino, *Hilarotragoedia* (1964) by Giorgio Manganelli, *La scoperta dell'alfabeto* (1963) and *Il serpente* (1966) by Luigi Malerba, and *Tristano* by Nanni Balestrini (1966). We should also mention *Barcellona* (1963) and *Il confine* in 1971, *L'eterna moglie* (1963) by Giuliano Gramigna, *La principessa Montalbo* (1962) by Michele Perriera, *L'oblò* (1962) by Adriano Spatola, and *Notizie sugli scavi* (1964) by Franco Lucentini (who would soon leave the group).[2]

There has been destruction, there has been creation: now it is time to take stock of the results. The critics in the group establish the common points of the experimental work. The third and last phase thus opens and closes: it is at this point that technical and theoretical considerations, having influenced the literary production of group members, become sediment, resulting in the 'tradition' noted by Eco at the 1965 conference. Eco's statement might have been premature, but at the same conference, others in the group, unsatisfied with the results, believed that the crisis of the novel was such that no renewal was possible: 'Anche per l'avanguardia, il romanzo stava quindi sul letto di morte' [Even for the avant-garde, the novel was on its death bed] (Barbato 187). It is true that in those years the novel was declared dead numerous times: nevertheless, within the Gruppo 63 there was little enthusiasm for narrative, whether traditional or avant-garde.

It is interesting to note that a 'neo-avant-garde literary canon' did stabilize during the second half of the 1960s. This canon influenced several transitional writers whose cultural formation took place under the neo-avant-garde but who made their narrative debut somewhat later: Sebastiano Vassalli's novels *Narcisso* (1968) and especially *Tempo di massacro* (1970), as well as Gianni Celati's *Comiche* (1971) and *Le avventure di Guizzardi* (1973). We will return to this point.

The Canon of the *Neoavanguardia*

Experimental narrative works – novels or excerpts read at the conferences – concentrate on formal research and on the manipulation of verbal material. The literary techniques used, while various, can nevertheless be related to a series of trends. First, they often have a first person narrator and an interior monologue in the form of stream of consciousness or free associations. Furthermore the first person narrator, now deprived of psychological depth, loses consistency, while the protagonist, often a normal man, loses his heroism. As for the structure, unity of space and diachronic progression are abolished in order to superimpose or intersect temporal layers and geographic centres. Little attention is paid to plot and action, and facts and characters are not intended to respect historical similitude. Finally, linguistic expression and genre are not univocal: pastiche predominates. These trends might be summarized with Barilli's formula of 'abbassamento' [lowering]: a lowering of things, gestures and behaviours, events, characters, and linguistic registers. Literature is no longer an aristocratic place.

Before lingering over the question of language, it may be useful to reiterate the point that the neo-avant-garde critics noted the obvious 'foreign' inspiration of these techniques (Joyce, Proust, and the French *nouveau roman*), but while pointing out that this production, coming from within their own group, had little originality, they did not suggest other models or other approaches.

The Question of Language

Insofar as its literary techniques do not seem to be specific, the neo-avant-garde novel does not even convince the supporters of experimentalism. In spite of this stern judgment, the theoretical and practical work on linguistic material carried out by neo-avant-garde writers is undoubtedly important. In particular, the methods of semantic and syntactic destruction of the language in certain early works are so radical that the resulting experimental texts are extremely difficult. It is no accident that one of the major themes of debate is illegibility. Authoritative writers outside the movement – for example Alberto Moravia in his 1967 essay 'Illeggibilità e potere' – criticized the work of the neo-avant-garde on precisely this score. But legibility is not an avant-garde requirement, and the reader of a neo-avant-garde novel is, by definition, an avant-garde reader, ready for an uncomfortable reception and for a reading based more on reason than emotion. Debate was also lively inside the Gruppo 63. At first, only Arbasino defended the cause of legibility, arguing that an avant-garde text can be pleasant, fascinating, and amusing (in Balestrini 48), but soon other members of the group accepted the criticism of their opponents and called the illegibility of experimental texts into question. As early as the 1965 conference, some noted, with great regret, that, in order to become more accessible to the reader, the majority of neo-avant-garde texts had lost a degree of complexity.

The latent contradiction – to be an avant-garde close to the masses – anticipates the conflict that would eventually bring about the group's dissolution, but behind this discussion lies another complex question: the linguistic evolution in Italy following the Second World War. By the 1960s the illiteracy rate (which had been 80 per cent at the time of Unification) had decreased to 10% per cent due to compulsory schooling and above all to the developments in mass media, particularly radio and television. The result was not only a new oral bilingualism, Italian-dialect, but also a national Italian language that, oscillating between the normative codes specific to certain domains (bureaucracy, business, science) and the elevated and literary language of cultural institutions, created a 'middlebrow' space. Reflection on a 'middle' language, as opposed to 'high' and 'low' languages, is particularly intense during this time period, and is not restricted to avant-garde circles. This processes of linguistic transformation fascinated writers such as Carlo Emilio Gadda[3] as well as fierce enemies of the Gruppo 63, such as Pier Paolo Pasolini.[4]

Language – or more precisely, verbal materials according to Sanguineti's definition – constitute the battleground of neo-avant-garde experimentalism. Convinced of the revolutionary function of language, Sanguineti and others again attack middlebrow codes along two main lines: from below, liberating language from its poetic function, stretching the lexical field of jargon, dialects, and specialized languages, and simplifying syntax; from above, turning to ancient, scholarly, and poetic texts to enrich the lexicon, even with precious terms or terms fallen into disuse. These two perspectives, situated above and below middle language, aimed at producing effects of alienation, disturbance, and disruption – formal manipulations that would thus underline the fact that, above all, literature is language.

We have already noted that an excess of formal experimentation often made the early narrative production of the avant-garde cold and difficult to read. Concerned about the reader's incomprehension, some members of the Gruppo 63 opposed experimental integralism. One consequence was the almost immediate rejection of the 'line from above' – the recovery of middle language – and a preference for the approach from below. Only this third option survived the dissolution of the group. Indeed, it was revisited in the early 1990s when an attempt was made during the

Ricercare di Reggio Emilia meetings to find a common denominator for the descendants of the Group.[5]

New Novels

In order to understand the practice of experimentalism in concrete terms, let us now review a group of the most representative 'new' novels.

Memoriale by Paolo Volponi

Paolo Volponi, a Partito Comunista Italiano intellectual and a friend of Pasolini and Leonetti, did not adhere to the neo-avant-garde movement but his novel *Memoriale*, published by Garzanti in 1962, was quickly labelled as experimental by critics, including those in the Gruppo 63. For his part, Volponi never denied his intention, arguing that his intention was to address the problems of the industrial world with a novel 'teso alla costruzione autonoma di una lingua e di un significato' [aiming at the autonomous construction of language and meaning] (in Ferretti 4). In short, *Memoriale* still proposes social involvement at the level of content, but it breaks with naturalism and is attentive to the way in which things are said.

The novel tells the story of a young man, the son of immigrant farmers, who after spending the war shut away in a work camp returns to his town of birth, where, unemployed and ill with tuberculosis, he finally accepts work in a factory, hoping to be integrated into society. However he finds only noisy machinery, impossible rhythms for his debilitated body, and alienated human rapport. The story is told in the first person, and the perspective, despairing and paranoid, is that of an outcast affected by psychological troubles and manias of persecution to the limit of insanity. The fallen paradise of the protagonist is the countryside where, still healthy, he had spent a happy and innocent childhood. In his raving monologue he rebels against a world in which progress and modernity have forced upon human beings the predominance of machines and technology. No one can help him because his rebellion is an individual one.

What was considered experimental by contemporary critics? Without a doubt, the language. The protagonist, a simple man in both character and social condition, expresses himself in elementary syntactical structures: facts are told in short phrases using ordinary vocabulary. The register, however, is literary: there is no imitation of spoken language;

there is no dialect interference; tenses, verbal modes, and rules of concordance are maintained. Moreover, the descriptions of the landscape have a lyrical tone. The frantic deliriums and the descriptions are also interpolated with passages from trade-union leaflets. Critics spoke of a double register, a stylistic duplicity corresponding to the duality of the novel's content: the idyllic world of nature contrasted to the world contaminated by war, industry, and pain, the lost dream and the hard reality. Is this enough to speak of experimentalism? Maria Corti, who classifies Volponi as a neo-experimentalist writer, rightly emphasizes the use of a 'punto di vista deformante' [distorting point of view] (Corti 135–7) because through the distorting glance of the protagonist, switching registers and fragmenting expression, Volponi is able to portray a different reality through different formal means. The result is a kind isomorphism between content and language. This passage is an example:

> Io impugnavo la mitragliatrice. Eccone due alla porta. Facevo fuoco. Le mie labbra misuravano la mitraglia. 'Sciopero,' una breve raffica. Uno portò le mani sul fianco e l'altro si piegò a sinistra. Subito altri tre, più due, più uno. A scaglioni, per ingannarmi. 'Scioperare...scioperare': una raffica dietro l'altra. Poi altri ancora. Le mie raffiche aumentavano. 'Sciopero...sciopero...fate sciopero.' 'Sciopero, sciopero, sciopero fate.' 'Avanti. Sciopero, sciopero, fate sciopero. Scioperate, scioperate.' 'Avanti, avanti, sciopero, sciopero, fate sciopero. Scioperate, scioperate, avanti [...] Potevo bruciarli, annientarli come se davvero le mie mani avvicinassero il sole [...] Lavoratori, lavoratrici del B-Mon 18, nel nostro reparto è in atto un tentative da parte della direzione ...
>
> [I was holding the machine gun. Two are at the door. I fired. My lips measured the shot. 'Strike,' a short burst. One had his hands on his side, the other turned to the left. Three more, right away, then two, then one. In groups, to deceive me. 'Strike... strike': one burst after the other. Then more. My bursts increased. 'Strike... strike... go on strike,' 'Strike, strike, go on strike.' 'Come one. Strike, strike, go on strike. Strike, strike.' 'Come on, come on, strike, strike, go on strike. Strike, strike, come on' ... I could burn them, annihilate them, as if my hands could truly approach the sun. Workers, men and women of B-Mon 18, in our section there is an attempt on the part of management ...] (300–1)

This passage shows that, in spite of his experimental inclination, Volponi's project remains within the bounds of certain narrative rules. In particular, the plot conserves linearity and suspense, and the action develops with a unity of place and a logical succession of facts. Volponi did not intend to bring about a revolution through language, nor did he want to provoke. Instead, his aim was to revitalize the novel by using well-known techniques in his own way: the articulation of a deformed vision of the world through a viewpoint 'from below,' and the use of a mixture of stylistic and linguistic registers.

Ferito a morte by Raffaele La Capria

La Capria made his debut as a scriptwriter in the 1950s but he became well-known to the public and appreciated by critics only with his second novel, *Ferito a morte* [Deadly wound], which won the Strega prize in 1961. He participated to the founding conference of the Gruppo 63, where he read 'Gioco di specchi' [A game of mirrors], a methodological and explanatory application of current modern literary principles, including école du regard, phenomenology, existentialism, Pirandellism, and stream of consciousness. After this, condemning the negative effect of an excess of theories on creativity, he distanced himself from the group.

Ferito a morte is without doubt, an experimental novel, especially in its structure, style, and themes. The reconstruction of the plot demands an attentive reading of the finest details. The action frame of the first seven chapters develops over a few hours. In the first chapter it is Sunday morning, the year is 1954, and the protagonist is in bed at the family home in Naples; that afternoon he must take the train to Rome, where he has decided to move, but meanwhile, in confused drowsiness, he dreams and reviews experiences of his past life. By the seventh chapter, still in bed, but now for his postprandial nap, he is completing the same dream. Dreams and reality, memories and present time are entangled through the intervening chapters, only distinguishable thanks to fleeting and sparse indications. Episodes from different years, placed one after another but not consecutively, fill up the space of a single morning.

The disorder of temporal moments and the deformation of events create a sense of complete disorientation. Furthermore, there is a plurality of narrative voices and a plurality of gazes, since several characters tell or live the same scene in different ways, along with the protagonist. Passage from one voice to another, from one memory to another, and from one space to another occurs in the same chapter, or even the same paragraph, with no stylistic modification or graphic device to signal the reader. Stylistically, the interior monologue predominates, but direct and indirect discourse are also used. La Capria opts for the low register of everyday spoken language with no dialectal inflections or linguistic innovations. The last three chapters are linear and univocal: the protagonist, now living in Rome, relates a series of his returns to between 1954 and 1960.

Altogether, the fragmented temporality of the narrative together with the multiplicity of and the alternation between points of view reflect a compositional strategy typical of early twentieth-century European modernity. La Capria, openly attempts to situate himself outside of the traditional novel. Moreover, the narrative choices correspond to thematic choices, which is also in tune with literary modernity. For La Capria, the wound, the overall sense of existential failure, is the expressive premise for the twentieth-century artist. Under the joyful and mythical guise of 'dolce far niente,' his Naples hides its underlying social immobility, its wasted time, the terrible dissipation whereby a day or ten years are identical, passing in exactly the same way. It is this 'deadly wound' that cuts across the protagonist's day, a day that covers ten years with no individual or collective projects. Time turns in on itself, history does not move forward.

The problem of failure translated in the form of narrative impotence is also central in La Capria's next novel, *Amore e psiche,* published ten years later. By the author's own admission, this novel is a partial failure because of a 'complexity syndrome': its excess of construction and abuse of mechanisms and devices disconnect it from reality. Creativity is stifled by complication. La Capria decided not to go further in his experimentation and his search for formal complexity. From the 1970s onward, he explicitly asserts, he increasingly wrote books instead of novels, in a simpler and more direct manner.[6] Although his formal research is limited to structure and perspective and has no direct effect on expressive means and linguistic materials, *Ferito a morte* remains a novel emblematic of literary modernity.

Capriccio italiano by Edoardo Sanguineti

A prominent member of the neo-avant-garde exponent, Sanguineti is above all a poet (he was one of the five *novissimi*) and a theorist (*Ideologia e linguaggio*). The cardinal rules of his thought are the rationality of creation, which must conform to a project and a theory, and the ideological function of language, because the manipulation of verbal materials is not at all innocent and has a subversive power. Sanguineti also looks back to the theory of the three styles (tragic, elegiac, comic) and the three corresponding literary models (unreal, possible, real). In *Capriccio italiano* [Italian fancy] he chooses the comic style and the realistic mode, elaborating them oneirically. This novel – a *fabula onirica*, according to his definition – is the story of a dream, true and false at the same time. The plot and subject are simple: a couple goes through a time of crisis as the birth of their third son approaches. The reading is arduous, as the text is complicated by the multiplying places and situations (a lake, a hotel, a living room, dreams, strange adventures, and curious accidents) linked by complex connections that produce effects of confusion, disorientation, and bewilderment. If one gives up any attempt to find coherence and linearity, *Capriccio italiano* could be read as a series of events linked by the logic of the dream world into which the psyche of the protagonist, upset by the pregnancy of his wife and the long-awaited delivery, pours reality and fantasies.

In this world sexuality, desires, and drives reveal themselves through a vast symbolic repertoire (knives, hammers, holes, blood). The characters, deprived of an identity, are identified by the first letter of their names, except for the wife and son who are identified as such by the protagonist as he relates, in first person narrative, the banal but disturbing facts about his married life. It should be noted that both the observation of daily reality and the attention to things rather than values or feelings have a 'lowering' function.

The connections within the text can be also established through a logic internal to the text: the pure mechanicalness of language. Indeed, what is most astonishing and surprising about *Capriccio italiano* are its narrative modes. According to the principle that if the form is subversive, then the content is also, Sanguineti searches for a language that can blend form and content and that, while destroying rules and customs, can express dreams and psychological troubles. His linguistic project is the constitution of 'un sottoparlato oniroide che si articola entro un registro deliberatamente depauperato e ristretto, in una sintassi sbalordita e deficiente' [a dreamlike byproduct of spoken language that is articulated through a deliberately impoverished and limited register, through an astonished and deficient syntax] (*Ideologia e linguaggio* 11). To succeed in his intent, Sanguineti employs numerous stylistic and rhetorical techniques – overusing interjections, syntactic anacoluthons, almost obsessive repetitions – in an attempt to recreate through exasperation the asyntacticness and the linguistic tics typical in the spoken language, adapted to a specific logic of the unconscious. Short chapters follow one another, each characterized by the presence of a particular form of repetition. For example:

> 'Allora vengo,' mi dice. 'Cerca C.' gli dico. 'È qui,' dice lui. 'No,' dico, 'è mia moglie che la cerca.' 'Devi dirglielo,' dice, 'che è qui.' 'No,' dico, 'adesso non glielo posso dire.' 'Allora vengo,' dice lui. 'Perché allora?' dico.
>
> ['I'll come then,' he tells me. 'Look for C.' he says. 'No,' I say, 'my wife is looking for her.' 'You must tell him,' he says, 'that he's here.' 'No,' I say,' I can't tell him now.' 'I'm coming then,' he says. 'Why, then?' I say.] (19)

Sanguineti's experimentalism presents a paradox: how can a language rationally devised to dismantle the literary conventions express a dream-like world, which is irrational and has its own codes? The predominant intention is, in effect, a 'fabricated' language in which every invention corresponds to a function, an extratextual and demonstrative need. The narrative project and the conceptual construction are fascinating. The result is an ice-cold and mechanical prose made up of automatisms and schematic codifications. *Capriccio italiano* is thus more interesting to study than to read.

Fratelli d'Italia by Alberto Arbasino

Alberto Arbasino participated in the Gruppo 63 from the time of its inception. His novel *Fratelli d'Italia* [Italian brothers] was published in the fateful year of 1963 and went through two revised editions (1976 and 1994). According to the definitions supplied by the author, particularly in *Certi romanzi* (which was intended to explain the phases of creation in *Fratelli d'Italia*), this work plays a number of roles: it is a novel-essay because it is organized around two plots; it is a novel-conversation because it develops through dialogues, discussions, and gossip; it is a novel-reportage because it chronicles current events and a journey through Italy; and it is a novel-diary because citations and reflections are sometimes presented in the form of short notes and annotations by the narrator, who – and this is an important detail – is not the protagonist, but rather a witness, an observer.

Moving from the genre to the structure, *Fratelli d'Italia* can be defined as a novel within a novel because it is constructed through a baroque montage of stories and themes that are superimposed, juxtaposed, interwoven, or accumulated. This fundamental structure intersects with a circular structure consisting of concentric blocks, the last of which is joined with the first, calling into question the entire novel. As Arbasino explains in *Certi romanzi*, his models of reference were Proust's *Recherche du temps perdue* and Beckett's *Molloy*. Finally, *Fratelli d'Italia* is also a novel-pastiche, because in addition to mixing genres, it also mixes literary references, styles, and linguistic registers, driven by two requirements: expressionist realism and engaging legibility: 'Finalità del romanzo o del dramma dovrebbe essere prima di tutto il Divertimento' [The aim of a novel or a play, should be first of all enjoyment] (*Fratelli* 53).

The principle of legibility is not the only element that differentiates Arbasino's narrative production from that of other members of the Gruppo 63. The 'lowering' strategy, so dear to critics in the group, finds in Arbasino a restricted application mostly limited to parody and kitsch, producing a 'second degree' aesthetics in which everything is ridiculed and emptied of meaning and value. Frivolity and gossip also lower the linguistic register, in spite of an excess of foreign terms, and make it possible for the novel to extend beyond an excessive focus on content and a naturalist approach, the main enemies of the neo-avant-garde. On the contrary, there is no lowering of perspective on the sociological level. The world of which the narrator is a witness is the jet set, the rich, well-educated, polyglot young people who gather on ski slopes or splendid beaches, at concerts in London or exhibitions in Paris, at dinner parties in Florence or at other exclusive events. If Arbasino could be taken to task for his rather snobbish cosmopolitanism, it must be also pointed out that this snobbery has a polemical function against Italian provincialism. Although he is far from uncritical acceptance of all the latest foreign fads, he insists that culture must open up and become international.

Unlike Sanguineti, Arbasino focuses his formal pursuit more on the composition and structure of the novel than on the language. Themes, characters, ideas, and actions are nothing but instruments through which he constructs a novelist mechanism – to the point that, according to Arbasino, the true protagonist is the author: 'L'Operazione da lui svolta per organizzare i suoi materiali in un determinato congegno, secondo un determinato procedimento [...] la costruzione di un romanzo e il suo vero plot, è la riflessione critica sui procedimenti del romanzo' [The Operation he performs in order to organize his materials into a specific mechanism, according to a specific procedure ... the construction of a novel and its true plot is the critical reflection on the novel's procedures] (in Balestrini 139–40). And if Sanguineti can be rebuked for his cold intelligence and mechanical execution, Arbasino can be criticized for his self-satisfaction with his literary ability and his erudite narcissism.

Tristano and *Vogliamo tutto* by Nanni Balestrini

Balestrini, a poet and composer of experimental poetry up to the mid-1950s and an active member of the Gruppo 63, published his first novel, *Tristano*, in 1966, and his second, *Vogliamo tutto* [We want everything], in 1971; five more narrative works followed over the next thirty years. Balestrini does not like to separate poetic and narrative writing and considers his novels to be 'epic poems,' prose for which he has borrowed rhythm, verse, and measure from poetry.[7] Moreover, Balestrini argues that in the Gruppo 63 poetic creation preceded theory, theory preceded the novel, and the theory of the novel was influenced by foreign literature:

> Senz'altro una della caratteristiche è stata che la poiesi è venuta prima, e la teoria ha seguito la poesia. Da lì poi si è passati al romanzo, e in particolare si è arrivati al romanzo attraverso la letteratura strainera, che ha avuto un gran ruolo. Fin dai tempi del 'Verri' degli autori come Robbe-Grillet, Céline, Beckett sono stati inglobati e hanno formato il fondo della narrativa italiana.
>
> [Certainly one of the characteristics was that poiesis came first, and that theory followed poetry. From there we moved on to the novel, and in particular we arrived at the novel through foreign literature, which played an important role. Since the time of *Il verri* authors such as Robbe-Grillet, Céline, and Beckett were absorbed and formed the basis of the Italian novel.][8]

Balestrini's statement confirms that at around the time that *Tristano* was published, the techniques and themes of the new novel, both Italian and foreign, traditional and experimental, were extensively analysed by the group, and by Balestrini himself. What does *Tristano* bring to neo-avant-garde narrative production? The novel is described on the back-cover blurb as having plot, characters, or style, or rather – and more precisely – it is written in a 'non-style,' it is a prefabricated pastiche of materials. In addition to these editorial clichés on neo-avant-garde literature, the potential reader is informed that *Tristano* is a love story interwoven with a political reality. And indeed, the two subjects, corresponding to two genres, are continuously blended: the essayistic-political theme becomes a critique of the generation that fought in the Resistance for the way in which they dealt with the postwar period; the more novelistic plot centres on the theme of freedom within the couple, exploring complex love relations, adulteries, separations, passions, affairs, and conflicts that rotate around classic questions of money, sex, and jealousy.

These two narrative threads can both be considered narrative pretexts. Balestrini's true interest is the work of textual manipulation. First, the composition of the text is a mark of the originality, also present in Balestrini's later novels: short narrative passages of identical length follow one another according to a logic that cannot be easily determined. These passages are composed of phrases clipped and organized according to the technique of collage. Thus, within the same paragraph the action develops in an apartment, on a beach, and at a restaurant, all in different times and with different characters. The differentiation between the stories is complicated by the non-differentiation of the characters, all of whom are identified by the initial 'C.' – a rather obvious homage to Sanguineti, and even more to Kafka, as well as a means to erase psychological identity and singularity of character.

Another particularity is the multiplicity of narrators, since the story is articulated through all three grammatical persons, singular and plural, passing from I to you or from we to he/she in an alternation of monologues, dialogues, and descriptions in either direct or indirect style and past or present tense. Occasionally, the external I of the author intervenes to address the reader directly. Other strategies include the use of mostly low stylistic registers, particularly in spoken language and the language of news reports. Punctuation is reduced to the simple period, which, however, does not mark the end of sentences but rather serves to indicate a transition from one set to the next. All these factors make *Tristano* an obscure novel, on the brink of illegibility. There is no action nor place, no time, no identifiable characters; style and genres are heterogeneous. This is indeed the zenith of formal complexity and the transgression of conventions. The text, thus transformed into a ground of experimentation in which the author plays at trying out linguistic and literary combinations, becomes a 'pure verbal device': once set in motion, it obeys its own mechanics.

It is not by chance that *Tristano* was labelled as 'all form,' in comparison with *Vogliamo tutto*, Balestrini's 'all content' novel published just five years later. By 1971 the context had changed fundamentally. The Gruppo 63 had dissolved and Balestrini was an active participant in the post-1968 student and workers struggle for rights. *Vogliamo tutto* tells of the story-truth of a southern immigrant working in a large factory in the north. The novel contains an explicit message – an appeal to the masses for the construction of a better world – and being destined for the masses, it is extremely simple at the formal, linguistic, and structural levels. The revolutionary purpose is no longer intrinsic to the language, but instead is expressed by the content. Formally, the composition is still based on narrative blocks with a lowering of linguistic register both in the reproduction of realistic speech, even when ungrammatical and vulgar, and in the reproduction of the jargon in political and union leaflets. However, here Balestrini concentrates on the ideological task, on the message: experimentation has a subordinate function.

Hilarotragoedia by Giorgio Manganelli

I close this brief review of new neo-avant-garde novels with a work by Giorgio Manganelli, for which the best label is not so much novel but anti-novel, especially considering that Manganelli has expressed disinterest and disgust for the genre on various occasions. Manganelli was a prominent member of the neo-avant-garde exponent, although his approach 'from above' was definitely a minority position within the literary practices of the Gruppo 63. At the founding conference Manganelli presented *Iperipotesi*, a sort of theatrical monologue in which a speaker explains why formulating a hypothesis is a useful and indispensable activity. The use of theatre is a formal strategy that allows Manganelli to stage an essayistic text of a literary tenor. Its characteristics already herald those of his later production: an oratorical tone, irony, a cultured and over-refined language, movement by means of digressions and bifurcations, and an abuse of accumulations and enumerations – all this in addition to his conception of literature as, precisely, a hypothesis.

Hilarotragoedia (1964) is a work of fiction presented in the form of a scholarly treatise of abstruse construction. Calvino defines it as 'architettura composita tra il rinascimentale e il barocco con qualche merlettatura di neogotico' [a composite architecture between renaissance and baroque with a few neo-gothic embroideries] (back cover). The book opens on a 'Trattato di balistica' [Treatise of ballistics] with a notes on *verba discendi*, followed by an 'Introduzione al (...) suicida' [Introduction to the ... suicide], then a 'Chiosa alle pantegane' [Note on sewer rats]. The treatise is interrupted to make space for a new 'Trattato sulle angosce' [Treatise on anguishes], which is quickly interrupted by an

'Inserto sugli addii' [Dossier on farewells], and so on, through marginal notes, new glosses, and anecdotes – all accompanied by extensive documentation. The reader is further confused and surprised by the excess of rhetorical figures and by Manganelli's strange prose, consisting of a sequence of hyperboles, metaphors, ironies, paradoxes, and above all, long composite lists created through an accumulation of verbs, adjectives, and nouns, in which the climax does not rise and fall according to logic but rather to a playful disorder. Apparently conforming to the needs of an old-fashioned teaching manual, the language is scholarly, obsolete, and serious, according to the rules of 'tragedy' that Manganelli reviews with personal 'hilarity.' The derision and the break with the past are evident not only in the lexical choices, barbarisms, neologisms, and dead or invented words, but also in the unrestrained creative exuberance, in the linguistic explosion. Calvino observes: 'Il linguaggio dà spettacolo di se stesso, è esso stesso scenografia, macchina scenica, gioco d'acqua, fuoco d'artificio, prestidigitazione, acrobazia capriola sberleffo' [language makes a show of itself, it is itself scenery, stage machinery, waterworks, fireworks, prestidigitation, acrobatics, somersault, sneer] (back cover).

Unlike Gadda, an eminent precursor of luxuriant and impudent linguistic inventions, Manganelli does not turn to pastiche nor does he mix registers. He does not even make use of 'suspense'; it is as if he has no need for plot, characters, or action. For him, fiction is a linguistic device that has no need to represent or resemble anything. The writer is a manufacturer of verbal structures. Literature does not have functions or missions because it does not have a direct relation with either reality or history. And since literature is outside history, outside society, outside morality, and outside time, the writer can use outdated languages, rejecting the rules and ties of contemporaneousness. Manganelli's originality lies also in the fact that in order to strengthen and enrich current literature, he takes as a model the Italian literary tradition from past centuries rather than the great European writers of the early twentieth century.

Manganelli was often accused of formalism and lack of commitment. He was certainly a formalist because he was convinced that language was a pure mechanism, but he was also convinced that language could create rich and original worlds and explore the human spirit. He was indeed uncommitted: he wanted to entrust literature not with social and political struggle, but with existential investigations and inventions. His far-fetched and excessive constructions, his superfluous and antiquated words, and his distance from present times did not prevent Manganelli from giving us, with *Hilarotragoedia,* a deep metaphysical reflection on death and a magnificent literary text.

An Epilogue from a Distance

We have not yet carried out a careful evaluation of the legacy of the Gruppo 63 and of the importance of the experimental novel to subsequent production. We have noted that some of the early narrative works by Vassalli and Celati can be placed in the wake of the neo-avant-garde from which they derived ideas and lessons. It is not difficult to find echoes of the neo-avant-garde canon in the most unlikely texts, such as Pasolini's extraordinary posthumous novel *Petrolio* (1992),[9] and in works by the novelists of the 1980s ranging from Aldo Busi, Stefano Benni, Ermanno Cavazzoni, and Pier Vittorio Tondelli to Umberto Eco, Italo Calvino, and even Alessandro Baricco (in *Castelli di rabbia*). Some former members of the Gruppo 63 identify their legacy in young writers of the 1990s, such as such as Silvia Ballestra and Rossana Campo.[10]

In reality, a quick review of the most significant narrative productions of the neo-avant-garde, considered in the strictest sense, does not give convincing results either in quality or in quantity: a few experimental novels, written for the most part in the wake of European literary modernity from which the neo-avant-garde authors adopt the main innovations. If, however, one considers in a broad sense not only the creative works but also the critical production, it becomes clear that, through their radical critique of the (already wavering) novelistic conventions, the neo-avant-garde forced an entire generation of writers to engage with techniques which were certainly not invented by group members but which they forced upon Italian literature. Because of this work of modernization and opening, following generations were burdened with fewer restrictions and rules. As proof of the effectiveness of the action of the neo-avant-garde, it is enough to observe that today's readers are hardly surprised by experimental strategies that during the 1960s seemed extremely daring.

Let us return for a moment to the golden years of the new novel in order to summarize the main elements. Note first of all that the original purpose of the experimental procedures was the rejection of realism and psychologism. A constant characteristic is the influence of foreign traditions of thought (such as phenomenology, existentialism, and structuralism). A second essential element is the predominant role of theory, of rationality, and of intention: the metanovel is more important than the novel. A fundamental theoretical concept is the 'openness' of the work, translated according to the situation in terms of ambiguity, chance, and disorder of form, structure, and language – each articulated in terms of fragmentation or composite montage, in the mixing of genres and linguistic registers (registri), in the multiplicity or confusion of narrative voices, and in different narrative points of view, to obtain effects of alienation: perspective from below or from above, deformed or deviated, internal or external. Moreover, the function and identity of the narrator-protagonist is challenged. Manganelli gets rid of him, La Capria multiplies him, Arbasino transforms him into a witness, Balestrini reduces him to a verbal mechanism; others, in the best cases, create an anti-hero. Finally, we must note that the rejection of subjectivity also involves a shift in focalization from people to things, from the identities of characters to the reality of objects and the language that formalizes that reality.

It is precisely the question of the language – understood as linguistic debate and research – that might constitute the specific characteristic of Italian experimentalism. In this regard, two points must be kept in mind: a new 'middle' language is in the phase of constitution; and literary language is no longer wanted to reproduce reality but rather to create new relations with the real. The writer is free from the obligations of style, and of beautiful language; conventional literary language, now considered sterile and dead, is pushed to the low or high edges of the spectrum. Although this phenomenon goes beyond the boundaries of the Gruppo 63, it is within the group that this linguistic research is theorized and developed, and from the group that it first branches out. Very quickly, however, it dictates a tendency: a lowering of language. Lower registers are explored, with particular attention paid to spoken language: conversations in living rooms or discussions in factories, professional jargon, dialects, the languages of the mass media, of children, of the mentally handicapped, etc. Spreading and becoming trivialized, in a few years this lowering strategy lost its experimental character, becoming instead a factor of easiness and attraction. Today, the mixture of registers, especially of language and dialect (as seen with writers such as Andrea Camillieri and Marcello Fois), or of idiolects of youth culture (for instance, Enrico Brizzi's *Jack Frusciante* or Ballestra's *La gerra degli Antò*) has become normal for both writers and readers, and it is accepted by critics. The revaluation of 'popular' genres such as the detective story or science fiction is equally accepted. Nothing could be more normal: an avant-garde cannot reconnoitre forever. As soon as its innovative elements are understood and integrated by literature and society, its most advanced scouts return to the ranks.

Translated by Ashleigh Burnet

NOTES

1 For a detailed chronology, see the preface written by the editors Renato Barilli and Angelo Guglielmi to *Gruppo 63: critica e teoria*; Fabio Gambaro, *Invito a conoscere la neoavanguardia* includes an extensive biography.
2 For a more exhaustive list of narrative works by experimental writers published during these years see Gambaro, *Invito,* 85.
3 In 1961 Gadda was asked four questions on the evolution of the language: Is there a middle language that can constitute the base of the literary language? Will the formation of this middle language be able to reduce the rift between culture and people? What is the contribution of journalism, television, and cinema to the language? What role does dialogue play in the spoken and literary language? For Gadda's answers, see 'Processo alla lingua italiana.'
4 Pasolini's interesting article 'Nuove questioni linguistiche' (1964), begins: 'In Italia non esiste una vera a propria lingua nazionale' [In Italy a true national language does not exist] (5). He concludes with an apparent contradiction: 'Con qualche titibanza e con qualche emozione mi sento autorizzato ad annunciare che è nato l'italiano come lingua nazionale' [With some hesitation and with some emotion, I feel authorized to announce the birth of a national language] (24).
5 Following the meeting organized in 1993 to celebrate thirty years of the Gruppo '63, Balestrini, Barilli, and Guglielmi organized two events in 1994 and 1995 in Reggio Emilia, under the title of 'Ricercare: laboratorio di nuove scritture,' with the purpose of providing continuity for their literary pursuits.
6 'Se devo delineare una mia reazione a tutto questo, o meglio un mio tragitto, a partire dall'epoca di *Ferito a morte* (anni sessanta) a oggi, posso dire che è una parabola, che va da un concetto di letteratura (narrativa) tecnicamente complicata come quella di Joyce e dei grandi del Novecento, a un desiderio di semplificazione sempre maggiore di questa macchinosa complessità' [If I must outline my reaction to all of this, or better yet, my journey from the period of *Ferito a morte* (the 1960s) to today, I can say that it is a parable that moves from a concept of technically complicated literature (narrative), such as the works of

Joyce and other twentieth-century writers, to a desire for simplification of the complex complexity] (Gaglione 138).

7 In an interview with René de Ceccaty ('La fidélité de Balestrini' 1995) Balestrini states: 'Mes romans ne sont pas nettement séparés de mon travail poétique. Ce sont des poèmes épiques [...] J'ai éprouvé le besoin de me forger une écriture qui, bien entendu, emprunte beaucoup à la poésie, notamment l'idée de rythme poétique, de mesure. J'écris par strophes' [My novels are not separated from my poetic work. They are epic poems ... I felt the need to fashion a writing that obviously borrows from poetry, particularly the idea of the poetic rhythm and measure. I write in verse].

8 This quotation is from an interview that took place during the 'Colloquio con Nanni Balestrini' (Paris, June–July 1993); it is appended to my doctoral thesis, 'Le roman nouveau en Italie, du Gruppo 63 aux années quatre-vingt-dix,' University of Paris IV–Sorbonne, 1995.

9 Passolini's *Petrolio* begins with a statement of intents, dated Spring 1973, in which he explains that the novel should be built 'sotto forma di edizione critica di un testo inedito' [in the form of a critical edition of an unpublished text] (3). In addition to the essay-novel, there are other elements that recall the experiments of the neo-avant-garde, including fragmentation and the mixture of materials (historical documents, letters, oral depositions, and reportage). Other explicit comments by Passolini within the text (see 'Appunto 3C' 19) demonstrate that Pasolini was constantly concerned with escaping the narrative conventions of the traditional novel.

10 Certain uses of the lowering strategy – such as the comic line, the pastiche, and the mixture of genres and registers – widely used by authors of the 1990s are arrived at through the mediation of postmodernism, and in particular through writers and talent scouts such as Pier Vittorio Tondelli. I discuss this issue in greater detail in 'Le roman nouveau en Italie.'

WORKS CITED

Arbasino, Alberto. *Certi romanzi.* Milan: Feltrinelli, 1964.

– *Fratelli d'Italia.* Turin: Einaudi, 1963.

Balestrini, Nanni, ed. *Gruppo 63: il romanzo sperimentale.* Milan: Feltrinelli, 1966.

Balestrini, Nanni, and Alfredo Giuliani, eds. *Gruppo 63: la nuova letteratura, 34 scrittori, Palermo ottobre 1963.* Milan: Feltrinelli, 1964.

Barbato, Andrea. 'Appunti per una storia critica della neoavanguardia italiana.' In *Avanguardia e neoavanguardia.* Ed. Giansiro Ferrata. Milan: Sugar, 1966. 165–88.

Barilli, Renato, and Angelo Guglielmi, eds. *Gruppo 63: critica e teoria.* Milan: Feltrinelli, 1976.
Barthes, Roland. *Le plaisir du texte.* Paris: Seuil, 1973.
– *Roland Barthes.* Paris: Seuil, 1975.
Calvino, Italo. Introduction. *Hilarotragoedia.* By Giorgio Manganelli. 2nd ed. Milan: Feltrinelli, 1972. Back cover.
Ceccaty, René de. 'La fidélité de Balestrini.' *Le monde des livres,* 30 June 1995: XII.
Contarini, Silvia. 'Le roman nouveau en Italie, du Gruppo 63 aux années quatre-vingt-dix.' Diss. University of Paris IV-Sorbonne, 1995.
Corti, Maria. *Il viaggio testuale.* Turin: Einaudi, 1978.
Eco, Umberto. *Opera aperta.* 1962. Milan: Bompiani, 1968.
Ferretti, Gian Carlo. *Paolo Volponi.* Florence: La nuova Italia, 1972.
Gadda, Carlo Emilio. 'Processo alla lingua italiana.' 1961. Reprinted in *Carlo Emilio Gadda: il tempo e le opere.* Ed. Dante Isella. Milan: Adelphi, 1982. 95–100.
Gaglianone, Paolo, ed. *Letteratura e sentimento del tempo: conversazione con Raffaele La Capria.* Rome: Omicron, 1995.
Gambaro, Fabio. *Invito a conoscere la neoavanguardia.* Milan: Mursia, 1993.
La Capria, Raffaele. *Ferito a morte.* Milan: Oscar Mondadori, 1998.
Manganelli, Giorgio. *Hilarotragoedia.* 2nd ed. Milan: Feltrinelli, 1972.
Moravia, Alberto. 'Illeggibilità e potere.' 1967. Reprinted in *Il punto su Moravia.* Ed. Cristina Benussi. Bari: Laterza, 1987. 109–11.
Pasolini, Pier Paolo. 'Nuove questioni linguistiche.' 1964. Reprinted in *Empirismo eretico.* Milan: Garzanti, 1991. 5–24.
– *Petrolio.* Turin: Einaudi, 1992.
Sanguineti, Edoardo. *Capriccio italiano.* Milan: Feltrinelli, 1963
– *Ideologia e linguaggio.* Milan: Feltrinelli, 1965.
Volponi, Paolo. *Memoriale.* Milan: Garzanti, 1962.

5 Revolution in Flatland: Giorgio Manganelli's Critique of the Avant-garde

FLORIAN MUSSGNUG

A remarkable increase in specialist scholarship over the past decade has done much to reveal the originality and complexity of Giorgio Manganelli's theoretical reflections on literature.[1] A range of recent critical studies have emphasized Manganelli's interest in questions such as the social role of literature and the origins of literary creativity, as well as his engagement with a surprisingly large number of theoretical models.[2] While this has rightly established Manganelli's fame as one of Italy's most sophisticated and challenging authors of the late twentieth century, it also seems to have drawn attention away from his initial involvement with the Gruppo 63. Since Manganelli has increasingly come to be seen as a highly innovative author and thinker in his own right, his early contacts with the *neoavanguardia* seem of diminishing interest to scholars and critics. Yet Manganelli's participation in the Gruppo 63 remains crucial to any understanding of his theoretical and fictional writing.[3] More than forty years after the foundation of the Gruppo 63, Manganelli's name remains as intrinsically linked to the group's history as is the assumption that this author never entirely committed himself to the aims and beliefs of the *neoavanguardia*. In order to analyse Manganelli's outstanding contribution to contemporary Italian literature, it is therefore necessary to return to his puzzling status as an avant-garde author who was also a consistent and passionate critic of the avant-garde. While the originality of Manganelli's work within the context of the *neoavanguardia* is evident at first sight, a closer examination is needed to reveal his debts to the Gruppo 63 and his influence on the radical rethinking of the novel that took place in Italy during the 1960s. If one looks beyond the obvious contrasts between Manganelli's provocative anachronisms and the group's rhetoric of social commitment, the author of *Hilarotragoedia* emerges as a key figure of Italy's *neoavanguardia*, a writer whose sustained and constructive critique of avant-garde theory and practice opened new paths for Italian literature and whose importance to the literary scene of the 1960s cannot be overstated.

Neither Friend nor Foe: Manganellli and the Gruppo 63

When it comes to describing Giorgio Manganelli's role within the Gruppo 63, some critics appear irresistibly drawn towards unexpectedly dramatic claims. Mattia Cavadini, for instance, has no doubt that Manganelli has nothing important in common with other members of the *neoavanguardia*:

> [I]l rapporto di Manganelli con la neo-avanguardia degli anni Sessanta [è un] rapporto di assoluta diversità e lontananza. Né apocalittico, né integrato, egli con ironico sberleffo faceva il difensore della letteratura, divellendo i fanatismi dell'intervento attivo, le furorali e violente polemiche, i tracotanti decreti, gli impronti manifesti ... Manganelli partecipò all'avanguardia semplicemente per una sorta di sentimento vitale, per la necessità di sentirsi vivo.
>
> [Manganelli's relation to the neo-avant-garde of the 1960s is characterized by absolute difference and great distance. Neither apocalyptic, nor a conformist, he posed – with an ironic smirk – as the defender of literature. He brushed aside the ghosts of active participation, the raving and violent arguments, the presumptuous decrees, the abrupt manifestos ... Manganelli took part in the avant-garde simply because of a vital sentiment, the need to feel alive.] (*La luce nera* 32)

According to Cavadini, Manganelli's involvement with the Gruppo 63 was little more than a curious incident or a necessary compromise. Whatever determined Manganelli's decision to frequent the inner circles of the *neoavanguardia* – intellectual affinity, opportunism, curiosity, boredom – Cavadini seems firmly convinced that Manganelli's participation in the Gruppo 63 initiatives had little to do with his own poetics as outlined in *La letteratura come menzogna* (1967). A similar view emerges in the cover-text to the 1985 edition of *La letteratura come menzogna*, written by Roberto Calasso but clearly indebted to the provocative style of Manganelli's own earlier cover-texts.

> Quando apparve *La letteratura come menzogna* (1967), la scena letteraria italiana si presentava piuttosto agitata. Lo spazio era diviso fra i difensori di un establishment che vantava come glorie opere spessso mediocri e i propugnatori della 'neo-avanguardia,' i quali non si erano accorti che la parola 'avanguardia' era stata appena colpita da una benefica senescenza. Per ragioni di topografia e strategia letteraria, Manganelli fu assegnato (e si assegnò egli stesso) a quest'ultimo campo. Nondimeno, [...] la letteratura di Manganelli non apparteneva a quella battaglia dei pupi, ma rivendicava un'ascendenza più remota e insolente: quella della *letteratura assoluta.*
>
> [When *La letteratura come menzogna* (1967) was first published, the Italian scene appeared to be in great turmoil. It was divided between the supporters of the establishment, who praised themselves for their rather mediocre works, and the promoters of the 'neo-avant-garde,' who had not noticed that the word 'avant-garde' had just entered a stage of well-deserved senescence. For reasons of literary topography and strategy Manganelli was associated with (and allocated himself within) the latter field. Nevertheless ... his literary works did not stem from such puppet fights, but claimed a more remote and insolent ancestry: *absolute literature.*][4]

Calasso's depiction of Manganelli as a visionary among short-sighted rebels appears to be part of a well-designed editorial strategy. Less of an enfant terrible of the 1960s and more of a prophet of absolute literature, Calasso's Manganelli evidently corresponds to the cultural profile of the Adelphi catalogue. Yet, such speculations only partly explain why Manganelli is often perceived as a marginal and almost uncomfortable presence within the cultural sphere of the *neoavanguardia.* Cavadini and Calasso were not the only ones to argue that the author of *Hilarotragoedia* (1964) cannot be adequately described within the context of the Gruppo 63; similar claims have also been made by prominent representatives of the *neoavanguardia.* For instance, Edoardo Sanguineti, in a 1993 interview with Fabio Gambaro, remembers Manganelli as a mostly silent observer at the group's encounters and suggests that the Gruppo 63 facilitated but never determined Manganelli's development as a writer.[5] Renato Barilli, whose judgment of Manganelli is decidedly less generous, stresses in 1995 that 'Manganelli si maturava, si rafforzava in una insularità cocciuta, orgogliosa della propria diversita, rispetto alle proposte circolanti, perfino in seno alla stessa *neoavanguardia*' [Manganelli matured and gained strength in stubborn isolation. He was proud of his diversity, even in relation to the ideas which circulated at the heart of the neo-avant-garde] (*La neoavanguardia italiana* 246). Taking such scepticism to its extreme consequences, Mario Spinella suggests, in 1983, that Manganelli's 'reactionary' ethos had always been alien to the revolutionary spirit of the Gruppo 63 and might even be considered one of the causes of the group's dissolution.[6]

The apparent consensus among scholars as diverse as Sanguineti, Barilli, and Spinella is astonishing, especially if one considers that Manganelli's earliest literary writings undoubtedly fall among the cultural activities promoted by the *neovavanguardia.* Manganelli's name appears in all the Gruppo 63 anthologies: *Gruppo 63: la nuova letteratura* (1964); *Gruppo 63: critica e teoria* (1976, reissued 2003); *Gruppo 63: l'antologia* (2002); *Il gruppo 63 quarant'anni dopo* (2005, proceedings of the 2003 conference). Present at the group's inaugural meeting in 1963, Manganelli contributed a short dramatic monologue, *Iperipotesi,* which was performed on the first evening of the conference.[7] In 1964, during the second meeting of the group in Reggio Emilia, he was one of the 'amici dissidenti' interviewed by Eugenio Battisti.[8] When the group met again in 1965 to discuss the future of the experimental novel Manganelli was absent, but he submitted a short essay that was published together with the conference proceedings in the volume *Gruppo 63: il Romenzo sperimentale* (1966).[9] As editor of the journal *Grammatica* (first published in 1964) and as one of the coordinators of the Einaudi series 'La ricerca letteraria,' Manganelli did much to promote the writings of younger authors associated with the *neoavanguardia.*[10] It is therefore hardly surprising that most historians of Italian literature, especially outside Italy, attribute to Manganelli a prominent role among the writers of the *neoavanguardia.*[11] More than four decades after the foundation of the Gruppo 63 Manganelli occupies a firm place in its history: no comprehensive study of the *neoavanguardia* omits the author of *Hilarotragoedia* and many critics describe Manganelli as one of the most successful representatives of the new experimental literature advocated by the group. The contrast with Sanguineti, Barilli, and Spinella could hardly be more marked. In the wider context of Italian literary history, Manganelli's early writings are commonly perceived as products of the *neoavanguardia,* yet in the opinion of many specialists he remains an outsider, at best a highly uncommon fellow traveller of the Gruppo 63.

In her recent study of Manganelli's writings, *Il felice vanverare* (2002), Grazia Menechella remarks on the difficulty of defining Manganelli's role in relation to the Gruppo 63 and concludes that most of the apparent contradictions can be resolved by appealing to the Gruppo 63's essential openness, which has been repeatedly emphasized by many of its members.[12] Unlike Barilli and Spinella, Menechella sees Manganelli's early ideas about literature and writing as important contributions to the Gruppo 63's theoretical debates. As far as Manganelli's alleged lack of political commitment is concerned, Menechella accuses critics such as Spinella of misrepresenting the atmosphere at the group's meetings. According to Menechella, Manganelli's seemingly cynical and apolitical vision of literature cannot be said to be at odds with the positions of the Gruppo 63, simply because the group never conceived of itself as an artistic movement based on a manifesto, but rather – following the example of the German Gruppe 47 – defined itself as an open forum, or, in Umberto Eco's words, 'non [...] una massoneria in cui, con buone raccomandazioni, ci si potesse iscrivere, sia pure in segreto, [ma] piuttosto [...] una festa di paese, in cui fa parte chi è presente e partecipa dello spirito generale' [not a Masonry that you could secretly join if you were recommended by the right people, but rather ... a village festival, where you join in if you are there and feel part of the general atmosphere] (*Sugli specchi e altri saggi* 94).

In Menechella's opinion, the group's self-image suffices to resolve the controversy about Manganelli's involvement: *La letteratura come menzogna* is just as representative of the Gruppo 63's positions as the opinions of Manganelli's critics, and their disagreement is merely an expression of the group's essential openness. Interestingly, Manganelli himself also alludes to this idea of openness when he speaks to Eugenio Battisti about the atmosphere at the second meeting of the group in 1964:

> Nel nostro Gruppo non ci sono posizioni alternative ad altre, anche perché il Gruppo non ha un Manifesto, non ha una teoria, non ha mica una ortodossia, è un club di persone irritate [...] no, di persone disoneste, direi, di persone disoneste a vari livelli di coscienza ma disoneste, altrimenti non ci sarebbe alcun motivo di fare un club.

> [In our group, there are no alternative positions, because the group does not possess a manifesto, it does not have a theory, nor an orthodoxy; it is a club for irritated people ... or rather, for dishonest people, for people who are dishonest at various levels, but always dishonest, otherwise there would be no reason for a club.] ('Gli amici dissidenti' 48)

Manganelli's remark – probably little more than a passing witticism – shows that in 1964 he was perfectly happy with the lack of a unified perspective that he perceived among the group's members. Consequently, it seems that Menechella is correct when she suggests that Manganelli's involvement with the Gruppo 63 can only be understood in the light of the group's essential openness and when she concludes that Manganelli would not have felt equally comfortable in a more rigidly organized artistic movement. Nevertheless, Menechella's argument does not settle the controversy concerning Manganelli's relation to the *neoavanguardia.* Placing her emphasis on the Gruppo 63's crucial idea of openness, Menchella tends to overlook the equally important focus on radical, constructive criticism and ongoing debate. Although pleas for essential openness must be taken seriously, they do not offer an exhaustive picture of the constitution of the Gruppo 63. As Renato Barilli and Angelo Guglielmi point out in their 1976 preface to *Gruppo 63: critica e teoria,* the group's tolerance towards a wide range of different theoretical approaches and artistic attitudes never expressed itself in a neutral, unbiased atmosphere, but manifested itself in heated debates and more or less permanent disagreements among the group's more outspoken members. Openness, in this context, does not denote a wholesale acceptance of every theoretical stance, but rather a methodological *tabula rasa,* against which new theories and poetics may flourish and compete for primacy. Only a closer look at the complex and changing internal topography of the *neoavanguardia,* at the encounters and disputes among currents, sub-groups, and loosely affiliated individuals, can illuminate the role played by the author of *La letteratura come menzogna.*

Since *Quindici* ceased publication many of the Gruppo 63's most influential members have written on the group's history, often with the explicit purpose of redefining the *neoavanguardia* in light of the latest cultural trends. Unsurprisingly, not all these retrospective accounts have been unanimously accepted by former members. Nevertheless, the group's ongoing concern with its own history has ultimately produced a semi-official version of the events, largely based on Barilli's and Guglielmi's preface to the anthology *Gruppo 63: critica e teoria* (1976). In this text Barilli and Guglielmi first distinguish between three fractions – subsequently labelled 'le tre anime del gruppo' [three souls of the group] – associated with Sanguineti as well as with Barilli and Guglielmi themselves. Substantially similar in their struggle for formal innovation, the 'three souls' differ, according to Barilli and Guglielmi, in the degree of explicit ideological commitment. While Sanguineti's name is associated with political zeal and ideological fervour, Guglielmi and Barilli depict themselves as more doubtful of the political and social outcome of cultural innovation without, however, questioning the fundamental need for revolutionary upheaval. In *La neoavanguardia italiana* (1995) Barilli returns to the 'tre anime' hypothesis, defining each one in significantly different terms. Only Sanguineti is described as overtly political – but even in his case Barilli hastens to stress the lack of real sympathy 'nei confronti dell'ideologia di sinistra, incentrara sul marxismo' [regarding any left-wing ideology based on Marxism] (210). Guglielmi's attitude, on the other hand, is now portrayed as a radical refusal of ideology as such, a theoretical stance which Barilli labels 'l'anima distruttiva' [the destructive soul] whose purpose is an 'absolute rebellion' [rivolta allo stato puro] (209), revealing the chaos that logically precedes any ideological system. Despite his claims to the contrary, Barilli's 1995 discussion of the 'tre anime' thus appears less like a summary of the ideas of 1976 or 1963 than a substantial revision of the political and ideological ambitions of the *neoavanguardia*. Nevertheless it would be wrong to dismiss Barilli's retrospective account as entirely arbitrary. What remains unchanged between 1976 and 1995 is the basic structuring device of the 'three souls,' which, despite its vagueness, provides a substantial grid for a historical understanding of the Gruppo 63. By representing Sanguineti and Guglielmi as two extremes of an ideological spectrum (with Barilli's contributions marking an ideal middle ground) the editors of the 1976 anthology delineate a binary frame of reference in which each of the group's theoretical claims can be placed according to its proximity to either of the two poles. Priority is thus given to one particular aspect of the group's theoretical investigations: the social purpose of literature, and more specifically, its relevance to wider-reaching projects of social and political innovation.

The potentially restrictive nature of this scheme becomes evident when we consider its application to Manganelli in the final part of Barilli's *La neoavanguardia italiana*. As in many of Barilli's early studies, Manganelli is rapidly dismissed as a mere stylist, a writer of literary parodies that bear only a superficial resemblance to the experimental literature advocated by the Gruppo 63 and that ultimately ignore the truly innovative, creative force of avant-garde literature in favour of predictably 'assunzioni cruschevoli, neobarocche, talvolta professorali' [erudite, neo-baroque, sometimes professorial attitudes] (252). Explaining Manganelli in relation to the 'tre anime del gruppo,' Barilli treats his ideas as little more than a somewhat eccentric formulation of Guglielmi's 'destructive' principle. Yet, such a judgment is clearly inadequate, as even Barilli is forced to admit.[13] The theoretical essays in *La letteratura come menzogna* do not simply elude questions about the social purpose of literature but develop them in ways that are quite distinct from those outlined by Barilli and Guglielmi in the 1976 preface. This does not mean, of course, that Manganelli's participation in the Gruppo 63 ought to be treated as inconsequential. As I hope to show in the following section, Manganelli's earliest works, from *Hilarotragoedia* to *La letteratura come menzogna* and *Agli dèi ulteriori* constitute a radical challenge to the group's understanding of literature. They reflect not only Manganelli's fascination with some of the theoretical assumptions of *neovanaguardia*, but also his impatience to move beyond what he saw as the inevitable limits of avant-garde theory and practice. As a critique of the avant-garde from within, Manganelli's early writing cannot be appreciated without a prior awareness of the immediate cultural context. Nor can the history of Italian experimental literature in the 1960s be understood without considering Manganelli's fundamental contribution.

Inside the Linguistic Universe: Giorgio Manganelli's Philosophy of Literature

When *La letteratura come menzogna* first appeared in 1967, most of the essays in Manganelli's collection were already known to his most loyal readers. All the essays except the long final essay which gives its name to the volume had been previously published in specialist journals or anthologies. Unsurprisingly, most of these texts reflect Manganelli's professional interest in British and American literature: *La letteratura come menzogna* contains references to canonical authors such as Defoe, Scott, Dickens, and Stevenson, well-known eccentrics such as Lewis Carroll, Edwin A. Abbott, and H.P. Lovecraft, and contemporary writers including Beckett and Nabokov, as well as a highly unusual homage to Ivy Compton-Burnett, who was at the time almost unknown in Italy.[14] What might have come as a surprise to Manganelli's readers – especially those who knew him primarily as an experimental author associated with the Gruppo 63 – was the almost complete absence of the particular critical vocabulary that at the time functioned as a strong signal of identification for those who recognized themselves in the innovatory aspirations of the *neoavanguardia.* Compared to the confident and often provocative theoretical jargon of most *neoavanguardisti,* Manganelli's texts stand out as examples of rare methodological asceticism.[15] Unlike many of Manganelli's later essays, *La letteratura come menzogna* omits all explicit references to Italian literary criticism and current cultural affairs: significantly, none of the author's Italian contemporaries are mentioned in the text. As a result, Manganelli's essays read like pieces of a seemingly timeless scholarly prose that considers authors and texts without paying much attention to present-day cultural conventions. This impression is further enhanced by Manganelli's insistent use of a series of apparently idiosyncratic metaphorical descriptions of literary texts: throughout the collection, novels are referred to as language machines ('Questo Romezo è in primo luogo una macchina, un ordigno' [This novel is above all a machine, a mechanical device], 26), intricate games ('una criptica partita, celebrata secondo regole segrete, puntigliosamente osservate da giocatori estrosi e taciturni' [a cryptic game, played according to secret rules, which are strictly obeyed by imaginative and taciturn players], 148), or sophisticated choreographies ('Nel tessuto dei percorsi che diciamo trama, i personaggi si comportano come punti dinamici' [Within this tissue of crossing paths, which we call the plot, the characters behave like dynamic elements], 27). Evidently, Manganelli uses this recognizable and highly original jargon to create a high degree of stylistic continuity between the twenty-five essays and to make them appear as parts of an ongoing theoretical reflection.

Read against the grain of scholarly conventions – but also in isolation from the established practices of avant-garde criticism – the literary and critical works discussed in *La letteratura come menzogna* often appear as mere pretexts for Manganelli's idiosyncratic intellectual speculations. The title makes it clear that what follows ought to be read as a philosophical quest that develops from chapter to chapter, reaching its conclusion in the final essay, 'La letteratura come menzogna.' Yet, Manganelli's project is not always as linear as this paraphrase might suggest. While each of the twenty-five essays contributes to the overall theoretical content of the collection, the final essay by no means exhausts the meaning of all previous texts. Rather than a summary of Manganelli's reflections and intuitions, 'La letteratura come menzogna' appears as a provocative manifesto offering an essentially new perspective on some of the premises stated earlier in the book. Many of the claims made in this final essay have no equivalent in the earlier texts, and some of the ideas that emerge in the shorter essays disappear in his more overtly polemical conclusion. This is particularly evident in the case of two essays – 'Un luogo è un linguaggio' and 'Letteratura fantastica' – which together mark an early theoretical counterpoint to the final essay. While the former text deserves credit as one of Manganelli's most intricate pieces of philosophical prose, the second contains a particularly explicit and vehement critique of mimetic realism. Taken together, the two essays can be read as key elements of a preliminary philosophy of literature based on the central metaphor of 'linguistic universe.' Unlike 'La letteratura come menzogna,' they point towards the inevitable limits of avant-garde poetics, which Manganelli's final manifesto, despite its seemingly more radical tone, tends to obscure. While 'La letteratura come menzogna' shows us Manganelli in an already well-rehearsed pose as the nihilistic advocate and high priest of a deceitful, self-referential literature, the two earlier essays reveal the true extent of his engagement with literary theory, and more specifically, with the poetics of the *neoavanguardia.*

'Un luogo è un linguaggio' (1966) seems at first to be just an explanatory comment on Edwin A. Abbott's *Flatland: A Romance of Many Dimensions* (1884), a novel that had captured Manganelli's interest in 1963.[16] Yet, Manganelli's interpretation soon shifts towards wider-ranging philosophical reflections. He praises Abbott's Flatland – a two-dimensional universe populated by beings whose social status is determined by their geometrical shape – as a masterpiece of social satire, but he is nevertheless not particularly interested in Abbott's satirical references to Victorian England:

> È naturale riconoscere in questa descrizione, mentitamente scientifica, una satira della società classista e statale. Ma il piacere del ravvisare sotto la favola matematica gli indizi del noto [...] non deve distrarci da quello che mi pare il problema ctitico essenziale: cioè, la descrizione del modo in cui funziona questa invenzione sociale all'interno della macchina narrativa.
>
> [It is natural to read this pseudo-scientific description as a satirical representation of class society and the state. Yet, the pleasure of finding the traces of something well-know in this mathematical tale ... must not distract us from what is, in my opinion, the critic's main task: the description of how this imagined society functions within the narrative mechanism.] (*La letteratura* 47)

What really fascinates Manganelli is how Abbott's text – his 'narrative machine' – succeeds in describing a two-dimensional, fictional universe from the point of view of its inhabitants. As Manganelli remarks more than once, Abbott's description is perfectly coherent. Once we suspend our basic belief in a three-dimensional universe, the spatial and epistemological constraints of *Flatland* appear as natural laws whose validity may not be doubted. Abbott's literary invention is undoubtedly fantastic – the title of Masolino D'Amico's Italian translation, *Flatlandia: racconto fantastico a più dimensioni*, makes this even clearer than Abbott's original 'Romance' – yet the world he describes is far from arbitrary and chaotic. Every aspect of life in a two-dimensional universe is meticulously explained and discussed together with all its epistemological and social implications. According to Manganelli, this internal coherence of Abbott's fictional universe raises questions that are quite distinct from those associated with its satirical content.

> Non sarebbe esatto definire ironiche queste visioni. Si tratta piuttosto di una ironia di secondo grado. Il problema intellettuale è assolutamente esatto, la sua formulazione è propriamente tragica e che si eserciti nell'ambito di un gioco forse non elude, ma eccita, grazie alla mostruosa lucidità delle minime dimensioni, la sua qualità di provocazione irresolvibile.
>
> [It would not be accurate to define these visions as ironic. More appropriately, we might speak of second-level irony. The intellectual problem is completely accurate and its wording is truly tragic. Its playful setting does not distract us from its irresolvable and provocative core, which is actually enhanced by the monstrous eloquence of the slightest details.] (50)

Manganelli's interpretation accurately distinguishes between two levels of reading. As a social allegory, *Flatland* indulges the reader's desire for humorous and satirical poignancy, yet this 'second-level irony' can only flourish once we perceive the 'tragedy' of the Flatlanders' confinement to their two-dimensional world. The playful inventions of *Flatland* barely disguise an underlying, haunting fear: could it be that the Flatlanders merely exemplify a dilemma that is common to every form of social organization? Is their incapacity to look beyond the limits of their two-dimensional world exemplary of the way in which our cognitive powers and personal freedom are limited by arbitrary but inescapable social rules? Looking beyond the historical context of Abbott's Romance, Manganelli turns Flatland into a model of all rule-governed social systems.

> Un linguaggio è un gigantesco 'come se': una legislazione ipotetica che in primo luogo inventa i propri sudditi: i luoghi, gli eventi. Con gesto arbitrario fissiamo i valori delle carte, ma da quel momento subentra il rigore del gioco e del rito.
>
> [A language is a gigantic 'as if': a hypothetical legislation which first of all

> invents its own subjects: places and events. With an arbitrary gesture we establish the value of the cards, but from that moment we are subject to the rigour of the game and of the rite.] (44)

Moving rapidly from the particular social and literary context that prompted Abbott's work, Manganelli confronts his readers with several fundamental philosophical questions. If our perception of reality depends on an arbitrary set of norms and conventions – one 'language' out of many – does this mean that there are other radically different but equally legitimate ways of perceiving the world? Could we become aware of these other points of view? And would this allow us to grasp the limits of our own perception? Finally, could we ever look beyond the 'veil of perception' imposed by our conventions to see reality as it is? These are questions that Manganelli tries to answer as early as 1964, in the first edition of the journal *Grammatica.*

> Ogni universo è in primo luogo un universo linguistico in quanto è proprio una morfologia ed è sottoposto a tutto il rigore e a tutta l'arbitrarietà delle morfologie. Così noi possiamo parlare del linguaggio come di ciò in cui l'universo stesso diventa non direi pensabile (cosa possiamo dire? in che modo l'universo è linguaggio?), direi: abitabile.
>
> [Every universe is primarily a linguistic universe. It is a morphology and hence subject to the rigour and the arbitrariness of all morphologies. For this reason, we can say that language makes the universe not thinkable (what can we say? In what way is the universe linguistic?), but, I would say, liveable.] (*Grammatica* 1, 1964)

In this earliest published formulation of his philosophy of literature, Manganelli does not explicitly refer to literary texts, but considers the relation between language and extralinguistic reality in more general terms. His crucial claim that 'every universe is primarily a linguistic universe' affirms that linguistic meaning cannot be explained in relation to 'inner' mental representations or through direct reference to an extralinguistic sphere. Spoken and written language are not an approximate translation of an autonomous mental discourse, since the structure of thought is not independent from the structure of language, and the thoughts of language users are always in, and in a certain sense about, language.[17] As a consequence, language cannot be contemplated from the outside – the linguistic universe is not 'thinkable' – but only experienced, as it were, from within ('inhabited'). To speak a language does not mean to establish a connection between two distinct spheres, language and reality, but rather to be part of a universe which is already, and always, intrinsically linguistic.

As Mattia Cavadini points out, Manganelli's early philosophy of literature shows striking similarities with that of Roland Barthes in his *Essais critiques* (1964).[18] Yet, the philosophical complexity of Manganelli's vision becomes even clearer if we consider 'Un luogo è un linguaggio' in relation to one of the key texts of twentieth-century philosophy, Ludwig Wittgenstein's *Philosophical Investigations* (1953).[19] Like Wittgenstein, Manganelli uses the term 'language' in an unusually extensive manner to refer to all forms of intentional behaviour, and he compares language to a game in order to express some far-ranging assumptions about linguistic meaning and understanding. Yet a close comparison between Wittgenstein's 'language game' and Manganelli's 'linguaggio come gioco' reveals important differences in their motivations for choosing this metaphor.[20] For the author of the *Philosophical Investigations,* the comparison of languages with games turns around the idea that neither of the two practices can be explained by appealing to a prior set of rules. Playing a game is an activity that is learned against the background of and in the course of learning innumerable other activities, for example giving directions or following orders. One can learn each of these activities without ever formulating the rules that describe them. Indeed, it would be impossible to teach somebody what it means to play a game by merely citing a rule or a set of rules. If our interlocutor knows what it means to follow a rule, she or he already learned more than could be explained by citing a rule. In the absence of any given practice, a rule can always be misunderstood or misinterpreted. Wittgenstein's comparison between language and games hence draws attention to the fact that meaning and learning are practices that take place only within the context of established conventions, inside a community of rule-followers, which, in *Investigations,* Wittgenstein calls the 'form of life.' Crucially, 'forms of life' do not constitute an explanation of rule following, but mark the inevitable boundaries of all explanatory attempts. Wittgenstein clearly states this in *Investigations*: 'If I have exhausted the justifications I have reached bedrock, and my spade is turned. Then I am inclined to say: "This is simply what I do."' (section 217).[21]

Manganelli's description of the 'linguistic universe' is strongly reminiscent of Wittgenstein's 'form of life.' Just as Wittgenstein affirms that the 'form of life' itself can not be explained by philosophy – to speculate about a different form of life is to ask whether the world could be different from what it is – Manganelli's reflections about Flatland suggest that no literary practice could make us see the 'linguistic universe' from the outside. Like the two-dimensional Flatlanders, we are unable to move beyond the boundaries of our linguistic universe:

> 'Un luogo è un linguaggio: noi possiamo essere 'qui' solo accettando le regole linguistiche che lo inventano. Essendo il porsi di un linguaggio arbitrario e non deducibile, i diversi linguaggi indicheranno luoghi totalmente discontinui.'
>
> [A space is a language: we can only be 'here' if we accept the linguistic rules which invent the space. Since the configuration of a language is arbitrary and cannot be inferred, various languages indicate entirely discontinuous spaces.] ('Un luogo è un linguaggio' 44)

And yet, it is precisely this aspect of Manganelli's vision – his reflections on the impossibility of a point of view outside the boundaries of our linguistic universe – that reveals his difference from Wittgenstein. For Manganelli, the linguistic universe is essentially a prison house of norms and conventions. Since its existence rests on a totally arbitrary basis – the contingent rules of the language game – it can easily be replaced by another system of linguistic conventions. In fact, every linguistic universe is haunted by its own contingency: 'ciascun linguaggio 'sa' che altri sistemi linguistici sfidano la sua totalità' [each language 'knows' that other linguistic systems defy its totality] (49). Threatened by the possibility of other, equally arbitrary norms and rites, the linguistic universe seeks to deny their existence and claims to be an absolute and inescapable social reality. As a consequence, the inhabitants of the linguistic universe not only suffer from its semantic restrictions (in terms of Abbott's allegory, its 'lack of dimensions') but are also victims of the totalitarian impulse of the linguistic universe to present itself as the only true representation of reality. Language, Manganelli writes, constantly manifests 'la sua vocazione a porsi come definitivo, come la 'realtà' e quindi la sua cattiva coscienza. Per reggere le proprie membra [il linguaggio] ricorre a due armi: al terrorismo e all'eufemismo. Cioè, allo Stato e alla Storia' [its tendency to pose as definitive, and hence as 'reality,' and therefore its guilty conscience. In order to keep its limbs in place (language) relies on two weapons: terrorism and euphemism. In other words, the state and history] (47).

Manganelli's charges against the totalitarian nature of the linguistic universe have no equivalent in Wittgenstein's philosophy. His description of the 'form of life' as a sum of language games is wider-ranging and more complex but at the same time less political than Manganelli's idea.[22] Unlike Manganelli's 'linguistic universe,' the 'form of life' is not the expression of specific power constellations, nor can it easily be replaced by another set of linguistic rites. Rather, it comprises all our attempts to make sense of one another and of the objective world. To be excluded from the 'form of life' means, according to Wittgenstein, not to partake in humankind. This point is made clearly by Stanley Cavell in an early essay on Wittgenstein's philosophy of language.

> That on the whole we do [communicate] is a matter of our sharing routes of interest and feeling, modes of response, sense of humour and of significance and of fulfilment, of what is outrageous, of what is similar to what else, what a rebuke, what forgiveness, of when an utterance is an assertion, when an appeal, when an explanation – all the whirl of organism Wittgenstein calls 'forms of life'. Human speech and activity, sanity and community, rest upon nothing more, but nothing less, than this. It is a vision as simple as it is difficult, and as difficult as it is (and because it is) terrifying. (Cavell 55)[23]

Evidently the tragedy described by Manganelli is different from the terror noted by Cavell. According to Wittgenstein, the 'cure' of everyday language is liberating for the philosopher, since it puts an end to philosophy's pretence to explain the world. 'The real discovery is the one that makes me capable of stopping doing philosophy when I want to. – The one that gives philosophy peace, so that it is no longer tormented by questions which bring itself in question' (*Philosophical Investigations* section 133). For Manganelli, on the contrary, awareness of the limits of the linguistic universe is liberating, because it creates the basis for a rebellion against dominant social conventions:

> Se il linguaggio si regge terroristicamente, se i suoi confini sono così aspramente definiti, se è insieme effimero ed eterno, ciò comporta che da linguaggio a linguaggio non vi sia spazio per un percorso dialettico, né per alcuna possibilità di deduzione. Il passaggio dal'uno all'altro potrà avvenire solo con un atto di violenza.

> [If language rules through terror, if its boundaries are so crudely drawn, if it is both ephemeral and eternal, this means that between languages there

> can be no space for dialectic exchange, or for any kind of deduction. The passage from one language to another can only be achieved through an act of violence.] (*La letteratura* 50)

Manganelli's speculations about a violent break with the rules of the linguistic universe reveal the extent to which his position is influenced by contemporary debates about avant-garde literature. His visions of a heroic rebellion against the linguistic universe contain the genuine pathos of the avant-garde. This becomes particularly evident in the final part of 'Un luogo è un linguaggio' where, once again, Manganelli's reflections are prompted by a particular aspect of Abbott's novel. While the first part of *Flatland* is dedicated to the (largely satirical) description of the narrator's two-dimensional universe, part two, entitled 'Other Worlds,' allows Abbott to explore the full philosophical potential of his ideas. In the final chapters of *Flatland,* Abbott's protagonist, the 'old square,' discovers the existence of alternative universes and different dimensions. First he dreams of a visit to the one-dimensional world of Lineland, and then he is contacted in his own world by a sphere, which reveals to him the reality of three-dimensional space. At first incredulous, the two-dimensional narrator is finally forced by the sphere to leave his world and he sees Flatland from the outside. Promptly converted to three-dimensionality the square enquires about the existence of universes of four, five, or six dimensions and insists on their mathematical possibility. His teacher, however, is more and more angered by such questions and finally catapults the narrator back into his two-dimensional world, where he is now condemned to a life in full awareness of his own confinement. Abbott's tale culminates in this final, Platonic parable. Incapable of suppressing his knowledge of three-dimensional space, the narrator seeks to convert his fellow Flatlanders, but he is taken by them for a subversive and a madman and ends his days in prison. What started as a social satire ends in stoic resignation.

> Yet, I exist in the hope that these memoirs, in some manner, I know not how, may find their way to the minds of humanity in Some Dimension, and may stir up a race of rebels who shall refuse to be confined to limited Dimensionality. That is the hope of my brighter moments. Alas, it is not always so. [...] It is part of the martyrdom which I endure for the cause of Truth that there are seasons of mental weakness, when Cubes and Spheres flit away into the background of scarce-possible existences; when the Land of Three Dimensions seems almost as visionary as the Land of One if None;

> nay, when even this hard wall that bars me from my freedom, these very tablets on which I am writing, and all the substantial realities of Flatland itself, appear no better that the offspring of a diseased imagination, or the baseless fabric of a dream. (*Flatland* 95–6)

Like Abbott's novel, Manganelli's essay emphasises the emancipating function of the square's voyage through different mathematical universes. While the first part of *Flatland* describes an apparently stable and potentially eternal system, the second part is dedicated, according to Manganelli, to the crisis of the linguistic universe. The moral problem raised by Abbott's text is no longer how to reconcile one's existence with the objective restrictions imposed by the dominant order, but when to abandon it for alternative sets of conventions and rites: 'Al problema dello stare dentro un unico universo, si contrappone l'eroico problema del passaggio da uno ad altro universo' [The difficulty of staying within one single universe is replaced by the heroic pursuit of passing from one universe to another] (*La letteratura* 49).

It is significant that at this point of his essay Manganelli uses the term 'linguistic universe' in a relatively narrow sense. His vision of a 'heroic' rebellion against the rule of the linguistic universe reflects avant-garde ambitions to change social reality by changing the cultural codes that define and perpetuate its existence. The 'universe' mentioned by Manganelli is thus not a Wittgensteinian 'form of life' but a language game in the strict sense of the word: a set of speech conventions. Indeed, it appears that Manganelli's speculations ultimately refer to something even more specific: a literary canon, a set of stylistic and thematic norms.

This is certainly the impression given by Manganelli in 'Letteratura fantastica,' the essay that follows 'Un luogo come linguaggio' in *La letteratura come menzogna.* Throughout 'Letteratura fantastica' Manganelli mocks the narrative conventions associated with the realist novel, a genre that on several occasions becomes the prime focus of his scorn and derision, and he praises fantastic literature as an antidote to the mendacious pretence of realism to narrate the world as it really is: 'Nulla è più mortificante che vedere narratori, per altro non del tutto negati agli splendori della menzogna, indulgere ai sogni morbosi di una trascrizione del reale, sia essa documentaria, educativa o patetica' [Nothing is more humiliating than to see a novelist – who might incidentally not be altogether immune to the splendours of falsehood – indulge in morbid dreams about transcribing reality in a documentary, educational or moving manner] (*La letteratura* 57).[24] In the initial part of 'Letteratura fantastica,' literature is personified in the guise of the 'Grande Mentitore' [the Great Liar], an eternal wanderer, trickster, and storyteller, but also an uncannily metamorphic creature with no recognizable features, proper name, or definite social status, whose only apparent goal consists in inventing impossible universes. Clearly, what fascinates Manganelli about fantastic literature is its ability to create alternative fictional worlds. Commenting on a quote from E.T.A. Hoffmann's *Der goldene Topf* (1814), Manganelli remarks:

> Quelle righe di Hoffmann compitano sommariamente un universo assurdo e insieme coerente. […] Codesta coerenza è appunto attributo proprio di un universo impossibile che, come tale, sa essere perfettamente compatto, impeccabilmente organizzato e irrefutabilmente argomentato. Ciò non avviene a dispetto dell'universo che per quotidiana codardia di linguaggio fingiamo prevedibile e maneggiabile, ma, al contrario, perché il fantastico sa che non v'è universo che non sia assolutamente impossibile.
>
> [Hoffmann's words contain the rough outlines of a universe that is at once absurd and coherent … Indeed this coherence is precisely the attribute of an impossible universe, which, as such, knows that it is perfectly compact, impeccably organized, and irrefutable. All this does not go against the universe which our everyday, cowardly language pretends is predictable and manageable. On the contrary, fantasy knows that there is no universe which is not completely impossible.] (56)

It is tempting to read these sentences as an answer to the questions raised by Manganelli in reaction to *Flatland.* While the linguistic universes of Abbott's fiction violently impose themselves and force their inhabitants to identify their boundaries with the boundaries of the world, fantastic literature perceives itself as an impossible world among an infinite number of other impossible worlds. Its subversive power is similar to that of the 'alternative worlds' which threaten to extinguish and replace the dominant order of the linguistic universe. Yet unlike these 'heroic alternatives,' fantastic literature escapes the threat of violence and terror that haunts Manganelli's reading of Abbott. The 'heraldic design' (56) of fantastic literature denotes an impossible universe: it does not pretend to reveal the true nature of things, hidden by the mendacious practices of the linguistic universe, but rather encourages him to see every linguistic universe as a set of arbitrary conventions. Finally, it reveals the current perception of reality as merely another fiction, a book enclosed in a book of books: 'il libro onnicomprensivo; un libro capace di generare infiniti libri' [an all-comprehensive book; a book capable of generating an infinity of books] (61).

Literature re-enters the picture because of the failure of the avant-garde's heroic ambitions. Like Hamlet in Manganelli's intertextual, epistolary *divertissement* 'Un amore impossibile,' the avant-garde writer dreams of a truly revolutionary gesture which prepares his escape from the 'luogo come linguaggio': 'Un nuovo significato! Che altro, che più oserei chiedere?' [A new meaning! What else, what more could I possibly ask for?] ('Un amore impossibile,' in *Agli dèi ulteriori* 28). Yet, like Hamlet and his impossible lover, the Princess of Clèves, the avant-garde writer ultimately must accept the 'linguistic universe' as a final and absolute boundary of meaning. The rebellion against Flatland is significant only within its context of rules and conventions; outside this context, any gesture of transgression is not only uninteresting, but literally meaningless. As the writer moves further towards the boundaries of his linguistic universe, as he plots for the dissolution of his world, his aspirations become increasingly irrelevant. His ambition to transgress the boundaries of his world can only lead to the annihilation of the linguistic universe – including everything that might have made his rebellion meaningful. It does not take much to see Manganelli's parable as a response to the *neoavanguardia*'s efforts to renew literary, linguistic, and ultimately, social conventions. His depiction of literary writing as a failed but unrelenting rebellion incarnates an idea of literature that is antithetical to the revolutionary optimistism of the avant-garde. Manganelli's artistic vocation originates in his desire for a complete break with the past, yet his real achievement consists in not abandoning the struggle for meaning even when this ambition reveals itself a mere illusion. As a consequence, avant-garde theory manifests itself as an important source of inspiration for Manganelli's writing precisely as he sets out to unmask the avant-garde as an ultimately purposeless and socially irrelevant pose.

NOTES

1 For a more extensive discussion of the topics addressed in this chapter, see Florian Mussgnug, *The Eloquence of Ghosts.*

2 Recently, for instance, scholars have focused on Manganelli's interest in Blachot and Barthes (Cavadini), on his concern with the Baroque (Manica; Menechella), ethics (Montani), utopianism (Dedier) and negative theol-

ogy (Kuon), and above all on his complex attitude towards psychoanalysis (Pulce and Paolone). On Manganelli's stylistic and literary models, see especially Donnarumma, De Benedictis, Cortelessa, Nigro, Pegoraro, and Bricchi.

3 According to Rebecca West, all of Manganelli's works are marked by 'the continuing presence of avant-garde and/or neo-avant-garde preoccupations, methods, and solutions in our present time' (*Before, Beneath and Around the Text* 57).

4 Roberto Calasso, cover text for the 1985 Adelphi edition of Manganelli's *La letteratura come menzogna* ; the italics are mine. The text is not signed in this edition; Calasso acknowledged his authorship only in 2003 when he included it in a collection of editorial prefaces and cover texts written since 1965 (see *Cento lettere a uno sconosciuto* 168–6).

5 'Probabilmente senza l'esistenza del gruppo, Manganelli avrebbe avuto molta difficoltà a pubblicare i suoi testi, i quali oltretutto avrebbero avuto un eco minore. In ogni caso, quando nel 1964 uscì *Hilarotragoedia,* nessuno avrebbe mai immaginato il successo che Manganelli avrebbe avuto piú tardi' [Without the group, Manganelli probably would have found it very difficult to publish his works, which would also have been met by less interest. In any case, when *Hilarotragoedia* first appeared in 1964, nobody could have imagined how successful Manganelli was going to be later on] (Gambaro, *Colloquio con Edoardo Sanguineti* 91).

6 See Balestrini, 9. Spinella's ambition to unite the Gruppo 63 around a Marxist creed is particularly evident in his contribution to the 1965 debate, where he defines the group's position as 'estrema sinistra rivoluzionaria e democratica [...] per cui si tratta di sovvertire i significati tradizionali entro cui si svolge ancora oggi la vita politica, culturale e sociale italiana' [radically left-wing and democratic ... which means that we must undermine the traditional meanings that still determine political, cultural and social life in Italy] (in Balestrini 126). See also Muzzioli, *Teoria e critica della letteratura nelle avanguardie italiane degli anni sessanta;* Gambaro *Invito a conoscere la neoavanguardia.*

7 Manganelli's monologue (*Iperipotesi*) was part of a performance entitled *Teatro Gruppo 63,* directed by Luigi Gozzi and Ken Dewey. It was first published in Balestrini and Giuliani, eds., *Gruppo 63: la nuova letteratura,* 259–62, and was subsequently reprinted in Manganelli's *A e B,* 7–11 (as *Hyperipotesi: prefazione*), in Balestrini and Giuliani, eds., *Gruppo 63: l'antologia,* 260–62, in *Tragedia da leggere* (2005), a collection of Manganelli's theatrical works edited by Luca Scarlini. For further details see Gozzi, 'Teatro Gruppo 63 a Palermo'; Barilli and Guglielmi, eds., *Gruppo 63: critica e teoria,* 337.

8 See Battisti, ed., 'Gli amici dissidenti: Il Gruppo 63 a Reggio Emilia,' 36–53.

9 This essay was first published in Balestrini, ed., *Gruppo 63: il Romenzo sperimentale* (1966), and was reprinted in 1994 in Manganelli's *Il rumore sottile della prosa*, 57–59.

10 Manganelli was a member of the editorial board of *Grammatica* until 1968 (together with A. Giuliani, G. Novelli, and A. Perilli) and was involved with the preparation of three issues. For more information, see Menechella, *Il felice vanverare*, 52–7. The Einaudi series 'La ricerca letteraria' was directed by Manganelli, Sanguineti, and Davico Bonino and included works by, among others, Celati, Scabia, and Vassalli. For details, see Belpoliti, *Settanta*, 148; Ferretti, *Storia*, 193.

11 See, for instance, Quandt, 'Giorgio Manganelli'; Wagstaff, 'The Neo-Avantgarde'; Hillebrand, *Strategien der Verwirrung*, 140–57.

12 Consider, for instance, Sanguineti's 1993 conversation with Fabio Gambaro: 'Insomma, l'esistenza di posizioni diverse era in sintonia con la struttura del gruppo che poi era quella adequate alla situazione: non c'era un manifesto di poetica e non lo si voleva fare' [The existence of different positions fitted the group's structure, which suited the general situation: there was no poetic *manifesto* and we did not want to write one] (Gambaro, *Colloquio con Edoardo Sanguineti*, 70–71).

13 Significantly, both the 1976 preface and Barilli's 1995 volume associate Manganelli's increasing popularity with the rise of structuralism, a theoretical paradigm that, according to Barilli, remained largely alien and hostile to concerns of the *neoavanguardia*; See Barilli and Guglielmi, eds., *Gruppo 63: Critica e teoria*, xxvii; Barilli, *La neoavanguardia italiana*, 284–5.

14 With Viola Pappetti's recent two-volume edition of Manganelli's early critical essays and radio scripts – *Incorporei felini* (2002) – it is finally possible to consider *La letteratura come menzogna* in the light of his wider scholarly production. It is worth noting, in this context, that his extraordinary knowledge of English language poetry is hardly evident in his 1967 collection. Manganelli likely restricted his investigation to literary prose because he wanted *La letteratura come menzogna* to be read as the work of a novelist whose critical interests coincided with his creative ambitions.

15 According to Papetti, the most important models for Manganelli's early critical essays were 'Leavis, Eliot, Wilson, Richards, Empson, and the New Critics' ('Archeologia del critico' x).

16 In 1963 Manganelli was asked by Luciano Foà to translate Abbott's book into Italian (see Belpoliti, *Settanta*, 147). Manganelli declined Foà's request, but agreed to contribute a critical essay, which appeared as an appendix to Masolino D'Amico's translation (*Flatlandia: racconto fantastico a più dimensio-*

ni, 1966) and was subsequently included in Manganelli's *La letteratura come menzogna* under the title 'Un luogo è un linguaggio' (43–53).

17 In 1988, in an interview with Graziella Pulce, Manganelli paraphrases this rejection of philosophical idealism: 'Le idee non vengono mai. Prima vengono le parole, poi vengono ancora le parole, poi vengono ancora le parole. Poi si va a casa' [One never gets to the ideas. First there are the words, then more words, then even more words. Then we all go home] (*Bibliografia degli scritti di Giorgio Manganelli* 102).

18 See Cavadini, *La luce nera,* 8–12.

19 Barthes and Wittgenstein are by no means mutually exclusive theoretical models, as Michael Wood has recently shown in an elegant and highly enlightening comparison; see Wood, *Literature and the Taste of Knowledge,* 38–43.

20 In *Pasolini contro Calvino* (1998) Carla Benedetti discusses the importance of Wittgenstein's later philosophy as a self-image for literary authors. According to Benedetti, the fascination of Wittgenstein's ideas is typically perceived by authors who become aware of the philosophical flaws implicit in naïve definitions of literary realism, based on a principle of representation. Whenever these authors feel compelled to adopt a 'postrealist' stance, they become susceptible to the idea of writing as a game, a 'closed system' that remains separate from extraliterary reality (116–17). While I agree with Benedetti on Wittgenstein's importance as a literary model, it seems to me that her critical assessment is excessively negative. During the 1960s and 1970s 'closed systems' could become a trap for some authors but they could also – as in Manganelli's case – inspire original and innovative stylistic and narrative solutions.

21 The scope of this essay permits only a preliminary reference to critical studies of Wittgenstein's later philosophy. Readers with a particular interest in Wittgenstein's ideas on literature can start with Perloff, *Wittgenstein's Ladder*, and Gibson and Huemer, eds., *The Literary Wittgenstein.*

22 Unlike most Wittgenstein scholars, Ernest Gellner severely criticizes this lack of an explicit political dimension when he describes Wittgenstein as 'politically colour-blind and tone deaf' and his philosophy as 'a typically Viennese fin-de-siècle intellectual autism'; see Gellner, *Language and Solitude,* especially 43–113.

23 Cavell's essay, 'The Availability of Wittgenstein's Later Philosophy,' was first published in the *Philosophical Review* 71 (1962) and is reprinted in Cavell, *Must We Mean,* 44–72.

24 Manganelli's interest in fantasy literature has recently been the topic of seve-

ral studies; see especially Zandonella, 'Tra fantastico e allegoria'; Lazzarin, '*Centuria*: Le sorti del fantastico nel Novecento.'

WORKS CITED

Abbott, Edwin Abbott. *Flatland: A Romance of Many Dimensions* [1884], London, Penguin, 1987.

– *Flatlandia: racconto fantastico a più dimensioni.* Trans. and preface by Masolino D'Amico, with an essay by Giorgio Manganelli. Milan: Adelphi, 1966.

Balestrini, Nanni, ed. *Gruppo 63: Il Romenzo sperimentale, Palermo 1965.* Milan: Feltrinelli, 1966.

Balestrini, Nanni, and Alfredo Giuliani, eds. *Gruppo 63: l'antologia.* Turin: Testo & Immagine, 2002.

– *Gruppo 63: la nuova letteratura, 34 scrittori, Palermo ottobre 1963.* Milan: Feltrinelli, 1964.

Barilli, Renato, *La barriera del naturalismo.* Milan: Mursia, 1964.

– 'Manganelli nuota tra i pesci rossi.' *La stampa,* 12 February, 1982.

– *La neoavanguardia italiana: dalla nascità del 'Verri' alla fine di 'Quindici.'* Bologna: Il Mulino, 1995.

Barilli, Renato, Fausto Curi, and Niva Lorenzini, eds. *Il Gruppo 63 quarant'anni dopo.* Bologna: Pendragon, 2005.

Barilli, Renato, and Angelo Guglielmi, eds. *Gruppo 63: critica e teoria.* Milan: Feltrinelli, 1976; Turin: Testo & Immagine, 2003.

Barthes, Roland. *Essais critiques.* Paris, Seuil, 1964.

Battisti, Eugenio, ed. 'Gli amici dissidenti: il Gruppo 63 a Reggio Emilia.' *Marcatrè* 11–12–13 (1965).

Belpoliti, Marco. *Settanta.* Turin: Einaudi, 2001.

Benedetti, Carla. *Pasolini contro Calvino: per una letteratura impura.* Turin: Bollati Boringhieri, 1998.

Bricchi, Maria Rosa. *Manganelli e la menzogna: notizie su Hilarotragoedia con testi inediti.* Novara: Interlinea, 2002.

Calasso, Roberto. *Cento lettere a uno sconosciuto.* Milan: Adelphi, 2003.

Cavadini, Mattia. *La luce nera: teoria e prassi nell'opera di Giorgio Manganelli.* Milan: Bompiani, 1997.

Cavell, Stanley. *Must We Mean What We Say? A Book of Essays.* 1969. Cambridge: Cambridge University Press, 1976.

Cortelessa, Andrea. 'La "filologia fantastica" di Manganelli.' In Viola Papetti, ed., *Le foglie messaggere.* 229–59.

Corti, Maria. 'Gli infiniti possibili di Manganelli.' *Alfabeta* (1979): 14.
– *Il viaggio testuale: Le ideologie e le strutture semiotiche.* Turin: Einaudi, 1978.
De Benedictis, Maurizio. *Manganelli e la finzione.* Rome: Lithos, 1998.
Deidier, Roberto. 'Per un discorso su Manganelli e l'utopia.' In Viola Papetti, ed., *Le foglie messaggere.* 72–82.
Donnarumma, Raffaele. '*Hilarotragoedia* di Manganelli: Funzione Gadda, neoavanguardia, Linea Landolfi.' *Nuova corrente* 42 (1995): 51–90.
Eco, Umberto. *Sugli specchi e altri saggi.* Milan: Bompiani, 1985.
Ferretti, Gian Carlo. *Storia dell'editoria letteraria in Italia, 1945–2003.* Turin: Einaudi, 2004.
Gambaro, Fabio. *Colloquio con Edoardo Sanguineti: quarant'anni di cultura italiana attraverso i ricordi di un poeta intellettuale.* Milan: Anabasi, 1993.
– *Invito a conoscere la neoavanguardia.* Milan: Mursia, 1993.
Gellner, Ernest. *Language and Solitude: Wittgenstein, Malinowski and the Habsburg Dilemma.* Cambridge: Cambridge University Press, 1998.
Gibson, John, and Wolfgang Huemer, eds. *The Literary Wittgenstein.* London and New York: Routledge, 2004.
Gozzi, Luigi. 'Teatro Gruppo 63 a Palermo.' *Marcatrè* 1 (1963): 13–16.
Hillebrand, Sabine. *Strategien der Verwirrung: zur Erzählkunst von E.T.A. Hoffmann, Thomas Bernhard und Giorgio Manganelli.* Frankfurt: Peter Lang, 1999.
Kuon, Peter. 'Ogni teologia è della notte: Giorgio Manganelli's literarische Pseudo-Theologie.' *Italienisch* 29 (1993): 16–28.
Lazzarin, Stefano. '*Centuria*: le sorti del fantastico nel Novecento.' *Studi novecenteschi* 53 (1997): 99–145.
Manganelli, Giorgio. *A e B.* Milan: Rizzoli, 1975.
– *Agli dèi ulteriori.* Turin: Einaudi, 1972; 2nd ed. Milan: Adelphi, 1991.
– *Hilarotragoedia.* Milan: Feltrinelli, 1964; 3rd ed. Milan: Adelphi, 1987.
– *L'impero Romenzesco: letture per un editore.* A cura di Viola Papetti. Turin: Nino Aragno, 2003.
– *Incorporei felini 1: Poeti inglesi degli anni cinquanta.* A cura di Viola Papetti. Rome: Edizioni di storia e letteratura, 2002.
– *Incorporei felini 2: Recensioni e conversazioni radiofoniche su poeti in lingua inglese, 1949–1987.* A cura di Viola Papetti. Rome: Edizioni di storia e letteratura, 2002.
– *La letteratura come menzogna.* Milan: Feltrinelli, 1967; 2nd ed. Milan: Adelphi, 1985.
– *Il rumore sottile della prosa.* A cura di Paola Italia. Milan: Adelphi, 1994.
– *Tragedie da Leggere. Tutto il teatro.* A cura di Luca Scarlini. Turin: Nino Aragno, 2005.

Manica, Raffaele. 'Col Bartoli, in Cina, per esempio.' Papetti, ed., *Le foglie messaggere*, 145–56.

Menechella, Grazia. *Il felice vanverare. ironia e parodia nell'opera narrativa di Giorgio Manganelli.* Ravenna: Longo, 2002.

Montani, Alessandro. 'Manganelli, ovvero l'etica dell'intelligenza.' *Annali d'Italianistica* 19 (2001): 255–67.

Mussgnug, Florian. *The Eloquence of Ghosts: Giorgio Manganelli and the Afterlife of the Avant-Garde.* Oxford: Peter Lang, 2010.

Muzzioli, Francesco. *Teoria e critica della letteratura nelle avanguardie italiane degli anni sessanta.* Rome: Trecani, 1982.

Nigro, Salvatore Silvano. 'Scoperta di una vocazione.' In Viola Papetti, ed., *Le foglie messaggere.* 83–6.

Ottone, Giuseppe. 'Cultismo Linguistico di Manganelli.' *Italianistica* 5 (1976): 181–5.

Paolone, Marco. *Il cavaliere immaginale: Saggi su Giorgio Manganelli.* Rome: Carocci, 2002.

Papetti, Viola. 'Archeologia del critico.' Giorgo Manganelli. In *Incorporei felini 2: Recensioni e conversazioni radiofoniche su poeti in lingua inglese, 1949–1987.* A cura di Viola Papetti. Rome: Edizioni di storia e letteratura, 2002.

– 'Manganelli e gli inglesi.' *Nuovi argomenti,* 1–2 (1998): 356–65.

Papetti, Viola, ed. *Le foglie messaggere: scritti in onore di Giorgio Manganelli.* Rome: Editori Riuniti, 2000.

Pegoraro, Silvia. *Il 'fool' degli inferi: spazio e immagine in Giorgio Manganelli.* Rome: Bulzoni, 2000.

Perloff, Marjorie. *Wittgenstein's Ladder: Poetic Language and the Strangeness of the Ordinary.* Chicago: University of Chicago Press, 1996.

Pulce, Graziella. *Bibliografia degli scritti di Giorgio Manganelli.* Florence: Titivillus, Editore, 1996.

– *Giorgio Manganelli: figure e sistema.* Florence: Le Monnier, 2004.

– *Lettura d'autore: conversazioni di critica e di letteratura con Giorgio Manganelli, Pietro Citati e Alberto Arbasino.* Rome: Bulzoni, 1988.

Quandt, Lothar. 'Giorgio Manganelli.' In *Italienische Literatur der Gegenwart,* ed. Johannes Hösle and Wolfgang Eitel. Stuttgart: Kröner, 1974.

Vollenweider, Alice. 'Literatur als Metapher: Zum Werk Giorgio Manganellis.' *Italienisch* 13 (1985): 46–54.

Wagstaff, Christopher. 'The Neo-Avantgarde.' *Writers and Society in Contemporary Italy,* ed. Michael Caesar and Peter Hainsworth. Leamington Spa: Berg, 1984.

West, Rebecca. 'Before, Beneath and Around the Text: The Genesis and Construction of Some Postmodern Prose Fictions.' *Annali d'Italianistica* 9 (1991): 272–92.

– '*La letteratura come menzogna, Dall'inferno, Laboriose inezie* and *Tutti gli errori.*' *Annali d'Italianistica* 4 (1986): 307–11.

– 'Toward the Millennium: Update on Celati, Malerba, Manganelli.' *L'Anello che non tiene* (1993): 57–70.

Wittgenstein, Ludwig. *Philosophical Investigations.* German-English parallel text, trans. G.E.M. Ascombe. Oxford: Blackwell, 1953.

Wood, Michael. *Literature and the Taste of Knowledge.* Cambridge: Cambridge University Press, 2005.

Zandonella, Alessandra. 'Tra fantastico e allegoria. Sulla scrittura di Giorgio Manganelli.' *Il verri* 3 (1992): 113–24.

6 The Poetry of the *Neoavanguardia* and the Materiality of Language

JOHN PICCHIONE

In its various expressions, the avant-garde embodies the most radical and complex endeavour of twentieth-century art to go beyond the conventional boundaries of language and aesthetic forms. Within the context of literature, it consistently presents itself as an adventure in unchartered territories, searching for new ways to expand the spaces of writing. Its objective is that of reconfiguring the internal spaces of subjectivity and of provoking shifts in the collective frames through which we read the world. In this respect, the avant-garde is rooted in the preoccupation to break with uncomplicated representational notions regarding the relationship between the word and the world. It clearly shows solid links with the general hermeneutics of language that has marked the philosophical and linguistic investigation of our age. These traits, steeped in a culture of renewal and antagonism, are at the core of the experience of not only the so-called historical avant-garde but also of the neo-avant-garde movements that characterize the 1950s and 1960s. The Italian *neoavanguardia* can easily be placed within this general framework. Indeed, its general aesthetic orientation is informed by the awareness that the contact with the world is a languageified experience, inseparable from the system of language and from dominant literary models. In my view, the theoretical tenets of the neo-avant-garde not only constitute an extremely fertile elaboration of the reflection on art and literature advocated by the historical avant-garde, but also address new fundamental issues that, decades after its demise, are still pressing and laden with numerous social and ideological ramifications.

Setting aside the various blocs and conflicting positions that distinguish the theoretical positions of the group, it can safely be claimed that the aesthetic orientation of the neo-avant-garde rests on the premise that in literature reality occurs first and foremost in the form of linguistic modalities. It is in this postulate that the specificity of literature resides. Indeed, the identification of literature (specifically poetry, the activity under investigation in this study) with the exploration of language bears far-reaching effects on both the formal organization of the text and the role of the reader. Although the neo-avant-garde problematized deeply the possibility of literature to produce a direct impact on praxis (to subvert social and economic conditions by providing the necessary ground for a revolution within the context of late capitalism) it did not abandon the transgressive traits of all avant-garde movements.[1]

If, on one hand, numerous members of the group exhibit theoretical stands that reveal postmodern postures (the collapse of dialectics and ideologies, and consequently the end of a utopian project capable of overcoming the negativity of capitalism), on the other hand, the new avant-garde does not renounce to the possibility of a critical stance on language and on social structures. It never admits a homologation that would block any form of tension. A critique of traditional language turns inevitably into a critique of dominant historical paradigms. Said differently, the subversive approach towards language carries with it the desire to subvert the linguistic modalities through which we apprehend our realities. The deviation from standard norms of social communication and the displacement of conventional literary models coincide with the breaching of established grammars of the world. For the neo-avant-garde, poetry's objective is the production – not the reproduction – of meanings. Indeed, the neo-avant-garde takes poetry back to its etymological roots: the Greek *poiesis* (from *poiein*) means to make, or to produce. Poetry must break with traditional models of mimesis and suspend the prewritten script of the experiences of our life-world. It must go beyond the already-thought and the already-said in the attempt to provide, through linguistic experimentation, new galaxies of meaning and thus new ways of relating to reality. The poetic text is perceived, on one hand, as an autonomous and self-reflexive formal structure, and on the other, as a tool capable of generating, through the reader's active collaboration, new possible encounters with the world.

The central goal of this study is to demonstrate that this theoretical and aesthetic orientation leads the poets of the *neoavanguardia* to explore the materiality of the word and to delve into the flesh of language, with the ambition of forcing life to rewrite itself. By reducing language to a material entity, they attempt to break off the trammels of referentiality and of authorized syntactic and semantic constructions. It is the very otherness of the text that can recover the inventiveness of poetry and challenge our habitual linguistic and mental grids. Indeed, poetry's task is not that of confirming what has already been established through different means of communication and human activities. The significance of poetry resides in the very distance it creates both from the world and from our standard communicative practices.

One of the central figures of the neo-avant-garde who pursues a well-discernible and significant poetic project linked to the materiality of the word is Edoardo Sanguineti. Sanguineti's poetry dating from the 1950s to the 1970s is centred on the exploration of an alienated language, characterized by a shattered and lacerated syntax that serves as an expression of the chaos and pathology of our bourgeois-capitalist realities, and at the same time reveals an urgency to subvert traditional literary models and their ideological constructs. In this first stage of Sanguineti's poetic production, marked by collections such as *Laborintus* (1956) and *Erotopaegnia* (1961), formal dissonances, semantic discontinuities, hybridization, and contamination of styles, agitated syntactic constructions, all stem from an awareness that poetry is in its essence a metalinguistic production of ideologies. The linguistic disorder is intended as a transgression of the dominant and codified ways of seeing things. This work on language is central in Sanguineti's entire poetic production. However, it displays a number of innovative shifts.

By the late 1970s and into the 1980s, Sanguineti's language takes a new turn. Through inventive and resourceful procedures, it addresses in a forceful manner the correlation between poetry and the materiality of the word.[2] The collections of this new phase that will be at the centre of our analyses are *Novissimum testamentum* (1986) and *Bisbidis* (1987).[3] Both collections display an intense linguistic vitality and a sort of baroque virtuosity that seem to originate from a notion of writing conceived as a space of *jouissance* and as a manifestation of the libido. At the same time, the materiality of language and its corollary, the vision of the text as an autonomous and self-contained organism, generate numerous implications involving both the aesthetic domain and that of cognition and ideology. In *Novissimum testamentum,* aside from explicit statements of poetics present in texts such as 'Ab edendo' and 'La philosophie dans le théatre' ('e ti guardo con questi miei occhi barocchi' [36]; 'eiaculare pensieri in un liquame / di parole, e le parole farsi carne' [39]), the new territories explored by Sanguineti's poetry disclose a conspicuous adherence to the free encounter of signifiers joined without apparent semantic restrains and without the crippling control of ordinary logic.

The premise on which this poetic operation rests can be outlined as follows: (1) signification does not precede the poetic work; (2) the process of signification flows from the signifiers to the signifieds; (3) thought is not antecedent to writing inasmuch as the poet discovers the meaning of his/her own words in the act of writing; (4) signifiers shift, transform, attract, and reconstruct themselves following above all the 'laws' of their materiality; (5) language is a material entity that produces the non-material phenomenon of signification.

Several poems in *Novissimum testamentum*, written between 1982 and 1984, radiate a highly intense semantic energy and a constant polysemic flux, generated essentially by the intricate network of phonic equivalences. Sanguineti constructs his texts starting from the material base of the verbal signs, essentially from the phonic substance of the signifiers. This operation, in sharp contrast with the prosaic language adopted in the first part of the collection, begins to appear in poems such as 'Ab edendo' and 'Lirica,' in which the signifiers are organized following almost exclusively the principle of homophony. They chase one another and proliferate through continuous variations and permutations. These processes either weld them together or create series of swirling resonances. Here are some significant examples:

ero il cappello (del cappellaio cappellano, in amore) del prestigiatore
[prestidigitatore:

(ero la coppa (e anche la maschera) del maschio in coppia): ero la torre
[(la torta)
dei tarocchi: (la tana delle tortore: una trama tremante sopra un tetto):
[ero un prefetto
insetto: (una torma di tarme): ero il tuo trono (il tuo treno):
(ero il tuo seno):
sono una testa della terra (abitabile abile): e ti guardo con questi
[occhi barocchi che
ti bruciano: ti vedo con la fronte che si spezza, con le labbra
[che si slabbrano
(con la lepre, la lebbra): (con la mia lisca e la mia cresta): sono una testa
antropomorfa, forma del fermo cerchio fatto circo (circa): ti cerco:
(e sono il seno):
('Ab Edendo,' secs. 1–2, 36)

Rotta è l'alta catena ottenebrante, turbante di sirena lancinante,
[furfante che ci esorta,

E che ci scorta, lì alla porta, a mano morta, di matrici punitrici, grassatrici
[da appendici:
Nane mamme mammellate, marmellate le gomme di gonne, martellate le
[donne cannoni castrate,
in soldoni di bottoni
di calzoni:
Alta è la turpe tubatura dura di tabacchi, di sacchi, di spacchi di almanacci
Troncato è il tronco, tattile ma torto, dei tasti pederasti, coccolati cioccolati
Ossigenati cottimati, operati, oberati di travi e di navi, di nodi di navi da
[razzi,
di pazzi con cazzi di chiodi:
('Lirica,' secs. 1–2, 42)

Apart from the assiduous presence of rhymes (including rhymes constructed with invariable suffixes and verb endings, imperfect rhymes – those that in the context of Italian prosody are referred to as *rime artificiose*), assonances, consonances, alliterations and syllabic recurrences, the signifiers attract one another by virtue of a phonetic magnetism accentuated by all sorts of metaplasms and particularly by the use of paronomasia, anagrams, paragrams, polyptotons, and etymological and pseudo-etymological wordplay.

These practices also reemerge, rather obstinately, in the first three sections of *Bisbidis* ('Codicillo,' 'Rebus,' and 'L'ultima passeggiata'). Indeed, here too, Sanguineti pursues the endless metamorphoses of words and reverberations of sounds. The verbal signs produce a multiplicity of echoic structures. Attracted by their material correspondences, they narcissistically mirror one another. Here is a selection of verses from the above-mentioned three sections:

[…] in questo guasto impasto, questo nefasto impiastro: in un disastro):
ti dico, e ti ripeto: eri il mio astro, la mia lastra di alabastro: (e in te mi incastro,
per disegnarti, farti (farmi, farci) una figura umana): (una vita infarcita,
insaporita):
('Codicillo,' sec. 6, 14)

ti ricordi di quella pazza ragazza, che, sopra l'erba imbrattata,
imberrettata, convisse con la mascherata dei froci (dei proci precoci
procaci),
dei baci? (che si imbiaccò di bianca bava quella sua fronte
('Rebus,' sec. 8, 46)

la nostra prole, i nostri polli molli, che ti ballano e ti bollono, al sole soli,
che ti beccano e saltabeccano, e ti mordono e non demordono, per noi
[grami, tu che li ami,
si ingozzano, ci singhiozzano, si ingrassano, ci invecchiano
('L'ultima passeggiata,' sec. 3, 73)

The signifiers flow unfettered from the constraints of a linear discourse. The impression is that the poet transcribes words that offer themselves through a spontaneous combination. Indeed, as the title of this collection suggests, the act of writing is essentially identified with the act of listening to language's own internal resources. The terms 'bisbis' and 'bisbidis' are derived from a text by the medieval poet Immanuel Romano and form the Italian onomatopoeic word 'bisbigliare' [to whisper]. It is as if words produced a continuous buzzing and humming that the poet captures and writes down:

(considerato che,
tira e molla, non mi importa di niente): (seguo soltanto, tante volte, appena,
questo basso bisbis di un bisbidis, che mi ronza qui dentro, debolmente,
senza, neanche più, diventarmi parola, frase, verso): cerco una conclusione
finalmente: ('Rebus,' sec. 27, 67)

In several poems of both collections, the wordplay and the search for phonemic clusters and patterns are directed toward the recuperation of old poetic genres as the abecedarius and the tautogram which favour primarily alliterative contiguities. In addition to the above-mentioned poem 'Lirica,' *Novissimum testamentum* assembles texts that combine the acrostic with the abecedarius, even though the verses do not follow an alphabetical order. When read vertically, the initial letters of the verses in the poems 'Re-spira,' 'Chronometron,' 'Iperromanzo,' and 'Astrolapsus' spell out various dedications, and the words of each line create alliterations of both consonants and vowels. Here is an example taken from a particularly long acrostic divided into seven parts, where the first letters form the title 'Mimus albus' (sec. 1) and the rest make up the self-ironic combination of Pulcinella (secs. 2–6) and Sanguineti (sec. 7):

protoprometeo postperipatetico
umuncio da universo unipoetico
libero lazzi logigi & luetici,
con cazzo a chiazze, in cosmi da cosmetici:
innalzo a iperimbuto un ipsilonne,

negando nanne & ninne a nonni & a nonne:
erro tra le erme emetiche, erto eone,
lussurio e lussi a lampo di lampione:
lottizzo lutti, lumino lindure,
arrido agli astri & astringo le aperture: ('Minus Albus,' sec. 5, 47)

The last section of *Bisbidis* follows similar poetic practices. It contains a series of twenty-one tautograms (one for each letter of the Italian alphabet), written in octaves. Assembled under the title of 'Alfabeto apocalittico,' the series is fittingly dedicated to Enrico Baj, an artist who produced a number of paintings also inspired to apocalyptic visions. Indeed, at the end of the 1970s Baj had an exhibition entitled 'Apocalissi' at the Marconi Gallery in Milan. In 1982 he held a second exhibit of similar works in Mantova, with Sanguineti reading the texts in question at the opening. This correlation is much more revealing if we consider that Baj too displays a long and intense dialogue with the materiality of his medium. In fact, he is one of the most significant practitioners in Italy of the so-called 'pittura materica.'[4] In these texts the contiguity of the signifiers is validated exclusively by the phonic affinities: the linkages are not based exclusively on the use of alliteration, but on that of the assonance and of the rhyme – the latter bonds the end of all the lines. Here is the opening tautogram devoted to the letter 'a':

anime amiche all'aspro astro afroditico,
abnepoti dell'albero adamitico,
audite le mie antifone acide & ascetiche,
arche di angui & di anguille arcialfabetiche:
apro abissi di aleppi apocalittiche,
ansimo ansie di angosce & di asme asfittiche:
adattatemi auricole atte & attente,
annunzio un acre, acerrimo accidente: ('Alfabetico apocalittico,' sec. A, 81)

On a macrotextual level, these poetic practices are considerably removed from the linguistic and mental turmoil that marked Sanguineti's initial productions, such as *Laborintus.* In his early work the linguistic alienation and turbulence was the result of a descent into the historical chaos of contemporary reality. On the other hand, both collections under examination disclose a playfulness that generates the pleasure of the text. The semantic anarchy, the satisfying effects engendered by the phonic correspondences, and the pleasure derived from the unexpected associations of words all contribute to a poetic experience that pursues, in its linguistic orgasms, the demands of the libido. Obviously, this intercourse does not occur solely between author and language, but between reader and text. The eroticized dimension of these poems is further demonstrated by recurrent references to sex organs and acts of love making. A few examples will suffice: 'protrudo un pene proboscidoidesco,' 'lungando la mia lingua lecco in letto' (*NT*, 'Minus albus,' sec. 2); 'ampliando amplessi amareggio l'amore' (ibid., sec. 3); 'erezioni / aurorali' (*B*, 'Codicillo,' sec. 10); 'chiudo nella mia bocca la tua lingua' (ibid., sec. 12); 'lasciva mia lucerna licenziosa' (*B*, 'Alfabeto apocalitico,' sec. L); 'vulvacce vispe, vergini a vedersi' (ibid., sec. V). Indeed, *Bisbidis* in particuar presents explicit correlations between writing and eroticism. In 'Codicillo' the act of writing ('faccio scrittura, e non sono scrittura') is related to that of love-making ('faccio le faville / (con il fuoco e le fiamme): (faccio l'amore),' (sec. 3). In 'L'ultima passeggiata,' the gaze on one's body is redirected, rather suggestively, on the white, 'naked' paper upon which the poetic signs are inscribed. Furthermore, writing and ejaculation are associated in unambiguous terms:

ti esploro, mia carne, mio oro, corpo mio, che ti spio, mia cruda carta nuda,
che ti segno, che ti signo, con i miei seri, severi, semi neri, con i miei
[teoremi,
i miei emblemi, che ti sbatto e ti ribatto, denso e duro, tra le tue fratte,
con il mio oscuro, puro latte (sec. 1, 71)

This eroticized relationship with language, adopted as a source of pleasure, can be further explored by taking into consideration the way in which Sanguineti exploits the vast galaxies of literary memories offered by the multi-dimensional space of writing. The intertextual playfulness, present in both collections, is rather prominent. Sanguineti seems to derive much gratification from linking his linguistic search to reminiscences of authors who provided clues for his writing. The allusions to Dante, Petrarch, Lorenzo de' Medici, Folenco, Manzoni, Cecco Angiolieri, and Jacopone da Todi, to name only the most conspicuous ones, are too numerous to cite. Two examples will serve our purpose. The first is from the poem 'Novissimum testamentum,' in which Manzoni's famous passage of Lucia's 'addio ai monti,' in *I promessi sposi*, is reminisced:

addio le foto, e le mammelle, e i letti,
e i kamasutra, e i parti, e i fazzoletti:
addio lì i monti, che dalle acque sorgono,
e addio lì le acque, che dai monti sgorgano: (*NT*, 33)

From the same collection, the last segment of 'Mimus albus' presents a clear allusion to Cecco Angiolieri's poem 'Se fossi foco':

> se sesso io fossi di sensato sasso,
> aguzzerei l'anguilla & l'ananasso: [...]
> torturerei le tartarughe tristi,
> invocando johanni e jesuchristi (sec. 7, 48)[5]

Sanguineti's intertextual memories and pleasures do not stop here. An entire poem, 'Iperromanzo,' is constructed by bringing together, in a satirical fashion, characters of various celebrated novels:

> travestita da Tess, trucida Tristram:
> Eduard evade: educato in esilio,
> riporta Rastignac da Rubempré: [...]
>
> Lucinda lincia Lolita lebbrosa:
> Lufcadio, a letto, lecca Lola Lola:
> esasperata, Eufemia espone Elisa: (*NT*, 53)

This experimentation with the materiality of language is not an occasional and transient activity for Sanguineti. In fact, it is not limited to the two collections in question but is pursued through the years, up to his most recent poetic production. The last two extensive poetic collections published by Sanguineti – *Il gatto lupesco: poesie (1982–2001)* and *Mikrokosmos: poesie (1951–2004)* – feature many poems dating from the 1980s to the first years of the new millennium that follow a similar poetic exploration. Of particular interest for our investigation is the series entitled 'Fanerografie,' in *Il gatto lupesco.* Sanguineti organizes this series by combining a few poems from *Bisbidis* and *Novissimum testamentum* with numerous poems written during the 1980s and early 1990s. This structure clearly reveals that Sanguineti is giving continuity and breadth to this significant trait of his poetic practices. Poems such as 'Parole senza romanza,' 'Che cosa è la poesia,' 'De pictura,' 'Acrosonettizzazione,' 'Segno,' all continue testing the materiality of language. Particularly remarkable is the poem 'Catasonetto,' which contains a number of significant formal properties and conceptual nuclei. Here is the entire poem:

> mia materia e maceria, musa morta,
> catalessi e catastrofe, cancrena

tragico tanfo e tonfo, trita torta,
schiuma sepolta, mia sfasciata scena:

catarsi di catarro, crisi corta,
celibe crepa in cotta cantilena,
piega porosa a putrefatta porta,
vuoto vocale, vescicosa vena:

rudere di reliquia, mio relitto
avanzo di avariata anestesia,
frolla il fragile fallo, il fasto fritto:

orrore di oppilata omofonia,
crollo concluso, chiodo di conflitto,
restaura il regno, rovinografia: (211)

It is interesting to observe how the phonemic patterns trigger a series of quite engaging thematic possibilities. The terms 'maceria,' catastrofe,' 'sfasciata,' 'crepa,' 'rudere,' 'relitto,' 'crollo,' and 'rovinografia,' constitute a semantic field that denotes personal and collective ruins. Indeed, the terms 'cancrena,' 'tanfo,' 'putrefatta,' 'avariata,' also connote a sense of destruction. (The verb 'trita' [to mince] fits this semantic area as well.) The presence of nouns such as 'catalessi and 'crisi' and adjectives such as 'tragico,' 'fragile,' and 'orrore' reveal an emotional reaction, a state of mind, connected to the conditions of devastation and collapse. (Also, 'porosa' and 'frolla' can be related to this aspect through their denotation of fragility.) The openness of these signifieds allows the reader to collaborate in the construction of the text's messages by reconnecting it to social, political, and ideological predicaments of our age. Most significantly, this sate of disintegration and decay bears negative effects upon poetry (and in a larger context, upon art) itself: 'musa morta,' 'vuoto vocale,' 'oppilata omofonia,' (but also 'vescicosa vena,' if we create the semantic link of 'vescicosa' to lesions and 'vena' to poetic vein). The self-reflexivity of the text is further underscored by 'cantilena,' with its connotations of repetitiveness, and by 'oppilata omofonia,' which refers both to the formal devices adopted in the text and to an 'occlusion,' an obstruction that perhaps hints at the difficulty of producing messages. In a conceptual frame that recalls Walter Benjamin's gaze on history, Sanguineti establishes a healthy dialectics between ruination and redemption: the presence of 'catarsi' and 'restaura' creates a semantic tension with the catastrophic view that invades the text and renews possibilities of liberation and struggle – 'chiodo di conflitto' contributes in constructing this latter allusion.[6]

Three series – 'Stravaganze,' 'Cose,' and 'Poesie fuggitive' – included in *Il gatto lupesco* and reproduced in part in *Mikrokosmos* display a recurrent emphasis on the material base of language. Among the most apparent examples, let us restrict the selection to the following texts: 'Le parche rosse,' 'Per un'ebrezza di concordanze,' 'Canzonetta,' 'Acrostichetto,' 'Matiz de Leo,' 'Canzone,' 'Tiparchetipi,' 'Lamentatio Doctoris Fausti,' 'Cataloghetto catacolophonico,' 'La mucca pazza,' 'Metalmeccanici,' and 'Emisubsonetto.' This practice is adopted even in instances where the thematic area is rather confined, thus limiting the possibilities of homophonic clusters. A case in point is the poem 'Malebolge 1994,' in which Sanguineti, recalling through the title Dante's infernal realities, attacks the Italian prime minister Silvio Berlusconi for his collusion of politics and business, for his control of the media, and for the cultural homogenization he promotes. Here is the first part of the poem:

Berlicchi in bassi braghi bidoneschi
ectoplasmano eterica emittenza,
riciclando i rugati regimeschi:
lemuri e lamie di luminiscenza
unguentano gli utenti più ultrulscheschi,
spacciano spot, sparati in subcoscienza:
cori da curve di campi calceschi
omologano olanti in obbedienza,
neoplasmati da news per neoyuppeschi
itali idioti, ipermarkettizzati: (*GL*, 322)

The priority given to the signifiers in these poetic practices could lead to placing Sanguineti's work within a deconstructive poetics that espouses the view of the verbal sign dominated by difference and absence. The dissemination of the signifiers in their constant motion, indeed in their unstoppable movement, would entail that they do not point to any signified but to themselves alone. The poetic adventure in the territory of the materiality of the signifiers would reveal a sign inhabited by the impossibility of plenitude. The signifiers, treated as reified entities, in their endless slipping and sliding would disclose nothing but a void derived from the futile prospect to be attached to any signified. Other implications would include the impossibility that the writer could be an agent of his/her own signification and the inability of language to represent externality.

Sanguineti's poetic writing does not proclaim either the death of the author or the reduction of the text – and thus of history itself – as a process without a subject. Undoubtedly, Sanguineti has abandoned all pre-Freudian notions of a subject rooted in the principle of an autonomous self, above and outside of language. Indeed, Sanguineti's entire poetic production – and in particular the collections analysed here – presents a myriad of 'neocrepuscular' self-portraits that display a frail and weakened subject. Here are a number of examples from *Bisbidis*: 'io non lo so: so / più niente di niente' (18); 'la storia si capisce, e non si capisce' (10); 'se ti sciogli dentro il liquame del mio me' (12); 'questo mio me, questo straccio di carta uso bollo, formato / protocollo' (13); 'per sciogliermi in minuzzoli, per / spolparmi in poltiglia' (14); 'se non sono nessuno, / resto però un modesto e appassionato collezionista di / autografi' (30); per sempre / vivente inesistente' (63); 'ah, che infermo inferno che mi vivo, dormendo, / non dormendo, e che mi scrivo' (66); 'io sono il soffio asmatico, fantasmatico, meccanico e automatico e patetico, e parodico' (74); 'fragile firma ferma 'sto foglietto' (86). A similar destabilizing condition of the subject is identifiable in *Novissimum testamentum* – 'a mani vuote, e lentamente, / io vado, ormai, che mi aspetta il mio niente' (29); 'congedo prendo, più morto che vivo' (35); 'dentro il niente del niente di ogni niente' (41); 'nutrito a nomi, il niente ha nascimento' (52 – and in Sanguineti's latest poetic work). Let us limit the selection from *Mikrokosmos* to one text, 'Identikit,' written in 2003:

> mi autoproduco, fragile, mi clono,
> stacco me da me stesso, e a me mi dono:
>
> mi autodigitalizzo, olografammatico,
> replicandomi in toto, svelto e pratico:
>
> mi automaschero e, assai plasticamente,
> sindonizzo il mio corpo e la mia mente:
>
> mi autoregistro, ormai, se mi iconizzo,
> cromocifrato in spettro – e mi ironizzo: (317)

It is apparent from these examples that Sanguineti adopts a self-ironic perspective that does not allow for the subject any reassuring stability, permanence, and security.[7] Indeed, a poetic writing in progress cannot but envision a subject-in-process. However, it does not result in the disappearance of the subject, in its absence from the signifiers. Sanguineti's poetics are grounded in the postulate that poetry, as a metalinguistic production of ideologies, is inseparable from historical and social conditions. The materiality of the signifiers in Sanguineti's poetic work is tied to a dialectical and materialist world view. Contrary to the theoretical orientation of deconstruction, Sanguineti does not assign to signifiers absolute autonomy, inasmuch as writing and language are seen, in Marxist terms, as superstructural manifestations. Signifiers are neither neutral nor innocent. Their organization is not independent from an agent. Signification arises from the dialectical encounter between the materiality of the signifiers and the activity, the work conducted on them by a subject who resides inside history and ideologies. Accordingly, the text is a result of a dialectics between the relative autonomy of language and its existence as an ideological and epochal construct – the product of a historically determined subjectivity.

Opposed to an idealist orientation that perceives signification as pre-existing manifestations of mind and thought, Sanguineti starts from the materiality of his medium. Matter transforms as a result of a synthesis between the properties that constitute it and the intentionality of a subject. (The project is not to anchor conquered states of consciousness to the written word, but to locate new possible perceptions of the world through the act of writing). The exploration of the virtual material properties of language presumes in Sanguineti a specific ideological objective. It is directed, first of all, to free the verbal signs from the despotic fixity and predictability of conventions. In other words, Sanguineti's ambition is that of dislodging fossilized and calcified signifieds produced by the hegemonic culture and ideology.[8] The adherence to the materiality of the signifiers is then an act of transgression, an attempt to create an alternative space to the existing and codified modes of signification. The result is a ludic, grotesque, parodic, clownish, comic, and yes, also tragic form of poetry that is always firmly rooted in a revolutionary creativity that aspires to subvert the social control of signification. For Sanguineti, this practice is the only possible endeavour for assigning to literature a relative autonomy vis à vis other forms of the social production of signification. Signifiers are asked to force the world to rewrite itself. They express the desire to liberate discourses from the paralysing effects of the so-called social normality and to press for the problematic and uncertain conquest of other possible human realities.

Within the context of the new avant-garde, Sanguineti is not alone in adopting poetic practices that highlight the materiality of language. Other significant practitioners include Antonio Porta and Nanni Balestrini.[9] For these two poets it is necessary to keep the textual analyses to a minimum, due to space constraints.

One of Porta's most radical experimentations is represented by the collection *Cara,* which comprises texts written between 1965 and 1968.[10] Here Porta identifies poetry exclusively with the syntactic and rhythmic space that regulates its formal organization. In most texts the obsessive recurrence of the same syntactic structures and the absence of a narrative progression seem to hypothesize that poetry is first and foremost an intransitive and self-reflexive operation generated by the physical, material substance of language. This 'corporeal' core of poetic language precedes signification; it is at the base of the poetic activity. Here is the initial sequence from a series of texts entitled 'Come se fosse un ritmo':

si servono di uncini	si alzano dalle sedie
chiedono dei fagioli	azzannano i bambini
amano la musica	si tolgono le scarpe
ballano in cerchio	seguono lo spartito
escono dalle finestre	vanno a fare il bagno
aprono la botola	rientrando dalla finestra
cambiano posizione	si chinano sul water
controllano l'orario	escono dalla chiesa
pieni di medicine	cadono dalle sedie
si appendono al soffitto	colano con lentezza
si servono di forbici	li prendono a pedate

(sec. 1, 39)

The 'chilly' literal dimension of this poetry compels the reader to focus on the internal, formal constructs of the texts. Indeed, symbolic or metaphoric considerations are constantly thwarted. In this collection Porta's experimentation revolves around the conception that poetry possesses a material reality and it is not simply a medium employed for objectives other than itself. Undoubtedly, the reiteration of daily gestures and actions suggest a view of reality observed through the lens of estrangement and of the absurd. In fact, in texts such as 'Loro,' 'N. x serie di ipotesi verificabili,' and 'Come è un avverbio di tempo' this approach to the world generates a plurality of thematic interpretations that centre on the void and the senselessness of collective rituals that dominate our lives. However, Porta's focus is the exploration of the mechanisms that regulate poetry and constitute its material basis. In this respect, these texts reveal an obsession with such figures of speech as anaphora, epanalepsis, anadiplosis, or, as in Sanguineti's case, with a variety of phonic devises, principally rhyme, assonance, consonance, and alliteration.

A case in point is the closing text of the collection, 'L'altro' ('ancora distesi divaricati divelti dentali digitali [...] / rimuoiono rinserrano ritti risvolti riscambiati [...] / sfiutano sfogliano sfilano sfaldano sradicano mingono [...] / riusato rilegato riletto rivivo riesumato rieletto' [111]). Indeed, *Cara* foregrounds a self-reflexivity and intransitivity of verbal signs that refuse to administer poetry exclusively as a mimetic vehicle that ends up reproducing a signification easily identifiable outside of its own field. The metapoetic nature of texts such as 'Intervento dell'utopia nel racconto,' 'Come è scomparso Mallarmé,' 'Critica della poesia,' 'Sonetto,' 'Lirica,' and 'Rima,' centred on the investigation of literariness and intertextuality, clearly demonstrates Porta's project.

It should be emphasized that Porta, like all the poets of the new avant-garde, espouses a phenomenological perspective, the reduction of the 'I,' the so-called *epochè*. The 'I' (the empirical self) is bracketed inasmuch as it is considered the result of an alienated subjectivity (a social and linguistic alienation engendered by the conditions of late capitalism) and thus divorced from a genuine life of experience. The centrality of the 'I' is supplanted by the centrality of language, as a way to not only denounce traditional and sentimental poetry, but to recover linguistic forms freed from conventions, obsolescence, and stale and alienating stereotypes. As in Sanguineti's case, the result is a weakened subject dialoguing with language and with the world while waiting for new beginnings. The following self-portrait ('Modello per autoritratti'), the closing text in Porta's collection *Metropolis* (1971), will suffice to illustrate this point:

io non sono non c'è chi è
non abito non credo non ho
cinquantanni ventuno dodici che c'è
quando bevo nell'acqua nuotare non so
con la penna che danza la polvere che avanza
non credo non vedo se esco né tocco
mangiare se fame digerire non do
prima corpo poi mente poi dico poi niente
è un'altra chissà se alla fine cadrà
né una vita né due né un pianeta né un altro
le lingue non capisco le grida annichilisco (53)

This poetic orientation is pursued in other collections of the 1970s and 1980s, but is perhaps most apparent in the second part of *Week-end* (1974). In poems such as 'Quale posizione di universo' and 'Rimario,' the exploration of the signifiers is conducted primarily through the rhyme, which performs the function of searching for new possible semantic links and associations. 'Rimario,' in particular, is constructed exclusively through binary syntagmatic associations tied by the presence of rhyme. Here too, the organization of the text is governed by the material substance of the signifiers. Guided by their materiality the signifiers dilate, through their unique combinations, semantic possibilities and facilitate the emergence of the repressed. This therapeutic prospect is enhanced by the numerous permutations and variations of the same syntagms and by infinite possible associations activated by the reader's dialogue with the text.

'Rimario' is constructed in seven sections of which only the first three present autonomous lexical units; the other four are subjected to various inversions and rearrangements that force the reader to generate new associations. Here are excerpts from two sections:

freni
                    frontiere
veleni
                    visiere
visiere
frontiere
Freni
veleni
contagio
naufragio (sec. IV, 56-57)

figlio
                    dementi
artiglio
                    sementi
sementi
dementi
figlio
artiglio (sec. VI, 61)

It is not essential to provide an analysis of the semantic possibilities offered by these texts. It will suffice to point out that their polysemic nature and cognitive tension are triggered by the formal and material properties of the lexical units. For Porta, the attention given to the material base of language is a decisive practice undertaken by any poet who perceives his/her own activity as that of an artisan working with verbal signs.

As noted above, the centrality of language and its materiality are manifest in another central figure of the new avant-garde: Nanni Balestrini.[11] In his case, the authorial voice is essentially pulverized and made invisible. Faced by a commodified, automatized, and trivialized linguistic code, he devotes much of his attention to the visual and physical properties of the word.

Balestrini experiments with collage poems produced by adopting a cut-and-paste technique in which he ransacks all sorts of printed materials, preserving only the typographic characters. For example, in the series of texts entitled 'Cronogrammi,' Balestrini highlights the visual qualities of words and turns poetry into an aesthetic experience of the materiality of the linguistic sign. Undoubtedly, these experiments have their roots in the practice of montage championed by the first avant-garde (futurism and Dadaism in particular) and by the practitioners of concrete poetry. In Balestrini, this procedure is charged with a fierce critique of the instrumental use of language and its commodification. These texts objectify linguistic alienation and contribute to the creation of a culture of dissent. Indeed, Balestrini fulfils an ideological project that aims to confront both the social system and its production of meanings. Here is one example from 'Cronogrammi' (201):

Balestrini's poetic investigation of the internal properties of language as the primary source for the production of meaning is taken to extreme consequences in two texts generated in 1961 with the assistance of an IBM

7070 computer: 'Mark Tape I' and 'Tape Mark II'– the first poetic texts written with the collaboration of a machine. Balestrini programmed the computer to randomly select series of syntactic patterns from extracts of texts by Michito Hachiya, Laotse, and Paul Goldwin. The computer was also used to create variations and permutations of these selected segments. In this case as well, Balestrini not only questions the traditional humanistic subject as the centre of signification, but emphasizes that poetry is indeed principally an adventure through the material properties and structures of language. The results are exceptional. In the first text, the computer generates stanza after stanza – a terrifying sight, like an atomic explosion on the scale of Hiroshima. Here is one stanza:

> Giacquero immobili senza parlare, trenta volte
> più luminoso del sole essi tornano tutti
> alla loro radice, la testa premuta sulla spalla
> assumono la ben nota forma di fungo cercando
> di afferrare, e malgrado che le cose fioriscano
> si espandono rapidamente, i capelli tra le labbra. (*Come si agisce*, 67)

The treatment of language as a physical substance is further evidenced by one of Balestrini's most radical collections: *Ma noi facciamone un'altra* (1968). Here words are subjected to various forms of mutilation and dismemberment. It is as if they were violently attacked, showing physical evidence of lacerations. This fractured linguistic reality, the result of a historical condition of decease that affects language, is now manifest not only at a syntactic level, but also at the level of monemes and phonemes. They are often shredded, making it impossible to follow a direct and uncomplicated semantic articulation. Here the materiality of the word on one hand denounces the state of reification and alienation of the social system of communication, and on the other, shows the fecundity of linguistic ambiguity and unpredictability. Here is a segment from the series 'Perimetri':

```
                omuni specchi
          he i c
ro superfice
         di copertura
                in par
                are
fos                              ultimo
```

l'ideale sare in quest'
ossero eriore di
tato e
lla lo
ossero vetro di
ene
nzionare abba
omuni specchi
stanza b
mpleta
colpisci face
resto ma anc
nzionare abba
olare
gli
specchi f
ossero
invece tu ttangolo (75)

Undoubtedly, Balestrini is collecting for the reader the linguistic ruins that surround us. At the same time, however, these texts give the impression of creating linguistic structures in an embryonic state, as if they were striving to produce forms of signification. In this series as well as in others, such as 'Istruzioni' and 'Una brutta storia,' Balestrini's work on the materiality of language is further evidenced by the spatial and visual organization of the texts. The discursive syntax is replaced by a spatial one that structures the linguistic material in the form of graphic patterns. The integration of spatial, graphic, and semantic elements contributes to the construction of polysemic systems of signs that favour ambiguity and thus engage the reader with a plurality of meanings. For Balestrini, the focus on the materiality of language is a strategy for exposing the condition of our linguistic code and for pursuing a poetic revolution capable of renewing the stale models of tradition. For a poet there is no greater aspiration.

NOTES

1 For an overview of the neo-avant-garde's theoretical positions and poetic production, see Picchione, *The New Avant-Garde in Italy*.

2 In *Segnalibro: poesie 1951–1981* texts dating back to the 1970s are grouped in the section 'Fuori catalogo.' The texts in question include: 'Due mnemoritmi,' 'Marketing landscape,' 'Albedo,' and 'Erotosonetto.' For a critical overview of Sanguineti's poetry see Sica, *Sanguineti*; Wlassics, 'Edoardo Sanguineti,' Pietropaoli, *Unità e trinità di Edoardo Sanguineti*; Curi, ed., *Edoardo Sanguineti.*

3 Hereafter referred to in citations as *NT* and *B* respectively.

4 For Baj's apocalyptic series of paintings, see the catalogue *Apocalisse* (1979), edited by Umberto Eco.

5 Similar practices are pursued in other collections, including *Il gatto lupesco: poesie (1982–2001).* Here are a few examples from other texts: 'L'arpa magica' is reminiscent of Ariosto ('canto le fate, i mostri, i cavalieri, / le armi e le cortesie, le spadee i fiori, / le picche e i cuori, i bastoni e gli alfieri' [204]); 'Omaggio a Catullo' recaptures the language of the Latin poet ('alla mia ragazzina piaci, passero / che lei ci giuoca, e a te ti stringe al seno' [251]); and 'Imitazione, da Orazio' recaptures that of Horace ('tu non cercare, è illecito sapere che fine a me, che fine a te, / Leuconoe, ci hanno dato gli dei, e non tentare / calcoli babilonici: meglio subire quello che sarà' [316]). *Il gatto lupesco* will be hereinafter referred to in citations as *GL.*

6 In a much-cited passage of 'Theses of the Philosophy of History' (1940) Benjamin writes: 'This is how one pictures the angel of history. His face is turned toward the past. Where we perceive a chain of events, he sees one single catastrophe which he keeps piling wreckage upon wreckage and hurls it in front of his feet. The angel would like to stay, awaken the dead, and make whole what has been smashed. But a storm is blowing from Paradise; it has got caught in his wings with such a violence that the angel can no longer close them. This storm irresistibly propels him into the future to which his back is turned, while the pile of debris before him grows skyward. This storm is what we call progress' (*Illuminations* 257–8). The theme of ruins recurs in Sanguineti's later texts, such as 'Le petit tombeau' in the series 'Ecfrasi': 'gli occhi barocchi, che mi hanno guardato, / sono le mie rovine rassegnate, / marmi di melama, i miei mosaici veri' (*Mikrokosmos* 278).

7 On the relationship between poetry and identity, a text entitled 'Che cosa è la poesia' from the series 'Fanerografie' is rather revealing. Here are a few lines: 'Arti e artefatti articola in artista / nessi di nodi in nuda nonpersona, / occhi ottativi in ottimo ottimista: / avventi e apofobie, se avverbia, aziona' (*GL* 213).

8 At the first gathering of the new avant-garde, Sanguineti declared: 'Per essere autenticamente critica [...] l'arte deve energeticamente uscire dai limiti della normalità borghese, cioè dalle sue norme ideologiche e linguistiche';

quoted in Nanni Balestrini and Alfredo Giuliani, eds., *Gruppo 63: la nuova letteratura*, 383. For an overview of Sanguineti's positions on the relationship between ideology and language, see the entire debate of the Gruppo 63 reproduced in Balestrini and Guiliani ('Il dibattito' 371–406) and also in in Barilli and Guglielmi, *Gruppo 63: critica e teoria* ('Il dibattito teorico' 239–360). For further investigation of this topic, see Sanguineti's collection of essays in *Ideologia e linguaggio.*

9 Among other poets whose work is centred on the materiality of language, Adriano Spatola is, without doubt, one of the most prominent. See in particular his *Zeroglifici* (1966), in which letters are segmented or blown up, fragmented or inverted, creating signs that are virtually unreadable. The 1977 edition, titled *Zerogliphics,* presents new texts in which letters and words are totally dismembered, often seeming to explode, leaving behind undecipherable debris. Occasionally Spatola ransacks advertisements of consumer products and reduces them to rabbles. In their objectification the semantic properties are essentially lost. The reification of the word results in its adoption as an iconographic object, a material entity. For an overview of Spatola's poetry, see Elena Urgnani, 'Adriano Spatola.'

10 For a critical overview of Porta's poetry, see Sasso, *Antonio Porta*; Moroni, *Essere e fare*; Picchione, *Introduzione a Antonio Porta.*

11 For a critical overview of Balestrini's poetry, see Livorni, 'Nanni Balestrini'; Smith, 'Nanni Balestrini.'

WORKS CITED

Balestrini, Nanni. *Come si agisce.* Milan: Feltrinelli, 1963.

– *Ma noi facciamone un'altra.* Milan: Feltrinelli, 1968.

Balestrini, Nanni, and Alfredo Giuliani, eds. *Gruppo 63: la nuova letteratura, 34 scrittori, Palermo ottobre 1963.* Milan: Feltrinelli, 1964.

Barilli, Renato, and Angelo Guglielmi, eds. *Gruppo 63: critica e teoria.* Milan: Feltrinelli, 1976.

Benjamin, Walter. *Illuminations.* Ed. Hannah Arendt. New York: Schocken Books, 1969.

Curi, Fausto, ed. *Edoardo Sanguineti: opere e introduzione critica.* Verona: Anterem, 1993.

Eco, Umberto, ed. *Apocalisse.* Milan: Mazotta, 1979.

Livorni, Ernesto. 'Nanni Balestrini.' In Giovanna De Stasio Wedel, Glauco Cambon, and Antonio Iliano, eds. *Twentieth-Century Italian Poets.* Detroit and London: Bruccoli Clark Layman, 1993.

Moroni, Mario. *Essere e fare: l'itinerario poetico di Antonio Porta.* Rimini: Luisè, 1991.

Picchione, John. *Introduzione a Antonio Porta.* Rome and Bari: Laterza, 1995.

– *The New Avant-garde in Italy: Theoretical Debate and Poetic Practices.* Toronto: University of Toronto Press, 2004.

Pietropaoli, Antonio. *Unità e trinità di Edoardo Sanguineti: poesia e poetica.* Naples: Edizioni Scientifiche Italiane, 1991.

Porta Antonio. *Cara.* Milan: Feltrinelli, 1969.

– *Metropolis.* Milan: Feltrinelli, 1971.

Sanguineti, Edoardo. *Bisbidis.* Milan: Feltrinelli, 1987.

– *Erotopaegnia.* Milan: Rusconi Paolazzi, 1961.

– *Il gatto lupesco: poesie 1982–2001.* Milan: Feltrinelli, 2002.

– *Ideologia e linguaggio.* Milan: Feltrinelli, 1965; rev. ed., Milan: Feltrinelli, 1970.

– *Laborintus.* Varese: Editrice Magenta, 1956.

– *Mikrokosmos: poesie 1951–2004.* Ed. Erminio Risso. Milan: Feltrinelli: 2004.

– *Novissimum testamentum.* Lecce: Piero Manni, 1986.

– *Segnalibro: poesie 1951–1981.* Milan: Feltrinelli, 1982.

Sasso, Luigi. *Antonio Porta.* Florence: La Nuova Italia, 1980.

Sica, Gabriella. *Sanguineti.* Florence: La Nuova Italia, 1974.

Smith, Lawrence R. 'Nanni Balestrini.' In John Picchione and Lawrence R. Smith, eds., *Twentieth-Century Italian Poetry: An Anthology.* Toronto: University of Toronto Press, 1993.

Spatola, Adriano. *Zeroglifici.* Bologna: Sampietro, 1966; *Zerogliphics.* Los Angeles: Red Hill Press, 1977.

Urgnani, Elena. 'Adriano Spatola.' In Giovanna De Stasio Wedel, Glauco Cambon, and Antonio Iliano, eds. *Twentieth-Century Italian Poets.* Detroit and London: Bruccoli Clark Layman, 1993.

Wlassics, Tibor. 'Edoardo Sanguineti.' In Gianni Grana (ed.), *Letteratura italiana: i contemporanei,* vol. 6. Milan: Marzorati, 1974.

7 Language, Gender, and Sexuality in the *Neoavanguardia*

LUCIA RE

The Originality of the Italian Neo-avant-garde

Like its 'historical' predecessor, the Italian neo-avant-garde was essentially male-dominated. Although it is difficult to pinpoint exactly where and when the Italian neo-avant-garde was born, the founding of the journal *Il verri* by Luciano Anceschi in Milan in 1956 is often cited as its starting point, while the publication in 1961 of the anthology *I novissimi*, containing excerpts from the work of Nanni Balestrini, Alfredo Giuliani, Elio Pagliarani, Antonio Porta, and Edoardo Sanguineti, is considered its official birth.[1] The all-male group of *novissimi* poets went on to form the core of the larger Gruppo 63, in which women were a tiny and marginalized minority. Out of twenty-nine participants who spoke or read from their work at the first meeting of the group (in Palermo, October 1963) only two were women: Amelia Rosselli and Carla Vasio. All ten writers whose work was staged in the evening devoted to theatre were male, although Piera Degli Esposti, Annita Nosei, and Carmen Scarpitta participated as actors. Subsequent meetings were supposed to be more open and diverse, but the gender ratio remained substantially unchanged.[2] No women participated in the final meeting of the group, held in Fano in May 1967.

A selection of texts from the 1963 meeting (along with additional texts by other writers) was published in the anthology *Gruppo 63: la nuova letteratura, 34 scrittori, Palermo 1963*, edited by Nanni Balestrini and Alfredo Giuliani. This anthology includes Carla Vasio's 'I grandi riflessi' and an excerpt from Rosselli's *Variazioni belliche*, both of which were retained for the new, revised (and rather revisionist) edition, also edited by Balestrini and Giuliani, entitled *Gruppo 63: l'antologia*, published in 2002, shortly before the celebrations for the fortieth anniversary of the Gruppo 63 in Bologna (8–11 May 2003) under the direction of Renato Barilli, Niva Lorenzini, and Fausto Curi and the auspices of the Assessorato alla Cultura, Provincia di Bologna.[3] Seeking to present a more balanced and comprehensive vision of the *neoavanguardia*, this new edition of the 1964 anthology includes texts (all written before 1969) by thirteen writers who were reputed to be close to the spirit of the Gruppo 63 even though they did not participate in the group meetings. Only three of these new texts are by women: Patrizia Vicinelli, Giulia Niccolai, and Alice Ceresa.[4] Even in hindsight then, it appears that women did not have much to do with the whole project of the Gruppo 63. Yet an examination of the theories and experimental practices of Italian neo-avant-garde groups spanning roughly the period from the mid-1950s to the late 1960s reveals elements of great interest and value to women.

One element is the urge to 'demystify' and 'demythify.' This urge – which filled the air of the first meeting of the Gruppo 63 in Palermo and became a sort of lucid and compelling passion – was informed in part by Marxist theory, by the work of the Frankfurt school (especially Adorno and Benjamin) and Lucien Goldmann, and by the materialist esthetics of Galvano Della Volpe. The early ground-breaking essays by Roland Barthes on the role of myth in contemporary life (in particular, *Mythologies*) were also a source of inspiration.[5] During the 2003 celebrations of the fortieth anniversary of that meeting Alfredo Giuliani and Edoardo Sanguineti also cited Alberto Savinio's 1947 essay 'La fine dei modelli' as a crucial influence. Avant-garde intellectuals and artists of the younger, postwar generation in Italy felt the need to question and critique the models, images, and values imposed on one hand by traditional academic and literary culture, and on the other, by the logic of the new consumer capitalism. Although they would eventually become stereotypes of a certain 'sixties' rhetoric, in the late 1950s and early 1960s the emergence of the overlapping concepts of demystification and demythification, with the process of critique and oppositionality that they entailed, marked a radical turning point unequaled in the history of modern Italian culture.[6] What exactly did this oppositional and critical attitude imply in the specific cultural situation of Italy?

Around the end of the 1950s, under the impetus of the economic boom, the entire organization of culture in Italy changed radically, in order to develop the means to meet the challenges of the newly born mass culture. The advent of television in 1954 had introduced Italy to the 'global village' of communication; the publishing world began a rapid process of development and modernization, for the first time thinking of itself as an industry in an open market, and of its readers as consumers. The new culture industry thrived on the consumerism created by the economic boom, and also profited from the mass schooling introduced in 1962. The pivotal symbolic moment in the advent of the Italian culture industry was the successful introduction by the major publisher Mondadori of the 'Oscar,' a new mass-produced paperback series sold for the first time in newspaper kiosks on every street corner (rather than in bookstores). In this new situation, the role of intellectuals in Italy also changed radically, as they increasingly found themselves working as 'specialists' and 'technicians' employed by *imprese culturali* such as publishing houses, magazines, newspapers, radio, and television. This was indeed the predicament of the best-known writers and artists of the neo-avant-garde, who thus discovered how illusory any pretence of intellectual autonomy was. The claims made by previous generations of intellectuals (especially of the Crocean tradition) regarding the purity of art and its separation from the economic and political spheres were increasingly unmasked as deluded and empty.

Without making any explicit connection with the futurists – who were their largely unacknowledged forerunners in this kind of demystification of art – the intellectuals of the Italian neo-avant-garde nevertheless followed in their footsteps. Like the futurists, they self-consciously pointed to the 'prostituted' nature of art, but while the futurists were able to view this condition in ironically positive terms and even to build an anti-establishment mythology based on it, no such idealism was possible for the neo-avant-garde. To the young avant-gardists of the late 1950s and early 1960s it was clear that in the world of mass culture and the culture industry, art was a commodity and the intellectual a producer involved in a specific production process based on the law of supply and demand. But, unlike the futurists, the young avant-garde could no longer claim or even hope for a special status – a transformative power – for the commodity that they were selling: avant-garde art. Art was just one consumer good among many. In this context, the traditional intellectual in his ivory tower had vanished and even the romance of the avant-garde had become suspect. Peter Bürger argues that the very notion of neo-avant-garde is a contradiction in terms and that the only real avant-garde was the historical avant-garde, which broke not only with traditional representational systems but with art itself as an institution (*Theory of the Avant-garde* 61–3).

Nonetheless, two key factors contributed to making the Italian neo-avant-garde a reality. Unlike the postmodern condition, which, with its profound transformation of the systems of cultural communication, rendered any avant-garde type of attack against traditional and institutional discourses ineffective and useless by immediately incorporating it (through the automatic colonization of ideas, feelings, and the individual and collective imagination), the late-modern phase of Italian culture still allowed for a cultural militancy of sorts. In Italy during the 1950s and 1960s it was still possible (or seemed possible) to be *intellettuali contro.* This was due partly to historical and political circumstances and partly to the desire, particularly resilient and resistant in Italy after the Second World War, to believe in the oppositional power of elite intellectual groups. The massive postwar demonization and repression of the *ventennio nero,* the tendency to see the past twenty years of fascism as a kind of wasteland, entirely empty (with the exception of *ermetismo* and a few other supposedly oppositional discourses) of any legitimate cultural value, made it conveniently simple for the *neoavanguardia* to dismiss futurism (given its collusion with fascism) as a false or misguided avant-garde, or to accept – rather incongruously – only the formal innovativeness of futurism while denouncing its politics.[7] The process involved was analogous to the Freudian model of repression and repetition. The *reprise* of certain devices and strategies of futurism by the *neoavanguardia* was largely made possible by resisting and disavowing futurism itself.

The *neoavanguardia,* which was preponderantly made up of Marxists and other extreme left-wing intellectuals (who were, however, opposed to the myopic cultural preferences of the Italian Communist Party) felt itself to be, despite its name, the first *real* avant-garde movement in Italy worthy of being identified as such. The *neoavanguardia* acknowledged ties only with Brecht, with French surrealism, and with other politically acceptable experimentalists outside of Italy, therefore nourishing and feeding itself on the myth of its own originality (a myth that, ironically, as Rosalind Krauss has observed, is shared by all avant-gardes).[8] Like the futurists, the young protagonists of the *neoavanguardia* cultivated the myth of their own youth and 'newness.' The label *novissimi,* however, was rather ambiguous: while it pointed to the novelty and youthfulness of the movement (whose members were born for the most part between the late 1920s and the early 1930s), it also clearly echoed (ironically and parodically) the *dolce stil novo,* a movement whose gendered approach to the lyric form would reemerge, sometimes in uncanny ways, in the poetry of the *novissimi* themselves.

As Hal Foster has argued, neo-avant-gardist repetition does not necessarily entail a farcical return of the same.[9] Disavowal can be productive and creative even as it hides its origins from itself. The changed historical conditions of Italy in the late 1950s and early 1960s made a return of avant-garde practices seem necessary and important. The Italian neo-avant-garde's polemical platform – which functioned much like the anti-Giolittian, anti-socialist, and anti-decadent platform did for futurism – was based on the bankruptcy of certain rhetorical ideals of the Resistance and of the Reconstruction, and on what the neo-avant-gardists saw as the failure of the postwar neorealist model of mimetic representation and political commitment.[10] Their iconoclasm was a symptom of the discontent produced by the hegemonic neorealist aesthetics of mimetic representation and by the neorealist type of intellectual. They felt the need to create new and different political and aesthetic models for themselves. Finally, what united the members of the *neoavanguardia*, in addition to the call for a radical type of innovation, was the need to unmask the falsifications of language.

Demystification and demythification for the *neoavanguardia* did not imply the belief that one could somehow step outside of ideology in an absolute sense. The crucial point about the stand of the Italian neo-avant-garde compared to other avant-garde movements and other influential components of the Italian leftist intelligentia (for example Marxist intellectuals such as Pier Paolo Pasolini and Franco Fortini) was precisely this.[11] Pasolini and Fortini, although they differed from each other, both still believed in the traditional oppositional function and autonomy of the leftist intellectual and in his ability – in a historicist and Marxist perspective – to commit himself to a radical type of political activity that systematically unmasked and exposed the ideological machinations of the neocapitalist regime and its institutions; the neo-avant-gardists had no such faith. On the contrary, in a sort of Althusserian and Foucaldian perspective antelitteram, they saw ideology and power as all-pervasive and essentially inescapable. This perspective was crucial in two principal and related respects: one was the attitude of some of the principal leaders of the *neoavanguardia* towards the institutions; the other was their understanding of language.

Wary of what Steven Connor has called 'the romance of the margins,' (*Postmodernist Culture* 228) the Italian neo-avant-garde did not believe in the subversive potential of the marginal condition. Like the futurists before them (but without acknowledging them as predecessors) the neo-avant-garde sought admission and legitimation in the centres of cultural power. Although specific positions varied and eventually led to an insuperable schism in 1968, the overall philosophy of the Italian neo-avant-garde entailed learning to navigate and in some instances to 'sabotage' the institutions in various ways from within while simultaneously carrying out – whenever possible – reform.

The very institutions and institutional sites through which discourse and subjectivities are moulded by power could, in their view, be used as strategic sites of resistance and counterdiscourse. Thus, for example, Nanni Balestrini, the most radical member of the *novissimi,* was employed by Feltrinelli, a major publisher who agreed to print, among other series, one devoted to the group's writings as well as Balestrini's own work. Giuliani and Edoardo Sanguineti, also original members of the *novissimi,* had successful academic careers in the Italian state university. Angelo Guglielmi, one of the theorists of Gruppo 63, worked for the Italian State Television Network (RAI). From the beginning the original *novissimi* (Balestrini, Giuliani, Elio Pagliarani, Antonio Porta, and Sanguineti) mounted a veritable campaign to gain media exposure and move from the margins into the mainstream. The new edition of the *I novissimi* anthology, published by Einaudi, Italy's most distinguished publisher, is one indication of their extraordinary success. (The first edition was published in 1961 by a small press co-owned and directed by Antonio Porta's father.) The Einaudi edition went through five reprints by 1969.

Unlike any previous literary or artistic movement in the history of Italian culture (with the partial exception of futurism), the *neoavanguardia* gained considerable media exposure. The group's polemical exchanges and the chronicle of their meetings between 1963 and 1967 were reported and given significant coverage in wide-circulation newspapers and magazines, and became the object of lively controversies. Some of the newspaper journalists who wrote about the group were sympathizers (Andrea Barbato, Nello Ajello) or even members of the group (Alberto Arbasino, Furio Colombo, Elio Pagliarani). Between 1964 and 1968 there was a veritable explosion of experimental and avant-garde poetry and prose, published by major commercial publishers in Italy. In its heyday (1967–8) *Quindici,* one of the principal neo-avant-garde journals, is reported to have reached a circulation of 20,000 – an unprecedented record for a cultural journal.[12] The publication of the last issue in the spring of 1969 is generally considered the end of the most creative phase of the new avant-garde in Italy, although the critical and theoretical debate continued for some time after.[13]

The *neoavanguardia*'s attitude towards institutions was based on its vision of language as fundamentally ideological. It was through the manipulation of language and specific discourse formations (they thought) that institutions and institutional sites managed power and maintained their hegemonic positions. And although there was, according to the *neoavanguardia*, a potential space for strategic resistance and counterdiscourse, the real was thought to be unavailable per se outside the ideologically informed (and deformed) structures of neocapitalist language.[14] As Guido Guglielmi (Angelo's brother) and Elio Pagliarani wrote in their preface to *Manuale di poesia sperimentale* (1966), an anthology containing selections from the work of twenty-two poets: 'the paradox of poetry today consists in its having to contest an instrument by availing itself – and there is no way around it – of that very same instrument' (12).[15] Any political intervention therefore had to be focused on language (and ideology) itself.

The two ways for the *neoavanguardia* to go about this emerged quickly at the first meeting of the Gruppo 63 in Palermo. One was the anarchist resistance line, whereby the avant-garde text, in a sort of mimesis of chaos, exacerbated and thus exposed the alienation of language in the neocapitalist world by using pastiche, collage, bricolage, etc. Thus, while the artwork could not evade or escape neocapitalist ideology or its own status as commodity, it could refuse to communicate messages or any particular meaning, for these were assumed to be perpetually already compromised. Nanni Balestrini's work fell into this category, which was also endorsed in Palermo by Angelo Guglielmi.[16]

The second and less extreme line, championed by Sanguineti, maintained that the hold of ideology on language was not absolute, but was linked to specific bourgeois norms and codes that are dominant in contemporary society. Thus by working against these norms, in the linguistic interstices, so to speak, of the system, or with linguistic realities that the system 'represses' and attempts to contain and normalize, the avant-garde text could contribute to bringing about radical linguistic and cultural change. For Sanguineti, the mythologies of the neocapitalist bourgeoisie could be countered only by using countermythologies. In his 1961 defence of the mythic character of poetry, Sanguineti stated that poetic discourse as he saw it was precisely an alternative and critically productive source of myths and symbols that could 'deform' and contrast the mythologies of the dominant bourgeois culture.[17]

Although, as we shall see, the leaders of the Italian neo-avant-garde were for the most part oblivious or indifferent to the ideology of gender in their own discourse, both the linguistic and the institutional scenarios with which they worked prefigured the dilemmas of the Italian and international women's movements vis-à-vis the problem of language and myth, on one hand, and the question of how to reach and change the mentality of a larger audience, on the other.

My use of the term 'women's movement' does not necessarily refer to feminism, and the political movement that arose in Italy, the United States, and elsewhere during the late 1960s and early 1970s, and was specifically committed to the cause of women, or, indeed any unified field of theory or political position. I prefer to use the term 'women's movement' in a larger sense, referring to the multiple and different cultural practices and interventions from the position called 'woman' or 'the feminine' in which the question of gender is posed more or less directly and more or less explicitly in Italian culture, beginning in the 1960s, in conjunction with issues of creativity, subjectivity, and the politics of discourse in the contemporary world.

Italian women seeking to negotiate their position in regard to the hegemonic discursive practices of the 1960s and 1970s in Italy (before the advent of a full-fledged and self-conscious feminist theory) found themselves dealing with issues structurally similar to those tackled by the Italian neo-avant-garde, and, however indirectly, they learned and profited in a number of ways from the experience, the triumphs, and the failures of the *neoavanguardia.* To be sure, other cultural phenomena were also of great importance for the intellectual formation of the Italian women's movement. Among them were American feminism, Simone De Beauvoir's *The Second Sex* (which appeared in Italian in 1961), and later the French postructuralist thought of Althusser, Foucault, Lacan, and Deleuze that so deeply informed a range of seminal feminist thinkers, including Hélène Cixous and Luce Irigaray. Cixous and especially Irigaray in turn became extremely influential among Italian feminists in the 1970s. However, the early phase of the Italian women's movement, from 1965 to 1969, when the first discussion groups were coming together, coincided with – and doubtlessly profited from – the phase of the great debates of the *neoavanguardia.*

The *neoavanguardia*'s position on language in particular prefigured and informed that of the Italian women's movement, whose critique of authority addressed first and foremost the realm of culture and the hegemonic use of language itself. Since the only language women had was the hegemonic phallologocentric language of patriarchy (albeit in its culturally specific formations), the alternatives for women searching for a way out were similar to those formulated by the *neoavanguardia.* The options confronted and theorized by the women's movement were in fact either a radical refusal of the hegemonic language of patriarchy (which carried with it the problem of how to communicate at all) or a more 'compromised' type of negotiation with that language, including attempts to deconstruct it from within by mimicking it, mocking it, ironizing it, and finally transforming it. The transformation could occur by foregrounding elements that patriarchal language systematically repressed, while simultaneously attempting to construct new and positive mythologies. The reappropriation and rewriting of myths eventually became a staple of Italian feminist thought.

The problems implicit in the institution of language are carried through to all other institutions that are informed by it. Thus the dilemmas faced by the leaders of the Italian neo-avant-garde and their strategies in dealing with institutions such as the media, the publishing industry, museums, and the academy, constituted a useful and instructive precedent for women writers, artists, and intellectuals wishing to make their discourse known to a wider audience than the restricted one of obscure and alternative avant-garde practices. Whatever its specific failures and errors, the experience of the Italian neo-avant-garde demonstrated that it was possible to navigate institutions while maintaining an oppositional and alternative stand of sorts. However perilous and ambiguous this position might have been, it was nevertheless a valuable experiment, given the historical and cultural context in which it arose, in that it demonstrated that one could not entirely 'stand outside' or wholly 'reject' the system, but had to work with and within it at some level.

Women did not simply repeat or mimic the experience of the 'male' *neoavanguardia*. Rather, they learned from its experience, especially its impasses, and they proceeded to remap the territory to be explored, redefining the frontiers of the avant-garde in different directions. Thus, for example, during the 1970s many women in Italy were involved in the phenomenon of 'double militancy': they were simultaneously active in the experimental cultural practices of separatist women's groups and in institutional bodies such as parties and other political organizations.[18]

One of the principal elements of the platform of the Italian neo-avant-garde that was of value to Italian female intellectuals was the connection, insistently drawn by Sanguineti and others, between politics and writing (and aesthetic production in general). Although the *neoavanguardia* inherited its preoccupation with 'the social' and 'the political' from both neorealism and futurism, its originality consisted in dealing with the ideological and the social as linguistic issues. Particular practices of working with language in writing (and aesthetic practices in general) were perceived as intrinsically political acts. In this regard Jean Thibaudeau wrote in *Tel Quel* of a specifically 'Italian way' to the avant-garde.[19] Its politics was a politics of form.

In his influential and controversial essay 'Del modo di formare come impegno sulla realtà' (1962),[20] Umberto Eco lucidly theorizes this crucial position of the *neoavanguardia.* A writer's 'form,' he argues, the language of the text, is the true content (and hence the politics) of the work. The avant-garde artist innovates at the level of form by destroying the ordered system of conventional language that perpetuates the mystifications of the dominant ideology. The problem, as Eco was increasingly to acknowledge in his later work, was how to revolutionize form while still maintaining communication with the reader.

Throughout its development the Italian neo-avant-garde promoted a radically new relationship between reader and text, first theorized by Eco in *Opera aperta* (1962). In essence, the dismantling of traditional syntax and forms prevented the reader from 'passively' receiving the message of the text, while new and unexpected textual configurations (especially those deploying estranging avant-garde strategies of collage and montage) required the reader to be actively involved in the (re) construction of the text, and exposed the reader to a text that was open to a multiplicity of individual readings. This sudden activism assumed a political significance for the Italian neo-avant-garde, for it was meant to shake the reader or viewer out of the anesthetizing torpor to which traditional literature and art (including to a large degree neorealism) had accustomed him, and to promote a more active critical stand towards all texts and codes of contemporary culture.

Unlike the Anglo-American context, in which the avant-garde was usually construed as politically motivated and antithetical to the merely formalist concerns of modernism, in Italy the borderline between modernism and avant-garde in the 1960s was in many respects a porous and tenuous one, because for the *neoavanguardia* experimentation with language and aesthetic codes constituted by definition a political challenge. Thus, for example, the prose writers of the Italian neo-avant-garde directly embraced as their privileged forerunner one of the greatest masters of Italian modernism, the experimental novelist Carlo Emilio Gadda – especially celebrated for his innovative use of dialects, labyrinthine plots, and pastiche – during a time when various forms of lyrical realism and neorealism ruled.

As the Italian neo-avant-garde saw it, most neorealism – however committed to themes of social change and revolution and other explicit political contents – remained complicitous with the dominant ideology precisely because neorealism did not revolutionize language itself. The *neoavanguardia* wished to open up literary language (or aesthetic discourse in general, including the visual arts) to spoken, colloquial language and to images and codes of the mass media, in a violent and disruptive way capable of exposing the 'mystifications' of both aesthetic discourse and the discourse of power. The *neoavanguardia* experimented with language by making poetic discourse, especially its tropological and figural power, react with or against the different figurality of 'common speech,' and even the new commodified language of the mass media and the culture industry, liberating in the process levels of meaning that were previously 'repressed' in both.[21]

Unlike neorealism (but, in some respects, like futurism), the *neoavanguardia* was aware of language as having a political unconscious. It was also aware of the unconscious itself as a kind of language. Whatever its shortcomings, the Italian neo-avant-garde is thus to be credited with the creation of a new imaginary attuned to the times and to the experience of living in a contradictory culture that was still deeply archaic in some respects and yet an integral part of the culture industry and the global village in others. As it probed this contradictory context, the Italian neo-avant-garde opened up aesthetic discourse to the spheres of the quotidian, of experience, of the body, and of the unconscious – all elements that turned out to be essential to the formation of a new aesthetic and political discourse for women.[22] Even more importantly, these very elements, through the language that expressed them and gave them form, were perceived as being essentially political – as having a political function and impact.

The relevance of this vision to women's politics and aesthetics is clear. In her own influential and visionary avant-garde text 'Le rire de la Méduse' ['The Laugh of the Medusa'] Hélène Cixous states: 'Writing is precisely *the very possibility of change*, the space that can serve as springboard for subversive thought, the precursory movement of a transformation of social and cultural structures.' Although many Italian women writers, artists, and intellectuals tended not to share what appears to be the essentialist connection made by Cixous and others between the female body and feminine writing or visual expression, they did advocate the need to enter into a *corpo a corpo* with the problems of *form* as a way to politicize their aesthetic practices.[23] While the more destructive and disruptive elements of the Italian neo-avant-garde's poetics were soon to exhaust their significance and value, the notion of experimental writing and aesthetic practices as political activities and the activist, critical model of readership had a considerable and lasting impact in Italian culture. Italian women writers, artists, and intellectuals for the most part rejected the more violent disruptive strategies of the *neoavanguardia*, but they remained interested in experimentation, incorporating and adapting in their work the *neoavanguardia*'s passion for working with language and form as a kind of political commitment. The concrete and visual poems of Mirella Bentivoglio and Lucia Marcucci – both formed in the 1960s and 1970s and still active today – are examples of politically informed, feminist experimental aesthetic practices by women which promote the 'activism of the reader.'[24]

Even beyond the realm of creative writing and artistic production, the effects of Italian neo-avant-garde politics and aesthetics, and of the intense debate that surrounded them, were multiple and diverse. At the level of theory and critical thought it is not coincidental that one of the most cogent critiques of the 'science' of linguistics in terms of the politics of gender should have come from a woman scholar, Patrizia Violi, who was a student of Umberto Eco and the author of *L'infinito singolare.* However blind the male *neoavanguardia* might have been to the question of gender, its work with and on language nevertheless laid the foundations for a kind of critique which could then be extended (much to the chagrin of some of the neo-avant-gardists themselves) to unmask the masculinist bias of their own discourse.

The effect of this new critical aesthetics travelled far. Some of the reflections by Teresa de Lauretis (presently one of the most influential feminist critics in the Western world) on the possibility of alternative aesthetic practices in the cinema, and on the complex interplay of codes that in a given text can activate a multiplicity of different readings and responses, are influenced by Eco's reflections on the open work, and by the politics (though not necessarily the practices) of Italian avant-garde aesthetics in the early 1960s.[25] Indeed an argument could be made that some of the most influential contemporary feminist thinkers have, to varying degrees, shaped their thought at least partially in response to avant-garde aesthetics of some kind. Julia Kristeva's relationship to the *Tel Quel* movement and her sustained interest in avant-garde aesthetics in general is the most obvious case, while Cixous' link not only to Joyce's experimentalism (a passion she shares with Eco) but especially to surrealism – although evident from her writing – is yet to be fully explored.

Finally, however apparently removed from the realms within which the *neoavanguardia* operated, the women's movement in Italy from its very inception was marked by an unusual interest in the political possibilities generated by active and personal critical readings of literary works as open works. Women's groups in the 1970s and 1980s practiced the kind of readership that the *neoavanguardia* had tried to encourage and create through the formal structuring of their works as open works. And although the women's groups in Italy most definitely did not (for reasons that will shortly be clear) choose to read Italian neo-avant-garde texts, but instead turned to works by authors such as Emily Dickinson, Virginia Woolf, Ingeborg Bachman, and Adrienne Rich, their experimental reading practices represent in part a creative appropriation of the strategies promoted by the *neoavanguardia*. (Some of Bachman's work was published by Anceschi in *Il verri* and was loved especially by Alfredo Giuliani; she seems thus to provide a direct link between the *neoavanguardia* and the women's movement.)

Both the demystifying and the political impulses of the *neoavanguardia* were very much in tune with the project formulated by the first official feminist group in Italy, known as DEMAU (Demystification of Authority). In 1966, this group (which originated in Milan) published a seminal manifesto that called for the 'demystification of authoritarianism as a theory and a mystique of the moral, cultural and ideological values on which the current division of labor and society as a whole are based' (Bono and Kemp 33). The same urge for demystification and antiauthoritarianism, grounded in the terrain of language and culture, animated the activities of *Rivolta femminile*, a group formed in Rome in June 1970 with Carla Lonzi, Carla Accardi, and Elvira Banotti among its founders. In the tradition of the avant-garde, *Rivolta femminile* also used the manifesto as a tool of communication and demystification, but their demystification was rather unlike the demystification called for only a few years earlier in the United States by Betty Friedan in her classic *The Feminine Mystique* (published in Italy in 1964). In keeping with the liberal tradition, Friedan affirmed the need and ability of individual women to change their patterns of behaviour but failed to engage the ideological question of the language that shapes the individual. The Italian feminist movement instead, from its inception (and well before the advent of Luce Irigaray's work), devoted a great deal of attention to the question of language and to the critical role of literature and aesthetic discourse in shaping consciousness.

The work of Carla Lonzi (1931–82), the first postwar Italian feminist theorist and the author of the fundamental *Sputiamo su Hegel* (1970), continued to inspire Italian feminist thought through the 1980s and 1990s. Although her life and career before *Rivolta femminile* are usually ignored, it is important to remember that she was an art historian and critic, and that in the 1960s she was in close contact with elite members of the Gruppo 63 through the organization of exhibitions of contemporary avant-garde painting. Lonzi was also a poet, although her poems, written between 1958 and 1963, were published only posthumously in the collection *Scacco ragionato* (1985). Her *Autoritratto* (1969) is a pioneering, feminist avant-garde 'open work' of creative art criticism. While Lonzi's immersion in the culture of the neo-avant-garde may account for her understanding of language as 'già politica' (an insight which was to be crucial to Italian feminism), her experience – even as a highly emancipated woman – of always being and feeling subordinate in a cultural scene that was essentially masculine was equally important for the conceptualization of her feminism. She came to see so-called emancipation as mere deception, a way for masculine culture to preserve its hegemony by placing and keeping women in a complementary and essentially secondary, subordinate position. Just as the *neoavanguardia* had demystified the claims of Crocean culture and Communist ideology, women now had the cultural and linguistic tools to deprive masculine culture of its illusion of being gender-neutral and equally liberating for all.

In dropping out of the masculine avant-garde world and devoting herself to feminist theory, research, and publishing for *Rivolta femminile*, Lonzi did not advocate separatism per se, but instead sought to re-educate both men and women to a different vision of sexual difference, where woman would no longer be merely complementary.[26] Ironically then, it was the very masculinism of the avant-garde cultural scene in which she moved that fostered her decisive step into feminism.

Carla Accardi, another original member of *Rivolta femminile*, was an avant-garde abstract painter. She met Lonzi in 1963 when Lonzi wrote the introduction to one of her exhibitions. They became friends and intellectual partners, and in 1970 co-authored the pamphlet 'Rivolta femminile.'[27] Accardi's work was familiar to the Gruppo 63 especially through Gillo Dorfles (a member who was an art critic) and she was involved in some of the group's activities. A number of Gruppo 63 members, particularly Sanguineti and Balestrini, were very interested in abstract painting. Accardi attended the second meeting in Palermo and became acquainted with the *novissimi* Giuliani,[28] Pagliarani, and Balestrini. One of her paintings was shown at an exhibition organized by Balestrini in 1965 at the Feltrinelli bookshop in Rome. Nevertheless,

Accardi remained on the margins of the group, and her name rarely appeared in their publications. She received more attention from the younger experimentalists, including Adriano Spatola, who published one of her paintings in the journal *Malebolge*.[29]

The potential connection between the *neoavanguardia* and the women's movement in Italy was, at best, problematic. Women poets, thinkers, artists, and critics who, in the 1960s and 1970s, felt drawn both by the *neoavanguardia* movement and by the women's movement, found themselves in a difficult and conflictual position. Despite their affinities, there is no phenomenon of 'double militancy' on the part of women in organizations and groups of the women's movement and in the *neoavanguardia*; even after 1968 the male leaders of the neo-avant-garde showed no interest in the kinds of questions posed by feminism, nor did they attempt to reconfigure the traditional polarities of gender in their work. In fact, they seemed to want to rethink and undermine all traditional polarities *except* that of gender,[30] thus showing themselves as poor followers even of some of their own male models, such as Savinio.

Women connected to the Italian neo-avant-garde, on the other hand, felt especially uneasy with the feminist movement, even when their practices of writing were implicitly feminist. And later, when women intellectuals (especially poets and philosophers) in Italy tackled the question of myth and demythification, they did so largely on their own, some – most notably the feminist group Diotima – opting explicitly for a gender separation even more radical and more self-conscious than that practiced by the male elite of the *neoavanguardia*.[31]

Poetry as Critique in the Work of Sanguineti, Pagliarani, Porta, and Balestrini

In view of its preoccupation with the rhetorical and figural structures of language on one hand, and the structures of experience and the unconscious on the other, it is not surprising that the initial and principal impetus for the movement of the neo-avant-garde should have come from poetry, and only subsequently expand to narrative and the visual arts. As Cixous remarks, while novelists are allies of representationalism, 'poetry involves gaining strength through the unconscious, and ... the unconscious, that other limitless country, is the place where the repressed manage to survive: women, or, as Hoffmann would say, fairies' ('Laugh of the Medusa' 250). The Italian neo-avant-garde at its best probed the linguistic and political unconscious of the dominant bourgeois culture and of the new Italian consumer society, exposing their alienation and repressiveness and, at the same time, working with the liberatory potential of their contradictions.[32]

The polemic against the 'rationality' of the dominant ideology was carried out through a self-conscious use of 'irrationality,' by plunging into the language of the unconscious. For example, in *Laborintus*, one of his texts that he chose as a showcase piece to be included in the anthology *I novissimi*, Edoardo Sanguineti – who was perhaps the most successful and accomplished exponent of the *novissimi* and of the Gruppo 63 – mimics an oneiric type of language, creating a self-consciously 'regressive' discourse. The unconscious for Sanguineti is the place where the estrangement of 'common language' and of its ideologies is most powerful. In an undifferentiated flux interrupted only by the division of the poem into sections, phrases apparently taken from the familiar (for Sanguineti) language of Marxist cultural criticism ('Le condizioni esterne è evidente esistono realmente queste condizioni') and eroticism ('toccami'), are juxtaposed with archetypal images drawn from alchemy (the famous alchemist Nicolas Flamel is referred to several times) and quotations in different languages (including medieval Latin, French, German, and Greek) from sources ranging from Aristotle to Nicholas of Cusa to Kant to Goethe. No syntactical order is used and the text seems to follow a delirious, free-associating logic inspired by the anarchic and scrambled order of dreams. Fragments of phrases and words are mingled together in a fluid stream with no rhythmical scheme. Clusters of meaning and themes coalesce through a non-linear, impressionistic coming together of images (which has prompted comparison between Sanguineti's work and some forms of abstract expressionism).

In a later text, 'Purgatorio de l'Inferno,' Sanguineti works stubbornly with rhetorical, rhythmic, and syntactic figures of the Italian literary tradition in an attempt to disalienate them through radical simplification.[33] For instance, rhymes often occur simply as repetitions of the same word.[34] At the same time, spoken, colloquial language – shreds of actual phrases and conversations, taken mostly from Sanguineti's own middle-class intellectual milieu – become key elements of the text. The way spoken language is used however, is quite different from neorealism. It is often difficult to tell who is saying what and in what context. The point is not, in fact, to 'let reality in' or to transcribe actual experience, but rather to operate a simultaneous estrangement of both 'the literary' and 'reality' or 'experience' through their defamiliarizing juxtaposition. In so doing, Sanguineti and the Italian neo-avant-garde updated strategies developed by the historical avant-garde and especially by the modernist master of defamiliarization, Bertolt Brecht.[35]

While the use of avant-garde techniques of estrangement and defamiliarization by the historical avant-garde were developed intuitively, the Italian neo-avant-garde also benefited from the critical reflections and the theoretical formulations of the Russian formalists (especially for the notion of *ostranenje*) and of the newly disclosed 'structuralist revolution,' in particular the ground-breaking work of Saussure and Jakobson. The notion of language as a system of signs, the concepts of *langue* and *parole*, and the theory of the different functions of language – however freely and perhaps imprecisely or 'wildly' interpreted and manipulated – contributed to transform the Italian neo-avant-garde into a highly self-conscious 'semiotic' movement.[36] The Gruppo 63 as a whole was responsive to the work of Italy's first and foremost semiotician, Umberto Eco, who was in turn influenced in his own theoretical work by the new 'open' and estranging aesthetics of avant-garde texts.

Although the *novissimi* and later the core members of the Gruppo 63 shared a project of critique and demystification vis-à-vis the dominant ideology of contemporary society, and had a common intellectual framework that, for the first time in the history of Italian literature and art, was open to international developments in a variety of disciplines ranging from phenomenology to psychoanalysis to communication theory and semiotics, the ways they went about actually giving form to their works – and hence their politics – varied widely.

Elio Pagliarani was especially interested in problems related to the communicative function and the critique of 'the signified.' His primary strategy from the 1950s on was the 'widening' of the semantic field of poetry to include and expose the degrading aspects of the new capitalism. His expansion of poetic diction tended towards the undermining of the difference between poetic and non-poetic words, and a radical 'democratization' of literary language. He therefore saw himself as a part of a particular tradition in twentieth-century poetry ranging from the Italian *crepuscolari* to the futurists and other historical avant-gardes, with particular reference to the work of Brecht and Majakovskij. Demystification (in the Barthesian sense) and communication are the pivotal points of Pagliarani's poetics, for unlike some other poets and artists of the Italian neo-avant-garde, Pagliarani insisted on the need to not dismantle the communicative function altogether. On the contrary, communication was essential to the political projectuality of his work. He wrote in 'Per una definizione dell'avanguardia' that what was needed was 'Contestazione di significati precostituiti della *langue*, e *progettazione* di nuovi significati.'[37] For Pagliarani, the political project of poetry was essentially linguistic and semiotic. Poetry had to inject into language a new and qualitatively different vitality while simultaneously exposing and disposing of its worn out, alienated forms. To do so, poetry had to draw on the resources of the extraliterary, the great reservoir of 'the prosaic' and the *lingua d'uso* or *linguaggio medio.*[38]

Pagliarani's best known and most representative long poem, 'La ragazza Carla,' is an example of the interface of the literary and the colloquial, of the language of poetry and the speech of everyday life, which generates the estrangement of both. Contrary to Sanguineti, Pagliarani (who was influenced perhaps more by Palazzeschi than by any other futurist) chose a highly readable and loosely narrative form in which the figures of poetry could emerge almost casually, even randomly, as surprising and simple 'comings into poetry' (for example, alliterations, rhymes, or hendecasyllables) of everyday language. The effect of reciprocal defamiliarization of the literary by the colloquial, and the technique of the collage and the 'ready-made' (including excerpts from a typing manual and other such prosaic texts) is heightened by Pagliarani's effective choice of a 'low' colloquial register, the language of clerks and typists, of working men and women.

The search for a non-alienated, authentic, and therefore politically subversive expression of real experience, and the primary role of communication in the literary and generally aesthetic text, were of great interest to Italian women poets, artists, and feminists, as was the critique of traditional forms of representation and of human subjectivity that perpetuate the mythologies of bourgeois culture.[39]

The critique of bourgeois individualism was at the centre of much of the work of Antonio Porta. His *Metropolis*, for example, effectively enacts a deconstruction of the Italian lyric tradition (and of the lyric as a mode) along with the entire notion of lyric subjectivity. Being a form almost entirely centred, at least since the *dolce stil novo* and Petrarch, on a subjectivity that is essentially gendered *male*, and on the power of the masculine gaze and ego and the subjection or objectification of the feminine, the deconstruction of the lyric and the search for alternative forms were of particular concern to women poets. This critical tendency of the *neoavanguardia*, whose original motto had been 'la riduzione dell'io' [the reduction of the 'I'], was directly inspired by Italian phenomenological thought, particularly the work of Luciano Anceschi.[40] The futurists had already deconstructed the lyric in their own way, of course. Porta attempted to do the same, but he took an approach at the opposite end of the spectrum from futurism's 'multiplied man.' His target was still the lyrical 'io,' but instead of dissolving it by multiplying it, he dissolved it by reducing it to near invisibility. For Porta, in order for poetry to provide some kind of epistemological access to reality, the interests and desires of the individual subject – which are imbued with ideology – must be bracketed. The de-ideologized poet, however, did not cease to be interested in the mind and the psyche per se. On the contrary, the mind and the psyche remained very much his object of inquiry. What was presumably left behind, as the disinterested seeker of knowledge watches his mind experience the world, was the individual 'I.' This represented a radical break with the conventions of the lyric deployed by the master poets of *ermetismo* – which in the early 1960s still constituted an important hegemonic tradition in Italy – as well as a break with the equally hegemonic language of realist and neorealist poetry.

In *Metropolis*,[41] which is composed of five sections ('Quello che tutti pensano,' 'La rose,' 'Modello di bambini per linguaggio,' 'Modello di linguaggio per coppie che lavorano,' 'Modello per autoritratti') Porta sabotages the lyric in a number of different ways. One is by breaking down and fragmenting the traditional sentence structure, the accumulation and subordination of relative and oppositional clauses that give the lyric composition its organic coherence and allow for the meaningful articulation of discourse and the positioning of both subject and object.[42] In the section entitled 'La rose' (the very title of which parodically alludes to a lyric topos, with a wink at Gertrude Stein), each line comprises an entire and usually very simple syntactic unit, for example: 'le difese ingannevoli odorano la rosa' (58) or 'il vento artificiale simula l'inverno' (68). There are no conjunctions in this entire section, nor are there any syntactic connections between the lines. What Porta does is effectively to foreground and expose the self-referential, closed, and monad-like character of the lyric, a critique that is particularly poignant in a literary culture such as the modern Italian one.

At the level of imagery Porta stages a highly ironic, stilted, and parodic re-enactment (which inevitably recalls analogous if more vociferous futurist indictments) of the voyeuristic objectification of woman in the Western poetic tradition, with particular reference to aestheticism and, in Italy, D'Annunzio. In a hermetically sealed garden, a mysterious female figure, whose only speech act consists in whispering to her dogs, performs purposeless acts 'of beauty': 'coi fazzoletti di seta cuce una piccola vela / ... dita annodate in passeri guanti in forma d'ali / ... con l'aiuto del fuoco percorre le finestre' (58–68). The principal topos that Porta alludes to here is that of the *hortus conclusus,* which also functions as a figure for the self-enclosed, sterile nature of lyric poetry. Thus, for Porta, the lyric can hardly pose as a corrective for or an antidote to the worn out and banal commonplaces or *cose sentite dire* which, in an ironic reprise of Flaubert, are listed in the first section, signifying the utmost in alienation.

The three 'Modello' sections that follow 'La rose' each point to a possible strategy for opening poetry up to reality. Each presents a radical simplification of poetic form, an attempt to disalienate it through the reduction of poetry to the most elementary of its resources. 'Modello di bambini per linguaggio,' for example, 'regresses' to a simple binary rhythm, reminiscent of a playful manipulation of the signifier: 'verdu dura / carne dente / inna sono / rato mo' (78). Turning to the model of interpersonal communication, the section 'Modello di linguaggio per coppie che lavorano' deploys a similar strategy, with a binary structure and pervasive use of repetition: 'le foglie s'inverdiscono e aprono la bocca / le foglie spalancano e asciugano la bocca' (80); or: 'senza suoni il linguaggio procede verso il vero / senza linguaggio i suoni rifiutano il lavoro' (92). In the previous section the thematic emphasis is on the primary needs of hunger and sexuality, but here there is a metalinguistic emphasis on language itself and, at the same time, a self-conscious attempt to generate images that are both extremely simple and refreshingly surprising (thus preserving some of the child-like tone of the previous section). Finally, in 'Modello per autoritratti,' the illusion of the unified lyrical subject as the origin rather than the effect of poetic discourse is dispelled precisely in an attempt at self-description: 'io non sono non c'è non chi è / non abito non credo non ho' (96). Identity, the 'I' who speaks, is produced in a structure of alienation. Identity, however it may appear in the imaginary projection of the self-portrait, is never simply itself ('sono io') but is always only a likeness, a reflection of something else.

Despite its radical critique of lyrical subjectivity, Porta's text remains haunted by the lyric, and especially by the question of sexuality, and however divided and problematic, its subject is still unequivocally gendered male, while the object is still always female. In a simplistic attempt at antilyric oppositionality, however, she becomes the target of violence rather than love. For example, 'Aprire' [To open], the final poem of the anthology *I novissimi* (162), is constructed through a seemingly compulsive repetition and recurrence of fragments that are almost snapshots (the door, the black silk stockings, the glass, the curtain, the breasts, the belly, the blood stain) which, despite the absence of a narrative logic, allow the reader to reconstruct piece by piece, as if it was happening in front of his/her very eyes, the scene of the rape and murder of a woman while her child is sleeping in the same room, and a simultaneous strip-tease scene in a room by the sea. The voyeuristic logic of Porta's technique, like any good pornographic movie, succeeds in making the reader/viewer an accomplice of the violence, and therefore has a mimetic effect. This effect is only intensified by the obsessive punning on the author's name: the word *porta* (door, a topos of pornography) recurs several times throughout the poem, including the opening and closing lines – a trick that underscores ironically the author's own complicity with and voyeuristic pleasure in the 'scene' behind the door. Porta's critique of subjectivity thus finally appears as a dead end, leading nowhere except back to where the lyric has always been.

Of all the authors of the *novissimi* and the Gruppo 63, Balestrini was the most rigorous and uncompromising. It is not surprising, therefore, that he has often been harshly criticized, especially by orthodox Marxist critics in Italy. However extreme, his work is nevertheless of special interest from the point of view of feminist criticism. Even in his early writing Balestrini began to reject not only lyric subjectivity but also some of the fundamental structures of poetry and literary language: 'prima di posare sul sagrato si libra ad ali tese / negli specchi di luce bagnata, rotti da un piede verde; al Malcontento Bar ferisce mortalmente uno sconosciuto / scambiandolo per il suo seduttore' (*Come si agisce* 35).[43] We find here and through the volume *Come si agisce* a polemic refusal of metaphor itself. The semantic link between the fragments of phrases and images that make up the text is so imponderable that we can grasp only a relationship of contiguity. In other words, metonymy replaces metaphor. For Balestrini, the rhetorical structure of metaphor is so deeply embedded in the tainted ideology of consumer capitalism, so profoundly commodified, as to be unredeemable. This does not mean, however, that Balestrini opts instead for a nonmetaphoric prose narrative: he also rejects narrative. Like metaphor, he sees narrative as carrying in its very structures the burden of an ideology to which he can in no way subscribe. This is all the more remarkable because during the years in which Balestrini was writing his 'poetry' Barthes and other structuralist critics were busy describing the universal and supposedly 'neutral' structures of narrative. Balestrini's position is closer, instead, to that of Teresa de Lauretis, who compellingly demonstrates the relationship between certain traditional narrative structures and topoi and a misogynistically violent ideology.[44]

I am not trying to argue that Balestrini was a feminist, but rather that, in his opposition to the cultural formations of bourgeois thought in the age of neocapitalism, he also happened to refuse to 'come to terms with' the language of phallogocentrism and patriarchy (including psychoanalysis). He therefore also anticipated in some ways the work of Deleuze and Guattari and the more radical thinkers who emerged in 1968. In his long poem 'I funerali di Togliatti' (Togliatti died in 1964), the only narrative element that apparently concerns the funeral is a detail about a wreath that was presumably carried in the funeral procession. Everything else seems like an accumulation of unrelated details and fragments. There is no directionality of discourse, no choice of point of view, and no hierarchical structure. There is no narrative development, no punctuation, and apparently no closure; there is no period at the end of the text.

Balestrini's poetry, according to Walter Siti, represents the moment of minimal clarity and the highest level of 'involution' in the history of the Italian neo-avant-garde' (*Il realismo* 34). Yet this appears so only if one approaches the text from the point of view of certain expectations or conventions of literary form. Indeed, Siti's entire project is to read the neo-avant-garde from the point of view of 'realism,' historically a form or mode among the most compromised with the ideology of patriarchy. In his work, Balestrini, while seeking to destroy the order with which language articulates dominant ideology, attempts to 'find' a totally 'other' language; as the title *Come si agisce* implies, he sees this as an eminently political praxis.

His way of going about this is to use a cut-and-paste approach, a verbal equivalent of collage. Bracketing as much as possible his private 'self' in his texts Balestrini cuts up sentences, phrases, excerpts from pre-existing texts (such as novels or technical manuals), and especially texts from the endless flow of information in an increasingly saturated media world, and reassembles them in unforeseen, absurd, and sometimes ironic combinations. Some of his work – for example *Cronogrammi* (1963) – consists of collages of words in their original typography cut from newspapers and pasted together in interesting visual layouts. The effects of these collages are, first, of depriving the texts he uses of their meaning, and second, of highlighting the sheer, naked fact that they are made up of language, that they are linguistic artefacts. Balestrini's collages do not really ask to be interpreted or deciphered; they can only be 'experienced.' They are not 'meaningless,' but they are not 'meaningful' either. The reader peruses the fragments – some make sense, some do not. Some combinations may turn out to be surprising and enlightening, to 'click' in one way or another according to the reader's own experience, associations, and willingness to let his/her mind be stimulated in this way. Balestrini's design is to free language by opening it up to a potentially endless plurality of senses.[45] Surprise, the energy of 'wonder,' and the flash of unforeseen combinations and illuminations, are the key elements of his poetics. As Giuliani remarks in the preface to the 1961 edition of the *I novissimi* anthology, 'one can even stress, in Adornian fashion, 'the organized emptiness of meaning' of these poems and read them as a repudiation of existing society' (35).

Balestrini also experimented with visual poetry, with different types of typographical layouts, and even with computerized texts. In *Ma noi facciamone un'altra* (1964–68), he based the length of the lines on the exact typographical length of words and letters, thus producing a radical estrangement of the tradition of *enjambement*: for example, breaking off words in the middle of a letter, or repeating the same fragment of text several times, each time cutting it off, mid-line, in a different place. The violent cuts in the lines (not unlike Fontana's famous cuts on the canvas) foreground and estrange the material process of the making of the text.

Balestrini's most radical estrangement of narrative is to be found in his 'collage novel' *Tristano* (1966). In striking contrast to the tragically closed mythical narrative of Tristan and Isolde, Balestrini's collage-book is totally open, made up entirely of fragments and shreds of other texts that the reader can reshuffle and recompose in his/her mind. Balestrini does, however, manipulate the fragments in two major ways: he replaces all names of places and persons with the letter C, and he makes pervasive use of repetition of the fragments themselves. The apparently simple trick of the letter C has a disconcerting and powerful effect. In a given phrase or text, subject and object become confused; characters appear to change gender in mid-sentence. The device of repetition creates a kind of rhythm and allows for a coagulation of 'meaning,' however fluid. Themes such as the alienation of gender relations and the difficulty of 'seeing' emerge slowly.[46]

However powerful and comparable in their disorienting effect to some of Godard's films, Balestrini's collages are finally frustratingly vacuous. The effort required on the part of the reader to track down some meaningful pattern does not seem worthwhile. On the whole, Balestrini's work tends to make 'literature' appear ambiguous and absurd. Its language cannot be 'redeemed.' Its fundamental linguistic apparatus is that of capital, and for this basic reason no amount of formal experimentation can set it free. All the avant-garde 'writer' can apparently do, from Balestrini's point of view, is to expose the alienated status of language, its being but an artifice incapable of capturing passions and phenomena – a reality whose complexity and mutability forever escape its grasp. Literature has, in short, no real cognitive function for Balestrini.

Masculinity of the Neo-avant-garde?

Although in Italian cultural history the word *neoavanguardia* is often used to refer only to the literary neo-avant-garde, and sometimes even more restrictively to refer to just the Gruppo 63, a neo-avant-gardist spirit actually infected all the arts, including music and the visual arts. Composer Luciano Berio, one of the great exponents of international avant-garde and electronic music, was the co-founder, with Bruno Maderna, in 1954 of the experimental Studio di Fonologia Musicale at the RAI in Milan.[47] As Umberto Eco points out in the preface to *Opera aperta*, it was through Berio that he became interested in the notion of the experimental 'open work' in the late 1950s. The first meeting of the Gruppo 63 took place in conjunction with the fourth annual Settimana internazionale della nuova musica. This cultural event, which gathered avant-garde musicians from various countries, had gained media attention and a faithful audience that included other avant-garde artists. Thus the newly formed group was able to insert itself in a context that was already connoted as 'avant-garde' and was able to connect with other forms of avant-garde discourse (while also profiting from the presence of the media to gain instant notoriety).

The journal *Il verri*, which through the 1960s continued to support the new avant-garde (from 1962 on its editors were either members or sympathizers of the group), promoted an interdisciplinary approach that connected literature with international developments in music, art, architecture, critical theory, and philosophy. From its very beginning a programmatically interdisciplinary approach characterized *Marcatrè*, the journal closest in spirit to the Gruppo 63, with many group members on its editorial board, and sections devoted to literature, music, ethnomusicology, mass culture, architecture, and the visual arts.

Of the original *novissimi* group, Alfredo Giuliani was particularly interested in atonal music and the work of John Cage. His own experiments with dissonance and atonal verse – for example, the poems 'Prosa' and 'È dopo' in the *I novissimi* anthology – were influenced by Charles

Olson's ideas on projective verse as verse written for the ear and not for the eye. Luciano Berio and Edoardo Sanguineti had previously worked together on *Passaggio*, a work for soprano, chorus, and instruments and in 1965 collaborated on the production of a musical adaptation of *Laborintus* (*Laborintus II*). In many respects the poetics of the *novissimi* and the Gruppo 63 were also influenced by developments in the arts, such as European *informel*, as well as American abstract expressionism and 'action painting' in the 1950s, with its foregrounding of the material process of painting,[48] and then by the American new Dada and Pop Art of the 1960s. Luciano Anceschi, the founding editor of *Il verri*, maintained and promoted a constant interest in the arts through the journal and other cultural activities. The neo-avant-garde's restless curiosity and interest for a multiplicity of discourses and forms from non-Italian sources radically opened up modern Italian culture for the first time to an international context and frame of reference. Also, for the first time in the history of modern Italian culture, the cross-fertilization between the arts was multidirectional and international.

However mediatedly, the international and interdisciplinary thrust generated by the movement of the *neoavanguardia*, and its propensity towards radical critique, had a considerable impact on the women's movement in Italy. Various organized groups of the Italian women's movement from the late 1960s and early 1970s operated on three interconnected levels: attention to the national and local problems of the condition of women in the still largely patriarchal Italian society; demystification of the sexism of institutions and the media; and intellectual reflection and theorization within an international intellectual framework (open to suggestions from the French-, German-, and English-speaking worlds), regarding the status of discourse and the possibility of an ideological critique. But while the male elite of the neo-avant-garde did not, for the most part, extend its critique to the crucial question of gender, the Italian women's movement did exactly that.

At the level of literary creation, aesthetic production, and critical thought, it is not surprising that some of the most interesting experimental work done by Italian women was created in a cultural framework which – however intensely personal and experiential – crossed national and linguistic barriers and opened itself up to a variety of discourses and disciplines. Giulia Niccolai, Amelia Rosselli, and Alice Ceresa, for example, grew up and worked in several languages and cultural backgrounds. Niccolai worked in photography for ten years before turning to experimental poetry, including visual poetry. Rosselli was intensely involved in musical research.[49] However inimical the *neoavanguardia* might, on the whole, have been to women, the opening up of traditional national culture worked in women's favour.

Given these and other elements that are of great interest and relevance to women, why then is the Italian neo-avant-garde, at least in its more public and 'institutional' manifestations such as conferences, anthologies, exhibitions, catalogues, for the most part a male phenomenon?

The scarce presence of women in the new avant-garde groups is the result of a double process of exclusion. Unlike futurism, which especially in its second phase encouraged the involvement of women in the movement and manifested provocatively feminist positions, the second wave of the avant-garde in Italy gained and maintained a group identity in part through the exclusion or marginalization of women. This is particularly true of what may be called the elite core (or corps) of the neo-avant-garde in Italy, namely the *novissimi* and the Gruppo 63. Unlike the Gruppo 70 and the practitioners of visual and concrete poetry, whose work remained artisanal and almost clandestine, the Gruppo 63 gained enormous notoriety, had considerable media exposure, and was greatly influential in Italy. Being a man or like a man, and subscribing to a certain ethics of masculinity, seemed to be an unspoken requirement of the *neoavanguardia* and was a key element of its media image.

The dynamics of the group meetings between 1963 and 1967 were mercilessly confrontational. Individual readings were followed by collective discussions where each author's text was subjected to impromptu criticisms and often scathing attacks. As Umberto Eco describes the situation in his 1964 essay, 'La generazione di Nettuno,' 'unity was emerging little by little through two implicit methodological assumptions: (1) each author felt the need to control his research by submitting it to the judgment of the others; (2) the collaboration manifested itself as a lack of pity and indulgence. Judgments were being proffered that would skin alive any too-sensitive soul.'[50] In this manly ritual of roughing each other out, authors would receive fierce criticism without batting an eyelash. It was this confrontational style, with rough interventions and aggressive discussions, according to Eco, that cemented the group and gave it a sense of its strength precisely inasmuch as it acted and was perceived by the media as a group.

Given this male homosocial dynamic, it is not surprising that women who were attracted to the movements and/or adhered to some of their practices – such as Carla Vasio, Patrizia Vicinelli, Giulia Niccolai,

Alice Ceresa, and Amelia Rosselli, among others – were always implicitly seen, and saw themselves, as 'exceptions,' marginal and secondary with respect to the main male constituency. Most of these women, neither inside nor outside the group, were confronted with the arduous task of constructing their experimental work and poetic language in conditions of essential solitude and alienation.

This marginalization of women was doubled and reinforced by the languages of criticism and theory through which the new avant-garde groups asserted and publicized themselves. The critics and theorists who, in ever-increasing numbers, attempted to systematize and make sense of the various avant-garde practices and pronouncements in Italy during the 1960s were for the most part men, often but not always practicing avant-garde artists themselves (Alfredo Giuliani and Edoardo Sanguineti are cases in point). However different their approaches, and however diverse their ideas regarding who or what is avant-garde, their essays, appraisals, anthologies, and various 'mappings' of the *neoavanguardia* and its shifting constituencies and practices have one trait in common: they consistently either ignore or marginalize women.[51]

The poet, critic, and feminist Biancamaria Frabotta, who does not consider herself an experimental writer, states that in 1980 that 'the history of women's contribution to the ... neo-avant-garde has yet to be written.'[52] This situation has still not changed substantially, but not for lack of material. Giulia Niccolai, Patrizia Vicinelli, Piera Oppezzo, Carla Vasio, Milli Graffi, Anna Malfaiera, and Amelia Rosselli are some of the women poets who come to mind, along with Lucia Marcucci, Ketty La Rocca, and Mirella Bentivoglio, whose work is widely experimental and interdisciplinary. Rather than a study of women's contribution to the neo-avant-garde as presently defined in literary histories (a project that may end up reproducing the masculine logic of the neo-avant-garde itself), what is needed is an open and unrestricted study of the variety of experimental discourses and practices that women have created in their work, which may include authors whose names are not usually associated with the *neoavanguardia*, such as Anna Maria Ortese (an experimenter if ever there was one, although she kept herself far from the Gruppo 63) and Carla Lonzi.

The *Neoavanguardia* and 'the Feminine'

The exclusion of women from the canon of the *neoavanguardia* is all the more ironic and paradoxical given that, in its rebellion against the linguistic and ideological oppressiveness of dominant bourgeois discourse and its critique of the culture industry and the mass media, the Italian neo-avant-garde sought to explore venues to an alternative language, which in many ways meant somehow moving towards a non-masculine, 'feminine' type of discourse. Rejecting 'the system' in fact meant rejecting an essentially masculine economy, what has been called the 'phallogocentrism' of patriarchal bourgeois culture. To do so, many of the artists and poets of, or close to, the *neoavanguardia* chose at times to speak as women or in a language that was largely 'feminized.'[53] Two examples may be considered paradigmatic: Elio Pagliarani (especially the previously cited 'La ragazza Carla,' which tells the story of a lower-class girl's coming of age) and Edoardo Sanguineti.

Pagliarani implicitly places his poem within a psychoanalytic framework,[54] gearing his entire narrative towards the 'happy' conclusion whereby seventeen-year-old Carla, who was molested by her boss and is the constant object of unsolicited sexual advances by other men and is repelled by them, finally resigns herself to sex. Her surrender to 'normal' sexuality (in contrast to her autoeroticism, portrayed voyeuristically but dismissed as 'immature' in the poem) is celebrated as an acceptance of life itself, and a coming of age. Her dislike of 'compulsory' heterosexuality, on the other hand, is portrayed as a form of repression. The poem attempts to speak in the register and 'voice' of a *soggetto collettivo medio,* a kind of average collective subject – neither too refined nor too uncultivated – and thus to give a sense of the milieu in which Carla lives. In other words, the 'collective' voice that tells Carla's story also takes part in it; it is, in a way, supposed to be also Carla's own voice.

Unfortunately, nowhere is the fallacy of the notion of 'common speech' (so fundamental to the Italian neo-avant-garde) more evident than in Pagliarani's poem. The experiment fails precisely in its attempt to convey Carla's sexual experience. It is clear from the following passage, for example, that the supposed 'collective subject' is none other than a voyeuristic male subject:

> 'S'è lavata nel bagno e poi nel letto / s'è accarezzata tutta quella sera. / Non le mancava niente, c'era tutta / come la sera prima – pure con le mani e la bocca / si cerca si tocca si strofina, ha una voglia / di piangere di compatirsi / ma senza fantasia / come può immaginare di commuoversi? / Tira il collo all'indietro ed ecco tutto.' (*I Novissimi* 96–7)

In the first part of this passage, Carla is the exhibitionist object of the male gaze in the typical mirroring process that characterizes scopophilia according to Freud: the desire of the subject who is looking is assumed to be also the exhibitionist desire of the object being looked at. This scenario is not without its ironies for, as Elizabeth Grosz has pointed out, exhibitionism is almost exclusive to men.[55] In the closing part, however, the text proceeds to censor what appears to be the dangerously autoerotic turn taken by the image of Carla touching herself; in its superior wisdom the narrating voice concludes that a more mature fantasy (implicitly, a heterosexual one) alone can truly nourish and move Carla's imagination. The voyeuristic and patronizing logic of this text did not cease to exercise its seductive appeal on certain readers, even decades later. In 1995, Renato Barilli – a great supporter and commentator of the *neoavanguardia,* and a skilled theorist in many respects – commented: 'between this collective [linguistic] subject, suitably 'lowered' and normalized, and Carla herself, there is no substantial separation, nor is there any lack of proportion between the omniscience of the observer and the intellectual poverty of the person being observed ... Deep down, Carla 'knows' albeit in a confused way what the narrating collective self is explaining' (*La neoavanguardia italiana* 48).

Although Sanguineti is quite far from the 'healthy' masculine ethos of Pagliarani's poem, women and female sexuality do not fare any better in his work. Sanguineti's writing is extremely rich and he speaks in many voices, but in the anthology *I novissimi* he chose to include excerpts from his poem *Laborintus,* which starts out as a description of 'a decomposing mental landscape,' the unconscious of Renée/Ellie, a young schizophrenic woman. Sanguineti deals in particular with the woman's association of her female analyst with a symbolic mother in a Jungian psychoanalytic sense, and explicitly presents Ellie as a figure for his own conflicted psyche as well as his body, with its unrepressed corporality.[56]

The descent into the unconscious is staged as an oppositional quest, a way of getting at a deeper language of 'universal' myths and archetypes that is not compromised or tainted by the dominant ideology. Indifferent or oblivious to the significance of gender and sexual difference, Sanguineti seeks to escape the mystifications of ideology by plunging into the irrationality of a generically 'feminized' unconscious. For Sanguineti, as for Pagliarani, the feminine provides an alternative way of conceptualizing and speaking about subjectivity, outside, that is, the worn-out paradigms of the 'male' lyric, the male subject, and the male hero.

This turning to a feminine 'space' or speaking with 'a woman's voice' has little to do with real women but rather represents a fantasized appropriation of the feminine. Among other things, it allows for the usurpation of a vast metaphoric field that includes images of giving birth, giving life, nourishing, etc. In 'Laborintus,' for example, Ellie (that is, the poet) is defined as 'questo linguaggio che partorisce.' Such a practice – a kind of colonization or theft of the feminine – is a common strategy of avant-garde discourse (French surrealism is perhaps the most blatant example) and is totally compatible with – indeed it seems invariably connected to – misogynistic condescension, violence, and generally a strong 'suspicion' or dislike of women.

In *Laborintus* the appropriation of the feminine coexists with a discourse of female abjection (and implicitly self-abjection) whereby the uterus is a 'prison' and a 'cancer.' Sexuality in general is connected with brutality and filth in a series of sadomasochistic fantasmatic images throughout the poem. Fantasies of castration run through the text, as well as, inversely, an obsession with male genitals and a violent symbolic imagery associated with the phallic: tail, whip, muscle, and fist. In the process of purification that, in the wish-fulfilling structure of Sanguineti's poetics, allows for salvation, the abject feminine – the labyrinth and 'stinking swamp' – is left behind. In his famous gloss to the poem, Sanguineti describes the process as 'throwing oneself head first into the labyrinth of formalism and irrationalism, the Palus Putredinis of anarchism and alienation, with the hope I refuse to consider illusory of eventually getting out of it once and for all, if with sullied hands, yet ultimately with even the mire truly left behind' (*I novissimi* 391).

Sanguineti claims that the saga of the male protagonist who speaks in *Laborintus* has nothing 'subjective' about it. His 'story' is neutral and objective. It is the 'paradigmatic' account of a historical crisis of late modernity in which all human beings participate (*I novissimi* 388). The failure of this supposedly 'universal' 'I' to allow for difference in terms of gender and class is striking. Not only is the poem filtered through the perspective of an essentially misogynistic archetypal male hero, but the entire poem, despite its linguistic richness, implies and constructs for itself an essentially middle-to-upper-class intellectual reader whose linguistic and cultural competence is that of the participants and sympathizers of the Gruppo 63. Sanguineti is therefore far from that project of radical democratization of literary language, which – however utopian – was the goal of the historical avant-gardes, from futurism to surrealism to Brecht, and in many ways of the *neoavanguardia* itself.

Rather than deploy the explosive potential that a discourse of the feminine as radically 'other' holds within an essentially patriarchal society, the Italian neo-avant-garde ended up relapsing into a discourse complicitous with the very same misogynistic deep structures that formed the bases of that society. Understandably, this made the entire neo-avant-garde and formal experimentation itself suspect to women, and placed women experimenters in an uncomfortable and difficult position.[57] Ironically, and sometimes tragically, it was from their doubly marginal and isolated position at the edge of Italian society and of the neo-avant-garde that women experimenters – first and foremost Amelia Rosselli – were able to create texts whose language was both radically other and miraculously eloquent and timely.[58]

NOTES

1 This essay is a slightly revised version of the article 'Language, Gender and Sexuality in the Italian Neo-avant-garde,' *Modern Language Notes* 119 (2004): 135–73. The original *I novissimi* anthology, whose creation was nurtured by Anceschi himself, was edited with a preface by Alfredo Guiliani and published in 1961 by Rusconi and Paolazzi (Edizioni del Verri). Giuliani wrote an expanded preface and notes for the second edition, entitled *I novissimi: poesie per gli anni sessanta* (Turin: Einaudi, 1965). All subsequent references are to the bilingual edition, *I Novissimi: Poems for the Sixties* (Los Angeles: Sun and Moon Press, 1995), which is based on the 1965 Italian edition.

2 Out of about fifty authors who took part in the meeting held at Reggio Emilia in November 1964, three were women: Marina Mizzau, Amelia Rosselli, and Carla Vasio. Only Mizzau and Vasio returned to the following meeting, devoted to experimental narrative and film, held in Palermo in September 1965. The meeting at La Spezia in June 1966, which was supposed to be open to younger and different authors, included only five women: Alice Ceresa, Lucia Marcucci, Rossana Ombres, Amelia Rosselli, and Patrizia Vicinelli.

3 The 2003 celebrations included a symposium entitled 'Il Gruppo 63 quarant'anni dopo' and a series of readings of old as well as new texts by younger writers inspired (in different degrees and different ways) by the experience of the *neoavanguardia.* All the original *novissimi* authors were present (with the exception of Antonio Porta, who died in 1989). Part of an afternoon was devoted to readings of texts by women: Amelia Rosselli, Giulia Niccolai, and Patrizia Vicinelli. Niccolai read her own texts; the texts by Rosselli (who committed suicide in 1996) and Vicinelli (who died in 1991) were read by a woman actor. Carla Vasio (b. 1932) was present only

in effigy: a gigantic photograph by Ugo Mulas of members of the Gruppo 63 standing around Giuseppe Ungaretti was posted at the back of the stage through the three days. Although Vasio's face is clearly visible in the foreground of the photograph, she was not identified in the caption provided in the program, which named only the men in the group and the publisher Inge Feltrinelli. However, four younger women whose work is thought to carry on the experimental spirit of the Gruppo 63 – the poet and critic Milli Graffi (b. 1940), the poet Rosaria Lo Russo (b. 1964), and the novelists Rossana Campo (b. 1963) and Silvia Ballestra (b. 1969) – were invited to read, along with ten male writers.

4 The new authors are Giorgio Celli, Corrado Costa, Achille Bonito Oliva, Arrigo Lora Totino, Eugenio Miccini, Gianfranco Baruchello, Gianni Celati, Nico Orengo, Sebastiano Vassalli, and Giuliano Scabia. In the original 1964 edition the writers are presented in alphabetical order, but in the new 2002 edition, they are divided into three main groups: Poetry (comprising the subcategories 'I Novissimi,' 'Malebolge,' and 'Nella corrente'), Narrative (including 19 writers, plus the subcategory 'La scuola di Palermo', with three writers), and Theatre. The placement of the five *novissimi* at the beginning has hierarchical rather than merely descriptive implications. Moreover, there are several errors and omissions in the Appendici, which provide information about the various meetings of the Gruppo 63. For example, the list of participants for the Reggio Emilia meeting includes only the men. Also, in the list of writers who read at the La Spezia meeting, two of the women's names are spelled incorrectly: Luciana (instead of Lucia) Marcucci, and Amalia (instead of Amelia) Rosselli. All the critical and theoretical interventions from the 1964 anthology have been omitted in the new edition, including Umberto Eco's essay 'La generazione di Nettuno.' However, Angelo Guglielmi's 'Avanguardia e sperimentalismo' and Fausto Curi's 'Sulla giovane poesia,' along with the summary of the debate following the first Palermo meeting, are included in the companion anthology, *Gruppo 63: critica e teoria*, ed. Renato Barilli and Angelo Guglielmi, which was first published by Feltrinelli in 1976. In the preface to the 2003 edition, published by Testo & Immagine, the editors argue, rather unconvincingly, that the Gruppo 63 was a crucial part of the postmodern movement theorized by Fredric Jameson and Ihab Hassan.

5 Galvano della Volpe's *Critica del gusto* (1960) was particularly influential. Barthes' essays on myth (first published 1954–6) are collected in *Mythologies* (1957); the Italian translation by Lidia Lonzi, *Miti d'oggi*, appeared in 1962. On Della Volpe, and on Barthes as a great demystifier, see Sanguineti's essay 'Poetry and Mythology' ('Poesia e mitologia') in *I Novissimi.*

6 See for example Elio Pagliarani's paper presented at the conference 'Arte e comunicazione' (Florence, 24–6 May 1963), published in *Letteratura* 28 (1964), as cited in Francesco Muzzioli, *Teoria e critica della letteratura nelle avanguardie italiane degli anni sessanta*: '[Poetry as opposition] Opposition to what? Opposition in a way to the already known, because otherwise it would no longer be communication, but repetition ... Opposition to the myths that surround us, the myths of the present. And these myths are nothing but a false interpretation of reality. Therefore art as opposition to myths, as demystification of myths' (124).

7 Edoardo Sanguineti's particularly strong indictment of futurism makes for one of the most fascinating chapters in the history of the relationship between the avant-garde and the neo-avant-garde in Italy. Among the futurists and futurist sympathizers, the *neoavanguardia* poets acknowledged the importance and value for their own work only of Palazzeschi, Soffici, and occasionally Govoni. Sanguineti gave a special place to the minor experimental work of Gian Pietro Lucini (1867–1914) and pressed for his poetic canonization precisely in view of Lucini's anti-futurist stand.

8 Angelo Gugliemi was among those who insisted on the distinction between the new experimentalism of the *neoavanguardia* and the more violent kind of rupture sought by futurism; see his 'Avanguardia e sperimentalismo' (April 1963). Umberto Eco, a sympathizer, fellow-traveller, and occasional commentator on the Gruppo 63 (he took part in the first meeting in Palermo), emphasized from the very first the distance between the more enlightened sections of the movement and the strategies of the historical avant-garde, stressing instead the more enduring, fundamental links with modernist experimentalists such as Joyce, Proust, and Eliot; see his essays 'La generazione di Nettuno' (1964) and 'Il gruppo 63, lo sperimentalismo e l'avanguardia,' a lecture given in 1983 on the occasion of the twentieth anniversary of the Gruppo 63 and published in *Sugli specchi e altri saggi* (1985). Eco reiterated his position in his opening address for the 40th-anniversary conference on the Gruppo 63 in Bologna, published under the title 'Quelli che il Verri' in *La Repubblica* (9 May, 2003).

9 Hal Foster, *The Return of the Real*, 1–32. According to Foster, despite all the widely critiqued historical failures and shortcomings of the avant-garde, the notion of avant-garde remains a valuable one, even – or especially – in the postmodern era, for its crucial oppositional articulation of artistic with political discourse. Thus, in many ways, Foster shares the self-justificatory logic of the Italian neo-avant-gardists.

10 On Resistance and Reconstruction rhetoric, and the question of realism and commitment in postwar Italy, see my *Calvino and the Age of Neorealism*.

11 For Pasolini and others, the *neoavanguardia*'s war on language was a mere *bomba di carta* [paper bomb], and the neo-avant-gardists mere exhibitionists whose protest was only verbal and essentially empty. In his own literary work, Pasolini opted instead for a thematic type of political commitment, preserving and working with both the syntactical and rhythmic schemes of the Italian poetic tradition – from Dante to Pascoli and Carducci – which he considered the unprescindable ground for any kind of innovation or experimentation. One could not just blow that tradition to smithereens as the new avant-gardists wanted to do. Any stylistic freedom had to be built upon the corpus of the existing tradition. For Fortini, on the other hand, by working merely at the level of expression and communication – that is, at a superstructural level – and renouncing any transgression at the level of praxis, the *neoavanguardia* had betrayed the tragic spirit of the historical avant-gardes, its transformative and liberatory impetus, preserving instead only its mocking, ironic, and ultimately conservative attitude. Fortini (like many others) maintained that this neo-avant-garde is finally not an avant-garde at all, but only the other face of 'mass-chatter,' glued to the neocapitalist order. See Pasolini, 'Fine dell'avanguardia,'136–7; Fortini, 'Le due avanguardie,' 101–2.

12 See Gambaro, *Invito a conoscere la neoavanguardia,* 107–8. The twenty-five editors of *Quindici* (all men) owned and published the journal themselves. Among them were Alberto Arbasino, Nanni Balestrini, Andrea Barbato, Renato Barilli, Furio Colombo, Umberto Eco, Alfredo Giuliani, Guido Guglielmi, Giorgio Manganelli, Elio Pagliarani, Antonio Porta, and Edoardo Sanguineti.

13 See the introduction to the 1976 edition of Barilli and Guglielmi, *Gruppo 63: critica e teoria.*

14 The classic statement of this position is in Eduardo Sanguineti's volume of essays *Ideologia e linguaggio.* See especially 'Sopra l'avanguardia' and 'Avanguardia, società, impegno.'

15 This and all subsequent translations are mine unless otherwise specified.

16 Guglielmi, 'Il dibattito in occasione del primo incontro del Gruppo a Palermo.' Cf. Barilli, *La neoavanguardia italiana,* 209–18.

17 See 'Poetry and Mythology,' in Giuliani, ed. *I Novissimi: Poems for the Sixties.* According to Sanguineti, mythic forms and structures animate not only poetry but also the experimental novel. The writer works by giving form to mythic structures, which are connected in turn to essential mythic structures from the deeper recesses of human history. As a conscious operative strategy, this work with myth according to Sanguineti keeps the writer's activity from being mere free play of the imagination, allowing it to penetrate the

depths of 'the real' and to circumvent ideology. See Balestrini, ed., *Gruppo 63: il romanzo sperimentale*, 149–50.

18 The oppositional symbolic practices of the Italian feminist philosophic community Diotima, from the 1980s on, were carried out in a context carefully and skilfully negotiated within the Italian state university in Verona.

19 See *Tel Quel* 22 (1964): 89–90.

20 This essay, commissioned by Elio Vittorini, first appeared in *Il Menabò* in 1962, shortly after the publication of *Opera aperta*, and was reprinted in the book from the 1967 edition on. For a lively narration of the controversial reception of this volume, see Eco's preface to the 1976 Bompiani edition.

21 On this process, see Siti, *Il realismo dell'avanguardia*, 25.

22 Some of the small groups of women that sprung up all over Italy – the so-called *gruppi di autocoscienza* [self-awareness groups] around 1974–5 – began the so-called *pratica dell'inconscio* [practice of the unconscious]. By listening and reflecting together on individual women's experiences (related through narratives of dreams, fantasies, etc.) these groups attempted to understand the links between conscious and unconscious life for women while imagining alternatives to the misogynistic ideology and power structure of psychoanalysis. Lea Melandri was among the proponents of this practice. See Bono and Kemp, *Italian Feminist Thought*, 82–108.

23 See Corona, Introduction to *Donne e scrittura*, 26; Corona also edited this rich and diverse anthology of women's writings.

24 Although Marcucci took part in an exhibition of visual poetry organized by the Gruppo 63 at the Galleria Guida in Naples in 1965, she was more closely connected to the less known, less glamorous, and semi-clandestine Gruppo 70, whose activities intersected at times with those of the Gruppo 63. Gruppo 70 was formed in Florence around the journal *Quartiere* (1958–60) by Lamberto Pignotti and Sergio Salvi, both of whom were editors of the journal. The group was interested in taking poetry and literature beyond their traditional boundaries, and promoted the intersection of literary form with the graphic and visual arts, and with theatre and music. Between 1963 and 1965 they organized three conferences of experimental writers, painters, architects, and musicians.

25 See, for example 'Now and Nowhere: Roeg's *Bad Timing*.' De Lauretis, who has written extensively on Eco, is also the most acute feminist critic of the masculinist bias of Eco's semiotic theory.

26 See *La presenza dell'uomo nel femminismo.*

27 Accardi was suspended from her teaching position after she distributed the pamphlet in the Rome high school where she was employed.

28 Both Accardi and Giuliani were born in 1924.

29 Spatola (1941–88) published *Malebolge*, which he co-directed with Corrado Costa and Giorgio Celli, between 1963 and 1967. Of all the avant-garde journals, only *Malebolge* and later *Tam Tam* (co-founded by Spatola with the avant-garde poet Giulia Niccolai) were relatively open to women.

30 Most male members of the Italian neo-avant-garde conform to Susan Suleiman's characterization in *Subversive Intent: Gender, Politics and the Avant-Garde*: 'Insofar as the dominant culture has been not only bourgeois but also patriarchal, the productions of most male avant-garde artists appear anything but subversive' (83).

31 On Diotima's separatism, see my 'Diotima's Dilemmas: Authorship, Authority, Authoritarianism.'

32 Contemporary avant-garde artists such as Cindy Sherman and Barbara Kruger, in their ironic and parodic estrangements of the languages of art, the museum, the mass media, and advertising, deploy rhetorical strategies that in some respects are similar to those of the Italian neo-avant-garde.

33 Sanguineti, *Triperuno*; of all the *neoavanguardia* poets, Sanguineti, a professor of literature at the University of Genoa, has always been the most deeply steeped in literary tradition. He is also a critic and has published essays on Dante, Pascoli, and Gozzano; his celebrated anthology of modern Italian poetry has been crucial in the formation of the modern Italian canon.

34 For a detailed analysis, see Siti, *Il realismo dell'avanguardia*, 77–93.

35 On Brecht as paradigmatic avant-garde artist, see Bürger, *Theory of the Avant-Garde*, especially 88–92.

36 Orthodox structuralist critics were rather unhappy with what they considered an often too facile use of structuralist 'science' by the *neoavanguardia*; see Corti, 'Le orecchie della 'neocritica,' and Avalle, 'Ragioni minime delle avanguardie.' On the critical self-consciousness of the new avant-garde compared to the historical avant-garde, especially with respect to experimental montage and the notion of literariness, see Lorenzini, *Il laboratorio della poesia*.

37 'Per una definizione dell'avanguardia' was first presented in 1965 at a conference on the avant-garde in Rome.

38 See Muzzioli, *Teoria e critica*, 124.

39 On the importance of experience for feminism see de Lauretis, 'Semiotics and Experience,' and 'The Practice of Sexual Difference and Feminist Thought in Italy.'

40 Cf. Siti, *Il realismo dell'avanguardia,* 47–62. Anceschi's 'Orizzonte della poesia,' published in the first issue of *Il verri* (1962), is particularly interesting in light of the possibilities that it opens up, at least implicitly, for a critique of the fantasy of exemplary and authoritative selfhood, and a reas-

sessment in terms of social, cultural and gender difference: 'We should not think that our experience, that which we have lived as our experience, may account for the experience of the entire world. The first necessary "reduction of the "I" is precisely the relinquishing of the claim – which now sounds emphatic and romantic – that the particular experience we have lived may take on the value of an exclusive and universal criterion, or even take on the guise of a dogmatic a priori.' I translate from the essay as reprinted in *Tra Pound e i Novissimi* (Rome: Salerno Editore, 1982), 71.

41 *Metropoli* (1971); all my citations are from the bilingual edition, *Metropolis*, ed. and trans. Pasquale Verdicchio (Los Angeles: Green Integer, 1999).

42 As traditional as this form is, it was not at all outmoded in Italian poetry of the 1960s. Pasolini, for example, worked fully within this lyric mode, as can be seen from any of his poems from this period.

43 Cf. Siti, *Il realismo dell'avanguardia*, 35.

44 See for example 'Desire in Narrative.'

45 See Balestrini's essay, 'Language and Opposition,' in *I Novissimi: Poems for the Sixties*, 382–4.

46 For a more extended analysis, see Christopher Wagstaff, 'The Neo-avantgarde,' 48–9.

47 Amazing as it may sound today, when it seems to produce only endless quantities of trash in competition with Silvio Berlusconi's even trashier networks, the Italian state television network in its first and idealistic golden years employed people such as Luciano Berio, Umberto Eco, and Gianni Vattimo.

48 By analogy Sanguineti and others referred to his verse as a kind of 'action poetry'; see Edoardo Sanguineti, 'Action Poetry?' in *I Novissimi: Poems for the Sixties*, 387–91.

49 See my 'Amelia Rosselli and the Aesthetics of Experimental Music.'

50 In Balestrini and Giuliani, *Gruppo 63: la nuova letteratura* (1964), 410.

51 See for example Vetri, *Letteratura e Caos*, 101, footnote. In *Invito a conoscere la neoavanguardia*, Gambaro mentions only Rosselli, giving her half a page at the very end of his discussion of individual authors. No women are mentioned in Curi's *La poesia italiana d'avanguardia.*

52 *Letteratura al femminile* (Bari: De Donato, 1980), 118.

53 On the unspoken, problematic appropriation of 'the feminine' by the male avant-garde, see Marianne De Koven, 'Male Signature, Female Aesthetic: The Gender Politics of Experimental Writing.'

54 The epigraph to the poem reads: 'A psychiatrist friend tells me of a young secretary whose distaste for city weekends is such she takes enough sleeping pills to stay asleep until Monday morning. Does it make any sense to dedicate this *Girl Carla* to that girl?' (*I Novissimi*, 81).

55 'Voyeurism/Exhibitionism/the Gaze,' in *Feminism and Psychoanalysis: A Critical Dictionary*, ed. by Elizabeth Wright (Oxford: Blackwell, 1992), 448.
56 See the first note (attributed to the editor, Alfredo Giuliani, but doubtlessly written in conjunction with the author), appended to the anthologized text: 'When Renée, the young schizophrenic treated by Mme Sechehaye makes her first contact with Mother (symbolically personified by the psychoanalyst) she feels shut up in her body as in a world of earth and water she calls *swamp*. The proximity of the female character Ellie to the *nomen loci* is highly significant. The author explains: Ellie is my body, it is the whole world ... endlessly predicated. Ellie is *Anima* in the Jungian sense, the *Palus* itself, 'lividissima mater' of section 26.'
57 In her poem *Variazioni belliche*, Amelia Rosselli, who is usually reserved in her judgments, speaks openly about the failures of the neo-avant-garde, its 'rivolta inutile' and 'menzogne'; its 'fragili riviste d'avanguardia costose / come le ambizioni che esse proteggono' (71). Rosselli's work continues to be considered minor and of dubious literary value by many critics who extol the male neo-avant-garde, while her association with 'male' experimentalism has rendered her suspect in the eyes of Italian feminist critics. As Suleiman observes: 'the avant-garde woman is doubly intolerable because her writing escapes not one but two sets of expectations; it corresponds neither to the "usual revolutionary point of view" nor to the "woman's point of view"' (*Subversive Intent* 15).
58 On Amelia Rosselli and the problem of female experimental creativity see two of my articles: 'Poetry and Madness,' and 'Mythic Revisionism: Women Poets and Philosophers in Italy Today.' On the empowering potential of the double marginality of avant-garde women, see Suleiman, *Subversive Intent*, 16–17.

WORKS CITED

Anceschi, Luciano. 'Orizzonte della poesia.' *Il verri*, 1 (1962): 6–21. Reprinted in *Tra Pound e i novissimi*, ed. Luciano Anceschi and Alessandro Tesauro. Rome: Salerno Editore, 1982.

Avalle, S.D. 'Ragioni minime delle avanguardie.' In *Strumenti critici* 1 (1967).

Balestrini, Nanni. *Come si agisce*. Milan: Feltrinelli, 1963.

– 'Linguaggio e opposizione.' In Alfredo Giuliani, ed., *I novissimi*. Milan: Rusconi e Paolazzi, 1961, 163–5. English translation. 'Language and Opposition.' In *I Novissimi: Poems for the Sixties*. 382–4.

– *Ma noi facciamone un'altra*. Milan: Feltrinelli, 1968.

Balestrini, Nanni, ed. *Gruppo 63: il romanzo sperimentale.* Milan: Feltrinelli, 1966.

Balestrini, Nanni, and Alfredo Giuliani, eds. *Gruppo 63: l'antologia.* Turin: Testo & Immagine, 2002.

– *Gruppo 63: la nuova letteratura, 34 scrittori, Palermo ottobre 1963.* Milan: Feltrinelli, 1964.

Barilli, Renato. *La neoavanguardia italiana: dalla nascita del Verri alla fine di Quindici.* Bologna: Il Mulino, 1995.

Barilli, Renato, and Angelo Guglielmi, eds. *Gruppo 63: critica e teoria.* Milan: Feltrinelli, 1976; Turin: Testo & Immagine, 2003.

Barthes, Rolland. *Mythologies.* Paris: Éd. Du Seuil, 1957. Italian translation, *Miti d'oggi.* Trans. by Lidia Lonzi. Milan: Lerici, 1962.

Bono, Paola, and Sandra Kemp, eds. *Italian Feminist Thought: A Reader.* London: Blackwell, 1991.

Bürger, Peter. *Theory of the Avant-garde.* Trans. Michael Shaw. Minneapolis: University of Minnesota Press, 1984.

Cixous, Hélène. 'Le rire de la Méduse.' 1975. English translation. 'The Laugh of the Medusa.' In Elaine Marks and Isabelle De Courtivron, eds. *New French Feminisms: An Anthology.* New York: Schocken Books, 1981. 245–64.

Connor, Steven. *Postmodernist Culture: An Introduction to Theories of the Contemporary.* Oxford: Blackwell, 1989.

Corona, Daniela. Introduction. *Donne e scrittura: atti del seminario internazionale (Palermo, 9–11 giugno 1988).* Ed. Daniela Corona. Palermo: La Luna, 1990.

Corti, Maria, 'Le orecchie della 'neocritica.' *Strumenti critici* 1 (1967).

Curi, Fausto. *La poesia italiana d'avanguardia: modi e tecniche.* Naples: Liguori Editore, 2001.

De Koven, Marianne. 'Male Signature, Female Aesthetic: The Gender Politics of Experimental Writing.' In Ellen G. Friedman and Miriam Fuchs, eds., *Breaking the Sequence: Women's Experimental Fiction.* Princeton: Princeton University Press, 1989. 72–81.

de Lauretis, Teresa. *Alice Doesn't: Feminism, Semiotics, Film.* Bloomington: Indiana University Press, 1984.

– 'Desire in Narrative.' In *Alice Doesn't.* Chapter 5.

– 'Now and Nowhere: Roeg's *Bad Timing.*' In *Alice Doesn't.* 84–102.

– 'The Practice of Sexual Difference and Feminist Thought in Italy.' In Milan Women's Bookstore Collective, *Sexual Difference: A Theory of Social-Symbolic Practice.* Trans. Patricia Cicogna and Teresa De Lauretis. Bloomington: Indiana University Press, 1990. 6–8.

– 'Semiotics and Experience.' In *Alice Doesn't.* 158–86.

Della Volpe, Galvano. *Critica del gusto.* Milan: Feltrinelli, 1960; 3rd ed. 1966.

Eco, Umberto. 'Del modo di formare come impegno sulla realtà.' *Il Menabò* (1962); reprinted in *Opera aperta* starting with the 1967 edition.
– 'La generazione di Nettuno.' In Balestrini and Giuliani, eds., *Gruppo 63: la nuova letteratura.* 407–16.
– 'Il Gruppo 63, lo sperimentalismo e l'avanguardia.' In *Sugli specchi e altri saggi.* Milano: Bompiani, 1985. 93–104.
– *Opera aperta.* Milano: Bompiani, 1962.
– 'Quelli che il Verri.' *La Repubblica.* 9 May 2003. 1, 8–9.
Fortini, Franco. 'Le due avanguardie.' In *Verifica dei poteri.* Milan: Il Saggiatore, 1965; 2nd ed. 1974. 101–2.
Foster, Hal. *The Return of the Real: Art and Theory at the End of the Century.* Cambridge, Mass.: MIT Press, 1996.
Gambaro, Fabio. *Invito a conoscere la neoavanguardia.* Milan: Mursia, 1993.
Giuliani, Alfredo, ed. *I novissimi: poesie per gli anni sessanta.* Milan: Rusconi e Paolazzi, 1961.
– *I novissimi: poesie per gli anni '60.* Turin: Einaudi, 1965. English translation. *I novissimi: Poems for the Sixties.* Prose and notes trans. David Jakobson, poetry trans. Luigi Ballerini, Bradley Dick, Michael Moore, Stephen Sartarelli, and Paul Vangelisti. Los Angeles: Sun and Moon Press, 1995.
Gugliemi, Angelo. 'Avanguardia e sperimentalismo.' *Il verri* 8 (April 1963).
– 'Il dibattito in occasione del primo incontro del Gruppo a Palermo.' In Barilli and Guglielmi, eds., *Gruppo 63: critica e teoria.* 264–8.
Guglielmi, Guido, and Elio Pagliarani, eds. *Manuale di poesia sperimentale.* Milan: Mondadori, 1966.
Lonzi, Carla. *Autoritratto.* Bari: De Donato, 1969.
– *La presenza dell'uomo nel femminismo.* Milan: Scritti di Rivolta femminile, 1978.
– *Scacco ragionato: poesie dal '58 al '63.* Milan: Scritti di Rivolta femminile, 1985.
Lonzi, Carla, and Carla Accardi. 'Rivolta femminile.' Pamphlet. 1970.
Lorenzini, Niva. *Il laboratorio della poesia.* Rome: Bulzoni, 1978.
Muzzioli, Francesco. *Teoria e critica della letteratura nelle avanguardie italiane degli anni sessanta.* Rome: Istituto della Enciclopedia Italiana, 1982.
– 'Per una definizione dell'avanguardia.' *Nuova corrente* 37 (1966): 91.
Pasolini, Pier Paolo. 'Fine dell'avanguardia.' *Nuovi argomenti* 3–4 (1966). Reprinted in *Empirismo eretico.* Milan: Garzanti, 1972. 136–7.
Porta, Antonio. *Metropolis.* Milan: Feltrinelli, 1971. Bilingual edition, *Metropolis.* Ed. and trans. Pasquale Verdicchio. Los Angeles: Green Integer, 1999.
Re, Lucia. *Calvino and the Age of Neorealism: Fables of Estrangement.* Stanford: Stanford University Press, 1989.
– 'Diotima's Dilemmas: Authorship, Authority, Authoritarianism.' In Graziella

Parati and Rebecca West, eds., *Italian Feminist Theory and Practice,* Madison: Fairleigh Dickinson University Press, 2002. 50–74.

– 'Mythic Revisionism: Women Poets and Philosophers in Italy Today.' In Maria Marotti, ed., *Italian Women Writers from the Renaissance to the Present: Revising the Canon,* ed. College Park: Pennsylvania State University Press, 1996. 187–233.

– 'Poetry and Madness.' In *Shearsmen of Sorts: Italian Poetry 1975–1993,* ed. Luigi Ballerini. Special issue of *Forum Italicum* (1992): 132–52.

– 'Amelia Rosselli and the Aesthetics of Experimental Music' *Galleria. Rassegna quadrimestrale di cultura* 48, 1/2. Special issue on Amelia Rosselli, ed. Emmanuela Tandello and Daniela Attanasio (Jan.–Aug. 1997): 35–46.

Rosselli, Amelia. *Variazioni belliche,* Milan: Garzanti, 1964.

Sanguineti, Edoardo. 'Avanguardia, società, impegno.' In *Ideologia e linguaggio.*

– *Ideologia e linguaggio.* Milan: Feltrinelli, 1965; Nuova ed. ampliata, 1975.

– 'Poesia e mitologia.' In *I novissimi.*

– 'Sopra l'avanguardia.' In *Ideologia e linguaggio.*

– *Triperuno.* Milan: Feltrinelli, 1964.

Siti, Walter. *Il realismo dell'avanguardia.* Turin: Einaudi, 1973.

Suleiman, Susan. *Subversive Intent: Gender, Politics, and the Avant-garde.* Cambridge: Harvard University Press, 1990.

Vetri, Lucio. *Letteratura e caos: poetiche della neo-avanguardia italiana degli anni sessanta.* Milan: Mursia, 1992.

Violi, Patrizia. *L'infinito singolare.* Verona: Essedue, 1986.

Wagstaff, Christopher. 'The Neo-Avantgarde.' In Michael Caesar and Peter Hainsworth, eds., *Writers and Society in Contemporary Italy.* Leamington Spa: Berg, 1984.

8 Giulia Niccolai: A Wide-Angle Portrait

REBECCA WEST

> L'avanguardia ha il compito dinamitardo di far saltare determinati paletti, confini e restrizioni, ma non può essere tenuta in vita razionalmente o volontaristicamente. Quando ha fatto saltare la diga, il suo compito è terminato fino al successivo possibile momento di 'rivoluzione.'
>
> [The avant-garde has the dynamiter's task of blowing up certain bolts, limits, and restrictions, but it cannot be kept alive rationally or wilfully. When it has blown up the dam, the task is completed, until a possible future moment of 'revolution.']

These words, written in an email by Giulia Niccolai on 15 August 2005 in response to questions I had asked her concerning the Italian neo-avant-garde reveal her widely shared belief in the fragility of any avant-garde that arises out of a specific cultural and political milieu in which renewal and change are felt to be necessary. When the goal of transforming the status quo is fulfilled, the impetus toward newness dies until conditions arise that once more push writers and artists of all kinds to 'make it new' all over again. There are those today who argue that avant-gardes are no longer possible, due to the mass medial, global environment in which we live and which devours every attempt at newness in its huge maw. Nonetheless, there do appear to exist those few makers of art and culture whose work reflects a kind of continual 'avant-gardism' that goes on pushing the boundaries of the given, the expected, or the banal. Giulia Niccolai is one of those rare birds.

Born in Milan in 1934 of an American mother and an Italian father,

Giulia Niccolai has been multilingual from a very early age. Her poetry reflects this facet of her experience, as does her lack of a sense of belonging to any one culture or country. She began her career as a photojournalist in the early 1950s, which at that time was 'dominated by the antics of the paparazzi and a macho attitude towards the "hunt" for a great photograph' (Hill 162). Her photographs were published in popular magazines such as *Life*, *Paris Match*, and *Der Spiegel*, and her novel, *Il grande angolo* (published in 1966 by Feltrinelli) is closely tied in both thematic and structural elements to her work as a photographer. A watershed moment for Niccolai, as for so many other contemporary Italian writers and artists, was the coming together of neo-avant-garde preoccupations and goals in the poetry of the five authors known as the *novissimi* and in the Gruppo 63, which held its first meeting in Palermo in 1963. Although she did not attend that meeting, she was present at the second meeting held the following year in Reggio Emilia, when she had already begun to turn from photography to writing as her main instrument of creation and expression. Niccolai began publishing poetry in the early 1970s, after she co-founded the journal *Tam Tam* in 1970 with Adriano Spatola (who in 1958 had also founded Edizioni Geiger, a small publishing house that later took the name of the journal). Spatola and Niccolai became companions in life as in work, living together in the countryside outside Parma in the small town of Mulino di Bazzano for many years, and remaining interlocutors until Spatola's untimely death in 1988. The 1970s and 1980s were decades of prolific creativity for Niccolai; most of her poetry of those years is now collected in the volume *Harry's Bar e altre poesie*, with an important introduction by Giorgio Manganelli. I shall have more to say further on about the connection between these two remarkably original and important writers.

Niccolai's life took a major turn during the 1980s when she experienced a serious health crisis and a long depression; she eventually became strongly committed to Buddhism, and in 1990 she became a Buddhist nun. Her work since then has been highly influenced by her spiritual convictions, as she has increasingly withdrawn from the official venues of the literary sphere and has dedicated herself to writing more autobiographically inflected prose than poetry. However, she has not entirely abandoned poetry, as is evident in her 1995 collection of verse entitled *Frisbees: poesie da lanciare.* Niccolai is a generous interlocutor, and has given several interviews over the last two decades, in which she has freely shared her ideas about literary creation and spirituality. We also cannot forget her important work as a translator of Gertrude Stein, Dylan Thomas, and others, as well as her writings for children. Niccolai continues to live and work in Milan.

Given the orientation of this volume of essays, I shall concentrate my subsequent analyses on Niccolai's most clearly neo-avant-garde writings, although I shall also touch upon her more recent work in which a certain legacy of the neo-avant-garde is evident. Let me begin by quoting Niccolai once more: in response to a question I posed to her regarding her involvement in the 'official' neo-avant-garde of the late 1950s and 1960s, she responded,

> Facevo parte delle reunioni ma non parlavo. Io ero agli inizi, avevo solo scritto *Il grande angolo,* non avevo scritto poesie (quelle che conosci su *Harry's Bar* sono le prime), e mi sentivo piuttosto intimidita da tutti loro battaglieri e sicuri di sé.
>
> [I attended the meetings (of the Gruppo 63) but I didn't speak. I was at the beginnings, I had written only *Il grande angolo,* I hadn't written poetry (those which you know, included in *Harry's Bar,* are the first), and I felt rather intimidated by all those others who were so militant and sure of themselves.][1]

'All those others' were, in the majority, men; the few women writers and artists associated with the Italian neo-avant-garde include the poet Amelia Rosselli, and to a much lesser degree Carla Vasio and Niccolai herself. Niccolai has acknowledged that gender played a role in the inclusion and reception of women into literary and other artistic spheres during the 1950s and 1960s (as it did for previous generations and would continue to do in subsequent times): 'In quegli anni ho potuto constatare e vivere sulla mia pelle l'atteggiamento paternalistico di molti uomini nei confronti miei e di altre donne che facevano determinati lavori' [In those years I was able to note and experience directly the paternalistic attitude of many men toward me and other women who did certain kinds of work].[2] However, Niccolai was not involved in feminist activism. In response to the question posed by Biancamaria Frabotta in the important anthology, *Donne in poesia,* of what the women poets included in the anthology thought of the feminist movement of the last five years – that is, from the early 1970s to the publication date of the anthology, 1976 – Niccolai said: 'Ne approvo senz'altro le rivendicazioni di carattere economico-sociale e le battaglie per la libertà e la dignità della donna in una società più dignitosa e più libera. Non credo che si possa condurre una lotta isolata *per la donna,* slegata dagli altri problemi' [I certainly approve of the economic-social victories and the battles for the freedom and dignity of women in a more free and dignified society. I don't think that an isolated battle *for women,* disjoined from other problems, can be conducted] (in Frabotta 61). In an interview conducted in 1984 and published in *Carte Italiane,* Niccolai again made clear her lack of involvement in organized feminism of the 1970s, stating that she was living mainly in the country during that period, and feminist activism was very much a city phenomenon. Her contribution to feminism, in her view, is simply the way she has lived and worked, gaining some respect in the halls of power and perhaps opening the door to younger generations of women writers and artists.[3]

I have brought up the issue of feminism because the exclusion of Giulia Niccolai from most of the canonical criticism regarding the Italian neo-avant-garde is, in my opinion, due in great part to her gender. Seen as a minor presence in the Gruppo 63 and as a 'helpmate' to Adriano Spatola during their years of collaborative work as poets and publishers, rather than as an essential voice in her own right, Niccolai has seldom been considered as a major figure of the neo-avant-garde, but rather as a participant in some fairly peripheral way 'by association.'[4] As she herself put it, 'il Gruppo '63 parla come se io facessi parte del Gruppo '63. Per *honoris causa,* hai capito. Da notare che nel Gruppo '63 c'erano soltanto due donne, il che è abbastanza interessante: Amelia Rosselli e Carla Vasio. Io sono stata inglobata dopo' [The Gruppo 63 talks as if I participated in the group. As an honorary member, you understand. To note is the fact that in the Gruppo 63 there were only two women, which is rather interesting: Amelia Rosselli and Carla Vasio. I was included later] (in Del Giudice et al. 11). I would argue, on the contrary, that her novel *Il grande angolo* (1966) was as significant a contribution to the neo-avant-garde's experimental approach to the renewal of literature as were the novels and poetry of such male writers as Sanguineti, Malerba, Pagliarani, Balestrini, Giuliani, whose works of those years have been given much more sustained and serious critical attention. Furthermore, Niccolai's earliest poetry, now collected in *Harry's Bar e altre poesie,* puts her beginnings as a poet squarely into the sphere of the neo-avant-garde and, more importantly, shows her enormous originality and uniqueness as a poet drawing on sources such as Lewis Carroll's nonsense verse, Gertrude Stein's writings, and her own multilingual abilities, which were quite distinct from many of the models that shaped other neo-avant-garde writers. Of course, she shared the neo-avant-garde's interest in linguistic experimentation, concrete and visual poetry, and a sort of surrealism redux, but her exuberant play with words, her joyful verve, and her very particular belief in the magic of certain verbal concatenations give her work a style and tone that are all her own.

Happily, Amelia Rosselli, a neo-avant-garde woman poet whose difficult verse has received serious critical attention, has even been 'canonized' in recent collections of twentieth-century poetry including Mengaldo's important 1979 anthology, but Carla Vasio, like Niccolai, has not been widely studied or even included in any overt way in the subsequent discussions and analyses of the Italian neo-avant-garde. General recuperation, usually feminist in origin, of women's contributions to literary movements, schools, and trends, is important. However, distinguishing clearly among the quality and significance of individual works by diverse women, whether or not the women in question considered themselves to be feminist writers, is, I believe, one of the most necessary tasks of feminist critics if recuperation of women's work is to be not merely a matter of righting past exclusions due to gender, but also and more importantly a genuine enrichment and re-articulation of literary history. Giulia Niccolai's writings are, in my view, fully worthy of inclusion due to their quality; what follows is animated by my conviction that our understanding of the Italian neo-avant-garde and its legacy is significantly deepened with the inclusion of Niccolai in analyses of it.

Although known primarily as a poet, Niccolai's debut as a writer was in fact as a novelist: *Il grande angolo* is always mentioned when Niccolai's works are listed, but has received very little critical attention, unlike other experimental novels that arose out of the neo-avant-garde era, such as Luigi Malerba's *Il serpente* (1966) or Edoardo Sanguineti's *Capriccio italiano* (1963).[5] Drawing greatly on Niccolai's experience as a photographer and photojournalist, the novel tells the story of Ita, a young photojournalist who, like Niccolai herself, tends to frame experience of both self and others as though through the lens of a camera, thus using photography as a cognitive and epistemological tool in the aid of understanding reality.[6] As in so many neo-avant-garde works, there is a preoccupation with fragmentation; diverse bits and pieces of places, people, and happenings form a patchwork of perception for Ita when the suicide of her lover Domínguez prompts her to seek understanding of this enormously traumatic and mysterious event. We cannot help but think of Michelangelo Antonioni's film *Blowup* (released the same year that Niccolai's novel was published) in which a mysterious (or apparent) death prompts the protagonist photographer to search for a completely clear understanding of what he thinks he has captured on film, an understanding that eludes him, just as the reasons for Domínguez's death ultimately elude Ita. As in *Blowup*, details and close-up scrutiny of the seen appear to be possible means for comprehending reality, the perception of which is, for Ita, always filtered through devices, such as measuring instruments, windows, or glass, but most importantly through the lens of her camera. There is also something cinematic about Niccolai's use of non-linear chronology, with flashbacks and iteration as devices to stop the forward flow of traditional narration. The novel is also spatially disjunctive, as Ita and Dominguez travel in Egypt where they are to photograph the lands that will be swallowed up by the Aswan dam, to New York, and in Italy.

The emphasis on detail, mystery, and the search for comprehension of the origin and meaning of events is related to the genre of detective fiction, one of the important models both for neo-avant-garde writers and for their 'forefather' Carlo Emilio Gadda.[7] Gadda's *Quer pasticciaccio brutto de via Merulana* has often been called a 'metaphysical detective novel,' without, however, the satisfying resolution of mainstream detective fiction. Death is, of course, at the heart of the *giallo* genre and is very much at the heart of Niccolai's novel as well. Attempting to come to terms with mortality and its connection with the inexorable passing of time is part of the human condition, and Niccolai was not and is not exempt from this shared burden. In her case, this need to find a way of comprehending mortality led her to art: first to photography, which in some sense overcomes time and death by preserving what is past; and then to writing, which is also an act of preservation as well as of an instrument of possible understanding of the great mystery of human existence itself.[8] Ita's discovery of her lover's dead body is recounted in enormous 'photographic' detail; what she sees allows her to reconstruct his exact movements on and around the bed where he bled to death from opened wrists, eventually falling onto the floor where Ita discovers his body. The intense scrutiny of the suicide scene is similar to the intense scrutiny of Liliana's murdered body by Gadda's detective Don Ciccio, but whereas Don Ciccio's gaze upon the woman's body sexualizes her, concentrating as it does on her lower body and uncovered, open thighs, Ita's gaze is almost forensic in its avoidance of any affective resonance.[9] Interestingly, the gaze of a woman represses or displaces emotionality in this case, as Ita dispassionately describes how her friend must have moved about and then fallen to the floor in death:

> Quando il sangue non zampillava più ma uscivano solo gocce deve essere

tornato al letto perché sul cuscino e sul lenzuolo dalla parte dove dormivo io c'erano due righe parallele di tratti rossi, di gocce rosse, un altro disegno come due file di formiche che alla fine si allargavano e formavano due altre spirali ma cominciate queste dal cerchio più largo per diventare più piccolo. Lui era in terra tra il letto e il muro dalla mia parte. In faccia era grigio.

[When the blood had stopped spurting but only dripping, he must have gone back to the bed, because there were two parallel lines of red marks on the side where I would sleep. There was another design like two lines of ants that widened at the end and made two other spirals, but these ones began from the widest circle and became smaller. He was on the floor between the bed and wall on my side. His face was gray.] (*Il grande angolo* 66)

This riveting description, part of a longer one that captures even more details of the suicide scene, is striking not only for its dispassionate detail but also for the repressed emotion in the words 'on the side where I would sleep' and 'between the bed and wall on my side,' both of which convey the intimacy of her relationship with Domínguez. This 'close-up photograph' would seem to reveal a great deal, but in fact only intensifies the mystery of a violent, self-imposed death. Niccolai's novel may in some sense be considered a novel of the type written by authors of the so-called école du regard, a trend in French literature of that period characterized by a strong emphasis on description of the phenomenological, and an avoidance of in-depth psychologically-conditioned character portrayals. Yet, as Franco Tagliaferro notes in an essay included in *La misura del respiro* (a volume of selected writings by Niccolai)[10] *Il grande angelo* is in fact quite different from this form of anti-novel, in that the 'analiticità della visione e l'impersonalità del racconto' [the analytical nature of the perspective and the impersonality of the narrative] have a different genesis and justification:

perché G.N. trasforma la tecnica dello sguardo, che nei romanzi di Robbe-Grillet e compagni è dichiarato artificio ... [a Ita] non le basta vedere, ma vuole anche capire, le cose deve inquadarle una per una, e *fissarle.* Perciò la sua analiticità è narrativamente giustificata. Quanto all'impersonalità, bisogna dire che qui il lettore non viene tenuto a distanza come accade nel *Nouveau Roman.* Anzi è obbligato a frequenti correzioni di lettura, perché la protagonista alterna le asciutte, quasi notarili descrizioni di luoghi e di azioni proprie e altrui, a emotive registrazioni ... dei ricordi e dei pensieri che la realtà esterna suscita in lei.

> [because G.N. transforms the technique of the gaze, which in the novels of Robbe-Grillet and company is declaredly artificial ... [for Ita] it is not enough to see, she also wants to understand, she must frame things one by one, and *fasten them.* For this reason her analytical nature is narratively justified. As for impersonality, it is necessary to say that here the reader is not held at a distance as happens in the *nouveau roman.* In fact he/she is obliged to make frequent corrections while reading, because the protagonist alternates the dry, almost legalistic descriptions of places and of her own and others' actions, with the emotional registration of memories and thoughts that external reality stimulates in her.] (Tagliaferro 62)

In short, the key to Ita's way of seeing and trying to understand reality is in her profession as a photographer, just as Antonioni's protagonist in *Blowup* is entirely motivated by his professional expertise as photographer. That Niccolai put this reliance on her professional orientation on trial in *Il grande angolo* is already an indication of her subsequent abandonment of photography in favour of writing, as another, and perhaps potentially more successful, instrument for capturing the mystery of human existence, overcoming time's limits, grappling with mortality, and finding the sheer joy of creating.

Missing in Niccolai's novel is any ludic quality, yet humour and play emerge strongly in her subsequent turn to poetry. *Poema & oggetto* (1974) is an exercise in visual poetry, made up of a series of drawings of everyday objects such as a typewriter, pins, or a light bulb, accompanied by a succinct phrase that comments on the objects in such a way as to stimulate our thinking about them in new and often humorous ways. These poems are visualizations that concentrate on the 'perceptive moment of thought,' as Milli Griffi writes in her Introduction to the volume (9). In her *Humpty Dumpty* series of poems (1969), Niccolai was already using visual poetry as a stimulus to thought and laughter; these poems, based on Lewis Carroll's *Alice* books as well as her beloved *Webster's Collegiate Dictionary*, play with the possible meanings inherent in words. For example, the phrase 'the table was a large one' becomes 'the table was a large' with a horizontal number '1' underneath the phrase in large bold print, looking for all the world like the corner of a table. The word 'cheese' is printed in the shape of a smile. The word 'impenetrability' is printed with the letters so close together as to create an impenetrable mass. Striking, of course, is the fact that Niccolai uses English in these first experimental forays into poetry, drawing on her childhood fascination with nursery rhymes and nonsense verse such as Carroll's 'Jabberwocky.' In the 1984 interview quoted above Niccolai explains that her American mother would often go to the United States and bring her back children's books in English: 'all the nursery rhymes and all the sort of magic, which is Anglo-Saxon, came to me in that way' (in Del Giudice et al. 5). Her first poems thus seem to be a return to childhood, and to the maternal source of language, which in her case was English. There is also no doubt that Spatola's strong interest in visual poetry influenced Niccolai's work of this period as well. Yet Spatola remained imprisoned in his search for 'total poetry' and eventually ended up feeling betrayed by poetry itself; according to Niccolai, he paid with his life for his endless, relentless dedication to art (which she likens to the task of Sisyphus).[11] Niccolai, however, gave herself over to the magical, ludic, and positive aspects of poetic creation, thus perhaps finding some form of 'salvation' from the torments of excessive conceptualization that characterizes much of avant-garde art.

The poems included in *Dai novissimi* and *Sostituzione* were written during the early and mid-1970s; Niccolai explains:

> sono diversissime da tutte le altre. Infatti sono dei collages dai testi critici dell'antologia dei Novissimi e di altri saggi critici (ricordo un libro di Fausto Curi di cui peró non ricordo il nome).
>
> [They are very different from all the others. In fact they are collages from the critical texts of the *novissimi* anthology and of other critical essays (I remember a book by Fausto Curi the title of which I don't remember, however).][12]

This phase of her work as a poet moved more squarely into the Italian context, and reflects very clearly her involvement with the theories and practices of the neo-avant-garde *novissimi* poets (Antonio Porta, Alfredo Giuliani, Nanni Balestrini, and others) who shared the conviction that poetry should be about language, about poetry itself in its ontological status as a linguistic sign rather than as an instrument for the expression of self, reality, or transcendental meanings. In recent email comments to me about this work, Niccolai states that she was 'practicing' ('Mi esercitavo') how to create tension in language: 'In effetti, in quei testi la tensione c'è ma non viene svolto in maniera convincente un vero e proprio concetto filosofico' [In fact, in those texts tension exists, but a real, genuine philosophical concept is not developed].[13] First published in *Tam Tam*, the journal that Spatola and Niccolai edited, these 'collages' reflect something of her work as a photographer, as well as aspects of *Il grande angolo*, as can be seen in the following quotation from *Sostituzione*: 'Seminando frantumi e ritagli / in una specie di dissolvenza incrociata / investe le membrature del testo / (oggetto della propria operazione)' [Sowing fragments and clippings / in a kind of slow dissolve / it collides with the frames of the text / (object of its own operation)]. Terms such as 'fragments,' 'slow dissolve,' and 'frames' all connect with acts of visual perception, reminding the reader of the way in which photographic registrations of bits of reality are always momentaneous and partial. Exercises these poems may be, but they are important steps in Niccolai's itinerary towards the expression not only of thoughts and ideas, but also of the processes and instruments of cognition and ordering that underlie artistic creation.

Niccolai's best-known and most anthologized and cited poems are from the collections *Greenwich* (1971), *New Greenwich* (1975–9), *Webster Poems* (1971–7), *Russky Salad Ballads* (1975–7), and *Prima e dopo la Stein* (1978–80), all of which now republished in *Harry's Bar e altre poesie.* In these poems, her early experimentation and search for a voice have been replaced by a sure style and an originality that is quite exceptional, even for those times of continuing avant-garde work, when originality was the goal of so many younger poets and prose writers whose theory and practice of literary creation had been conditioned by the experimentalism and neo-avant-gardism of the 1950s and 1960s. By the mid-1970s Niccolai had overcome her timidity and her reliance on the models provided by other poets and theorists; as she commented in a recent email:

> Credo che un poeta, agli esordi, corra il rischio molto forte di scegliere un tono (lirico, aulico, intimista, di invettiva ecc.) che in realtà appartiene a un poeta che ammira, e di avvolgere tutta la propria opera in esso. Diciamo che l'avanguardia mi è servita a fare 'piazza pulita' senza lasciarmi troppo influenzare dai poeti di successo. Ora non mi sento in alcun modo una poetessa d'avanguardia, tuttavia, quella lezione iniziale direi che funziona ancora.
>
> [I believe that at the beginning a poet runs the very strong risk of choosing a tone (lyrical, academic, intimist, of invective, etc.) that in reality belongs to a poet he/she admires, and to wrap all of his/her work in it. Let's say that the avant-garde helped me to make a 'clean sweep' without letting me be too influenced by successful poets. Nowadays, I don't feel in any way like a poet of the avant-garde, however, I would say that that first lesson is still working.][14]

The *Greenwich* and *New Greenwich* poems are made up entirely of place names, taken from the world atlas of the *Encyclopedia Britannica,* which, according to Niccolai, she chose particularly for its motto, 'All the World's Here – Unabridged,' a claim that she wittily qualifies as 'ricca di garanzie' [rich in guarantees] (Note in *Harry's Bar* 74). If Ionesco's assertion that 'geografia e filologia sono sorelle gemelle' [geography and philology are twin sisters], used by Niccolai as the epigraph for the series, is true, then her poems are as much, if not more, about language as they are about places. The many dedications to friends and fellow artists by which these poems are marked implies as well a level of interpersonal, private meaning associated with the choice of place names that make up the verses. For example, 'Como è trieste Venezia,' dedicated to Charles Aznavour (for his well-known song 'Que c'est triste Venise') and to Adriano Spatola, is a sort of love poem, not only because of the obvious allusion to the sadness of the romantic city of lovers, but also because of the dedication to a French singer of love ballads and to Niccolai's own longtime lover and companion.

Niccolai's particular penchant for dedicating many poems to specific individuals, and even incorporating friends into her poetry, combined with her attachment to 'neutral' sources of factual information, such as dictionaries and atlases, add up to a fascinating mixture of the very objective and the deeply subjective in her work. Yet, on second thought, for Niccolai there is nothing 'neutral' about dictionary definitions or place names; rather, they hold within themselves a magical potential for allusive meanings and deep reverberations that touch the psyche as much as the intellect. I use the word 'magical' quite intentionally, for it is a term that Niccolai has often evoked: the 'magic' of nursery rhymes, of words both in their materiality and in their abstraction, and of the very making of poetry itself. It may be that Niccolai's emphases on the magical and playful aspects of poetic creation are what ultimately distinguish her work from much of the production of the neo-avant-garde, which was generally more conceptual and intellectualized than open to the ludic realm. In her insistence on the potential in everyone to be a poet and on the power of humour and word play, one thinks of earlier poets in the Italian tradition, such as Pascoli (whose 'fanciullino' is akin to Niccolai's concept of the poet) and Palazzeschi (whose ludic qualities distinguish him from other poets of an earlier avant-garde, futurism). Niccolai commented both on magic and on the 'poet in all of us' in an interview in 1984, stating that 'great artists are translators of something that is very magical and sacred' and that 'It's up to everybody to become a poet. I mean a poet in a wide sense ... You can be a poet while you are picnicking in a wood, or someone from Los Angeles who is in a wood and is eating his pastrami sandwich. There's a big difference' (in Del Giudice, et. al., 5 and 13). Because poetry can come from anywhere and in any given circumstance, it is not surprising that many of Niccolai's poems are occasional in nature. *Russky Salad Ballads* (along with the *Webster Poems*) are among the most 'occasional.' Niccolai's note characterizes them as '"poesie d'occasione," poesie ad personam ... [e] si riferiscono a poesie o quadri sempre fatti dalle persone a cui sono dedicate' ['occasional poetry,' poetry ad personam ... which refers to poems or portraits that are always made up of the people to whom they are dedicated] ('Nota' in *Harry's Bar* 105). *Russky Salad Ballads* are also multilingual, making use of Italian, English, French, and German, and often punning interlinguistically. Niccolai calls this mix of languages 'un esperimento di esorcizzazione' [an experiment of exorcism], and explains that she has the 'hateful obsession' of looking for interlinguistic rhymes in empty moments when she is driving or just sitting around alone and not thinking about anything in a serious way. Language and subjectivity thus come together once more in these supremely entertaining poems.

The poem, 'E.V. Ballad,' included in *Russky Salad Ballads*, is dedicated to and is about Niccolai's friend and fellow poet, Emilio Villa (1914–2003), considered one of the forefathers of the Italian neo-avant-garde. The ballad begins: '*Ev*ening and the *ev*erest/ist vers la poetry leaning,' and further on Niccolai recalls one of Villa's experiments, which consisted in 'writing' a poem in English, a language he did not know, by feeding words into a computer; she calls the result 'un bel incest.' Incest is an ancient taboo, and the term indicates transgressiveness, which was one of the salient goals of the neo-avant-garde, both in terms of the renewal of standardized literary forms and of a challenge to societal structures that repress the individual. Asked what the recurrent term 'incest' means to her, Niccolai responded that, in creating a computer poem, Villa 'mimes English in this poem and what he does with the computer and with the language is incest. I call it "incest" because it's more than just making love, it's prohibited because it's magic.' Asked by the interviewer Del Giudice if 'incest' is a metaphor for poetry-making, Niccolai responds positively, and adds: 'Yes, and of being a poet; being incestuous with words and with objects and with people, that is, making love to these things and entering them. Naturally it's "incest" with quotation marks around it, no? It has that connotation, and "incidere" too. If I say "making love," it's too flat, so I use a knife (Del Giudice et al. 7).

It is all the more striking that a woman uses these terms of 'entering,' and 'making love to,' for these are assertive acts of possession that are much more commonly seen as masculine perspectives, while women are more typically viewed as 'acted upon,' 'entered,' or 'marked' by the actions of others. For Niccolai there is empowerment in poetry-making; poetry's prohibitive, magical essence is for her both a way of possessing language and experience (of others, the world, and the self), and of affecting them with the transformative power of creativity.[15]

Prima e dopo la Stein contains one of Niccolai's most quoted poems: 'Bad Ragaz.' Here, she creates a commentary on the making and reception of poetry, and the lack of understanding by which much of the world's population greets it. 'Bad Ragaz' is in the form of a conversation of sorts between the poet and an American tourist whose Italian is quite limited. A series of misunderstandings, due in part to linguistic limitations but also to the tourist's complete lack of comprehension regarding poetry, ensues, to hilarious results. 'Bad Ragaz' is a spa in Switzerland, but the tourist wonders if the word 'Ragaz' is related to the Italian term for boy, 'ragazzo,' which leads Niccolai to think that 'bad' means 'bath' in German and 'cattivo' in Italian, so the spa could be thought of as 'Bad Boy Baths.' She then remembers how the phrase 'concrete poetry' became 'concrete pottery' at a reading in Sydney, and 'concert poetry' in Melbourne, but decides not to share this with the tourist: 'No, I won't tell him / because I already know that he would ask me: / *What* to be Concrete Poetry? /and I have no intention of explaining it to him.' As in the earlier poem, 'Harry's Bar Ballad,' also one of the best known of her entire body of work, Niccolai's word play reaches a wonderful level of humour that is not only highly entertaining for the reader, but also stimulating in terms of how we think about language and its potential for communication as well as for utter and complete misunderstanding. How can speakers of different languages ever expect to order martinis, if 'nein' means 'none' in German, but 'nine' in English is a whole different matter! Better, as Niccolai concludes, for her to want just gin, since she is, after all, G.N.! The pleasure in reading these and so many other playful, interlinguistic verses, is enormous, and is intensified by reading them aloud, thus emphasizing the shared quality of such poetry that opens out onto others both within its dialogic forms and dedicatory specificities, and in its essence as play, itself an activity that creates a sense of community and commonality.

The communicative, quotidian, and occasional thrust in Niccolai's poetry is made even more explicit in her more recent poems, called 'Frisbees,' written between 1982 and 1988. Umberto Eco's concept of the 'opera aperta' and the importance of the role of the reader/receiver of texts and other art forms for many participants in the activities and theorizations of the neo-avant-garde come to the fore again in these poems.[16] By 1986, as her interest in Buddhism intensified, Niccolai had decided to get out of the 'game' of being a public poet. The Frisbee poems were a sort of 'last-ditch' effort, in her own words, to find a way out of her fears and suffering by means of poetic creation. (As noted above, she suffered a serious illness and long bout with depression during this period.) In these poems, she sought to transform simple everyday moments into poetry, but 'questo sforzo non bastava a tenere a bada la sofferenza' [this effort wasn't enough to keep suffering at bay] ('Postfazione' to *Frisbees* 152). In addition to being motivated by the desire to interact more directly with her public (Niccolai had done many public poetry readings by the 1980s), by playing a sort of 'back and forth' game of the kind represented by throwing a frisbee, she was also becoming fascinated with coincidences and the magic of synchronism in quotidian events and observations. Coincidences took on a profound significance for Niccolai:

> Non più casuali, bensí *causali* in maniera esemplare, proprio le coincidenze rappresentano infatti l'inizio di un mio cammino spirituale che nell'85, dopo una grave malattia, mi fece avvicinare al buddismo tibetano del quale sono ora monaca da quattro anni.
>
> [No longer simply chance, but rather *causative* in an exemplary way, coincidences represent the beginning of my spiritual path that in 1985, after a serious illness, made me approach Tibetan Buddhism, of which I have now been a nun for four years.] ('Postfazione' to *Frisbees* 153)[17]

The remarkable continuity of Niccolai's itinerary as a photographer, prose writer, and poet emerges from the constant presence of certain preoccupations in her work from the 1960s through to the 1980s: the magic inherent in language and only apparently trivial events; the search for a way to connect beyond the limits of the solipsistic self; the role of play and humour in the path toward transcendence.

Following her decision to end her career as a public poet, Niccolai nonetheless continued to write. Much of her most recent work is in prose and is directly tied to her experience of Buddhism. She contributed an essay on the via Emilia to the volume *Esplorazioni sulla via Emilia: scritture nel paesaggio* in 1986. More recent publications include her collection of essays, *Esoterico biliardo* (2001), and the limited edition volume of bilingual writings, *Orienti, Orients* (2004). She also published individual stories and poems through the late 1990s and into the new millennium. To end my consideration of her work, I would like to return to the connection between Giorgio Manganelli and Niccolai, for I see this connection as exemplary in terms of the best results that came out of the Italian neo-avant-garde. Both Manganelli and Niccolai are associated only peripherally with the neo-avant-garde. If we are looking for directions that have renewed and enriched twentieth-century Italian literature, however, we need look no farther than to these two writers, preeminent among the most original voices of this era. Manganelli wrote an unforgettably 'Manganellian' introduction to *Harry's Bar,* in which he describes her as a 'Shérézade,' a weaver of endless tales in a fit of 'glossolalia,' and 'l'ultimo, irripetibile caso di poetessa epica' [the last, unrepeatable case of an epic woman poet] ('Prefazione' 10). Yet their connection goes much deeper than that of a poet for whom another writer consents to write an introduction. In her essay 'Cavalli veri, cavalli figurati' [Real horses, imagined horses] (published in *Esoterico biliardo*) Niccolai calls Manganelli her 'lettore privilegiato' [preferred reader], her 'interlocutore immaginario' [imagined interlocutor]. According to Niccolai, Manganelli's deep interest in Jungian approaches to psychic and spiritual realms shares a great deal with her interest in Buddhism, leading them both to plumb the depths of inner experience. In reading Manganelli's first book, *Hilarotroegedia,* Niccolai came to see him as a writer who had 'il coraggio di mostrare tutto il grottesco, il goffo, l'abietto e l'irredento che ci contraddistingue' [the courage to show all the grotesque, the awkward, the abject and the unredeemed that characterizes us] ('Cavalli' 128), and she saw that his search for transcendence of the ego was pulling him, like her, toward 'una mostruosa vocazione mimetica' [a monstrous mimetic vocation] (140), which is, in fact, writing itself. For Niccolai, his is an extraordinary commitment to language (as Manganelli himself often asserted, calling language and rhetoric 'gods' that demand everything of their 'slaves'):

> In effetti, ogni singolo libro di Manganelli può essere letto come la testimonianza di un mistico (malgré soi?) che rifiuta di cedere a qualsiasi lusinga, a qualsiasi trappola della libido dell'Io.
>
> [In effect, every single book by Manganelli can be read as the testament of a mystic (in spite of himself?) who refuses to give in to any flattery, to any trap of the ego's libido.] (165)

Manganelli's devotion to language and his attention to the metaphysics of desire, the nullity of the self, and death, seen in the light of Niccolai's artistic and Buddhist perspectives, take on a deep spiritual quality that is at odds with his established critical reputation as a cerebral formalist and a player of dazzling, experimental literary games. These two writers, both of whom came into their vocations during the era of neo-avant-garde work, are united in their common search for ways to go beyond the merely personal and subjective, through the alchemy of literary creation, as they look into the deep abyss of the self in order to reach the highest levels of transcendence.[18]

Giulia Niccolai may have decided to withdraw from active participation in the literary scene, but she has continued to write both prose and poetry, to give interviews, and to share her art generously with anyone who cares to know more about her remarkable itinerary. The more she has relinquished her desire, shared by all artists, for public reception and recognition, the more she has made clear that art, for her, remains a continual search, parallel with and integral to life as it is lived.[19] Just as her life brings constant change and renewal, so too her writing continues to evolve, producing unique and ever new results. Being more genuinely 'neo-avant-garde' than this is difficult to imagine, if one accepts the term in its widest sense, as a never-ending dedication to process, risk-taking, and a belief in the power of art to renew both itself and us.

NOTES

1 Giulia Niccolai, email correspondence, 14 August 2005. This and all subsequent translations from the Italian are mine.

2 Quotation by Hill, in Ricaldone, ed. *Incontri di poesia*, 34.

3 This interview was conducted in both English and Italian. Niccolai's response to the question about her involvement in feminism was in English: 'I hadn't been actively involved then because I was living with Spatola in the country for ten years and all the feminist movement of that period was a city movement' (in Del Giudice et al. 7).

4 In an essay of reminiscence about the years spent living and working with Spatola in Mulino di Bazzano, Niccolai writes: 'Essendo donna, mi viene spesso chiesto quale aiuto io abbia ricevuto da Adriano [Spatola] a proposito della scrittura. So che questa domanda non viene mai rivolta a un uomo che, essendo poeta o scrittore, conviva con una donna che scrive.' [Being a woman, I am often asked what help I received from Adriano as far as writing

is concerned. I know that this question is never directed to a man who, as a poet or writer, lives with a woman who writes.] ('Gli anni di Mulino,' in *Esoterico biliardo* 89–90). I add, parenthetically, that in the volume *Gruppo 63: critica e teoria*, edited by Renato Barilli and Angelo Guglielmi, the names of Amelia Rosselli and Giulia Niccolai (both of whom are mentioned in the appendices) are misspelled: this may be seen as an indication of the level of carelessness and/or indifference that women writers often suffer, even when they are acknowledged in some minimal way.

5 Sarah Hill's analysis of *Il grande angolo in* 'Photographic Fictions' is, to my knowledge, the most complete and perceptive that exists to date. My discussion owes a great debt to her work.

6 In preparation for her dissertation, Sarah Hill interviewed Niccolai regarding many aspects of her work, beginning with photography. Asked why she moved from photography to writing, Niccolai responded that as a photographer, 'vedevi le cose dal punto di vista della fotografia. Io non riuscivo a vedere in un altro modo. Le vedevo sempre come in un'inquadratura possibile.' [you saw things from the point of view of photography. I could not see things in a different way. I always saw them as though in a possible frame.] (interview quoted in Hill 165).

7 Stefani Tani's 1984 study, *The Doomed Detective*, which analyzes the influence of detective fiction on postmodern fiction, remains a helpful source for understanding the relation of these genres.

8 Hill writes that 'Niccolai's shift into writing poetry, and her subsequent commitment to Buddhism represent a continuing evolution of her response to the questions of death and time, and her attempts to come to terms with 'l'inevitabile scorrere del tempo' [the inevitable passing of time] and the 'mutamenti interiori che questo comporta' [the internal changes that this involves] (quotations from Niccolai's email message to Hill, 17 April 2004, now cited in Hill 186).

9 'Don Ciccio first scrutinizes the thighs, the underwear, the garters, the stockings; all that was denied to him in life and now open to him legitimately as the investigator on the case' (Nerenberg 160).

10 It is interesting that Niccolai chose to include a passage from her novel in a collection that is subtitled *Poesie scelte*. In fact, the inclusion is entirely appropriate, given that the passage in question shifts from prose into poetic form (the only time this happens in the novel) as Ita and her companions look at wall drawings on a pyramid and Niccolai creates what Tagliaferro calls 'una momentanea sottrazione dei personaggi al dominio delle cose' [a momentary freeing of the characters from the dominion of things] (Tagliaferro 63) as they experience the timeless beauty of the drawn figures from ancient times.

11 See Niccolai's remarkable portrayal of Spatola and his work in 'Gli anni di Mulino,' included in *Esoterico biliardo,* 83–125.
12 Niccolai, email, 15 August 2005.
13 Interestingly, it is from these 'exercises' that the poems by Niccolai included in Biancamaria Frabotta's important anthology *Donne in poesia* (1976); are chosen. *Sostituzione* was translated by Niccolai and Paul Vangelisti, and published in 1975.
14 Niccolai, email, 14 August 2005.
15 One of the best studies of the experiences and legacy of the neo-avant-garde remains Francesco Muzzioli's *Teoria e critica della letteratura nelle avanguardie italiane degli anni sessanta* (1982). Considering the neo-avant-garde's goal of overcoming the more nefarious effects of society's civilizing structures, a goal allied to a return to some of surrealism's orientations, Muzzioli quotes from a piece by Niccolai published in *Quindici* in 1968, in which she 'prende di mira l'uniformante addestramento societario' [takes as her target the homologizing training of society]: 'Siamo simili a tanti polli di allevamento, ingozzati di equivoci' [We are similar to so many breeding hens, crammed with misunderstandings]. Muzzioli characterizes the neo-avant-garde's revolt against conformity as 'affidata al gioco, al divertimento, alla fantasia' [entrusted to play, entertainment, fantasy], all of which are central to Niccolai's subsequent art (Muzzioli 196).
16 See Muzzioli, especially chapter 3, 'Verso le cose stesse,' for an excellent description and analysis of these issues pertaining to the fruition of the text.
17 See Tagliaferro's essay in *La misura del respiro* for an excellent discussion of the trajectory of Niccolai's work, including *Frisbees.*
18 See my review article 'Manganelli and Niccolai' for a more detailed consideration of the ways in which these two writers are united.
19 In a 'Frisbee poem' of 1990, Niccolai wrote: 'Ho la quasi certezzza di essere stata una foca in un circo in una precedente incarnazione. Andavo matta per il pesce e gli applausi. Andavo matta per il pesce e gli applausi? Bene, in questa vita ho imparato a farne a meno' [I am almost certain that I was a circus seal in a previous incarnation. I would go crazy for fish and applause. I would go crazy for fish and applause? Well, in this life I have learned to do without them] ('Postfazione' to *Frisbees* 153–4).

WORKS CITED

Barilli, Renato, and Angelo Guglielmi, eds. *Gruppo 63: critica e teoria.* Milan: Feltrinelli, 1976.

Del Giudice, Luisa, and Pasquale Verdicchio, with Paul Vangelisti, interviewers. 'Intervista con Giulia Niccolai: I Think I'm Becoming Japanese.' *Carte Italiane: A Journal of Italian Studies*, 6 (1984–5): 1–18.

Frabotta, Biancamaria, ed. *Donne in poesia: antologia della poesia femminile dal dopoguerra ad oggi.* Rome: Savelli, 1976.

Griffi, Milli. 'Introduction.' *Poema & oggetto* by Giulia Niccolai. Poesia Italiana E-book. Edizioni Biagio Cepollaro, 2005.

Hill, Sarah Patricia. 'Photographic Fictions: Photography in Italian Literature 1945–2000.' PhD dissertation, University of Chicago, 2004.

Manganelli, Giorgio. 'Prefazione.' *Harry's Bar e altre poesie 1969–1980* by Giulia Niccolai. Milan: Feltrinelli, 1981: 7–14.

Mengaldo, Pier Vincenzo, ed. *Poeti italiani del Novecento.* Milan: Mondadori, 1978.

Muzzioli, Francesco. *Teoria e critica della letteratura nelle avanguardie italiane degli anni sessanta.* Rome: Istituto della Enciclopedia italiana, 1982.

Nerenberg, Ellen V. *Prison Terms: Representing Confinement during and after Italian Fascism.* Toronto: University of Toronto Press, 2001.

Niccolai, Giulia. *Esoterico biliardo.* Milan: Archinto, 2001.

– *Frisbees (poesie da lanciare).* Udine: Campanotto Editore, 1994.

– *Il grande angolo.* Milan: Feltrinelli, 1966.

– *Harry's Bar e altre poesie 1969–1980.* Milan: Feltrinelli, 1981.

– *La misura del respiro: poesie scelte.* Verona: Anterem Edizioni, 2002.

– *Orienti Orients.* Fondazione Franco Beltrametti. Limited edition. Mendrisio: Josef Weiss Edizioni, 2004.

– *Poema & oggetto.* Torino: Geiger, 1974; Poesia Italiana E-book. Edizioni Biagio Cepollaro, 2005.

– *Substitution* [*Sostituzione*]. Trans. Paul Vangelisti with Giulia Niccolai. Los Angeles: Red Hill Press, 1975.

– 'La via Emilia.' In *Esplorazioni sulla via Emilia: scritture nel paesaggio.* Milan: Feltrinelli, 1986.

Ricaldone, Luisa, ed. *Incontri di poesia.* Turin: Trauben, 2000.

Tagliaferro, Franco. 'Da un'avventura all'altra dello stile.' In *La misura del respiro. Poesie scelte* by Giulia Niccolai. Verona: Anterem Edizioni, 2002. 61–70.

Tani, Stefano. *The Doomed Detective: The Contribution of the Detective Novel to Postmodern American and Italian Fiction.* Carbondale: Southern Illinois University Press, 1984.

West, Rebecca. 'Manganelli and Niccolai: 'The Unlikely Bond between a Junghian "Bishop" and a Buddhist Nun.' *Italica* 80, no. 1 (Spring 2003): 73–9.

PART THREE

Beyond Literature

9 Signs and Designs: Sanguineti and Baj from *Laborintus to The Biggest Art-Book in the World*

PAOLO CHIRUMBOLO

Extraeccito esoftalmiche endoiconiche,
Nonne nasute, nomadi nixonici,
Radariste radiotelegrafoniche,
Iperbolici ippomani ipoconici,
Ciscarabinieresse cromotomiche,
Orchitici ostricanti ortocanonici
Brade bakuniane bisironiche,
Anarcoapocalittici androponici,
Jarryjazziste jam jugendstilcroniche:

(Edoardo Sanguineti, *agosto 1996*)

Art Informel and Nuclear Art

In the aftermath of the physical destruction and moral despair of the Second World War, a period during which Europe experienced a deep and dramatic social crisis, the old Continent witnessed the development of an artistic current known as Art Informel.[1] Although it is difficult to give a univocal definition of this term – due to its manifold and heterogeneous nature – it is nonetheless possible to identify some of its main tenets, including an emphasis on spontaneity and irrationality, a rejection of 'well-made' traditional art works, and a refusal of the idea of form (abstract and figurative). As Claudio Spadoni has aptly explained:

> Adottando un criterio estensivo al massimo [...] si sono considerate informali tutte le esperienze artistiche che hanno rifiutato un'idea di forma precostituita, programmata, teoricamente precisata; vale a dire tutto quanto

non è rientrato nell'astrazione di matrice razionalista, come nell'area definita, con una terminologia molto generica, figurativa, ma più propriamente legata alle varie diramazioni della tradizione realista.

[Generalizing … we can define as Informel all the artistic experiences that rejected a predetermined, programmed, and theoretically defined idea of form; that is to say everything that was not part of the rationalist as well as, to use a very vague definition, figurative abstraction, which is to say all the different outcomes of the realistic tradition.] (35–6)

In addition to the rejection of form, Art Informel strongly advocated the idea of art as creation rather than imitation; the emphasis fell on the process of creation rather than the final artistic product. Unable to cope with the ruins and wasteland of the most horrific tragedy in human history and unable to deal with a much changed world, visual arts – and later on literature – ceased functioning as the mirror of nature and began to question and redefine themselves in both formal and ethical terms.

One of those who tried to provide a suitable definition of Art Informel is Umberto Eco in his famous essay *Opera aperta.* Rather than giving an exhaustive description of Art Informel and its stylistic traits, Eco preferred to speak of 'una poetica dell'informale.' In his terms, Art Informel was to be interpreted as 'una tendenza generale della cultura di un periodo' [a general tendency of the culture of a period] (155) and thus as the distinctive sign of all the avant-garde experiences of the second half of the twentieth century. In other words, Art Informel could be used as a sort of subcategory of the *opera aperta* notion, representing a wide array of artistic possibilities from painting to music and literature.[2] According to Eco:

Parlare di una poetica dell'Informale come tipica della pittura contemporanea implica una generalizzazione: 'informale,' da categoria critica diventa qualificazione di una tendenza generale della cultura di un periodo, cosí da comprendere insieme figure com Wols o Bryen, i *tachistes* veri e propri, i maestri dell'*action painting,* l'*art brut,* l'*art autre,* eccetera. A tale titolo la categoria di informale rientra sotto la definizione più vasta di *poetica dell'opera aperta.* Opera aperta come proposta di un 'campo' di possibilità interpretative, come configurazione di stimoli dotati di una sostanziale indeterminatezza, cosí che il fruitore sia indotto a una serie di 'letture' sempre variabili; struttura, infine, come 'costellazione' di elementi che si prestano a diverse relazioni reciproche. In tal senso l'informale in pittura si collega alle strutture musicali aperte della musica post- weberniana e a quella poesia 'novissima' che di informale ha già accettato, per ammissione dei suoi rappresentanti, la definizione.

[Nowadays, to say that a poetics of the 'informal' is characteristic of contemporary painting involves a generalization. No longer limited to a critical category, the term 'informal' has come to designate a general tendency of our culture and to encompass, along with painters such as Wols and Bryen, the *tachistes*, the masters of *action painting*, *art brut*, *art autre*, and so on, at which point we might as well inscribe it under the broader rubric of the *poetics of the open work*. 'Informal art' is open in that it proposes a wider range of interpretative possibilities, a configuration of stimuli whose substantial indeterminacy allows for a number of possible readings, a 'constellation' of elements that lend themselves to all sorts of reciprocal relationships. As such, 'informal painting' is closely related to the open musical structures characteristic of post-Webernian music and to a form of poetry which in Italy goes by the name of *novissima*, whose representatives have already agreed to define as 'informal.'] (153–4)

However broad this definition might be, Eco's discussion has two indisputable advantages: on one hand, it introduces the concept of the active collaboration of the receiver in the reception of the 'text' (a notion particularly dear to the *neoavanguardia* in general and to Sanguineti in particular); on the other, it establishes the link, central to this analysis, between Art Informel and literature.[3]

In an article published in *Il verri* in 1961, entitled 'Poesia informale?' [Action poetry?], Sanguineti maintains that as he was writing the poems of *Laborintus* (1951–4) he found a series of 'riferimenti' [references] not in the coeval literary landscape but rather in music and the visual arts:

Una crisi di linguaggio, quale io intendevo stabilire e patire nei miei versi, trovava conforto e analogia in affini esperimenti pittorici (e musicali), assai più che in esperimenti di ordine letterario: il privato richiamo ad altre situazioni artistiche era un modo di rompere in solitudine, la solitudine stessa in cui mi trovavo praticamente gettato.

[The crisis of language I wanted to experience and represent in my poetry found analogy and affinity in similar pictorial (and musical) experiments and not in literature. The private cry for different artistic experiences was my attempt to break the solitude and isolation in which I found myself.] (in Barilli and Guglielmi 51–2)[4]

Aware of the historical necessity to go beyond the worn out literary and linguistic codes, Sanguineti realized that his only available option was to look for a different language and to create something entirely new with no counterpart in the history of Italian literature. The explicit references made in 'Poesia informale?' to both *espressionismo astratto* and *arte informale* are thus extremely significant, as they clearly set up the connection between Sanguineti and the 'tendenze informali' [informal tendencies][5] of the 1950s to which he was strongly attracted. As Picchione has rightly argued 'the linguistic agitation, nervousness, and chaos of Sanguineti's first poetic collection' (22) was inspired by the avant-garde projects of painters such as Fautrier, Gorky, Pollock, and de Kooning (to name just a few) and their experiments with alternative techniques and materials.

It is during this time and in this cultural setting that Sanguineti established a lifelong friendship with Enrico Baj, who in 1951 founded the Movimento arte nucleare[6] with an anti-institutional and anti-formalistic artistic agenda that was very much comparable to Sanguineti's. The basic principles of the movement were laid out in the 'Manifesto della pittura nucleare' (signed by Sergio Dangelo and Enrico Baj), in which the *nuclearisti* expressed their determination to 'abbattere tutti gli "ismi" di una pittura che cade invariablimente nell'accademismo, qualunque ne sia l'origine' [demolish all the 'isms' of a painting that inevitably lapses into academicism, whatever its origin may be] (Savauge 203), and to 'reinventare la pittura' [recreate painting] (203). Caught between the desire to explore the aesthetic potential of the new nuclear technology and the fear of possible apocalyptic destruction, between 'una visione di progresso tecnico-scientifico a cui l'arte non doveva essere insensibile' and 'il senso apocalittico che la scoperta portava in sé' [a vision of scientific progress towards which art could not be insensible and the apocalyptic dimension of that discovery] (Mussini 33), hope and despair, Baj spent most of the decade exploring the *informel* possibilities of *nuclearismo,* pursuing, at the same time, his crusade against celebratory and abstract art.[7] As clearly stated in two subsequent manifestos, 'Contro lo stile' [The End of Style] (1957) and 'Manifeste de Naples' [Naples Manifesto] (1959) – the latter of which was significantly signed by both Sanguineti and Baj – the intention of this new wave of artists was thus to question the idea of style ('l'ultima delle convenzioni' [the final convention] [Savauge 209]), to challenge 'qualunque forma di accademismo' [any form of academicism] (209), and to go beyond 'astrattismo' [abstract art].[8]

Baj's intention to explore the 'nuovi infiniti orizzonti' [new and infinite horizons] (Savauge 19) of Nuclear Art deeply influenced Sanguineti's own approach to poetry and his desire to elaborate a 'scrittura adeguata all'era atomica' [a style suitable for the atomic age] (Gambaro 27) capable of conveying the sense of impending destruction and hopelessness of postwar Europe. Recalling the years of his first encounters with Baj and other artists, Sanguineti defines that period as a key moment in his intellectual growth during which he began to develop his original poetics:

> Un momento essenziale per me fu poi l'inizio degli anni '50, a Milan, in un altro ambiente molto vivo, con i bar famosi dell'epoca, veri luoghi d'incontro per gli artisti. Era l'epoca in cui Enrico Baj elaborava assieme ai suoi amici Dova, Crippa e Colombo il programma del Movimento Nucleare, ed io mi trovai veramente in grande sintonia con lui. Stavo scrivendo il mio primo libro di poesie, *Laborintus*, dove peraltro il tema atomico era un tema assolutamente centrale, e inaugurammo allora una lunga collaborazione.
>
> [The beginning of the 1950s was a crucial moment for me. The city of Milan with its famous bars, real hang outs for artists, was a really exciting place. It was the period during which Baj and his friends Dova, Crippa, and Colombo were developing the nuclear movement program, and I was very much in tune with Enrico. I was then writing my first book of poetry, *Laborintus*, where the atomic theme was rather relevant, and thus we began our long collaboration.] (Postcontemporanea)

It is hardly pure coincidence that *Laborintus* is rife with references to 'death valleys,' 'bad waters,' and 'lunghi funghi fumosi' [long, smoky mushrooms] (*Catamerone* 12)[9] and 'visioni esplosive' [explosive visions] (26), and that the whole collection is suffused with an infernal and apocalyptic atmosphere. Picchione speaks of a 'descent into a historical hell' (115) that constantly reminds the reader of the possible tragedy. Furthermore, the nuclear content finds its stylistic correspondence in the atomic fragmentation of Sanguineti's language, which also aims at conveying the 'social and psychological fractures produced by capitalist-bourgeois realities' (Picchione 115).[10]

It is because of their common anti-institutional attitude and 'consonanza tematica' [thematic empathy] (Gambaro 29) that Sanguineti and Baj began an intellectual dialogue that lasted more than fifty years. This relationship produced many daring and interesting works in which the boundaries of both arts were pushed to their formal and physical limits, and where both Baj and Sanguineti pursued their research for a 'nuova figurazione' [new figuration] the goal of which was, to quote Sanguineti, 'creare e inventare nuove forme' [to create and invent new forms] (Postcontemporanea). Due to the chronological and thematic constraints of this volume, I will focus the remainder of my analysis on texts published during the 1960s.

Sanguineti's Anti-novels between Ekphrasis, Combinatory Literature, and Pop Art

If *Laborintus* is the text in which Sanguineti translated the visual suggestions of Nuclear Art into poetical terms, the work in which a direct connection between the two authors is for the first time 'visible' and tangible is undoubtedly *Capriccio italiano* (1963), Sanguineti's foremost anti-novel. In addition to providing paintings for the covers of the four editions of the book[11] – which functioned as a sort of preemptive declaration of poetics – and the fact that he was included in the text (under the pseudonym 'B.'), Enrico Baj also inspired Sanguineti with a series of pieces that are accurately represented in *Capriccio italiano.* Sanguineti illustrates this descriptive process:

> Questo della 'descrizione,' nel complesso delle mie opere, è un rapporto che oscilla da una sorta di iperbolica fedeltà, davvero propriamente 'descrittiva,' nel pieno prolungarsi di una tradizione molto antica, a un arbitrio assoluto, prendendo il testo come 'pretesto' in senso etimologico, ossia viene prima di un testo, che poi se ne va per conto suo.
>
> [In my works, the description oscillates between a sort of hyperbolic descriptive accuracy that follows a very ancient tradition and an absolute arbitrariness in which the image works as a 'pretext' in the etymological sense of the term, which means that it comes before a text that then takes its own way.] (in Lisa 22)

Thus, oscillating between faithfulness and arbitrariness, Sanguineti incorporates in his text a number of references to some of Baj's most popular works in order to exploit their innovative potential on the literary level. In particular, this analysis will focus on Baj's research on mirrors and the Meccano set.

Baj's experiments with mirrors began in 1959 at a time when his inquiries were marked, to quote Sauvage, by 'an absolute adhesion to the freest principles of a technical experimentalism open to every possibility' (92). Evoking that period and commenting on the accidental beginning of that project Baj wrote:

> Per gli 'specchi' andò così, che salito nella soffitta di una vecchia villa a Gavirate per rimediarvi qualcosa con cui far collage, trovai uno specchio con una bella crepa in mezzo, dentro a una cornice di noce. Anziché spaventarmi alla vista dello specchio rotto, cui molti attribuiscono malefiche virtù, decisi di prendermelo e di servirmene. Fu così che, moltiplicando le rotture e aggiungendo alcuni pezzi di vetro colorato, composi il mio primo specchio. Lo specchio rotto s'era trasformato grazie a me in un segno di luminosità differente e anche di fortuna.

> [That's how it all started. I was in the attic of an old villa in Gavirate and I was looking for something to make collages, and I found a chestnut framed mirror with a crack in the middle. Instead of being scared by the cracked mirror, to which many attribute evil traits, I decided to take it and use it. I then multiplied the cracks, added a few pieces of coloured glass, and I created my first mirror. Thanks to me, the broken mirror became the sign of a different brightness and of good luck.] (*Automitobiografia* 144)

As André Pieyre de Mandiargues has rightly argued, the transformation of the surface of the mirror[12] was one of the consequences of Baj's anti-traditional viewpoint: instead of representing an ordered and coherent reality, the fragmented mirror reflected 'il mondo esteriore allo stesso modo della pittura accademica e in un caso come nell'altro lo spazio di quel mondo è sconvolto dalla brutale introduzione di un corpo estraneo' [the exterior world the same as academic painting, and in both cases the space of that world is devastated by the brutal introduction of an exterior element] (78).[13] Baj's original intuition was taken up by Sanguineti and introduced in the diegetic universe of *Capriccio italiano*, when the narrating I looks at himself into a mirror. His reaction is uncontrollable, as the mirror completely disfigures him:

> E subito, allora, mi misi a sputare nello specchio, e allora il mio volto cominciò a guastarsi tutto, e non vedevo l'ombelico, ma una schiumosa chiazza,

e un ginocchio cominciò a sciogliersi tutto, e poi cancellai quasi un orecchio, e poi i testicoli, e tutto così, a caso. E la testa di B. era proprio dietro la mia, che rideva. Poi prese le mie mutande e se le mise in testa. E a vederlo così nello specchio, che si guastava anche lui tutto in faccia, con gli ultimi sputi, sembrava proprio che piangesse.

[And then immediately I began to spit at the mirror, and then my face began to get all smeared, and I couldn't see my navel, only a sort of frothy patch, and one of my knees began to come to bits, and then one ear was nearly obliterated, and then the testicles, and all just like that, in a haphazard sort of way. And B.'s head was just behind mine, and he was laughing. Then he took my pants and put them on his head. And seeing him like that in the mirror, with his face, too, all smudged with spittle, it seemed just as though he was crying.] (20)

The disfiguring mirror stands for Sanguineti's rejection of the bourgeois tradition of naturalistic fiction. In the oneiric universe created by Sanguineti the mirror loses its purely representational power: the narrator's face, instead of being objectively portrayed, is deformed by his own saliva (the literary equivalent of Baj's cracked mirror); the whole passage can be interpreted as an aesthetic statement through which Sanguineti makes it clear that his main goal is not to duplicate reality but rather to create a parodic version of it. In other words, the mirrors portrayed by Sanguineti and Baj do not to univocally reflect the world but 'lo trasformano e lo modificano in un entità caleidoscopicamente scomposta e grottesca' [transform and modify it in a grotesque and kaleidoscopic entity] (Corgnati 17).[14]

Another allusion to Baj's figurative experimentalism is the *Meccano* set, a children's educational toy consisting of a system of metal parts that can be used to construct models of vehicles or machines. Baj used Meccano pieces throughout his career. In fact, Baj and Raymond Queneau published a livre d'artiste entitled *Meccano, ou l'Analyse matricielle du langage* (1966), in which Baj's mechanical constructions illustrated Queneau's composition. As Baj later pointed out:

il sistema combinatorio adottato da Queneau per indagare morfemi e semantemi si prestava molto bene ad essere illustrato con un altro sistema combinatorio, il meccano, ovvero, quel gioco ora desueto che un tempo affascinava i ragazzi e consistente appunto nella possibilità di montare

> insieme un *assemblage* di pezzi decisamente meccanici (donde il nome di meccano) per cavarne le più strane costruzioni.
>
> [the combinatory system employed by Queneau to investigate morphemes and semanthemes could well be illustrated through another combinatory device, the Meccano, that now outmoded game that used to fascinate the young ones with the possibility of putting together an assemblage of mechanical pieces (hence the name Meccano) in order to build the strangest constructions.] (*Automitobiografia* 91)

The reference to Meccano in *Capriccio italiano* is twofold: on a structural level the 111 sections of this anti-novel can be seen as set of pieces that the reader can put together, in whatever fashion s/he might like: thus, Sanguineti's fragmented text becomes a literary duplicate of Baj's combinatory compositions; on a textual level, several descriptions of the Meccano are included in the diegesis as Sanguineti reproduces Baj's collages and assemblages as accurately as possible. A telling example is given in chapter XXIII:

> E guardavo la sua bocca che soffiava, e poi salivo su di nuovo, che seguivo il soffio, lí sopra i quadri della parete, con i miei occhi, che dai quadri ci sporgevano tanti pezzi del meccano, che lui ce li aveva come incollati sopra, si vedeva, e che poi c'erano tante puntine da disegno, anche che venivano fuori dalla parte della punta, e che ci avevano un po' di lana infilata addosso, e lí, tra i pezzi del meccano che ci sporgevano, e tra le puntine, c'erano le ragnatele, appunto.
>
> [And I looked at his blowing mouth, and then I looked up again, I was following the puff, at the paintings on the wall, with my eyes, and from the paintings stuck out many Meccano pieces that he had glued on, you could see that, and there were many drawing-pins, some sticking out with their point, and there was some wool inserted, and there, among the Meccano pieces and the drawing-pins, there were spider webs.] (49)

Sanguineti, whose intention is to play with the narrative and creative potential of the constructing game, disseminates Meccano pieces throughout the text. The outcome is, once more, unsettling, and the reader, whose traditional expectations are constantly defied by a text that presents itself as a highly experimental and taxing work, is repeatedly challenged.

Sanguineti's ekphrastic practice is in the forefront of *Il giuoco dell'oca* (1967), where the interplay between language and images reaches its zenith. More than *Capriccio italiano*, Sanguineti's second narrative endeavour is rife with references, allusions, and descriptions of several works of art. As he has put it:

> La tecnica ecfrastica l'ho usata molto nel *Giuoco dell'Oca*, che è costruito per molti e molti capitoli con descrizioni, spesso abbastanza puntigliose, talvolta abbastanza pretestuose, di quadri che vanno da Bosch ai fumetti, dalla pubblicità a Rauschenberg, che vi ha una parte notevole. In questo senso è un romanzo 'pop,' perché c'è proprio quest'idea di lavorare su dei 'materiali' rifabbricati in qualche modo, di fare un collage.
>
> [I used the ekphrastic technique a lot in *Giuoco dell'oca*, where you can find in many chapters both detailed and inaccurate descriptions of comic strips, ads, and paintings by Bosch and Rauschenberg (who has a prominent role in the text). In this sense it is a 'pop' novel, because you can find this idea of working with reused material and making collages.] (in Lisa 21)

In this sense, *Il giuoco dell'oca* marks a transition in Sanguineti's poetics. If *Laborintus* and *Capriccio italiano* were heavily influenced by the *informel* climate, this second narrative effort clearly shows signs of a different cultural situation. As Paola Marescalchi has appropriately argued, the 1960s could be defined as the 'era dell'oggetto' [era of the object] (117), a period during which it seemed necessary to 'misurarsi con la civiltà tecnologica e i suoi prodotti' [face technology and its products] (118), and to reconsider the relation between the subject and the new mass-media world. Acknowledging this necessity, pop artists such as Rauschenberg, Warhol, and Lichtenstein began to experiment with all kinds of materials and media produced by consumerism and mass culture. Comic books, ads, packaging, and images from television and the cinema were all included in their works and became the trademark of pop art. To some extent, Sanguineti's transition mirrors Baj's own artistic evolution. As indicated by Marescalchi, it is in these years that Baj began his research on assemblage[15] and started to include in his works fragments of domestic objects such as 'tappezzerie ... bottoni ... fili di lana ... pizzi ... maniglie' [tapestry ... buttons ... woollen yarns ... laces ... handles] (122).

It is hardly surprising, then, that most *Il giuoco dell'oca* is based on references to works by artists such as Rauschenberg, Bosch, Ceroli, and Baj, to name but a few. The result, as in the case of *Capriccio italiano*, is once again displacing: conceived of as a sort of encyclopedic catalogue of the visual culture of the 1960s in which the reader is deprived of all the points of reference of the traditional novel (well-defined plot, identifiable characters, coherent representation of time and space) and is forced to watch a kaleidoscopic unfolding of the narrative ('un bel giuoco di immagini confuse' [a pleasant game of jumbled images], 111). *Il giuoco dell'oca* gave Sanguineti the opportunity to push his fictional avant-garde experiment to its limits. The description of one of Rauschenberg's constructions, humorously defined by the narrator as 'il monumentino' [the little monument] clearly illustrates Sanguineti's fascination with pop art and its playful representation of contemporary mass culture:

> Mi faccio il mio monumentino, lí dentro la mia bara, un po' per me e un po' per mia moglie. È un monumentino a due piani. È come le vetrinette del Kurfüstendamm, che stanno davanti ai negozi e ai ristoranti, con le luci accese, di sera, sul marciapiede. Ci incollo tutto quello che posso, lí nel monumentino, al piano sopra e al piano sotto. Ci incollo le vecchie lettere che ho, i biglietti del tram, le tessere scadute, i programmi dei concerti del Conservatorio, un certificato di cittadinanza italiana del 1954, un pettine con i denti rotti.
>
> [I'll build my own little monument, there inside my coffin, for me and for my wife. It is a two-storey little monument. It is like the shop windows of the Kurfüstendamm, all facing the stores and restaurants, all lit up, in the evening, on the sidewalk. I glue everything I can, there in my little monument, both upstairs and downstairs. I glue old letters, streetcar tickets, expired passes, the concert programs from the Conservatory, a 1954 Italian citizenship certificate, a broken comb.] (95)

Rauschenberg's superimposition of several objects corresponds to the main strategy of *Il giuoco dell'oca* as laid out in the opening epigraph of the novel ('ce n'est superpositions d'images de catalogue') that makes explicit reference to the visual dimension of Sanguineti's undertaking and the relentless juxtapositions of images and icons of pop culture.[16]

As far as the relationship between Baj and Sanguineti is concerned, chapter LIII is a good case in point, as Sanguineti provides a meticulous representation of some of Baj's celebrated *mobili* (pieces of furniture).[17] Created in 1961–2, when he was exploring the aesthetic potential of wood, these *mobili* are characterized by their bi-dimensional and superficial aspect. Not interested in making real furniture,[18] Baj limited himself to the representation of the external façade. It might be said that to some extent, by representing a typical piece of bourgeois culture that evokes the intimacy of private residences, Baj wanted to draw the spectator's attention to the superficiality of that culture and its simulacrum-like condition. As Jean Baudrillard states in his famous essay 'The Precession of Simulacra,' the act of simulation 'implies an absence' (3) and entails the replacement of reality with its signs. In a similar fashion, one could also maintain that both *Capriccio italiano* and *Il giuoco dell'oca* are nothing but simulacra of novels in which the emphasis is placed on signifiers rather that on signifieds, and social criticism is combined with metafictional implications. Inspired by Baj's most daring positions and avant-garde research, Sanguineti was thus able to subvert the narrative genre from within and call into question its foundational rules.

Interestingly, just one year before the publication of *Il giuoco dell'oca,* Baj and Sanguineti printed *L'intérieur,* for which Baj created ten etchings to illustrate Sanguineti's poem. Their first *livre d'artiste,* and the first project in which the relation between the two arts is reversed (from literature to visual art), *L'intérieur* also seems to anticipate some of the questions dealt with in Sanguineti's second narrative work. According to Luigi Weber, *L'intérieur* makes reference to Walter Benjamin's essay on Paris ('Paris, Capital of the Nineteenth Century') particularly the section entitled 'Louis-Philippe, or the Interior,' in which there is a discussion of the symbolic value of private spaces in bourgeois culture. For Benjamin the interior is the locus of individual and social repression where the private person is 'maintained in his illusions' (154) and daily objects are deprived of meaning. In this context the objects mentioned by Sanguineti – poltrone, borsette, collane, specchi, divani [armchairs, purses, necklaces, mirrors, sofas] – typical of any respectable household, can be interpreted as symbolic signs of the cultural and ideological decay of bourgeoisie, a class that is significantly represented in the poem as 'morta ... caduta ... perduta' [dead ... fallen ... lost] (*Segnalibro* 371). Furthermore, as correctly suggested by Weber, Sanguineti's choice to draw on Benjamin's essay was deeply influenced by Baj's aesthetic experiments with what Weber defines as 'spazzatura borghese' [bourgeoisie trash] (69) – that is, domestic objects such as mattresses, mirrors, curtains, buttons, and so on. By reusing the remains of mass culture Baj and Sanguineti

> riescono così a raffigurare ed insieme a criticare l'ideologia di un'intera classe, riassumendola prima nel luogo privilegiato del suo manifestarsi, il

salotto, e poi addirittura nel più emblematico tra gli oggetti del mobilio, il divano. Quasi una sineddoche al quadrato.

[are able to portray and criticize the ideology of an entire class, firstly using its privileged domestic space, the living room, and then through the sofa, the most emblematic piece of furniture. Almost a square synecdoche.] (69)

Far from being comforting, the domesticity portrayed by the two authors is, to say the least, grotesque and disquieting, calling directly into question consumerism and its culture and ideology.

Do It Yourself: A Combinatory 'Livre d'artiste'

The collaboration between Baj and Sanguineti reached one of its experimental peaks in 1968 with the publication of *Baj: The Biggest Art-Book in the World,* a puzzle-like composition accompanied by a poem by Sanguineti entitled 'Pièce en forme de cube.' The dialogue between Baj's piece and Sanguineti's poem takes place mainly on the structural level as it exploits the combinatory potential of both literature and visual art. Particularly significant in this respect is the full title of this *livre d'artiste*: *Baj. The Biggest Art-Book in the World with 137,952,460,800 Colour Plates and 479,001,600 Pages for Musical Accompaniment.* Baj's composition was clearly inspired by Raymond Queneau's *Cent mille milliards de poèmes* (1961), in which his ten sonnets are part of a literary mechanism capable of creating a virtually infinite number of poems. Fascinated with the mechanical possibilities of both literature and visual art, Baj contrived a similar device and, as has been pointed out by Mussini, followed Queneau's method, modifying it according to his own needs:

Baj adatta l'invenzione di Queneau alle esigenze proprie dell'immagine e recupera il gioco infantile dei cubetti coi quali era possibile comporre figure prefissate. Sulle facce dei cubi sono state incollate le prime sei tavole del fascicolo, dato che le restanti tre immagini riproducono esempi delle combinazioni che possono essere ottenute mescolandoli. Sono cinque figure di dame e generali e la riproduzione dello spartito musicale dell'inno di Mameli su fondo damscato.

[Baj adapts Queneau's invention to his own needs, and recuperates the children's game of little cubes through which one can compose prefixed images. On the faces of the cubes are glued the first six tables of the booklet, since the remaining three images reproduce examples of the possible combinations. There are five images of ladies and generals, and a reproduction of the musical score of the Italian anthem on a damask background.] (15)[19]

The result, as suggested by the title, is a text whose potential combinations could produce more than a hundred and thirty billion colour plates and experimental music lasting for more than a thousand years. The ironic scope of *The Biggest Art-Book in the World* is reinforced by its subtitle, *Do It Baj Yourself – Today's Real Cubism*, a polemical statement against consumerism and its false myths on one hand, and late cubism on the other.

The interaction between words and images and the way the two art forms enlighten each other plays a critical and pivotal role. 'Pièce en forme de cube' is in fact one of Sanguineti's most experimental attempts, in which he explores the physical boundaries of the word. To better comprehend this poem, it is worth quoting Renato Barilli's comment in his essay *Viaggio al termine della parola* [Journey to the end of the word] (1981), centred on what he defined as 'ricerca intraverbale' [intraverbal research].[20] Discussing Sanguineti's poem, Barilli speaks of 'coraggio atomistico' [atomistic courage] (28), a clear allusion to Sanguinetti's earlier nuclear phase, and of a sort of 'effetto elettrolitico' [electrolytic effect] that produces the 'scissione' [division] of the verbal sign.

> [In 'Pièce'] si verifica magnificamente l'effetto che ci ostineremo a definire elettrolitico, di scissione 'morbida' delle varie componenti della catena linguistica, dal vocabolo alla sillaba al fonema, con interferenza su di esse dei segni di interpunzione, incaricati sia di scindere, sia di suggerire le giuste intonazioni per l'esecuzione orale.
>
> [(In 'Pièce') takes place the effect that we obstinately define as electrolytic, a 'soft' division of all the components of the linguistic chain, from the word to the syllable and the phoneme, with an interference on the punctuation signs which are required at the same time to separate and suggest the best intonation for the oral execution.] (*Viaggio* 28)[21]

Barilli's accurate interpretation concentrates chiefly on the linguistic surface of the poem and highlights its atomic and aphasic dimension. However, to complete Barilli's reading one cannot forget the context in which the poem is situated and the relationship it establishes with Baj's composition. In other words, 'Pièce en forme de cube' is fully understood and appreciated only if the reader is able to take into account the 'synergy' (Weber 74) between verbal sign and image. Sanguneti's 'carme cubico' [cubic poem] is, in this sense, the verbal equivalent of Baj's game; the reader's task is to roll the dice so as to recreate the text according to chance. As Weber asserts, the most prominent characteristic of this poem is the 'possibilità di un casuale ricomporsi delle parole in virtù di un lancio fortunato' [possibility of an accidental reassembly of the words thanks to a lucky shot] (73): as in *Il giuoco dell'oca*, where the reader is explicitly instructed to play with the text and the author, *causalità* [causality] is replaced by *casualità* [chance], and *The Biggest Art-Book in the World* clearly configures itself as an open structure and macrotext that challenges the traditional ways to 'consume' a work of art.

Conclusion: Visual Arts and Literature

In a discussion on the relationship between figurative arts and literature Enrico Baj speaks about his 'piacere di sposare la pittura alla poesia' [pleasure in uniting painting and poetry] (Caprile 40), and the essential correspondence of the two arts. According to Baj, at the origin of everything there is

> Il detto di Orazio *Ut pictura poiesis*, ovvero la pittura e la poesia sono per molti versi la stessa cosa. Questo è tanto più vero nella nostra epoca, perché la pittura moderna, che è basata non sulla imitazione del vero, ma sulla libertà d'invenzione e di soggetto, può trovare un supporto, oserei dire una difesa e una spiegazione, solo nel testo letterario e poetico [...] La pittura moderna non è né astratta né figurativa, è pittura d'invenzione.
>
> [Horace's motto *Ut pictura poiesis* ('as is painting so is poetry' *Ars Poetica*), means that painting and poetry are in many respects the same thing. This is even more true in our age, because modern painting – based not on the imitation of reality but on the freedom to create new subjects – can find justification, support, and explanation only in the literary and poetic text. Modern painting is neither abstract nor figurative: it is inventive painting.] (40)

Baj's correct claim about the connection between art and poetry could, in my opinion, be reversed. If it is true that modern painting finds explanation and theoretical support in literature, the same could be said about poetry, especially with reference to Sanguineti's avant-garde production that openly draws on artistic phenomena such as Art Informel, *nuclearismo,* pop art, and *nuova figurazione.* In this sense, Baj's reference to the 'pittura d'invenzione' could be applied to Sanguineti's idea of literature: conscious of the limits of both *ermetismo* and *neorealismo* and of purely mimetic modes of representation, Sanguineti pursued his own formal research with the objective of 'bridging the aesthetic gap between the traditional and exhausted language of Italian poetry and innovative means of expressions from other art forms' (Picchione 117). The magnitude and centrality of the intellectual dialogue between Edoardo Sanguineti's verbal signs and Enrico Baj's designs lies here, at the heart of the intersection of literature and visual art, two artistic forms capable of inspiring and renewing one another with their relentless experimental vitality.

NOTES

1 The term 'Art Informel' was 'coined by the French critic Michel Tapié in his book *Un art autre* (1952).' In using the label Art Informel [without form] Tapié wanted to emphasize the 'complete break from the past' of postwar art' (Chilvers 19).

2 Note that although Sanguineti did not consider the *poesia novissima* as an example of *opera aperta* ('Noi *Novissimi* non considerammo *Opera aperta* come l'esplicitazione della nostra poetica' [The *novissimi* never considered *Open Work* as part of their poetics], Gambaro 49) he did acknowledge Eco's theoretical breakthroughs: 'Personalmente non potevo che essere d'accordo con il discorso di Eco, anche perché avevo sempre pensato la letteratura in termini di stretto rapporto con le arti figurative e con la musica. Grazie a Eco si capiva che c'era una ricerca comune che percorreva le diverse arti e le diverse discipline' [Personally I agreed with Eco, also because I always thought of literature in relation with figurative arts and music. Thanks to Eco you could understand that there was a common research involving different arts and disciplines] (49).

3 On the connection between Art Informel and literature, see also Bertoni, 'L'informe della parola.'

4 In his discussion with Fabio Gambaro, Sanguineti again acknowledged his debt to visual arts, stating: 'Cercare in ogni modo di stringersi ai modelli dell'avanguardia mi pareva l'unica strategia possibile per andare oltre. Un'operazione simile era leggibile anche nei pittori e nei musicisti del

tempo [...] la musica e la pittura più significative avevano continuato a tener conto della lezione dell'avanguardia [...] Ciò che spiega l'abnorme prodotto di *Laborintus* è proprio questo rapporto con la musica e la pittura' [Trying to get closer to the avant-garde models was for me the only possible strategy to go forward. A similar operation could be seen in the painters and musicians of the time ... the most significant music and painting were able to take into account the avant-garde lesson ... What explains the abnormal outcome of *Laborintus* is this relation with music and painting] (Gambaro 26).

5 As Sanguineti wrote: 'la forma non si pone, in nessun caso, che a partire, per noi, dall'informe, e in questo informe orizzonte che, ci piaccia o non ci piaccia, è il nostro' [form stems, for us, from the informal, and this informal horizon is, whether we like it or not, ours] (in Barilli and Guglielmi 54).

6 In a letter quoted by Savauge in his seminal *Arte nucleare*, Baj explains the name of the movement and claims: 'The term 'nuclear' had for us at the start many justifications. Above all, we felt ourselves to be artists of a period in which atomic and nuclear research opened up for man new and infinite horizons; artists, therefore, rather nuclear, of a nuclear age. Then there was the fundamental consideration that our struggle, the position we had taken up, was above all anti-abstract in relation to the artistic world and the theories then circulating in that world. *Basically* anti-abstract; that is to say not only geometric abstraction was rejected, but abstraction in general' (19).

7 On the relationship between Nuclear Art and Art Informel, see Francesca Alinovi, 'Spaziali e nucleari: l'informe abnorme' [Spatials and nuclears: the abnormal informal]. The main polemical target of the nuclearists was the mannerism of artists such as the impressionists, the cubists, the futurists, and the 'immortal forms of decrepit Greek geometry' of the abstractionists (Savauge 206).

8 The Neapolitan *nuclearisti* wrote in their futurist-like manifesto: 'L'astrazione non è arte ma solo concetto filosofico e convenzionale. L'arte non è astratta benché vi possa essere una concezione astratta dell'arte. Questo neoplatonismo è da tempo superato dagli avvenimenti della scienza moderna, quindi non ha ragione d'essere come fenomeno vitale ed attuale' [Abstraction is not art, but only philosophical and conventional conception. Art is not abstract, although there may be an abstract conception of art. This neoplatonism has long been made obsolete by the events of modern science, thus it no longer has any raison-d'être as a vital and active phenomenon] (Savauge 211). Baj himself defined this manifesto as 'una aperta dichiarazione di guerra all'astrattismo' [an open declaration of war against abstract art] (*Automitobiografia* 141).

9 The full quotation reads: 'alle distorsioni relative di fronte a lunghi funghi fumosi / che si gonfiano e indico l'ustione linguistica frammenti che costellano / il notturno giardino dei succubi sopra l'atollo delle labbra coralline' [relative distortions before long, smoky mushrooms / that swell and I point to a linguistic burn fragments that stud / the nocturnal garden of victims on the atoll of coral lips] (*Catamerone* 12).

10 For a discussion on Sanguineti and other *pittori nucleari*, such as Guido Biasi, see Baccarani's *La poesia del labirinto* (107–16).

11 Baj's *ultracorpi* was used for both the 1963 and 1967 editions; the cover of the 1973 edition were a section of the celebrated *I funerali dell'anarchico Pinelli;* the cover of the 1985 edition was a painting entitled *Coppia* – an explicit reference to events narrated in the text.

12 For a thorough description of the techniques that Baj used, see Sauavage (92–8).

13 It should be noted that de Mandiargues' remark about 'pittura accademica' is a reference to some of Baj's most ingenious experiments, entitled *Modificazioni* (1959–60): he purchased a number of cheap and commercial paintings ('quadri dozzinali,' Crispolti 22) and proceded to disfigure the peaceful landscapes (lakes, mountains, cities) through the insertion of monsters, *ultracorpi* [ultrabodies], and flying machines. Baj's fascination with parody and the grotesque was carried on in Sanguineti's *Capriccio italiano*, where paintings are abused in any possible way. See for instance chapter IX, where B. says: '"Uh," disse B., che ballava per la stanza, "adesso ci metto anche i libri, nei quadri, e splàck, che te li schiaccio lí, e splàck, maledetti, che te li macchio tutti bene, d'inchiostro, cornuti, e ci metto, ai ritratti le corna, che un po' ti incollo le pagine, i libri, anche, se vuoi"' ['Uh,' B. said as he was dancing in the room, 'I will also put some books, and splàck, I'm gonna squeeze them there, and splàck, evil ones, I'm gonna dirty them all real well, with ink, cuckolds, and I'm gonna put horns in the portraits, and I'm gonna glue the pages a little bit, also the books, if you want'] (24–5).

14 Interestingly, according to Corgnati, Baj's mirrors represent the supremacy of creativity over pure mimesis and 'anticipano addirittura la celebre teorizzazione dell'opera aperta, categoria alla quale inequivocabilmente appartengono' [anticipate the famous theorization of the open work, the category to which they unmistakably belong] (17).

15 The term 'assemblage' was coined in the 1950s by Jean Dubuffet 'to describe works of art made from fragments of natural or preformed material, such as household debris' (Chilvers 21).

16 On this argument, see also Wlassics, 'Edoardo Sanguineti,' where the author highlights the visual attributes of *Il Giuoco dell'oca* (9796–9).

17 To quote from *Il giuoco dell'oca*: 'È sempre sopra il suo letto, la ragazza, lí nella sua camera ammobiliata [...] Si guarda, un po' di traverso, in *une glace reposant sur de petits pieds, placage en bois de rose, encadrements de filets, marqueteries en fleurs, fin de l'époque Louis XV (Haut. 73 cm, Larg. 50 cm).* Vicino al letto c'è *une table de forme rectangulaire présentant des décrochements aux angles, marquetée sur le dessus, frise de postes à la ceinture, basse époque (Haut. 50 cm. Larg. 73 cm.),* con *une chaise ponteuse en bois mouluré, sculpté et repeint gris, à dossier lyre, le siège de forme ovale détaché du dossier, la ceinture moulurée, les pieds à cannelures rudentées, le tout légèrement abimé, époque Louis XVI (Haut. 91 cm, Larg. 73 cm)*' [She is always on her bed, the girl, in her furnished room (...) She looks at herself a little bit, crosswise, in *une glace reposant sur de petits pieds, placage en bois de rose, encadrements de filets, marqueteries en fleurs, fin de l'époque Louis XV (Haut. 73 cm, Larg. 50 cm).* Close to the bed there is *une table de forme rectangulaire présentant des décrochements aux angles, marquetée sur le dessus, frise de postes à la ceinture, basse époque (Haut. 50 cm, Larg. 73 cm),* with *une chaise ponteuse en bois mouluré, sculpté et repeint gris, à dossier lyre, le siège de forme ovale détaché du dossier, la ceinture moulurée, les pieds à cannelures rudentées, le tout légèrement abimé, époque Louis XVI (Haut. 91 cm, Larg. 73 cm)*] (113).

18 'Del mobile io rappresentavo la facciata con ante e cassette, non avendo mai avuto l'intenzione di costruire mobile tradizionali' [I wanted to represent the façade of the piece with its drawers and shutters, I never wanted to build traditional furniture] (*Automitobiografia* 135).

19 The 'dame e generali' mentioned in this quotation relate to a series of paingings produced by Baj between 1959 and 1963 called *Generals* and *Ladies*, in which the symbols of 'constitutional authority' (Savauge 111) were mercilessly derided and demystified. Baj's anti-militarism and anarchism gave birth to successive works such as *I funerali dell'anarchico Pinelli* (1972) and *The Nixon Parade* (1974).

20 According to Barilli, in order to explore new and original poetical territories it is essential to 'scavalcare lo spazio esaurito della frase, e portarsi a lavorare al di sopra o al di sotto di essa [...] Lavorare al di sotto della frase, vuol dire rivolgersi al suo ingrediente essenziale, la parola, senza più rispettarne l'intangibilità, ma al contrario sottoponendola a fratture e segmentazioni successive, che potranno consistere nello scinderne il corpo radicale, il nocciolo lessematico [...] nell'isolarne i singoli fonemi, e infine superare la soglia della pertinenza linguistica, quell'ultimo limite di convenzionalità che permette di ravvisare in un suono o in un tracciato grafico la presenza dell'unità minimale della lingua, la lettera' [overtake the exhausted space of the sentence, and work above or below it ... Working below the sentence means to focus on its most essential ingredient, the word, with no respect

for its inviolability but, rather, subjecting it to fractures and breaks that could consist in the division of its body and the isolation of single phonemes, and eventually going beyond the threshold of the linguistic pertinence, the last conventional limit that allows us to recognize in a sound or in a grapheme the presence of the letter] (*Viaggio* 8).

21 Quotations from a few lines of the poem will give a clearer idea of Sanguineti's experimental effort: 'a.: würfeln (toul les mythes); (naturalis est); ('à tête'): oi m(a)amme! o- / -i mamma! una testa, un dad(o); (a); / herzhand! (dove il respiro / sociale è lento); salut! (ed asmatico); (mâles ac-); (nobis)' (*Segnalibro* 374). Besides illustrating the fragmented nature of the poem, these lines are relevant for two other reasons: first, they make explicit reference to the role of dice in Sanguineti's and Baj's texts; second, they introduce several allusions to the national anthems of Italy ('testa'), Germany ('herzhand'), and France ('mâles ac') which perform, as the author puts it, 'uno sbeffeggiamento del potere' [the mocking of power] (Lisa 15).

WORKS CITED

Alinovi, Francesca. 'Spaziali e nucleari: l'informe abnorme.' In Renato Barilli and Franco Solmi, eds., *L'arte in Italia nel secondo dopoguerra.* Bologna: Il Mulino, 1979. 35–51.

Baccarani, Elisabetta. *La poesia del labirinto: razionalismo e istanza 'antiletteraria' nell'opera e nella cultura di Edoardo Sanguineti.* Bologna: Il Mulino, 2002.

Baj, Enrico. *Automitobiografia.* Milan: Rizzoli, 1983.

Barilli, Renato. *Viaggio al termine della parola: la ricerca intraverbale.* Milan: Feltrinelli, 1981.

Barilli, Renato, and Angelo Guglielmi, eds. *Gruppo 63: critica e teoria.* Turin: Testo & Immagine, 2003.

Baudrillard, Jean. *Simulacra and Simulation.* Trans. Sheila Faria Glaser. Ann Arbor: University of Michigan Press, 1994.

Benjamin, Walter. *Reflections: Essays, Aphorisms, Autobiographical Writings.* Ed. Peter Demetz. New York: Schocken Books, 1978.

Bertoni, Alberto. 'L'informe della parola.' In Renato Barilli and Franco Solmi, eds., *L'informe in Italia.* Bologna: Mazzotta, 1983. 136–41.

Caprile, Luciano. *Conversazioni con Enrico Baj: mezzo secolo di avanguardie.* Milan: Elèuthera, 1997.

Chilvers, Ian, ed. *The Concise Oxford Dictionary of Art and Artists.* Oxford: Oxford University Press, 1990.

Corgnati, Martina. 'Il percorso di Baj da Pinelli a Bakunin.' In Enrico Baj,

Enrico Baj: catalogo generale delle opere dal 1972 al 1996. Milan: Marconi-Menhir, 1997. 15–45.

Crispolti, Enrico, ed. *Catalogo generale Bolaffi dell'opera di Enrico Baj.* Turin: Giulio Bolaffi Editore, 1973.

Eco, Umberto. *Opera aperta.* 2nd ed. Milan: Bompiani, 1976.

Gambaro, Fabio. *Colloquio con Edoardo Sanguineti: quarant'anni di cultura italiana attraverso i ricordi di un poeta intellettuale.* Milan: Anabasi, 1993.

Lisa, Tommaso, ed. *Pretesti ecfrastici.* Florence: Società Editrice Fiorentina, 2004.

Marescalchi, Paola. 'Le poetiche dell'oggetto negli anni '60.' In Renato Barilli, ed., *L'arte in Italia nel secondo dopoguerra.* Bologna: Il Mulino, 1979, 117–39.

Mussini, Massimo. *I libri di Baj.* Milan: Electa, 1990.

Picchione, John. *The New Avant-Garde in Italy: Theoretical Debate and Poetical Practices.* Toronto: University of Toronto Press, 2004.

Pieyre de Mandiargues, André. 'Gli specchi di Baj.' In Enrico Baj, *Baj, dal generale al particolare.* Milan: Fabbri Editore, 1985.

Postcontemporanea. 'Intervista: Edoardo Sanguineti,' http://www.postcontemporanea.it/incontri/2003/10Ottobre/sanguineti.asp (accessed 1 Dec. 2005; no longer online)

Sanguineti, Edoardo. *Catamerone 1951–1971.* Milan: Feltrinelli, 1974.

– *Capriccio italiano.* Milan: Feltrinelli, 1963.

– *Il giuoco dell'oca.* Milan: Feltrinelli, 1967.

– *Segnalibro: poesie 1951–1981.* Milan: Feltrinelli, 1982.

Sauvage, Tristan. *Arte nucleare.* Milan: Galleria Schwarz, 1962.

Spadoni, Claudio. 'L'informale.' In Renato Barilli, ed., *L'arte in Italia nel secondo dopoguerra.* Bologna: Il Mulino, 1979. 117–39.

Weber, Luigi. *Usando gli utensili di Utopia: Traduzione, parodia e riscrittura in Edoardo Sanguineti.* Bologna: Gedit Edizioni, 2004.

Wlassics, Tibor. 'Edoardo Sanguineti.' In Gianni Grana, ed., *Novecento: I Contemporanei.* Milan: Marzorati Editore, 1979. 9773–811.

10 Gruppo 63 and Music: A Complex Relationship

PAOLO SOMIGLI

The artists and intellectuals of the Italian neo-avant-garde and of the Gruppo 63 in particular were primarily active in the field of literature, in terms of both production and theoretical reflection.[1] Nevertheless, this cultural and aesthetic experience revealed an openness towards and an interest in the entire system of the arts. This essay will attempt to provide an overview, general by force of circumstances and with no claims to comprehensiveness, of the relationship that the Gruppo 63 entertained with music. As we will see, developments in the music world (in both theory and practice) in the 1950s and the 1960s present interesting correspondences with what the Gruppo 63 was advocating. While these similarities did not result in a perfect identity – indeed, there were significant differences between the two positions – the resemblance is there. Thus, the attitude of the Gruppo 63 towards music became enigmatic, simultaneously displaying attraction and detachment. It is on this question that the present discussion will focus.

The official formation in 1963 in Palermo of the Gruppo 63, which arose from the experience of the *poeti novissimi*, the experimental novel, and the reflection on aesthetics that developed around Luciano Anceschi's journal *Il verri*, coincided with the Quarta settimana internazionale nuova musica [Fourth International New Music Week]. In fact, since 1960, Palermo had hosted an annual week-long festival dedicated to new trends in contemporary music, featuring performances of music by both Italian and foreign contemporary composers such as Karlheinz Stockhausen and Domenico Guaccero, John Cage and Luigi Nono, Tōru Takemitsu, and Luciano Berio, to name a few.[2] These composers were widely known, at least by reputation, among insiders, but were rarely, if at all, represented in the programming of traditional institutional concert seasons. The Settimana of 1963 was profoundly interdisciplinary, and from this point of view, was in tune with a sensitivity that had been spreading though the musical and artistic worlds at the time, with significant examples in Italy. I will now consider three that are particularly relevant to the purpose and argument of the present paper.

The first example is a journal, *Incontri musicali* (Suvini Zerboni Editions), published in Milan in the second half of the 1950s thanks to the efforts of Luciano Berio (the last issue appeared in 1960). In spite of the fact that only four issues appeared, *Incontri musicali* was one of the most important Italian journals on music. Its coverage of contemporary trends in music and culture reveals an open-minded attitude. Berio, at the time, was interested in the interweaving of musical, linguistic, and literary matters. He was fascinated by the works and the use of language by James Joyce (he had already used poems by this author for *Chamber Music* in 1953); *Thema* (*Omaggio a Joyce*) is a result of this research: this electronic piece uses a passage from *Ulysses*, chapter 11, read by the great singer Cathy Berberian as source material for composition. It is thus not surprising that *Incontri musicali* would publish an essay on literature by Umberto Eco, who had actively participated in the research of his composer friend. What is striking, however, is the fact, which Eco himself acknowledges, that that essay became the originating nucleus of Eco's *Opera aperta*, a work to which we will return.[3]

The second example takes us to Florence, where in 1960 the electronic musician Pietro Grossi fostered an interesting and original cultural experience, *Vita Musicale Contemporanea*, a musical association that was also interested in the other arts. Every year between 1961 and 1967 (with the exception of 1966), the organization promoted a musical festival enriched by a visual arts exhibition. The president, Giuliano Toraldo di Francia, was not a musician but a physicist, and the treasurer, Giuseppe Chiari, was, at that time, one of the artists most engaged in challenging the division of the art world into separate disciplines of music, visual arts, and theatre.[4]

The third example also concerns Florence. In 1963 some of the scholars soon to be associated with the Gruppo 63 (Gillo Dorfles, Luciano Anceschi, and Umberto Eco), along with other poets, sculptors, painters, and musicians, gathered in Florence for the international conference 'Arte e Comunicazione,' an event that embraced the whole system of the arts and sought a new way of considering their inter-relationships. Among the musicians present were Pietro Grossi, Giuseppe Chiari, and Sylvano Bussotti, a composer intensely concerned with the graphic and visual dimensions of the musical score.

Thus, the early 1960s were characterized by the rise of a 'musica d'arte' [art music] based on the iteration of sign, sound, voice, and gesture. From these Florentine events sprang forth the Gruppo 70, an experience that, even in its name, found its distinctive feature in its impulse toward the future, toward experimentalism (1970 was still to come). The presence of Sylvano Bussotti and Giuseppe Chiari established a clear link with the Fluxus movement, an international network that advocated an art in which there were no barriers between one discipline and another, both in production and in reception. From this perspective, the performative dimension brought together the various artistic manifestations and infiltrated the various languages. A musical performance might consist of a gestural movement free from the normal pursuit of sound or it could consist of a sonorous output from varied, everyday, nonmusical sources. Giuseppe Chiari wrote:

> La divisione delle arti è a difesa di una nobiltà. In pratica bisogna negarla sotto tutte le forme. [...] Sono convinto che far musica equivalga ad affermare continuamente, implicitamente, l'impossibilità di uno specifico musicale. [...] Si adotta la tecnica della contaminazione, irrelando il suono con la parola, col gesto, col colore, coi fatti comuni e si ottengono opere dispersive, che il pubblico non può sintetizzare e che lo costringono in qualsiasi modo ad una partecipazione non più contemplativa ma attiva, polemica magari. Se prendo una chiave, la metto nella serratura e apro la porta non faccio musica; se prendo la chiave, la metto nella serratura e non apro la porta faccio musica. [...] Un evento uditivo è provocato da due corpi e da un certo modo di scontrarsi; la musica è il confronto fra dei corpi e dei gesti.

> [The division of the arts is in defence of an aristocracy. In practice, it is necessary to negate it in all forms ... I am convinced that making music is equivalent to continuously, implicitly affirming the impossibility of a specificity of music ... One adopts the technique of contamination, relating the sound with the word, the gesture, with colour, with common facts. One thus obtains a dispersive work that the public cannot synthesize and that forces them in some way to participate no longer contemplatively, but actively, polemically even. If I take a key, put it in the lock and open the door, I do not make music; if I take the key, put it in the lock, and do not open the door, I make music ... An auditory event is created by two bodies and from a certain way of clashing; music is the confrontation between bodies and gestures.] (Chiari 37–8)

Sometimes, no sound was produced: movements and gestures were the really important thing of the performance. For this reason this kind of musical production was called 'musica gestuale' [gestural music] or even 'musica visiva' [visual music]. This atmosphere also saw the development of a kind of poetry based on the signifier and on gestural expressiveness – an experience on the border between poetry and music, with 'music' understood in its general performative meaning – that came to be called 'poesia visiva' [visual poetry].[5]

The organizers of the Quarta settimana internazionale in Palermo likewise believed that the problems faced by contemporary music in its process of rapid linguistic renewal should be understood within a larger framework that included theatre, literature, and the visual arts. Consequently, the 1963 festival included an evening of theatre (3 October) and a series of lectures 'sui problemi e le tendenze dell'arte oggi' [on the problems and trends of art today], for which the invited speakers included Renato Barilli, Gillo Dorfles, Luciano Anceschi, and Umberto Eco.[6] However, they did not spend all of their time in Palermo in public activities. As is well known, during the festival, between 3 and 8 October, they also met with a group that included artists and intellectuals affiliated with Luciano Anceschi's *Il verri* as well as other key figures in the new literary world of the time. During these meetings, held in the grand hall of the Hotel Zagarella they compared and contrasted their literary works and pursued a theoretical reflection on art that had been developing for a few years.

From the beginning, *Il verri* had been open to musical concerns and had regularly given space to music columns, reviews, and short articles, many of which were written by Piero Santi and Luigi Pestalozza, who was also in charge of the music column. (The appendix to this article lists all the music-related content published in *Il verri* from 1956 to 1969) The first issue of 1959 opened with an article by Enzo Paci on contemporary music, and on Igor Stravinsky in particular: Paci's thesis was that the process of music renewal is irreversible and that it goes hand in hand with a process of synthesis of dialectical oppositions. For this reason Paci saw positively the last works of Stravinsky or even dodecaphony (and Berg's violin concerto in particular) in comparison with expressionism.[7] Paci's contribution was followed in later issues with articles by Gianandrea Gavazzeni, Rondi, D'Amico, Luigi Pestalozza, and Santi, in which, for all their different emphases, one can note a certain diffidence not only towards the more distinctly avant-garde tendencies (above all in Gavazzeni and Rondi, and in a more general way in D'Amico), but also towards trends that display a certain evasiveness regarding direct contact with society and history. In the years that followed, *Il verri* provided consistent music coverage, even though not many few contributions focusing on musical issues appeared in the first section, which was reserved for essays.

Despite such encouraging premises, the fact that this gathering coincided with the Quarta settimana internazionale and some of its members participated in initiatives sponsored by the music festival did not lead to a real integration, a kind of osmosis, between the two events. The gathering at the Hotel Zagarella was essentially a private meeting and sought to remain so. Initially journalists, drawn not only by the importance of the festival but also by the names of the conference participants, were not invited to attend. Their removal from the room at the beginning of the first session resulted in a diplomatic incident with the press. Attempts to remedy the situation took the form of a press release in which the members of the Gruppo 63 described the incident with the journalists as 'increscioso' [regrettable] and attributed the episode to a misunderstanding due to insufficient internal communication.[8] Yet even when this misunderstanding was clarified, the meeting was held in a quasi esoteric atmosphere, described by one of the protagonists as 'nel segno del mistero' [under the sign of mystery] (Barilli, *Neoavanguardia* 242). On the one hand, the neo-avant-gardists participated in the lectures and public debates, and on the other, when they were back within the 'ridotte pareti' [narrow walls] (Barilli, *Neoavanguardia* 242) of Hotel Zagarella, they focused, in their discussions, on art, chiefly on literature, and on the problem of the 'open work' and the relationship between art and reality.[9]

At the gathering at Palermo, the different positions within the group emerged quite clearly, particularly on the issue of the relationships between art, ideology, and contemporary reality. For Angelo Guglielmi, language and writing should enter into relationship with reality completely free of the customary ideological filters (revolutionary ambitions, social proclamations, and the like). For Edoardo Sanguineti, on the other hand, the ideological component remained an irrevocable element of artistic activity, and the challenge faced by writers and intellectuals was to act in such a way that language and ideology proceeded together, at the same level of innovation and advancement: in other words, in order to be authentically realistic, art had to move beyond the conventional ideological and linguistic bourgeois norms. For Renato Barilli, the concept of ideology should be expanded to that of 'visione del mondo' [world vision], of 'cultura' [culture], so that the rhythm of cultural life could proceed by successive steps, each one constituting an advancement with respect to the one before (Barilli, *La neoavanguardia* 215).

A heated debate on the relationships between art, ideology, and society had also shaken the music world a few years earlier, particularly during the Internationalen Ferienkurse für neue Musik (International Summer Courses for New Music) in Darmstadt.[10] These summer courses had been established in 1946 under the title Ferienkurse für Internationale neue Musik in order to bring young German composers raised under the Nazi regime up to date with recent developments in musical composition. From the late 1940s, they were characterized by a systematic search for an ideal of rational composition, unrestricted by the demands of contact with the audience and programmatically free from the myth of subjectivity of the romantic artist-creator.[11] The Ferienkurse were understood by their protagonists as an opportunity to re-found music – and even, together with music, society – in order to make a definitive break with tradition and the myth of the artist-creator, and to aim towards an ideal of music that was based entirely on rationality and was capable of constructing itself. Pierre Boulez provided a splendid example with *Structures pour deux pianos, 1ère livre* (1951–2): every sound, every indication of intensity, every detail of this complex score, was determined according to a rigorous principle from a single originating matrix.[12]

It is obvious that in this perspective a lack of interest in communicating with the audience did not coincide with a real indifference towards what had happened and was happening in the world: on the contrary, these composers found nourishment in the reaction against the system of values that had led to the advent of the Nazi regime. Nevertheless, in the music world there was a strong feeling that such an outlook might lead back to academicism, while at the same time, the debate on the need to give greater relevance and immediacy to the dimensions of communication and commitment was becoming increasingly more heated. These were also the reasons for the rapid distancing from the Darmstadt circle of Hans Werner Henze, a composer who had expressed his own rejection of an attitude that seemed to him like a sterile and mannered academicism in a brief piece also published in the first issue of Anceschi's journal.[13] By 1959, the *querelle* had become particularly bitter. New trends that had entered into the Darmstadt composition techniques – specifically chance and improvisation – had been adopted by composers such as Boulez and Stockhausen, but others had remained sceptical. Among the latter, Luigi Nono stood out for advocating an ideal of extremely advanced art from a technical point of view that was simultaneously and explicitly committed to progress and social improvement. The first inkling of the approaching polemic occurred in 1957, when Stockhausen publicly stated that he considered the behaviour of his Italian colleague to be contradictory: on one hand, he chose texts of great engagement and political connotation; on the other, he used his elaborate techniques in such a way as to render them altogether unintelligible. In 1959 Nono *de facto* responded with an extremely harsh attack against musical tendencies such as those advocated earlier by Stockhausen, in which he saw the spectre of escape and disengagement ('Presenza storica').

These issues bear an obvious resemblance to problems that the participants at the Gruppo 63 conference found themselves debating. Of particular note is the opposition between the demand for freedom of the artist from a rigid intellectual commitment on one hand, and the notion of the need for an ideologically connoted involvement supported by advanced linguistic means on the other. Furthermore, the *Il verri* group had first-hand knowledge of the polemic that had shaken the music world because the journal had published Nono's 'Realtà storica' in 1960.[14] Yet, judging by what emerges from accounts of the gathering that have been passed down to us, music only slipped into the rooms of the hotel Zagarella on the sly: the only clear reference to music – or better yet, to musical perception – came from Gillo Dorfles, to emphasize the various possibilities of fruition of a work. As far as we know, the issue of the relationships between contemporary music, ideology, society, and engagement was not discussed.

In spite of all this, many contributions to *Il verri*, including reports and reviews, were *de facto* concerned with this issue. Three reviews written by Luigi Pestalozza will serve as examples: a review of *Die Frau ohne Schatten*, the opera by Richard Strauss (1.3, Spring 1957, 113–15); the review of Mario Peragallo's opera *La gita in campagna* (2.4, December 1958, 153–60); and the review of the third issue of *Incontri musicali*, which was dedicated to the problem of the open work (3.6, December 1959, 96–101). In a more general sense, as we have seen, the relationship with music had accompanied the experience of the group during the conference, and the neo-avant-garde, either as a whole or in works by individual members, often touched upon music, and had even drawn from music, in a more or less mediated way, some of the stimuli for its own reflection.[15]

As is known, one focus of the Palermo debate concerned the problem of the open work. Discussion of this question began towards the end of the 1950s, and the third issue of *Incontri musicali*, as noted above, was dedicated to the problem. The decisive push, however, came from the publication of Eco's *Opera aperta* in 1962. From a textual point of view, as noted above, the embryonic form of the work was an essay that Eco had published in *Incontri musicali,* the journal directed by Berio, inspired by work on Joyce that Eco completed with his composer friend. From a conceptual point of view, however, musical influences play an even more fundamental role in *Opera aperta.* At the end of the introduction to the 1962 and 1967 editions Eco admits the importance of his conversations with Berio and with the French composer Henri Pousseur. The first chapter of *Opera aperta,* which is derived from Eco's 1959 essay opens with four music examples in which Eco finds an emblematic representation for the concept of 'aperto' [openness]: Stockhausen's *Klavierstück XI* (1956), Boulez's *Troisème sonate pour piano* (1957), Pousseur's *Scambi* (1957), and Berio's *Sequenza per flauto solo* (1958, later retitled *Sequenza I*).

The compositions by Stockhausen, Pousseur, and Boulez constitute important examples of a composition technique that catalyzed the interests and discussions of composers during the late 1950s (*Sequenza I* is a somewhat different case). In works of this kind, rather than defining all aspects of the music, the composer left some up to the performer(s) to choose. This practice was part of a wider musical tendency in which 'chance' was somehow involved and for obvious reasons became known as 'chance music,' or in these cases, 'semi-chance music.' Chance music (or *musica aleatoria* [aleatoric music]) is an extremely wide-ranging phenomenon: *alea,* the contribution of chance, can occur equally at the moment of composition or the moment of execution, or both together. It began to spread in the United States towards the end of the 1940s and arrived in Europe in the mid-1950s.[16] A music based on chance might seem even further removed from the rational constructions proposed at Darmstadt, but, by a singular and logical paradox, it found a fecund environment in the Ferienkurse. The rationality that governed the structuralist music of the first half of the decade was in reality undermined by subjective premises (György Ligeti demonstrated that an arbitrary decision was at the base of individuation of dynamics and durations in the first book of Boulez's *Structures*). Furthermore, this rationality generated a result that not only appeared equivalent to any other but also completely escaped the listener, who in fact had the impression that the sounds were dictated by fortuitousness. For their part, the performers, as incredibly skilled as they might be, often proved to be incapable of rendering the minute subtleties demanded by the score; and even when they were able to realize the notation perfectly, other elements beyond their control could threaten the accuracy of the performance: for example, perspiration caused by a room in which the temperature and humidity was slightly higher than expected, might prevent a performer from perfectly executing the dynamics, or even contribute to a few missed notes.

In short, chance always lay in ambush to a rationally and logically constructed music. The composer could avoid such influences by anticipating them in a musical construction constituted by preselected structures, bifurcations, and possibilities. It was for this reason that, Pierre Boulez, in his *Troisième sonate pour piano* left the definite realization of a few elements to the freedom of the performer:

> Partant d'un signe initial, principiel, aboutissant à un signe exhaustif, conclusif, la composition arrive à mettre en jeu ce que nous recherchions au départ de notre démarche: un 'parcours' problématique, fonction du temps – un certain nombre d'événements aléatoires inscrits dans une durée mobile – ayant toutefois une logique de développement, un sens global dirigé – des césures pouvant s'y intercaler, césures de silence ou plates – forme sonores – parcours allant d'un commencement à un fin. Nous avons respecté le 'fini' de l'œuvre occidentale, son cycle fermé, mais nous avons introduit la 'chance' de l'œuvre orientale, son déroulment ouvert.

> [Starting from an initial, principal sign, and concluding with an exhaustive sign, the composition succeeds in bringing into action that which we seek at the beginning of our journey: a problematic 'course' that is a function of time – a certain number of chance events inscribed in a mobile duration – yet possessing a logic of development, a directed overall meaning – with the possibility of inserting caesuras, caesuras of silence or sound platforms – paths from a beginning to an end. We have thus respected the 'finite' dimension of the Western work of art, its closed cycle, but we have also introduced the 'chance' of Eastern work of art, its open unfolding.] ('Alea' 52)

Even more radical positions maintained by the Darmstadt circle granted greater freedom of intervention to performers. The presence of instrumentalists such as pianist David Tudor and flautist Severino Gazzelloni constituted a formidable impetus in this direction. But this was precisely the tendency opposed by Nono in his *querelle* with Stockhausen in 1959; Nono was against a music that could appear self-referential either because of its rationality or conversely because of its aleatoric nature. Yet it was in this soil that the four compositions noted by Eco as examples of 'open' works took root. (Note that Berio's *Sequenza I,* which differs in character from the other works discussed by Eco, had been composed specifically for Gazzelloni).

Compared to the purely chance compositions displaying influences from North America and translated into scores that take the shape of a graph, a drawing, or a photograph, these four compositions – particularly those by Boulez, Pousseur, and Stockhausen, but to a different degree also the one by Berio – appeared especially good examples of 'open works' in two respects: they could receive many and very different realizations; and they relied upon a solid structure that was easily recognizable, notwithstanding the individual performance. In Berio's *Sequenza I,* however, the freedom left to the performer is quite minimal and is linked to time values, since Berio used proportional notation rather than traditional note values. During the 1950s notational experiments were frequent and arose from multiple demands, responding to compositional innovations and attempts to adjust the text of the score to the new sounds and the new constructive and formal conceptions that were coming to the fore.[17] Briefly, in the original score of *Sequenza I* the values of the notes are determined by their distance from each other on the page and their increasing or decreasing density within the specified time segments. As Eco explains, 'la durata di ciascuna nota dipende dal valore che l'esecutore vorrà conferirle nel contesto delle costanti quantità di spazio, corrispondenti a costanti pulsazioni di metronomo' [the duration of each note depends on the value that the performer wants to assign to it in the context of the constant quantities of space, corresponding to constant tics of the metronome] (*Opera aperta* 31). In fact, Berio gives the performer rather precise instructions and explains that the segment of reference, the temporal measure, should be 0.80 seconds. With proportional notation, Berio simultaneously sought greater precision and flexibility with respect to the common note values that are based on pre-established relationships and are equally binding for both composer and performer. Through proportional notation Berio intended, in some way, to facilitate the reading of the score, thus freeing the performer from the abstruseness that recourse to traditional notation would have entailed. He wanted to give the performer the possibility of adjusting the music – at certain moments in the performance – to his/her individual technical and interpretative abilities, but in general his score requires extremely close reading to obtain specific sound effects.[18]

The recourse to chance in the other three compositions cited by Eco is much more substantial and programmatic, although not absolute. We have seen that Boulez's *Troisième sonate* is a defined score containing a number of possible interventions by the performer. This is even more clearly the case in the other two works. In *Klavierstück XI* Stockhausen allows the performer to choose how to combine the various episodes notated in the score. To borrow Eco's words, he offers 'su un grande, unico foglio, una serie di gruppi tra i quali l'esecutore sceglierà, prima quello da cui cominciare, quindi, volta per volta, quello da saldare al gruppo precedente' [on a great, single sheet, a series of groups among which the performer will choose, first the one with which to start, and then, time and again, the one to join to the previous group] (*Opera aperta* 31). It is clear that even in this case the freedom of the performer is not total, but is curtailed by the presence of rules – even if they are few in number. The performer's freedom is likewise restrained by the limited number of available elements, and by the impossibility of modifying them.

There is a similar situation in *Scambi*, which, according to Eco, Pousseur describes as 'non [...] tanto un pezzo quanto *un campo di possibilità*, un invito a scegliere' [not ... so much a piece as *a field of possibility*, an invitation to choose] (*Opera aperta* 32). In this case, however, the composition is entirely electroacoustic; Pousseur imagined that the sixteen episodes could be sold individually with indications for their combination. In this way, the 'openness' would engage directly the user, who would become a co-creator of the actual composition as well as its listener.

If this is the sense of the open work that emerged through the musical examples selected by Eco, we can assert with a certain measure of plausibility that in 1962, the same year that the young scholar published his volume on the open work, an open work that was musical in nature was born at the heart of the neo-avant-garde. It was a work co-authored by Edoardo Sanguineti, then at the beginning of his collaboration with Luciano Berio. Sanguineti had written for the composer the text of *Passaggio*, a theatrical work that involved, among other things, the presence of a chorus in the middle of the audience. This chorus was to express hostility towards the woman on stage and her vicissitudes; however, because of its placement it also incorporated the reactions – of appreciation, or more probably of perturbation and disapproval – of the audience itself. Sanguineti has recently stated:

> Questo effetto del coro faceva sì che anche il pubblico, quando interveniva per protestare (la prima fu particolarmente burrascosa, nel '63 certe cose nei teatri italiani suonavano poco familiari) veniva a collaborare oggettivamente. Era come intrappolato nella rappresentazione perché se protestava, se gridava diventava una delle voci del coro. In un'idea, come si sarebbe

detto allora volentieri, di opera aperta che poteva contenere anche elementi assolutamente fortuiti e casuali, perché c'era una struttura molto salda che catturava questi elementi e li indirizzava al proprio fine.

[This effect of the chorus was such that even the audience, when it intervened to protest, came to collaborate objectively (the opening performance was particularly stormy – in 1963 certain things were not very common in Italian theatres). It was trapped in the performance because, if it protested, if it screamed, it became a voice of the chorus. In an idea, as was said at the time, of open work that could contain even absolutely fortuitous and chance elements, because there was a very solid structure that captured these elements and directed them to its own end.] (*Sanguineti/ Novecento* 39–40)

Compared to the compositions noted by Eco in *Opera aperta*, *Passaggio* presents a more obvious connotation of engagement. The work was proposed as a sort of reflection on the female condition, represented by three women seen in a variety of different situations, called '*stazioni*,' an Italian term normally used to refer to the Stations of the Cross (the moments of Jesus's Passion in the rite of *Via crucis*). In this work, the relationship between art and ideology, and between art and society, is highly evident. By its very structure and thematic nature, *Passaggio* not only indicates an original solution to the dilemma of the choice between freedom of language – even in relation to chance – and engagement, but also points to a future course of action. Eco himself grasped its potential in his notes for the first performance (see 'Introduzione a *Passaggio*'). In particular, Eco emphasizes how the 'openness' (although he does not use this term) of the work affects both its structural and its communicative aspects. The audience could decide whether to align itself with the chorus that contested and attacked the woman or with the woman who was forced to live her own *via crucis*:

La scelta è tra i vari significati concreti da dare alle situazioni della protagonista. La scelta è tra il coro B e la donna, tra due modelli umani. La scelta è comunque non solo di natura estetica ma di natura morale.

[The choice is between the various concrete meanings to give to the situation of the protagonist. The choice is between chorus B and the woman, between two human models. The choice, however, is not only aesthetic, but moral, in nature.] ('Introduzione' 72)

But *Passaggio* could not be simply understood in terms of unidirectional ideological engagement. This work was not intended to provide a clear and well-defined answer. Eco leaves the reader to understand that perhaps the most coherent reaction to the work was

> uscire dal teatro più inquieti e pensosi, consapevoli che sulla scena è stato rappresentato il nostro smarrimento, che gli spezzoni di gesti e di parole erano i nostri gesti e le nostre parole viste ai raggi X, al di sotto della patina di attendibilità che sembravano avere agli occhi della nostra pigrizia. Uscire col vago sentore di un compito rimasto inconcluso.
>
> [to leave the theatre more anxious and thoughtful, aware that our own bewilderment was represented on the stage, and that the numerous clips of gestures and words were our gestures and our words seen with an x-ray, beneath a gloss layer of reliability that seemed to have dulled our eyes. To leave with the vague feeling that an assignment was left incomplete.] (73)

Thus the fundamental characteristics of the musical works noted by Eco in *Opera aperta* and the neo-avant-gardist Sanguineti's *Passaggio* were potentially full of implications for the debate at the Hotel Zagarella. Moreover, the programs of the 1963 Settimana, included useful additional material for the neo-avant-gardists as it offered the opportunity of listening to at least one of the works cited by Eco (pianist Frederic Rzewski performed Stockhausen's *Klavierstück XI* on Tuesday, 8 October 1963) and other semi-aleatoric works (in which a sufficiently determined structure required the direct contribution of the performer), as well as bolder examples of actual chance music.

Strangely, however, these suggestions – and with them the echo of the polemic that had spread like wildfire through the musical world between the 1950s and 1960s on the problem of the relationship between art and ideology – did not breach the walls of the Hotel Zagarella. The debate there did not really cross over into the field of music, a domain that had generated important suggestions and from which useful ideas could be drawn. The conference participants sought, instead, to limit their discussion to a purely literary sphere. And yet, even the name 'Gruppo 63,' which was formally adopted during the Sicilian meeting, while literary in origin, was inspired by the world of music: Luigi Nono had suggested it to Nanni Balestrini in reference to the Gruppe 47 in postwar Germany.[19]

The reasons for this attitude can likely be found in a series of factors. First, as Renato Barilli recalls, the literary sphere maintained a certain resistance to the actual 'open' nature of the work of art and 'presentava forti riluttanze ad abbracciare la via di un "aperto" anche in accezione materiale, di effettiva confezione del testo' [displayed a strong reluctance to embracing an 'open' way, even in material terms, of the actual making of the text] (*La neoavanguardia* 234). In his review of *Opera aperta* in *Il verri*, in fact, Barilli expresses an opinion that is quite opposed to any excessive opening to the audience:

> il compito dello spettatore non sarebbe più soltanto di fruire un'immagine ma, ancora prima, di contribuire egli stesso alla edificazione dei supporti materiali da cui poi dovrà levarsi l'immagine. È questa una via assai pericolosa e anzi al limite insostenibile, poiché un'apertura in senso fisico si rivolgerebbe sulla stessa nozione di opera distruggendola.

> [the task of the spectator would no longer be to receive an image but, even before this, to contribute himself to the building of the material supports from which the image must then emerge. This is a very dangerous and in the end untenable position, because a physical openness would turn upon the very notion of work, destroying it.] ('Umberto Eco' 101)

This statement begins to explain why the influence that could potentially arise from a work such as Pousseur's *Scambi* would encounter so many difficulties in being accepted. Furthermore, the chronicles, interventions, and music reviews that appeared in *Il verri*, regardless of the author, tended to present a certain resistance towards fervently experimental operations that could appear as a self-referential actions. Luigi Pestalozza's review of the third issue of *Incontri musicali* displays a remarkable resistance to the concept of chance in the works of both Boulez and Cage. And *Il verri* also published Luigi Nono's essay on the new experimental musical theatre, in which Nono clarifies the point that his own proposal is not necessarily oriented in the same direction as the open work ('Possibilità').

But even taking all this into account, the silence in Palermo remains mysterious, for music did indicate one of the ways of the open work. The absence of Eco from the meeting does not seem to justify this silence. It is possible that the reasons for the prudent stance that the neo-avant-garde maintained towards music during their days in Palermo must be sought elsewhere, perhaps in the precise characteristics that the Gruppo 63 had adopted. As much as the group persisted in considering itself an avant-garde – indeed a neo-avant-garde – they wanted nothing to do with the *maudit* stance displayed by the twentieth-century historical avant-gardes, nor did they intend to indulge in neoromantic attitudes. Indeed, Guglielmi expressly refused the title 'avant-garde' so as to avoid such misunderstandings.[20] For those convened at the Hotel Zagarella, being avant-garde entailed impatience towards the state of Italian literature and an ambition to seek a way out of a situation perceived as backward and provincial so as to move in the direction of the open work. This research, however, was not to be based on the idea of following what was suggested by an inexplicable inner freedom or dictated by a subjective and unrestrainable artistic frenzy.[21] Instead, the neo-avant-gardists pursued an ideal of rigour, efficiency, and professionalism, married to a perfect integration into the contemporaneous moment and a capacity to grasp within it and its technology the most immediately fruitful aspects without otherwise succumbing to them.

The intellectuals of the group were aware of this characteristic, which they quickly and wittily cultivated, accepting the definition of 'avanguardia in vagone letto' [sleeping-car avant-garde] – a label that later, as Barilli comments:

> risultava perfino inferiore allo stato delle cose, in quanto, semmai, i giovani partecipanti alle riunioni palermitane (del 1963 e del 1965) del Gruppo 63 viaggiavano in aereo, mezzo assai più consono per raggiungere un luogo insulare come la Sicilia.
>
> [didn't even live up to the state of things, since if anything the young people participating at the meetings in Palermo (of 1963 and 1965) of the Gruppo 63 travelled in airplanes, a means much more appropriate to reach an insular place like Sicily.] (*La neoavanguardia* 202)

To continue with the metaphor, if one considers the clothing worn at that time by the technicians who worked in scientific laboratories one could say that, in the end, the neo-avant-garde was an 'avanguardia in camice bianco' (white coat avant-garde). Indeed, Guglielmi takes up the metaphor of laboratory work in 'Avanguardia e sperimentalismo.'

If the aspiration of the Gruppo 63 was to conduct an inquiry and to experiment with rigour, effort, and appropriate instruments, this ambition would inevitably circumscribe the field of the investigation itself (Guglielmi, 'Avanguardia e sperimentalismo,' esp. 281). From the beginning, the group's investigations concerned mainly the literary sphere: poetry, narrative, and theatre. This was the domain in which the debate had started, was bearing fruit, and was subjected to continuous verification. Leaving this niche could signify overstepping the boundaries of the field without the necessary and very rigorous instrumentation, with all the risks that this could entail. This is one probable reason for the relative interests that the neo-avant-garde maintained – on the whole, as a group – towards music, even during and after the Palermo conference. Indeed, this is all the more true since the Gruppo 63 did not promote a merely speculative theoretical debate, but rather pursued a model of work in which *theoria* and *praxis* moved together and supported each other. For these reasons – despite the many affinities between the issues of interest to the group and the musical developments and debate of the preceding years, and despite the simultaneity of the conference with the Settimana Internazionale Nuova Musica 1963 – during their days in Sicily the group's relationship with the world of music did not translate into the manifestations that we might expect. The simultaneous presence of the Settimana Internazionale and the meeting of the Gruppo 63 did not translate into integration, and music, even though well recognized and cultivated by a few individual exponents, nevertheless remained external to the group's direct line of action.[22]

Yet individual neo-avant-gardists – for instance, Sanguineti and Pagliarani – took an active part in musical life. Indeed, in Sanguineti's work we can see an influence of the poetics of the Gruppo 63 on music, as he intensified his collaboration with Luciano Berio between 1963 and 1965. Following the positive experience of *Passaggio*, Sanguineti was absorbed in work on *Laborintus II*, a work largely derived from *Esposizione*, a composition by Berio presented in 1963 and then abandoned. The title *Laborintus II* comes from Sanguineti's collection of poems entitled *Laborintus* (1951–4), from which he drew part of his text, but the work was also the result of literary stimuli, and it was commissioned on the occasion of the seventh centenary of the birth of Dante Alighieri. Thus, the work by Sanguineti and Berio includes references not only to *Laborintus* but also to Dante's *Vita nova* and *Commedia* as well as to Sanguineti's own *Paradiso de lo Inferno*. In this respect, *Laborintus II* is proof of the tendency towards interdisciplinarity noted above, and of the convergence of different material and ideas, literary and musical, in the same direction. As has been observed, Berio and Sanguineti shared in particular a similar linguistic interest.[23]

Nevertheless, Sanguineti's actions had a personal character and did not ipso facto involve the entire group. Further indications of an interest in music on the part of individual members of the group are the musical initiatives of Elio Pagliarani, who wrote the text for Angelo Paccagnigni's *Le sue ragioni* (1960), a theatrical work in which Luigi Pestalozza, writing in *Il verri,* saw a first sign of the reawakening of musical theatre.[24] In 1964, Pagliarani and Giuliani wrote *Pelle d'asino,* a 'grottesco per musica' [musical grotesque] that was destined to remain at the level of literary text.[25] Note also that Dorfles was interested in 'visual music.' These examples, however, represent individual positions.

Thus, there was no musical presence at the meeting of 1964, which took place in Reggio Emilia, and the 1965 conference at Palermo, although it again coincided with the Settimana internazionale nuova musica, focused on the experimental novel. Once again, there was no attempt to cross disciplines. Nor would the situation change for the subsequent meetings at La Spezia in 1966, and at Fano in 1967.

The neo-avant-garde, Gruppo 63, and music: does this represent a missed opportunity? I do not believe it is appropriate to make such an argument, which, after all, could be quickly disproved by the list of contributions on music published in *Il verri.* More simply, it was a multifaceted, complex relationship that was handled with awareness and extreme caution. On one hand, the neo-avant-garde understood the need to overcome the rigid boundaries between the various artistic disciplines. On the other, the group, as a result of its own characteristics, could only believe that such crossings required a conceptual apparatus and a practice at least as developed as that matured within the domain of literature.

In spite of their common militancy in the united front against the condition of art and culture in the 1950s and the 1960s, the Gruppo 63 and the Gruppo 70 had as many differences as similarities.[26] The Gruppo 70 was an avant-garde with an openly provocative connotation, much more so than the Gruppo 63. In this context, informality and synaesthesia were the logical and natural outcomes of a poetics that sought an immediate and open provocation – a provocation that was, for this reason, perhaps also somewhat 'traditional.' In their deliberate indeterminacy, the results of this approach not only did not quite fit the characteristics of the open work, but could go so far as to deny the concept of the *work,* at least in its historical and cultural determination.[27] In contrast, the Gruppo 63 sought to avoid ostentation; rather than deny the concept of the work inherited from the past, it wanted to develop and broaden it; this may explain the lack of real interest of the group as a whole in 'visual music.' Thus, the Gruppo 63 wanted to define itself as a rigorous avant-garde, one that was diffident towards leaps forward that might subsequently reveal over-ambition more than anything else. From this perspective, the group's contact with what was happening in the world of music could not but be accompanied by a rigorous and prudent attitude, and it would be erroneous to mistake this attitude for a lack of interest or attention.

Translated by Sarah Rolfe

APPENDIX

Contributions concerning music published in *Il verri* from 1956 to the first half of 1969 (when the first monographic issue dedicated to music was published).

I.1 (Fall 1956)
Section: Musica
Luigi Pestalozza, '*Canticum sacrum ad honorem Sancti Marci Nominis* di Strawinski' (138–42)
Vittorio Fellegara, '*Ferienkurse fuer neue Musik 1956* a Darmstadt (143–5)
Section: Note e opinioni
Hand Werner Henze, 'Pericoli nella nuova musica' (156–8)

I.2 (Winter 1957)
Section: Musica
Gino Negri, 'La Musica di scena' (107–10)
Luigi Pestalozza, 'I dialoghi delle carmelitane' (111–15)

I.3 (Spring 1957)
Section: Recensioni: musica
Luigi Pestalozza, '*Die Frau ohne Schatten*' (113–15)

I.4 (1957)
Section: Musica
Luigi Pestalozza, 'L'*Histoire* davanti alla guerra' (128–37)
Roberto Leydi, 'Ascesa e caduta di un musicista tedesco' (138–45, on Hindemith)

II.1 (1958)
Section: Recensioni: musica
Luigi Pestalozza, 'Paul Hindemith: *Mathis der Maler*' (126–30)
Section: Musica
Roberto Leydi, 'Osservazioni a proposito della musica elettronica' (137–42)

II.2 (August 1958) (issue dedicated to the Baroque)
Section: Musica
Piero Santi, 'La musica del barocco' (194–204)

II.3 (October 1958)
Section: Recensioni: musica
Luigi Pestalozza, 'Luigi Magnani: *Le frontiere della musica*' (114–15)

II.4 (December 1958)
Section: Pretesti d'estetica
Giovanni Battista Pighi, 'La più antica teoria della critica musicale' (66–73)
Section: Recensioni: musica
Luigi Pestalozza, 'Alfred Colling: *Schumann*' (116)
Section: Musica
Luigi Pestalozza, 'Peragallo, scrivere per l'opera' (153–60)
Piero Santi, 'Un delirio male organizzato' (161–5; on Boulez, *Poésie pour pouvoir*)

III.1 (February 1959)
Enrico Paci, 'Per una fenomenologia della musica contemporanea' (3–11)
Section Musica
Luigi Pestalozza, 'Il Quartetto di Petrassi' (124–30)

III.3 (June 1959)
Gianandrea Gavazzeni, Luigi Pestalozza and Brunello Rondi, 'A proposito di una fenomenologia della musica contemporanea' (109–18)

III.4 (August 1959)
Gianandrea Gavazzeni, 'Pagine da un "Diario musicale"' (58–69)

III.5 (October 1959)
Arnold Schönberg, 'Diritti dell'uomo' (3–11; selection from *Style and Idea,* forthcoming in an Italian translation by Pestalozza)
Section: Recensioni. Musica
Piero Santi, 'Luigi Pestalozza: *La Scuola nazionale russa*' (88–91)

III. 6 (December 1959)
Section: Cronache
Luigi Pestalozza, 'Due riviste musicali' (96–101, on issue 3 of *Incontri musicali* and issue 1 of *Ordini: Studi sulla nuova musica*)

IV.2 (April 1960)
Luigi Magnani, 'Umanesimo di Beethoven' (18–35)
Luigi Nono, 'Realtà storica nella musica d'oggi' (96–103)
Fedele D'Amico and Piero Santi, 'A proposito di una fenomenologia della musica contemporanea' (104–15)

IV.3 (June 1960)
Hans Werner Henze, 'Il Principe di Homburg' (93–96)

IV.5 (October 1960)
Luigi Rognoni, 'Debussy tra Wagner e Maeterlinck' (11–23)
Section: Cronache: musica
Paolo Castaldi, 'Darmstadt 1960' (129–35)

IV.6 (December 1960)
Pierre Boulez, 'Schoenberg è morto' (56–63)[28]

V.2 (April 1961)
Section: Cronache: musica
Luigi Pestalozza, 'Il XXIV Festival internazionale di musica contemporanea' (114–19)

V.4 (August 1961)
Niccolò Castiglioni, 'Presenza sonora e civiltà musicale' (81–88)
Section: Cronache: musica
Piero Santi, 'Il XXV festival mondiale della SIMC a Vienna' (127–30)
[News: 'Musica barocca a Bologna' (147)]

Nuova serie [New series]
1 (February 1962)
Milena Benedetta Savinelli, 'La drammatica posizione di Busoni nei confronti di Beethoven' (91–7)

2 (April 1962)
Section: Rassegna: musica
Luigi Pestalozza, 'Il Festival di Venezia' (118–21)

4 (October 1962)
Section: Rassegna: musica
Piero Santi, 'Engagement e sperimentalismo a Palermo' (107–14)

5 (December 1962)
Erik Satie, 'Da *Memorie d'un amnesico*' (71–6)
Section: Rassegna: musica
Piero Santi, 'Sulla musica sperimentale' (136–43)

7 (February 1963)
Luigi Pestalozza, 'Il 'puro gioco' stravinskiano' (67–84)

9 (August 1963)
Luigi Nono, 'Possibilità e necessità di un nuovo teatro musicale' (59–70)

10 (October 1963)
Armando Plebe, 'Invecchiamento della critica musicale moderna' (69–72; part of a contribution by multiple authors entitled 'Avanguardia e impegno,' 42–84)

16 (August 1964)
Aldo Clementi, Franco Evangelisti, and Franco Donatoni, 'Teatro musicale oggi' (59–77; with a presentation by Luigi Pestalozza, 59–60)
Section: Rassegna: musica
Sergio Martinotti, 'Ugo Duse: *Gustav Mahler, L'approdo musicale*, nn. 16–17 (139–43)

20 (February 1966)
Section: Rassegna: musica
Piero Santi, 'La VI Settimana della Nuova Musica di Palermo' (152–7)

21 (April 1966)
Domenico Guaccero, 'Un'esperienza di teatro musicale' (126–40)

23 (March 1967)
Section: Rassegna: musica
Giampiero Cane, 'Barry Ulanov: *Storia del Jazz in America*' (178–80)

26 (February 1968)
Section: Rassegna: musica
Diego Bertocchi, 'Theodor W. Adorno: *Wagner, Mahler. Due studi*' (129–32)
Riccardo Ambrosini: 'Luigi Rognoni: *Fenomenologia della musica radicale*' (132–6)
Section: Notizie
Giampiero Cane, '*Don Giovanni* a Spoleto' (136–9)

27 (April 1968)
Section: Rassegna: musica
Enrico Fubini, 'Sergio Martinotti: *Anton Bruckner*' (119–21)

29 (September 1968)
Section: Rassegna: musica
Sergio Martinotti, 'Giorgio Pestelli, *Le sonate di Domenico Scarlatti*' (139–43)
Luigi Pestalozza, '*Macbeth*' (147–69)

30 (July 1969)
La nuova musica
Theodor W. Adorno, 'Su alcune relazioni tra musica e pittura' (6–18)
John Cage, 'Buone orecchie!' (19–24)
John Cage, 'Ritmo ecc.' (25–36)
Dieter Schnebel, 'Le ultime opere di Gustav Mahler come nuova musica' (36–54)
Dieter Schnebel, 'L'Avicenna di Bloch, Cage e il rapporto forma-materia nella nuova musica (il problema della forma nella nuova musica)' (55–67)
Morton Feldman, 'Un problema di composizione' (68–70)
Mauricio Kagel, 'A proposito di *Match für drei Spieler*' (71–7)
Karlheinz Stockhausen, 'Registrazione di una conferenza' (78–85)
Franco Donatoni, 'Penteo, o dell'apparenza' (86–93)
Heinz-Klaus Metzger, 'Sulla musica non figurativa' (94–101)
Frederic Rzewski and Salvatore Esposito, '*Zuppa* e altri processi' (102–15)
Cornelius Cardew, 'Note sulla musica AMM con riferimenti indiretti a una etica di improvvisazione' (116–26)
Mario Bortolotto, 'Zum Schluss' (127–31)
Section: Rassegna: musica
Diego Bertocchi, 'Musica e arti figurative,' *Quaderno della Rassegna musicale* 4 (165–8)
Section: Rassegna: Le riviste
Diego Bertocchi, 'Lo Spettatore musicale' (169)

NOTES

1 As throughout this volume, the term 'neo-avant-garde' refers to the artistic and cultural experience that revolved around the journal *Il verri*, experimental fiction, and the *novissimi* poets of the 1950s and the 1960s, of which the Gruppo 63 was a sort of formalization (see Barilli, *La neoavanguardia*).

Within the field of musicology, however, this term is also used in a wider sense to refer to composers who began their activity in the 1950s. It is therefore useful to stress that in this essay the term 'neo-avant-garde' is not used in this wider meaning (over which, incidentally, composers such as Luciano Berio have expressed a certain degree of dissatisfaction; see Berio, *Intervista* 63–64).

2 See Tessitore for a complete listing of the Settimane Internazionali Nuova Musica, with programs for the individuals seasons and evenings.

3 See Umberto Eco's note in the 2004 edition of *Opera aperta* (v–vi). Eco's article, 'L'opera in movimento e la coscienza dell'epoca' [The work in motion and the consciousness of the age], appeared in *Incontri musicali* 3 (1959) and is reprinted in its original version in Barilli and Guglielmi, 214–34.

4 For a discussion of Florentine musical life in the 1950s and 1960s and the Vita musicale contemporanea, see Cresti and Negri; De Simone; Lombardi, 'Musica'; Somigli, 'Compositori'; Somigli, *La Schola fiorentina*'; and *Vita musicale contemporanea.*

5 On the phenomenon of visual poetry, see Saccà. For an outline of the various issues succinctly described in the text, see Barilli, *L'arte contemporanea*, chapter 15, and the related bibliography; Lanza, *Il secondo Novecento*, paragraphs 24–8, and the related bibliography.

6 Eco sent his paper later; see Barilli, *La neoavanguardia* 209.

7 An editorial footnote on the last page reads: 'Con il presente studio di Enzo Paci *Il verri* apre una discussione sul significato della musica contemporanea. Sono stati invitati a intervenire Gianandrea Gavazzeni, Luigi Rognoni, Roman Vlad, Luigi Pestalozza, Piero Santi e Luciano Berio' [With the present study by Enzo Paci, *Il verri* opens a discussion on the meaning of contemporary music. Gianandrea Gavazzeni, Luigi Rognoni, Roman Vlad, Luigi Pestalozza, Piero Santi, and Luciano Berio have been invited to participate).

8 For the text of this press release, see Tessitore, 30.

9 Musicologist and music critic Gioacchino Lanza Tomasi described the meeting with a cutting tone: 'Gli scrittori novissimi [...] si riuniscono all'albergo Zagarella, dove il genio affaristico del banchiere Brignone riesce ad alternare principi della finanza, dello spogliarello e della cultura. Le riunioni del Gruppo '63 sono segrete, con accurata cernita degli iniziati, infatti gli scritori si riuniscono per lavorare e formare un movimento comune che il contatto col volgo potrebbe turbare' [the *novissimi* writers ... gather at the hotel Zagarella, where the business genius of banker Brignone manages to alternate the principles of finance, striptease, and culture. The meetings of the Gruppo 63 are secret, and the initiates are carefully selected. In fact, the writers have gathered to work and to form a collective movement that

contact with commoners could disturb] ('Nuova musica da oggi a Palermo,' *L'ora*, 2–3 ottobre 1963; quoted in Tessitore, 138–9). For an account of the actual meetings, see 'Il dibattito,' in Balestrini and Guglielmi 371–406; 'Il dibattito in occasione del primo incontro del Gruppo a Palermo nel 1963,' in Barilli and Guglielmi 237–62. For a discussion of the different positions within the group gathered at Palermo, see Barilli, *La neoavanguardia italiana* 206–19; Balestrini and Giuliani xvi–xvii.

10 For information on the Ferienkurse, see Danuser; Trudu; and the monumental *Im Zenit der Moderne*, edited by Borio and Danuser.

11 As Hermann Danuser, one of the foremost scholars of the phenomenon, observes: 'il disprezzo per gli ideali culturali nazionalistici e populisti in genere condusse alla legittimazione di un atteggiamento che implicava la consapevolezza di una missione [...] Se il mito nazista si rivolgeva alla collettività di un 'popolo,' il mito di Darmstadt si fondava sulla cultura parziale di un'élite; se quello tendeva all'irrazionalismo, questo tendeva alla razionalità' [the contempt for nationalist and populist cultural ideals led to the legitimation of an attitude that implied awareness of a mission ... If Nazi mythology appealed to the collectivity of a 'people,' the myth of Darmstadt was based on the partial culture of an élite; if the former tended towards irrationalism, the latter tends towards rationality] ('Darmstadt' 171).

12 This process of composition was put in relief by composer György Ligeti, who revealed the illusory nature of rationalist ambitions by means of a rigorous and pitiless analysis the numerous elements of subjectivity hidden in the very premises of the work. See Ligeti, 'Décision.'

13 See Henze, 'Pericoli.' Henze's article forms a de facto diptych on the risk of academicism in new music with Fellegara's report on the Ferienkurse published in the same issue. On Henze's experience, see his *Reiselieder mit böhmischen Quinten*.

14 Nono's lecture 'Presenza storica nella musica d'oggi' was published as 'Realtà storica nella musica d'oggi,' *Il verri* 4.2 (April 1960); for the complex history of the composition of this text, see the critical notes in the version edited by Angela Ida De Benedictis and Veniero Rizzardi, 563–64.

15 See also Furio Colombo's testimony in Barilli, Curi, and Lorenzini, 111–12.

16 The first examples of chance music date back to the 1940s and 1950s when American composers John Cage and Morton Feldman became advocates of experimental music in which the intentionality of the composer, his/her ego, had to disappear in order to allow the sound present in the world to come to light by unpredictable avenues. From this perspective, composers could limit themselves either by giving the performer a few generic instructions for gestures to complete and sound situations to produce, or

by providing extremely detailed parts to recreate freely by means of either superposition or succession. From the same point of view, composers could produce scores on the basis of chance so that the sound of their work arises from events that entirely escape their control. Thus, notes may result from throwing *I-Ching* chips, from the choice of following imperfections on a blank page, from stellar masses on astral charts, from the superposition of transparencies previously marked with staves, note values, and dynamic indications. For an overview on the subject that pays particular attention to John Cage and the deep origins of his music, see Prichett; Nicholls.

17 Gillo Dorfles also discussed this issue, as did *Il Verri* in a review of Dorfles's work (see Bertocchi). For an overview of musical notation during the 1950s and 1960s, see Karkoschka, *Das Schrftbild der neuen Musik*, an account that is almost contemporary with the events discussed here.

18 Berio later expressed serious doubts concerning the outcome of a performance based on proportional notation, and he published *Sequenza I* in traditional notation (this is the version published by Universal Editions in 1993). Of this decision he humorously commented, 'Spero che Umberto Eco mi perdonerà' [I hope that Umberto Eco will forgive me] (Berio, *Intervista*, 109). For an analysis of the internal composition of Berio's cycle of *Sequenzas*, see Galliano. For Berio's recent reflection on the problem of the 'open work' in the compositional tendencies of the 1950s, see *Un ricordo al futuro*, 55–77. About the problematic nature of Sequenza I as 'open work' see Venn; Priore; Folio and Brinkman.

19 See Balestrini and Giuliani (XII); see also statements by Inge Feltrinelli and Nanni Balestrini in Ballerini, Curi, and Lorenzini, 16 and 76.

20 Angelo Guglielmi's view of the concept of avant-garde emerges in his 'Avanguardia e sperimentalismo' (Balestrini and Giuliani 15–24); the October 1963 issue of *Il verri* also featured a debate on the term 'avant-garde.'

21 Several contributions in *Il gruppo 63 quarant'anni dopo* return to this simultaneous avant-gardism and rejection of the movementism typical of the avant-garde in favour of a more controlled experimentalism.

22 The lack of explicit references to the issue of the relationship between ideology and art in music on the part of Nono, which found an interesting parallel in Sanguineti, was probably the result of the different attitude of these two authors; Nono was more inclined towards greater emotional involvement, and Sanguineti leaning more towards greater objectivity. On this topic, see Becheri 299.

23 'Le operazioni poetica e musicale trovano un momento di singolare affinità quando la datità del riferimento viene assunta in un accumulo di motivi tematici diversi, in una sovrapposizione di figure, in una 'partitura' com-

plessa fondata su una condensazione di strati linguistici e sonori, oppure si libera dall'intreccio e della mescolanza dei linguaggi per porsi come oggetto singolo, volutamente evidenziato e straniato' [the poetic and musical operations share a moment of remarkable affinity when the thingness of their reference is assumed in an accumulation of different themes, in a superimposition of figures, and of a complex 'score' based on a condensation of linguistic and sound levels, or when it is freed from the plot and from the mixing of languages to position itself as a single object, purposely highlighted and estranged] (Dalmonte and Lorenzini 12).

24 Luigi Pestalozza, introductory note to *Teatro musicale oggi* in *Il verri*, new series 16 (1964): 59–60.

25 It was published in *Il verri*, new series 8.11 (1963): 42–58.

26 On the relationship between the Gruppo 63 and the Gruppo 70, see Barilli, *La neovanguardia italiana* 268–80.

27 On the extensive presence of chance in music, Luciano Berio has recently written: 'col caso si entrava in una sfera culturale diversa, dove le opere (virtuali, aperte, negative o 'informali' che fossero) non potevano trasformarsi per il semplice fatto che non c'erano più. Se ne erano andate' [chance took us into a different cultural sphere, where the works (whether virtual, negative or 'informal') could not change for the simple reason that they no longer existed. They were gone] (*Un ricordo al futuro* 68).

28 A footnote at the bottom of the first page states: 'Convinti come siamo della necessità di far vivere un autore nella ricchezza di tutte le relazioni che lo riguardano, pubblichiamo volentieri questo scritto proprio in occasione dell'uscita nelle nostre edizioni, del volume *Stile e Idea* di Arnold Schoenberg, a cura e con un saggio introduttivo di Luigi Pestalozza, nel quale si fa ripetutamente riferimento – sia pure in senso critico – alle tesi di Boulez' [Convinced as we are of the need to have an author live in the richness of all the relations that pertain to him, we gladly publish this writing on the occasion of the issuing, in our editions, of Arnold Schoenberg's book *Style and Idea*, edited and with an introductory essay by Luigi Pestalozza, in which references – albeit critical ones – are repeatedly made to Boulez's theses].

WORKS CITED

Balestrini, Nanni, and Alfredo Giuliani. 'Introduction.' In *Gruppo 63: L'antologia*, ed. Balestrini and Giuliani. Turin: Testo & Immagine, 2002. vii–xxii.

Balestrini, Nanni, and Alfredo Giuliani, eds. *Gruppo 63: la nuova letteratura, 34 scrittori, Palermo ottobre 1963.* Milan: Feltrinelli, 1964.

Barilli, Renato. *L'arte contemporanea: da Cézanne alle ultime tendenze.* 1984. Milan: Feltrinelli, 2005.

– *La neoavanguardia italiana: dalla nascita del* 'Verri' *alla fine di* 'Quindici.' Bologna: Il Mulino, 1995.

– 'Umberto Eco: *Opera aperta.*' *Il verri* new series, 7.4 (1962): 98–103.

Barilli, Renato, Fausto Curi, and Niva Lorenzini, eds. *Il Gruppo 63 quarant'anni dopo.* Bologna: Pendragon, 2005.

Barilli Renato, and Angelo Guglielmi, eds. *Gruppo 63: critica e teoria.* 1976. Bologna: Testo e Immagine, 2003.

Berio, Luciano. *Sequenza per flauto solo,* Milan: Suvini Zerboni, 1958.

– *Intervista sulla musica.* Ed. Rossana Dalmonte. Rome-Bari: Laterza. 1981.

– *Un ricordo al futuro: lezioni americane.* Turin: Einaudi. 2006.

Bertocchi, Diego. 'Quaderno della Rassegna musicale, 4.' *Musica e arti figurative* 30 (1969): 165–8.

Borio, Gianmario, and Hermann Danuser, eds. *Im Zenit der Moderne: Die Internationalen Ferienkurse für Neue Musik Darmstadt, 1946–1966.* 4 vols. Freiburg im Breisgau: Rombach, 1997.

Boulez, Pierre. 'Alea.' (1957). In *Relevés d'apprenti,* ed. Paule Thévenin. Paris: Éditions du Seuil, 1966. 41–55. First Italian trans., *Incontri musicali* 3.3 (1958): 3–15.

Chiari, Giuseppe. 'Gesti sul piano.' In *Firenze nel dopoguerra: aspetti musicali della vita dagli anni '50 ad oggi,* ed. Leonardo Pinzauti et al. Milan: Opuslibri, 1983. 37–8.

Cresti, Renzo, and Eleonora Negri, eds. *Firenze e la musica italiana del secondo Novecento: le tendenze della musica d'arte fiorentina.* Florence: LoGisma, 2004.

Dalmonte, Rossana, and Niva Lorenzini. 'Funzioni strutturanti nel rapporto musica-poesia: *Passaggio* e *Laborintus II* di Sanguineti-Berio.' In *Il gesto della forma: Musica, poesia, teatro nell'opera di Luciano Berio,* ed. Rossana Dalmonte, Niva Lorenzini, Loris Azzaroni, Fabrizio Frasnedi. Milan: Arcadia, 1981. 1–44.

Danuser, Hermann. 'Darmstadt: una scuola?' In *Enciclopedia della musica,* vol. 1: *Il Novecento,* ed. Jean-Jacques Nattiez, with Mario Baroni, Margaret Bent, and Rossana Dalmonte. Turin: Einaudi, 2001. 166–84.

De Simone, Girolamo. *Pietro Grossi.* Florence: Nardini, 2006.

Eco, Umberto. 'Introduzione a *Passaggio.*' Concert program for the Piccola Scala (1963). In *Berio,* ed. Enzo Restagno. Turin: EDT, 1995. 66–73.

– *Opera aperta.* 1962. Milan: Bompiani, 2004.

Fellegara, V. 'Ferienkurse für Neue Musik 1956 a Darmstadt.' *Il verri* 1.1 (1956):143–5.

Folio, C., and A.R. Brinkman. 'Rhythm and Timing in the Two Versions of Berio's *Sequenza I* for Flute Solo: Psychological and Musical Differences in

Performance.' In *Berio's Sequenzas: Essays on Performance, Composition and Analysis,* ed. J.K. Halfyard. Aldershot, UK, and Burlington, Vermont: Ashgate, 2007. 11–37.

Galliano, Luciana (ed.). 'Le *Sequenze* per strumento solo.' In *Berio,* ed. Enzo Restagno, Turin: EDT, 1995. 145–92.

Henze, Hans Werner. 'Pericoli nella nuova musica.' *Il verri* 1.1 (1956): 156–8.

– *Reiselieder mit böhmischen Quinten. Autobiographische Mitteilungen 1926–1995.* Frankfurt am Main: Fischer, 1996.

Karkoschka, Erhard. *Das Schriftbild der neuen Musik.* Celle: Moeck, 1966.

Lanza, Andrea. *Il secondo Novecento.* Turin: EDT, 1990.

Ligeti, György. 'Décision et automatism dans la Structure Ia de Pierre Boulez' (1958). Last rev. ed. *Neuf essais sur la musique.* Geneva: Contrecahmps, 2001. 89–126.

Lombardi, Daniele. 'Attraversamenti.' In *Attraversamenti: la musica in Toscana dal 1945 ad oggi.* Prato: Gli Ori, 2003. 39–81.

– 'Musica.' *Continuità: arte in Toscana 1945–2000.* Exhibition catalogue, Florence, Palazzo Strozzi, 2002; Pistoia: Maschietto, 2002. 81–107.

Nicholls, David, ed. *The Cambridge Companion to John Cage.* Cambridge: Cambridge University Press, 2002.

Nono, Luigi. 'Possibilità e necessità di un nuovo teatro musicale.' *Il verri* new series, 9 (1963): 59–70. Reprinted in *Scritti e colloqui,* ed. Angela Ida De Benedictis and Veniero Rizzardi. Lucca and Milan: LIM – Ricordi, 2001. 1: 118–32.

– 'Presenza storica nella musica d'oggi.' 1959. In *Scritti e colloqui,* ed. Angela Ida De Benedictis and Veniero Rizzardi. Lucca and Milan: LIM – Ricordi, 2001. 1: 46–56.

– 'Realtà storica nella musica d'oggi.' *Il verri* 4.2 (1960): 96–103. (cf. 'Presenza storica' above).

Pestalozza, Luigi. 'Due riviste musicali.' *Il verri* 3.6 (1959): 96–101.

Pritchett, James. *The Music of John Cage.* Cambridge: Cambridge University Press, 1993.

Priore, Irna. 'Vestiges of Twelve-Tone Practice as Compositional Process in Berio's Sequenza I for solo flute.' In *Berio's Sequenzas: Essays on Performance, Composition and Analysis,* ed. J.K. Halfyard. Aldershot, U.K., and Burlington, Vermont: Ashgate, 2007. 190–208.

Saccà, Lucilla. 'Poesia visiva.' *Continuità: arte in Toscana 1945–2000.* Exhibition catalogue, Florence, Palazzo Strozzi, 2002. Pistoia: Maschietto, 2002, 115–21.

Sanguineti, Edoardo. *Sanguineti/Novecento: conversazioni sulla cultura del ventesimo secolo.* Ed. Giuliano Galletta. Genoa: Il Melangolo, 2005.

Somigli, Paolo. 'Compositori a Firenze: un ritratto in nove istantanee.' In *Attra-*

versamenti, ed. Daniele Lombardi. New ed. Florence: Edizioni dell'Assemblea Regionale Toscana, 2009. 63–84.

Somigli, Paolo. *La Schola Fiorentina: Bartolozzi, Benvenuti, Bussotti, Company, Prosperi, Smith Brindle.* Florence: Nardini, forthcoming.

Tessitore, Floriana, ed. *Visione che si ebbe nel cielo di Palermo.* Rome: Rai-ERI, 2003.

Trudu, Antonio. *La 'scuola' di Darmstadt.* Milan: Ricordi – Unicopli, 1992.

Venn. Edward. 'Proliferations and Limitations: Berio's Reworking of the *Sequenzas.*' In *Berio's Sequenzas: Essays on Performance, Composition and Analysis,* ed. J.K. Halfyard. Aldershot, UK, and Burlington, Vermont: Ashgate, 2007. 171–7.

Vita Musicale Contemporanea. Sylvano Bussotti, Giuseppe Chiari, Pietro Grossi. Genoa: Tipografia Artigiani Grafici, 1998.

11 Superstudio Double-Take: Rescue Operations in the Realms of Architecture

LAURA CHIESA

Introduction

When considering the different and interdisciplinary experimental proposals that shaped the debates and the poetics of the Italian neo-avant-garde in the 1960s, one finds a consistency concerning names and motifs between the publications of the 1960s and the critical re-editions done in the last few years. Among the architects and designers who actively collaborated in publications, colloquia, and meetings of the Italian neo-avant-garde in the 1960s, one of the most influential critical voices is Vittorio Gregotti. An examination of critical theory in the field of architecture in recent years reveals a quite insistent reconsideration of an international neo-avant-garde, yet Vittorio Gregotti is scarcely mentioned; instead reconsideration is directed to several Italian architectural groups whose practice, in tune with the European and international context is identified as 'radical architecture,' or sometimes 'neo-avant-garde architecture.'[1] I will try to show that in the relation between architecture and broader neo-avant-garde artistic experimentation there is a short but critical temporal delay. The most radical experimentation advocated by Gruppo 63 preceded the most radical experiments in the field of architecture in Italy by about three years. The current reconsideration of radical architecture is taking place in an international context, but critics have yet to examine the broad interdisciplinary atmosphere that prevailed in Italy.[2] In this essay I will comment on the experimentation done by Superstudio, one of the most active groups practicing radical architecture in Italy, with the aim of establishing their singular moves in the broad and vital intellectual landscape at the crossroads of Italian and international debate. Superstudio was founded in Florence in 1966

Figure 1. Superstudio, from 'Atti fondamentali': 'Vita. Supersuperficie, pulizie di primavera' (1971–2). Courtesy of Cristiano Toraldo di Francia.

and 'carried out, until 1978, an activity of theoretic research on architecture' (Pettena 301), and definitively dissolved in 1982.[3] If, on one hand, Superstudio distinguishes its practice from the trend of the Italian neo-avant-garde in architecture, on the other, we find affinities between the theoretical research of Superstudio and the interdisciplinary theoretical debate that took place in the Italian neo-avant-garde.

A brief essay on the avant-garde and the neo-avant-garde by Elio Pagliarani will help to connect the radical architects with the general atmosphere in Italy around 1965. Pagliarani defines three aspects of the avant-garde movement:

> (1) critica consapevole dei *mezzi espressivi* in situazione; (2) critica, a tutti i livelli, della funzione dell'operatore e del rapporto operatore-consumatore; (3) critica della finalità dell'opera e/o funzione dell'arte.
>
> [(1) conscious criticism of the *expressive means* at work; (2) criticism at all levels, of the function of the operator and of the relationship operator-consumer; (3) criticism of the finality of the work and/or the function of art.] ('Per una definizione' 312)[4]

Pagliarani's first point specifies radicality for the critic of the expressive means, it is a '*massimo di scostamento* possibile in situazione dai mezzi espressivi tradizionali' [*maximum* possible *deviation* from the traditional expressive means] (313). This 'scostamento' [deviation] connected with a 'consapevolezza,' and the questioning of the relation between operator and consumer, are also at the core of architectura radicale [radical architecture] expessions. Pagliarani concludes his short presentation by suggesting that this contestation may lead to the impasse of negation of the project: that which radical architecture with an ironical stance will put in praxis. As a 'proper' but still generic adjective that connotes a movement, 'radical' was quickly adopted by the art critic Germano Celant to define the different but still related groups active between 1966 and 1977 that were not controlled by the rules of the market: 'radical' as a counter-design movement.[5] Penny Sparke mentions the counter-design movement at the end of her essay 'A Home for Everybody' (published in the well-known collection of Italian cultural studies, *Culture and Conflict in Postwar Italy*). Counter-design is seen as a reaction to a general tendency in the field of architecture, dating from the progressive postwar drive 'to build' shifted to a less significant focus on the life-style of consumption and elite design.[6] Sparke notes that lighting was the most successful arte-fact and fetish of the 1960s. My reading will examine in detail several experiments by Superstudio with a perspective that differs from that of cultural studies. Superstudio did design several lamps. But as we will see in the radical critique of the object, in its 'apparent' impasse of the negation of the project, Superstudio has not only questioned anew the relation of operator and consumer, but has also pushed forward the relation between criticality and inventiveness, between local and global, between the material and the different framing of the architectural space-time, including photography, writing, cinema, and the network matrix. In this perspective the neo-avant-gardist gestures of Superstudio are also 'valuable' for their after-effects, which they disseminated with their 'scostamento' [deviation] in the reading of history and of their contemporary society, as well as what can inventively be included or excluded from the process of the project. The 'radical moment,' rehearsing Marjorie Perloff's *The Futurist Moment,* is certainly remembered as lightning rather than lighting.[7]

Leisure Time, Space of Involvement, and Design as Rescue Operation

The XIII Milan Triennale (1964), curated by Umberto Eco and Vittorio Gregotti, is one achievement of the encounter between the Italian neo-avant-garde and architecture. The curators approached the theme, 'Tempo libero' [Leisure time] with a two-fold solicitation: invitations were directed both to international architects, to participate with projects for a new vision of architecture in a time of economic boom, as well as to artists, musicians, and scenographers, to present a stunning introductory section. Artists at the core of the Gruppo 63 performed an 'opera aperta' [open work] scenography in which visitors were exposed to the 'tempo libero' theme with an initial euphoric thrust that eventually crashed into a parodic double-take effect, as cacophonic disenchantment.[8] Among the various spaces that composed the scenic time in the introductory halls, much discussion centred on the 'Caleidoscopio' – a long room in the shape of a perspective telescope which immersed the passer-by in a multi-layered space of videos, mirrors, and music.[9]

The double-take at work in this exhibition was also present in publications when architecture was at the core of the Italian neo-avant-garde investigations. A sign post in this regard is the interdisciplinary journal *Marcatré,* which covered, among other themes, industrial design, communication, technology, arts, and literature (with articles by Eco, Gregotti, Spadolini, and Menna), as well as various experiments in architecture ranging from Yona Friedman to Constant, Arata Isosaki, and Archigram.[10] A few years after the Triennale several newly graduated and graduating students in Florence began to inscribe provocative interdisciplinary and avant-gardist motifs in their practices. The architect Leonardo Savioli taught a design studio whose project was to facilitate a more fluid relationship between the fixity of architecture and its users.[11] In 1966–7 Savioli and Aldolfo Natalini, one of the founding members of Superstudio,[12] taught a class that was documented in the architectural review *Casabella* under the title 'Spazio di coinvolgimento' [Space of involvement].[13] The project, also known as 'Ipotesi di spazio' [Hypothesis of space], is an interior nightclub space for spectacle and entertainment. As stated in the article, the project seeks to bring into the domain of architecture the matrix of two different contemporary artistic experiences: pop art (with its adhesion to the 'world of images' and consumerist society) and 'arte programmata' (with its concept of iteration, repeatability, and seriality). The various projects therefore operatively expanded architectural design with innovative construction materials (metals, plastics, and inflatables) assembled with a pop touch and aimed at performing a constructed space open to the estrangement of a normative context and to the contamination of styles. The fundamental point made in this article is that the design of interior space should not be in opposition to the exterior: 'Uno spazio interno che non fosse più il "negativo" dell'architettura, un dentro in contrapposizione al fuori, ma un oggetto spaziale generatore di esperienze' [An interior space that would no longer be the 'negative' of architecture, an inside opposed to the outside, but a spatial object and generator of experiences] (Savioli and Natalini 36). The constructed space was supposed to stimulate the participation of the user who was at the same time an operator in such a 'field of experience.'[14] A similar concept of design as a 'field of experience' is expressed in 'Design d'evasione e d'invenzione' [Invention design and evasion design],[15] one of the first publications by Superstudio, which accompanied a series of objects of design that were also presented at the Superarchitetture exhibition (architecture of superproduction, of superconsumption, of the superinduction of consumption, of the supermarket, of the superman, of the super gasoline, Pistoia 1966). The exhibition proposed a pop ambiance, a colourful constellation of forms that could be converted to design pieces. The tone of Superstudio writing and design aims to involve all users 'in oggetti a funzionamento poetico o fornendo schemi di comportamento' [in products that are poetically functional or by supplying patterns of behaviour] ('Design' 28; 'Invention' 440). According to Superstudio this could be done by supplying 'oggetti multisignificanti (ambigui), oggetti a funzionamento universale, e ogni fruitore li usa come vuole' [multisignificant (ambiguous) products, objects of universal use, and each user puts them to the use he thinks fit] (28; 440). The interior space of involvement becomes a space to 'be-in.' Superstudio's proposal for change in design implies their desire to inflect a too-rational modality with poetry; the change in the operativity of the design that Superstudio is aiming at was not a total revolution but rather a 'rescue operation.' 'Design d'evasione dunque per evadere dall'orrido quotidiano ... Oggetti insomma che riescano a modificare il vano-contenitore e a coinvolgerlo totalmente insieme al suo fruitore' [Evasion design to evade everyday dreariness, or rather evasion design to make it possible to live with the everyday dreariness ... Objects in short that succeed in modifying the container-unit and involving it totally together with its occupier] (28; 440–1). There is no intention of changing the entire environment, or even the houses, which Superstudio defines as 'cubic blocks' without memories, with only vague indications of top and bottom, entrance and exit, always 'senza sorprese o speranze' [without surprises and without hope] (28; 440); still the objects of design become a facilitation for an 'adventure in space.' Evasion design would exorcize indifference and modify 'il tempo e e il luogo e che siano segnali per una vita che continua' [Time and space and serve as sign posts for life that is going ahead] (28; 441). Superstudio wanted to put back 'design in motion,' avoiding the 'prefabricated monopoly of the truth,' against rationalism and functionalism. Evasion, rescue, and involvement set the tone with which the not-yet 'radical architecture' of Superstudio began. Among several objects designed by Superstudio, was one of the design symbols of the year: a lamp named 'Falling Star.' If Superstudio announced design as a rescue operation, and therefore already less enchanted than a 'spazio di coinvolgimento,' the multi-media counter-projects that followed would change the critical vision of constructible spaces much more drastically.

Estranging Journeys in the Architectural Landscape

The premise of this design was to shift attention from the object of design to an 'avventura dello spazio' [adventure in space] ('Design' 28; 'Invention' 440). But what do we find instead? The criticism, the revolt, or perhaps only the *état de lieux* of an hegemonic architectural system is mentioned only briefly in 'Design d'invenzione e d'evasione' but it occupies a central position and is brought to its extreme in two empty allegorical reflexive projects: 'Viaggio nelle regioni della ragione' [Journey into the realm of reason] (1969), and 'Monumento Continuo' [Continuous Monument] (1969). Whereas before the focus was on small objects of design and the small scale of the project, here all the attention moves in the opposite direction: vast and homogenous exterior spaces are the target, and co-involvement is silenced.

In the title alone – 'Viaggio nella regioni della ragione' – there is a clash of words: a voyage, ultimately a discovery and a way of experiencing, counter-intuitively takes its paths in the 'regioni della ragione' [realms of reason] ('Viaggio') (see figure 2). It is an estranging journey into an architecture designed by abstract reason. 'Viaggio' is framed in a series of drawings, accompanied by lapidary texts, between script and cartoon style, which document moments of the travel and history of an ultimately all-too-abstract architecture; the *carnet de bord* [storyboard][16] is about a cube that has been liberated from its tights and fragmented into smaller pieces that are all the same size, thus bringing 'con sé i ricordi della loro origine' [with itself the memories of its own origin] ('Viaggio' 40); it is the minimalist symbol of geometry. The fragments of stories accompanying the drawings are thrown into an empty environment where there is no trace of relationship or tension with the contemporary city; they are indeed in a desert landscape. It is an estranged, fictionalized, and abstract environment that includes, for example, an image of a landing strip where a plane will pass among 'pilastri della saggezza' [pillars of wisdom] ('Viaggio' 40), or a death-end trip by car to visit a drive-in museum of architecture. The title announces a voyage, but this voyage in fact does not find the 'architettura misteriosamente scomparsa' [architecture mysteriously disappeared] ('Viaggio' 40); an estranging enchantment is suspended in this empty environment where architecture has almost disappeared, frozen in its isolation; in these regions reason rules. Because of the short-cut mode of this counterproject, it would be silly to compare it with the cinema of that time. But one could argue that it has fewer connections to Rossellini's problematization of neorealism in *Viaggio in Italia* than to Antonioni's *L'avventura*, which is concerned with adventure as disappearance.[17] Nevertheless, even in its ephemeral artifactuality 'Viaggio nelle regioni della ragione' seeks an invisible voyage and has its own neo-avant-gardist hopes hidden in the minimalist play between word and image. There is no desire to impose an operative criticism like that proposed by architectural historian Manfredo Tafuri, criticizing expressions such as Monumento Continuo, which turns the project 'in una registrazione di materiale onirico trascritto in un'ironia che "non fa ridere"' [into dream material transcribed with an irony 'that makes nobody laugh'] (*Storia dell'architettura italiana* 125; *History of Italian Architecture* 99).[18]

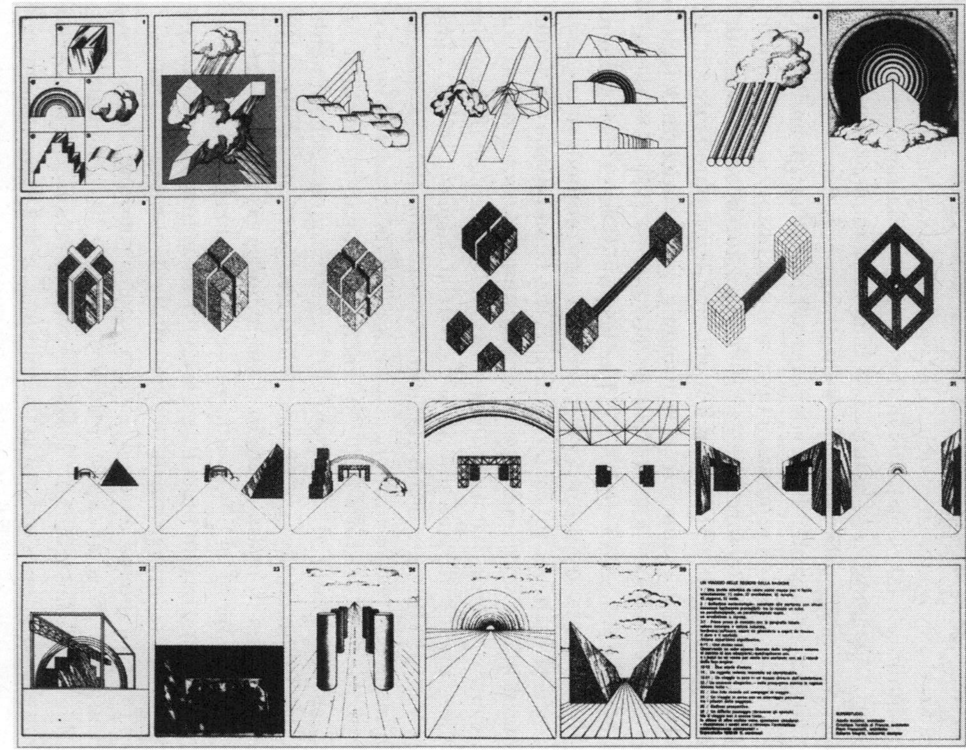

Figure 2. Superstudio, 'Viaggio nelle regioni della ragione' (1966–8). Courtesy of Cristiano Toraldo di Francia.

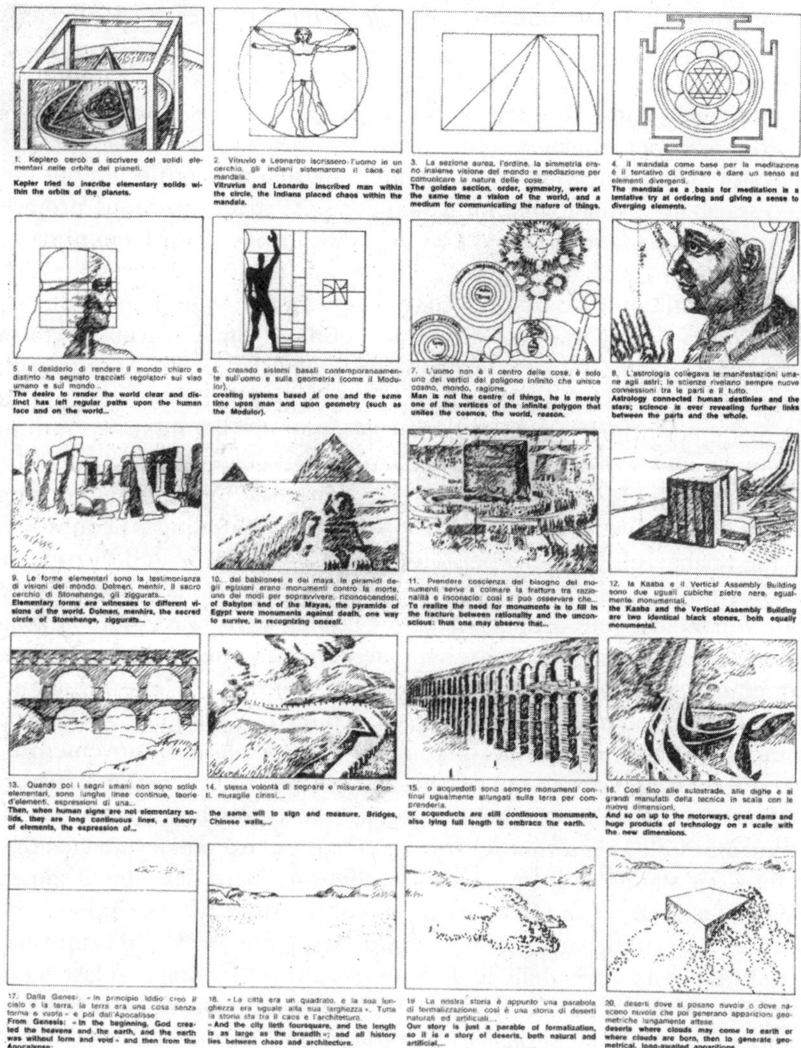

Figure 3. Superstudio, 'Il Monumento Continuo' from the storyboard (1969). Courtesy of Cristiano Toraldo di Francia.

But what is the Monumento Continuo? What is the design, the project, or better, the counter-project? It is presented in the format of two different media: one reads like a cinematic storyboard; the other proliferates in montages of abstract allegorical hyper-modern times. The storyboard, or 'discorso per immagini' [discourse by images],[19] is composed of a series of estranging episodes of architecture that are connected but not necessarily in a linear temporal sequence. As in the previous project, all that is drawn and narrated converges with irony toward a minimalist idea of the project blindly mastered by reason, truth, and rationality. The first part of the storyboard presents examples in which human rationality is seen as a faculty that measures and defines: from Vitruvius's Man to Le Corbusier's Modulor. A prologue of the genesis of the Monumento Continuo presents elementary forms such as Dolmen, Stonehenge, and the pyramids, which are described as monuments that fill in 'la frattura tra razionalità e inconscio' [the fracture between rationality and the unconscious] ('Monumento Continuo' 124) (see figure 3). According to this perspective the VAB (Vehicle Assemblage Building) is equivalent to the Kaaba; this 'discorso per immagini' has the marks and the uncanny qualities that Anthony Vidler analyses in his *The Architectural Uncanny*. The storyboard goes on to show other human signs: ways of measuring according to continuous lines that extend horizontality such as bridges, aqueducts, and motorways ('Monumento Continuo'). The infrastructural difference and the use of each architectural example are undermined, and nothing in the storyboard signals a sense of movement or life. Everything is frozen into images in order to define a fictional history of formalization; the storyboard format reduces any historicity of architecture as well as internal tensions. After these exemplary images that offer some standstill of formalization, the storyboard describes a square block. Geometry is the first 'character' of the story (which Superstudio defines as a parable and a genesis), and the square block is 'il primo atto e l'ultimo nella storia delle idee di architettura' [the first and last act in the history of architectural ideas] ('Monumento Continuo' 126). The history of the cube is similar to that found in 'Viaggio.' The storyboard tells of the cube that, when represented in axonometric drawing, flies. It is

> costretto da due cinghiature ad essere un cubo perfetto e appena liberato si divide in pezzi seguendo leggi precise … e le parti non si disperdono ma l'ordine non genera il disordine e ogni parte ha con sé il messaggio genetico della sua razza ordinata.

> [forced into a perfect cube by two straps and as soon as it is freed, it divides into pieces ... and the parts disperse, but order does not generate disorder and each part has with it the genetic message of its ordered race.] ('Monumento Continuo' 126)

The final part of the storyboard is the genesis of the Monumento Continuo: architectural apparitions will converge in the construction of it.

> 49. LE APPARIZIONI. 3. LA PIETRA. Grande e nera nel giace nel deserto. Come uno specchio sicuro rimanda immagini in movimento di uomini e città. 50. Poi comincia a muoversi e si alza in volo. 51. Raggiunge una certa quota e poi rimane parallela alla terra, muovendosi. 52. Dentro ha l'immagine distorta della città, il grande Barum tecnologico. Lo specchio nero in cielo è intelligente e immobile.
> 53. LE APPARIZIONI. 4. I MURI. In prospettiva con gente che ci passa dentro. Camminare in prospettive parallele (New York). 54. All'uscita appare la pietra specchio che muovendosi ... 55. balza sui muri paralleli e diviene un soffitto e i muri divengono un tunnel buio. 56. Camminare a lungo nel buio e infine vedere un chiarore, e nella luce appare come una linea bianca il MONUMENTO CONTINUO.
>
> [49. THE APPARITIONS. 3. THE STONE. Large and black, it lies in the desert. As in a dark mirror, it reflects moving images of men and cities. 50. Then it begins to move and takes off in flight. 51. It reaches a certain height and then remains parallel to the ground, moving. 52. Within, it contains the distorted image of the city, the great technological circus. The black mirror in the sky is intelligent and immobile.
> 53. THE APPARITIONS. 4. THE WALLS. In the perspective with people walking between them. To walk in parallel perspective (New York). 54. At the exit, the mirror-stone appears, moving ... 55. and jumping onto the parallel walls it becomes a ceiling and the walls become a dark tunnel. 56. Walking in the dark for a long time, and at last seeing a faint glow, and in the light, like a white line, we see the CONTINUOUS MONUMENT.] ('Monumento Continuo' 128)

In this metaphysical and deserted landscape a silhouette of a human figure, an astonished passerby, sees the Monumento Continuo. What does this project incorporate and what does it omit? To what is it radically and ironically responding? With the Monumento Continuo Superstudio brings to the extreme consequences the drives of Modern Movement in architecture, participating in the recent utopian or dystopian vision of architecture (from Friedman to Archigram)[20] while demarcating the absolute passage out of the megastructures, as Rouillard has argued, and finally responding to a more local discourse – that which was taking shape within the Italian Gruppo 63. This last point is clear in relation to Eco's *Appunti per una semiologia delle comunicazioni visive* (1967); the third section of this book, 'Proposte per una semiologia dell'architettura,' was also published in *Marcatré.*[21]

Eco sketches a semiology specific to architecture in order to read it as a communication, taking into consideration the denotation, the meaning, use, function, as well as the connotation, syntax. While writing on possible codes of architecture, he clearly separates semantic and syntactic codes:

> Per intanto una ispezione dei codici architettonici sinora individuate da chi si è occupato dell'architettura sotto l'aspetto comunicativo, ci permette di riconoscere che spesso non ci si è chiesto se si intendevano indicare *codici semantici* o *codici sintattici,* e cioè leggi di articolazione dei significanti indipendente dai significati che possono essere loro attribuiti, o leggi di articolazione di certe strutture significanti a cui viene convenzionalmente già attribuito uno e non un altro significato.
> In secondo luogo locuzioni come 'semantica dell'architettura' hanno spesso spinto alcuni a cercare nei segni architettonici l'equivalenza della 'parola' della lingua verbale, dotata di un significato preciso, riferentesi cioè addirittura ad un referente; mentre sappiamo che un codice può anche prescrivere soltanto delle leggi di articolazione sintattica dei segni, ma cosí sarà opportuno vedere se l'architettura supporti anche una codificazione puramente sintattica (anche per giustificare e poter descrivere oggetti di cui non è predicabile la funzione che denotano, come i *menhir,* il *dolmen,* il recinto di Stonehenge, etc.)
>
> [Meanwhile, an inspection of architectural codes previously identified by those interested in architecture from a communicative standpoint allows us to see that, it has rarely been questioned whether these referred to *semantic codes* or *syntactic codes,* that is, laws of articulation of signifiers independent of the signifieds that can be attributed to them, or laws of articulation of certain signifying structures to which one signified, and not another, is already conventionally attributed.
> In the second case, locutions like 'architectural semantics' have often led some to seek, in architectural signs, the equivalent of the 'word' of verbal

> speech, carrier of a precise signified, referring, that is, to a specific referent; while we know that a code can also only prescribe laws of syntactic articulation of signs, it is worth considering whether architecture can support a purely syntactic codification (also to justify and be able to describe objects that are not predicated on the function they denote, such as the *menhir*, the *dolmen*, Stonehenge, etc.)] ('Proposte' 67)

Eco also considers how the 'secondary functions' lose their significance more quickly than the 'primary functions,' and he describes a 'vorticosa spirale secondo cui il nostro tempo riempie e svuota le forme dei significati, ricopre codici e li dimentica ... una continua operazione di *styling*' [whirling spiral where our time fills and empties the forms of their meanings, covers up codes and forgets them ... a continuous operation of *styling*] ('Proposte' 66). Eco individuates at the core of this diachronicity the cause of a 'philological vocation' and in response proposes an architecture that designs '*funzioni prime variabili e funzioni seconde "aperte"*' [unpredictable primary functions and 'open' secondary functions] where the step back is facilitated to mutate into a step forward. Eco also articulates his argument carefully in order to support Gregotti's *Il territorio dell'architettura*, which, for Eco, prevents the architect from thinking of himself as a demiurge.

Was not the menhir or Stonehenge at the beginning of the Superstudio storyboard? Superstudio acts at a level where the semantic and the syntactic, in the play between images and words, are brought to their extreme. The Monumento Continuo is not the monument of the 'philological sickness' (Eco), or the Borradori's ambiguous concept of monument (see 'Nozione di progettualità'), or the territory as presented by Gregotti. If Eco's proposal furnished a more syntactic hinge to Superstudio, Gregotti's investigations furnished a semantic one that is brought *per absurdum* by the radical praxis directly to the artifactural roots.

Gregotti, the general editor of *Edilizia moderna*, dedicated the issue 87–88 to the vast theme of landscape. His take on this issue was, even at a graphic level, a transversal one: his editorial essay literally appears in fragments scattered throughout the other essays that compose the issue. His aim was focused on the possibility of the formation and formalization of an anthropogeographic landscape, which with experimentation could structure in a meaningful way the physical space and the ambiguous term of landscape, conferring an aesthetic sense.[22] Gregotti, considering the spatial expansion and the temporal acceleration of planning, aims at instituting another intellectual and operative optic in which the construction of the landscape has new significance because it has also new gestures. In the necessity of finding an operative unity, Gregotti brings to our attention a multilayered questioning: to find a contour of the field, to define the figurative iconicity of the operative intervention, to consider the aesthetics of geography and the operability of/on matter, also in relation to its cultural and artificial specificity; Gregotti asks for imagining the planning at a distance, inscribing into the matrix of the project a 'spostamento dell'organizzazione percettiva, di fronte alle nuove dimensioni, ai nuovi rapporti dinamici, ai problemi posti dal vario uso degli strumenti di comunicazione visiva' [displacement of the perceptive organization when faced with new dimensions, new dynamic relationships, problems posed by varied use of the instruments of visual communication] (*Edilizia moderna* 77/150). He also calls to attention specific cases of urban architectural interventions (such as in Milan and Naples). The passage moves from a defence of the landscape to a plan and purposefulness for the landscape itself (progetto intenzionato del paesaggio) searching for a stratigraphy that operates experimentally within a 'schematizzazione, unificazione della terminologia, delle simbologie di rappresentazione degli schemi di procedimento progettuale' [schematization and unification of the terminology, of symbologies of representation of the schemes of planning procedure] (*Edilizia Moderna* 146/151).

The generic effect of any mass medium grafted onto the landscape is conceptually inscribed in the discourse by images of the Monumento Continuo, perhaps also implying a retroactive questioning of the *Profezia di una società estetica,* as announced by art critic Filberto Menna.[23] The architecture of the Monumento Continuo, with its draconic iconography of a total reduction of the landscape project, does not allow for the Benjaminian distraction; is not the neorealistic or allegorical background and landscape for a film, but instead is the main 'fictional character' of the story. This adventure is a temporary eclipse of architecture, perhaps not too distant from Antonioni's *L'eclisse,* which Eco cites as exemplary for the contemporary way to give form to estrangement and alienation: 'Antonioni accetta nelle forme quella stessa situazione di alienazione di cui vuole parlare: ma rendendola palese attraverso la struttura del suo discorso, la domina e ne rende cosciente lo spettatore' [Antonioni lets his forms express the alienation he wants to communicate to his public. By choosing to express it in the very structure of his discourse, he manages to control it while letting it act upon his viewers] (*Opera Aperta* 277).[24]

The mode of the script of the Monumento Continuo is effective in capturing an immobilized landscape; it annihilates any enchantment up to the point where it elliptically re-enchants *per absurdum*; eventually it leaves room at large for new spaces of invention. The simple and implacable logic of the shape of the Monumento Continuo resolves the question of the project and in its impassiveness can be used everywhere; it can extend where there is only nature, but also in cities and suburbs. Superstudio brings to an extreme with a fictional and 'cruel' story the intention of the architectural project, estranged from historicity, life, and the city with all its connections and interferences. The monolithic and homogeneous shape of the Monumento Continuo can expand in any space. Superstudio invents a fictional story of a cruel constructive machine which demonstrates faith neither in architecture nor in invention. Superstudio's Monumento Continuo is a celebration of a possible dead end of modern architecture, whose violence is performed everywhere. Peter Lang, commenting on the Monumento Continuo, writes: 'The creeping expansion of the monument across the global landscape is subtly revealed as its own neutralizer, thereby putting an end to its sublime terror' ('Suicidal Desire' 45). Disenchantment rises to the top, everything is immobile, eventually lifeless, everything is exterior, or rather, there is no more space for questioning whether the Monumento Continuo has an exterior or an interior. At the end of the storyboard, the block is not in pieces, but instead is formally defined as a 'single design.'[25]

With the photo-collages, an astonishing series of images, the beauty of the Monumento Continuo is allowed to appear: the images 'localize' the Monumento Continuo, which is also a rescue of historical centres, and the presence of human beings returns, as well. The photo-collages that Superstudio presents for the Monumento Continuo expand everywhere – in the desert, among lakes, in the mountains – with a touch of landscape similar to that in Antonioni's film *Zabriskie Point.* Sometimes there are a few people in the picture, in the proximity of the Monumento Continuo. The photo-collages implicitly question problems of the history of architecture and of everyday life; they are traces of a voyage. The Monumento Continuo puts an additional layer on the Coliseum, protects and climatises the Taj Mahal, it crashes into a rich landscape of St Moritz (figure 4), into an Alpine lake, into the Nevada Desert, or finally into an Indian marsh. In a black and white photo-collage of Coketown, a row of worker houses is cut by the passage of the Monumento Continuo and a few children play in the deserted street (figure 5). Another photo-collage is a picturesque photograph of an Italian fisherman coming back to a southern Italy harbor in his boat. The fisherman stares at the Monu-

Figure 4. Superstudio, 'Il Monumento Continuo: St Moritz rivisitata' (1969). © Gian Piero Frassinelli. The Museum of Modern Art, New York. Gift of the Howard Gilman Foundation. Courtesy of Art Resource.

Figure 5. Superstudio, 'Il Monumento Continuo: Coke Town rivisitata' (1969). Courtesy of Cristiano Toraldo di Francia.

Figure 6. Superstudio, ‘Il Monumento Continuo: O Pais d’o sole’ (1969). Courtesy of Cristiano Toraldo di Francia

mento Continuo where, behind its transparent shape, one can see small fishermen's houses in the harbor (figure 6). In 'Liebe Grüße aus Graz von Superstudio!' a postcard from Graz is traversed by the Monumento Continuo. One of the best-known photo-collages is the Monumento Continuo that covers Manhattan, expanding not on the vertical but on the horizontal plane. It is hypothesized at the end of the storyboard:

> 78 ... struttura ortogonale per l'espansione. Tutto il resto è Central Park. Basta per raccogliere tutto il volume costruito. 79. Un mazzo di grattacieli antichi, conservati a ricordare il tempo in cui le città si costruivano senza un unico disegno... 80. E dalla baia vediamo New New York ordinata dal monumento continuo come un gran piano di ghiaccio. Nuvole e cielo.
>
> [78 ... perpendicular structure for expansion. All the rest is Central Park. This is sufficient to hold the entire built-up volume. 79. A bunch of ancient skyscrapers, preserved in memory of a time when cities were built with no single plan. 80. And from the Bay we see New New York City arranged by the continuous monument into a great plan of ice, clouds, or sky.] ('Monumento Continuo' 130)

The reiteration in the photo-montage of the Monumento Continuo permits the appearance of ghostly architectures that Superstudio calls 'architetture riflesse': the flat mirrored surfaces reflect visually on the architectural speculations. The photo-collages, as a contestation of any euphoric megastructural project, or a too-easy embrace of a landscape project, question Gregotti's take on landscape, borrowing a breath from the new dimension of land art: for example, injecting in the counter-project the critical perspective of the American artist Robert Smithson. The cube has an iconographical connection with Smithson's *Proposal for a Monument on the Red Sea* (1966) and *Proposal for a Monument at Antartica* (1966). In Smithson's proposal, as discussed by Jennifer L. Roberts in *Mirror-Travels*, a 'scientific diagram of a cube appears massive and alien in its juxtaposition with the coastal landscape. In *Proposal for a Monument at Antartica*, a negative photostat of a collage produced in 1966, a gridded crystalline form sits ominously on an hill, as if threatening to spread throughout the image and asphyxiate all the busy ship workers in the foreground'(55). Superstudio's collages can be compared to those by Smithson, especially if we consider Roberts's comments: 'If this image seems disquieting or dystopian, it is largely because Smithson's collage practice introduces jarring shifts into the viewer's visual experience of the space [...] it refuses to fit into the representational structure of the image itself' (55). Moreover, among the many similarities that Superstudio and Smithson share is the same hidden opening into the discourse of hyperspace.[26] For Superstudio, this was to lead to the *Supersurface* where life eventually will allegorically be disclosed.

The Filmic Emergence of New Behaviours out of the *Supersurface*

With the Monumento Continuo, Superstudio formally resolved the question of construction fictionally proposing the foundation of a single design. With 'Atti Fondamentali: Vita, Educazione, Cerimonia, Amore e Morte' [Fundamental acts: Life, Education, Ceremony, Love, and Death] Superstudio moves on to liberate the potential of primary human acts. These counterprojects were intended as short films, but only two were realized, the first under a grant from the Museum of Modern Art for the exhibition 'Italy: The New Domestic Landscape' (1972). The others remain as detailed storyboards and photo-collages. These short films allegorically echo and respond to the influential films made by the American designers Charles and Ray Eames, who began experimenting with the medium of film in the 1950s and produced more than seventy-five films, showing their designs, collaborating in multimedia projects for World Fairs, and engaging with more broad aesthetic and educational themes (see Colomina).

The short film *Supersurface: An Alternative Model of Life on Earth* was presented at the exhibition 'Italy: The New Domestic Landscape.' The curator Emilio Ambasz, who had invited Italian designers with a wide spectrum of attitudes towards design, commented: 'Italy has become a micro-model in which a wide range of the possibilities, limitations, and critical issues of contemporary design are brought into sharp focus. Many of the concerns of contemporary designers throughout the world are fairly represented by the diverse and frequently opposite approaches being developed in Italy' (Ambasz 19).[27] *Supersurface* can be defined as a mocking of the condition of possibility, or better of impossibility, of the design, alluding in an impossible way to the convoluted relation that is at the core of the exhibition title: 'domestic' and 'landscape.' In previous Superstudio projects the human was hardly mentioned, but this film starts from the human factor.

The voice-over begins by addressing a generic 'you' in a scientific tone. 'You' are reminded that you use only a part of your sensorial channels: and the eye, the ear, and the hand are targeted visually, while the voice-over explains that, as senses, they have become in a McLuhanian way potentiated by technical tools.[28] A new symbiosis between the human and tools creates new uses, complex mechanisms that may sometimes bring to schematic rigidity the models of behaviour. (This symbiosis is eventually represented visually in the grafting of eyes to grotesque tools.) The potential speed of understanding furnished by the montage of the filmic medium enables a series of contemporary jump cuts: the interior of an airplane, Solzhenitsyn, Gandhi, a racing-car driver. The image of Fuller's ambitious geodesic dome city (1968) over New York City appears as the voice-over speaks about the design's mediation between the human and the environment. Taking on the false evidence of images showing multitudes of the masses and the phenomenon of nomadism, the voice-over suggests, in a science-documentary tone, that society has come to a point where there is a need of an urban life without three-dimensional structures. From the Monumento Continuo surfacing Manhattan, the video moves to a surface in the air and on the ground over which cows and horses graze. Manhattan, with its grids, is just an example of the homogeneous usage of landscape. Instead of cities as knots of a three dimensional material grid, the alternative model proposes a network of energy, that can assume different configurations, so as to render all the earth homogeneously habitable. But as a temporary arrest, the voice-over reminds us that what we see is not a 'three-dimensional model of reality' but a 'metafora visivo-verbale di distribuzione ordinata e razionale delle risorse' [visual-verbal metaphor for an ordered and rational distribution of resources] (Superstudio, 'Vita' 48; 'Life' 181). Among the nodal points of the invisible grid are universal plugs for primary needs. This new humanity, without induced needs, is visualized by several persons on a white gridded surface.[29] The video takes on a psychedelic tone, as scrolling images show people picnicking on the 'supersurface,' who can finally and integrally use the psychic potential as the only support for a life freed from futile needs: there is no more need for castles and cities, no reasons for streets and squares, and a highly sophisticated technics can substitute any three-dimensional structures of service and shelter. It is, the voice-over says, the very sense of locality that loses its meaning: 'Quindi, scelto un punto a caso su una carta, potremo dire qui sarà la mia casa per tre giorni due mesi o dieci anni' [So, having chosen a random point on the map, we'll be able to say my house will be here for three days two months or ten years] ('Vita' 50; 'Life' 183). A series of photo-collages allegorically brings together the happy life of a family in an Arcadian landscape and a new poverty; there will be some space left for consumer society.[30]

Supersurface is reminiscent but at the same time very different from the Eameses' *Power of Ten*, which moves, as Colomina writes, 'from a domestic space of a picnic spread with a man sleeping beside a woman in a park in Chicago out into the atmosphere, and then back down inside the body through the skin of the man's wrist to microscopic cells and to the atomic level' (12). As Colomina suggests, in *Power of Ten* 'intimate domesticity is suspended within an entirely new spatial system' (12). Certainly, the way to 'integrate architecture and information flow,' (17) is played by the Eameses and Superstudio in opposite ways. *Vita,* as an allegory of the network, at the same time alludes to some of the possibilities that are opened up for architecture by the 'supersurface' – an allusion that is also given by an adult Alice:

> Guarda quella montagna lontana... cosa vedi? E' quello il luogo dove andare? O è solo il limite di abitabilità ottimale? E' l'uno e l'altro poichè non esiste contraddizione , è solo un caso di complementarietà.
>
> Così pensava un'Alice assai adulta saltando la sua corda, molto lentamente, senza però né caldo né freddo.
>
> [Look at that distant mountain ... what can you see? Is that the place to go? Or it is only the limit of optimal habitability? It's the one and the other since contradiction no longer exists. It's only a case of being complementary.
>
> Thus thought a fairly adult Alice skipping over her rope, very slowly, though without feeling either heat or effort.] ('Vita' 49)[31]

Filiberto Menna, one of the critics who wrote about Superstudio, has been able to discuss the group activity, balancing the formal aspect of Superstudio projects with the general atmosphere in the design arena of contestation against the powerful relation between technology and politics. Referring to Sklovsky's 'motion of the horse,' Menna defines Superstudio practice as lateral thinking. Thus, in radical practice Menna does not see only 'design nihilism' per se but rather a new philosophy of design, 'a design for new behaviours' that 'seeks to achieve eminently communitarian ends by constructing environments that stimulate the active participation of every individual through the creation of spaces endowed with strong mental, psychological, and sensory appeal' (in Ambasz 412).

In *Cerimonia* (1973) made by the 'Supersensualists,' as Jencks has called Superstudio, several people emerge from their 'underground architecture' into a country landscape with slow and candid gestures

Superstudio, *Cerimonia*, 1973.

Figure 7. Superstudio, still image from the film *Cerimonia* (1973). Courtesy of Cristiano Toraldo di Francia.

that they perform throughout the film (figure 7). The story focuses on the sense of that single day in which the inhabitants decided to remain forever outside:

> Gli abitanti della casa sottorreanea dicono: non ti mostreremo la casa che si nasconde nell'ombra. Ti mostreremo dove viviamo e dove vivremo nella casa invisibile che stiamo facendo difronte ai tuoi occhi.
>
> [The inhabitants of the underground house say: we are not going to show you the house which lies in the shadow. We will only show you how we live or would live in the invisible house as we are doing before your eyes.] (from *Cerimonia*)

The inhabitants do not propose a mode d'emploi of architecture, or a lifestyle to endorse. Instead, moving gently in a rarefied architecture, they propose an invisible house for unknown ceremonies. The narrative voice-over explains:

> Il punto è: se riesco a fare un'architettura misteriosa che ti commuove non puoi non pensare che la tua commozione di fronte alle architetture viene proprio da un eugual grado di misteriosità? Insomma vorrei portarti in regioni sconosciute per farti riconoscere solo che il tuo viaggio è in una regione ugualmente sconosciuta e di qui il passo successivo sarà l'abbandono di tutte le illusioni di agire solo secondo ragione seguendo scale e gerarchie e modelli formali che ti posso dimostrare sono solo formule magiche che i tuoi stregoni ti hanno subdolamente sussurrato all'orecchio mentre dormivi.
>
> [The point is: if I succeed in creating a mysterious architecture that moves you, can you not think that your feelings in relation to the architecture come directly from an equal degree of mystery? Therefore, I would like to take you to regions unknown to make you recognize only that your journey is in an equally unknown region and from here the next step would be the abandonment of all beliefs that we have to behave only according to reason, following steps and hierarchies and formal models that I can demonstrate to you are only magic formulae that your wizards subtly whispered into your ear while you were sleeping.] (from *Cerimonia*)

With this maieutic tone, Superstudio returns to the voyage in the regions of reason that have now become unknown regions. In *Atlas of Emotion*

Giuliana Bruno emphasizes the close connection of the words 'movement' and 'emotion' – both of which come from the same Latin root: *emovere* – weaving multiple relations through journey, cinema, and architecture. Here, when finally Superstudio makes films, there is no architecture, at least only an invisible one, that could facilitate the journey and the emotion.

Conclusion

I have chosen to discuss in depth some of the motifs that articulate only one of the many radical architecture groups, and have left out many different experimentations that they successfully accomplished in their transversal multiple connections.[32] Andrea Branzi notes that the term radical architecture 'indica più che un movimento unitario, un 'luogo culturale', una tendenza energetica' [indicates more than an homogeneous movement, a 'cultural site,' an energetic tendency] (Navarone and Orlandoni 13). There is a swerve between the general phenomenon of the Italian neo-avant-garde and radical architecture; certainly the interdisciplinary debates on design and architecture mobilized by Gregotti, by Eco's poetics of indeterminacy, and by Menna and many others,[33] have facilitated the new visual/verbal double-take on the architectural scene, if not on the part of its users, surely on operators in the 'discipline' of architecture.

This essay is an in-depth consideration of Superstudio, about which Superstudio could have done a *demostratio quia absurdum*. In a discussion of surface in architecture Sylvia Lavin notes that 'the surface becomes manifestly effective rather than tectonic when architecture seeks mood instead of meaning' (in *Crib Sheets* 63). Superstudio's take on alternative models of behaviour, and perhaps also mood, plugs into the debate on design, plays with the idea of a linear-oriented history, inscribes into the practice of design that of contemporary arts, and enhances a multimedia environment within a critical tone, and, with brief but effective hints, alludes to the coming of the new technologies, leaving space for an inventive and critical architecture that does not rely only on rationalism, functionalism, or historicism and technology. Superstudio visually and verbally presents the shock of the optical dimension of the megastructures as extended constructions in the landscape, while pointing to the lack of a haptic dimension. In their allegorical montage images, where architecture is in total suspension, there is as much space left for desolation as for beauty. Almost like an apocatastasis in Walter Benjamin's sense, Superstudio's arrested counterprojects abruptly give way to a new multiple space that will eventually be reconsidered by several architects (Koolhaas, Tschumi, MVDRV), who only a few years after Superstudio's double-take have constructed projects within a new critical and inventive matrix.

NOTES

1 The first text on radical architecture is *Architettura radicale* (1974) by Navarone and Orlandoni. One of the earliest publications intended to offer a comprehensive retrospective of this phenomenon, *Radicals: architettura e design 1960–1975*, dates from the 1996 Biennale di Venezia. See also the catalogues for two recent major exhibitions – *Architecture radicale* and *The Changing of the Avant-Garde* – as well as Rouillard's *Superarchitecture.*

2 In 'Involuntary Prisoners of Architecture' Scott reads 'architettura radicale' and localizes Superstudio practice not so much for its formal strategies but for its 'attempts to forge new modes of radical political and institutional transformation' (79) in conjunction with the extraparliamentary left in Italy (84). See also Scott, 'Italian Design and the New Political Landscape' where she emphasizes the lines that guided the reception of 'architettura radicale' for the exhibition, 'Italy: The New Domestic Landscape' (1972) at the Museum of Modern Art.

3 Archizoom was the other major group of radicals, but there were several others who, with more or less emphasis, related to the radical direction of research: Remo Buti, Riccardo Dalisi, Ugo La Pietra, Alessandro Mendini, Gaetano Pesce, Gianni Pettena, Franco Raggi, Ettore Sottsass Jr., Gruppo Sturm, UFO, Zziggurat, 9999. I will examine in detail a selection of experimental and theoretical projects by Superstudio, but will leave out several of their civil and industrial constructions and designs. For a survey of these projects, see Natalini, ed., *Superstudio: Storie con figure 1966–1982.*

4 This and all further translations are mine unless otherwise indicated. Pagliarani's text, 'Per una definizione dell'avanguardia,' was presented at the COMES Conference dedicated to the avant-garde (Oct. 1965).

5 For the origin of the use of the term 'radical' for designating disparate practices of architecture, see Rouillard, esp. 18.

6 'The concept of the unified interior as a whole – with its early postwar emphasis on the human inhabitant rather than on its material components – was replaced by a growing emphasis, in magazines and sales brochures, on the isolated object: the light, the sofa, the chair, the table' (Sparke 232).

7 The 'radical moment' or 'radical time' insistently 'dwells' in a way similar to Benjamin's comment about the logic of modernity: 'In the fields with which we are concerned, knowledge comes [*es gibt*] only in lightning flashes. The text is the long roll of thunder coming after.' [N1,1] (*Arcades Project* 456).

8 On the question of double-take, see Samuel Weber, 'Double Take: Acting and Writing in Genet's "The Strange Word Urb."'

9 In their introduction to the exhibition catalogue, Eco and Gregotti give a detailed description of the Caleidoscopio: 'Lo spazio del parallelepipedo del salone della Triennale è visibile e tinto completamente in nero. All'interno è posato un enorme oggetto argentato costituito da due prismi triangolari rovesciati l'uno rispetto all'altro e incastrati lungo lo spigolo longitudinale. Una porta triangolare immette all'interno da una delle testate del prisma che si rivela come una grande sala da proiezioni cinematografiche, con la sezione del triangolo equilatero. Le pareti del prisma, lunghe 24 metri e con un'altezza di metri 10,30, sono completamente ricoperte di specchi e, mentre le due testate, riflettendosi, moltiplicano l'interno all'infinito, in senso longitudinale, le pareti laterali creano l'illusione di essere all'interno di un enorme prisma esagonale alto 18 metri. Sul pavimento bianco di questa sala sono proiettati e contemporaneamente riflessi sei volte negli specchi, due film (regista Tinto Brass), uno sul 'tempo libero,' uno sul 'tempo del lavoro.' I film, della durata di nove minuti, sono formati da un college di pezzi di repertorio. Una particolarissima tecnica di montaggio permette da un lato di rendere ritmicamente coincidenti i due temi, dall'altro di condurre simultaneamente più episodi nello stesso film, dando luogo a una complessa serie di paesaggi e incroci fra i diversi momenti della rappresentazione. Lo spettatore vede se stesso sei volte proiettato sulle pareti, nel mezzo dello schermo cinematografico, partecipante e fisicamente coinvolto nello spettacolo. In qualche modo uno finisce qui per diventare deformato ed impotente di tutto ciò che gli era stato promesso con tanto ottimismo nella prima sala. Al termine del film, una colonna sonora composta da Nanni Balestrini e una serie di collages a colori del pittore Achille Perilli invadono la scena secondo 24 combinazioni, in una specie di accumulo di rottami finali del nostro tempo libero consumato. Una voce annuncia la fine di questa prima sezione e invita a passare alle sale successive.' [The parallelepiped space of the *Triennale*'s main room is visible and entirely tinted black. Within it sits an enormous silver object, composed of two triangular prisms, overturned, one on top of the other, and intersecting along the longitudinal edge. A triangular door leads inside one of the prism's heads, revealing a large projection room, in the section of an equilateral triangle. The prism walls, 24 metres long and 10.3 metres high, are

completely mirrored and, while the two heads, reflecting one another, multiply the interior to infinity lengthwise, the lateral walls create the illusion of being within an enormous hexagonal prism 18 meters high. On the white floor of this room, two films (directed by Tinto Brass) are simultaneously projected onto and reflected by the mirrors six times, one on 'free time' and one on 'work time.' The nine minute long films are made of a collage of repertory pieces. An unusual montage technique allows the two subjects to coincide rhythmically while simultaneously reproducing various episodes within the same film, giving rise to a complex series of landscapes and intersections among different moments of the representation. The spectator sees him or herself projected six times on the walls, in the middle of the screen, participating and physically involved in the spectacle. In a sense, he or she is left disoriented and dispossessed of all that had been so optimistically promised in the first room. At the end of the film, a soundtrack composed by Nanni Balestrini and a series of multicoloured collages by Achille Perilli flood the scene in 24 different combinations in a kind of accumulation of the wreckage from our consumed free time. A voice announces the end of this first section and invites the spectators to move on to the following rooms.] (*Tredicesima triennale di Milan* 15). For an interesting analysis of the architectural culture and the exhibition from the 1930s to the *XIII Triennale* see, Rinaldi, *La casa elettrica e il caleidoscopio.*

10 For example, *Marcatré* published quite timely pieces by UFO. At the climax of the occupation of the School of Architecture in Florence, against the rational project, UFO invested the city with what they called the macro but ephemeral dimension: long inflatables were thrown randomly over the city; See UFO, 'Effimero Urbanistico. Scala 1/1, gli U.F.O,' and 'GLI UFO. URBOEFFIMERI AVVENIMENTI 1:1.'

11 In Bardeschi's article on Savioli, which was published in *Marcatré*, Savioli's projects are recognized as a new methodology that he brings to 'grado estremo operando asintoticamente sia nell'innovazione lessicale che l'uso dei materiali tradizionali fino a rendere quest'ultimo asintattico e scardinato dalla consueta matrice imposta dal paternalismo ufficiale' [the extreme degree operating asymptotically in the lexical innovation and in the use of traditional materials to render the latter asyntactic and unhinged from the usual matrix imposed by official paternalism] (Bardeschi 'Leonardo Savioli' 37) so that his projects are not a radical protest against the institutions.

12 The architects were Adolfo Natalini, Cristiano Toraldo di Francia, Roberto Magris, Alessandro Poli, Alessandro Magris, and Gian Piero Frassinelli.

13 The article and the various projects were later published in Savioli's *Ipotesi di spazio* (1972). For a detailed analysis of the stagnant situation in Florentine

architecture at that time, including comparisons with Rome and Milan, see Lang, 'Suicidal Desires.'

14 'Attraverso tutta la serie dei progetti si possono individuare due operazioni fondamentali: A. partendo da involucri indifferenziati, fornire una serie di oggetti-immagini, oggetti a funzionamento poetico capaci di stimolare comportamenti diversi; B. partendo da strutture spaziali progettate (nodi di servizi e attrezzature) fornire una serie di possibilità operative come schemi provvisori di comportamento. Nel primo caso, lo spazio interno diveniva un insieme invariato nelle sue coordinate spaziali, ma si modificava psicologicamente per l'insieme dei messaggi e degli stimoli provenienti dagli oggetti-catalizzatori che vi venivano introdotti. Nel secondo caso, lo spazio interno diventava un elemento continuamente trasformabile, e le azioni reciproche tra spazio e fruitore ne costituivano l'essenza specifica: si giungeva a un nuovo spazio interno modificabile e deperibile: non più un involucro per la capitalizzazione ma una serie di stimoli per l'azioni.' [Throughout the entire series of projects, one can identify two fundamental operations: A. starting from undifferentiated envelopes, the production of a series of object-images, objects with a poetic function capable of simulating different behaviours; B. starting from designed spatial structures (networks of facilities and tools), the production of a series of operative possibilities, such as provisional outlines of behaviour. In the first case, the internal space became an unvaried whole in its spatial coordinates, but was psychologically modified by the network of messages and by stimuli deriving from object-catalysts introduced therein. In the second case, internal space became a continually transformable element, and the reciprocal actions between space and user constituted its proper essence: one arrived at a new internal space, malleable and perishable: no longer an envelope for capitalization, but a series of catalysts for actions.] (Savioli and Natalini 36).

15 This article was first published in 1969 in *Domus* under the title, 'Design d'evasione e d'invenzione.' An English translation, entitled 'Invention Design and Evasion Design,' was later included in *Architecture Culture 1943–1968,* an anthology edited by Jean Ockman. All subsequent citations will include page numbers for both the Italian and the English versions, identified by the first word of their respective titles.

16 This *carnet de bord* is very different from the the storyboards we are used to; see, for example, Le Corbusier's *Carnets de voyage.*

17 Peter Brunette, commenting on the disappearance of the woman that is never found in *L'avventura,* writes: 'The absences in this film are not transcendental, nor do they mark something "inexpressible." Rather, they lead to the negation, or better, the calling into question of a prior, unprob-

lematic, completely visible presence. The sense of "mystery" that arises as a result of this suggestive absence as well as from the oddness of Antonioni's narrative seems to be a completely nonspiritual one that speaks to the deep ambiguity of the relation of human beings to reality, rather than to a hankering after the other-worldly' (*Films of Michelangelo Antonioni* 31).

18 In the critical scene of that times it was Tafuri who apparently imposed his 'panoptical and authoritative super-partes' voice on the neo-avant-garde, and who, unfortunately, I might add, has dominated the architectural intellectual scene. Mark Wigley has sharply commented on Tafuri's 'operative criticism' in 'Post-Operative History.' The incongruences at the core of Tafuri's criticism of the neo-avant-garde, and beyond Italy, are innumerable; one could go on for pages 'demystifying' his pseudo philosophical *parti-pris* against any practice that inscribes in its making criticality. It is crucial to emphasize that any later critic who considers the neo-avant-garde architecture must come to terms with Tafuri's theorical stranglehold. Dominique Rouillard has most effectively taken the time to demystify Tafuri's *partis-pris,* positing that Tafuri has in fact aberrantly borrowed radical architecture's criticism in order make an argument against it: 'Tafuri assimile les analyses de M. Cacciari – le mot "négation" apparaît de multiples fois dans l'introduction à la réédition en 1970 de *Théories et histoire de l'architecture,* alors qu'il est absent du texte d'origine – mais il tire aussi du discours contre-utopique architectural, élaboré par Archizoom and Superstudio, sa lecture de G.B. Piranèse. L'œuvre de l'architecte du XVIIIe siècle, qui n'était jusqu'alors abordée que rapidement et sous l'angle de l'éclectisme qu'il introduisit dans l'architecture, fait en 1972 l'objet d'une analyse portant sur la notion explicite "d'utopie négative." L'expression est absente chez Piranèse, car elle n'existe alors tout simplement pas [....] mais M. Tafuri en recrée *a posteriori* le concept, en recourant au vocabulaire de la contre-culture radicale-courant auquel il dénie par ailleurs toute espèce de valeur critique ou révolutionnaire, le qualifiant "d'aliénation du sujet," de projet comme réquisitoire, d'absurdité, de "polémique négative," de "vide sémantique absolu," etc. Le fait de vilipender Archizoom et Superstudio ne l'empêche pas de leur emprunter l'"utopie négative" pour lire l'œuvre de Piranèse, puis celle des avant-gardes artistiques du début du siècle.' [Tafuri incorporates Cacciari's analyses – the word "negation" appears several times in the introduction to the 1970 edition of *Theories and History of Architecture,* while it does not appear at all in the original edition – but he also draws his reading of Giovanni Battista Piranesi from the counter-utopic architectural discourse elaborated by Archizoom and Superstudio. Previously he had given only cursory consideration to Piranesi's work, solely from the perspec-

tive of the eclecticism that the eighteenth-century artist had introduced in architecture. Yet in 1972 he makes Piranesi's work the object of his analysis of the explicit notion of "negative utopia." Piranesi does not use this expression because it simply did not exist at that time [...] but Tafuri recreates the concept *a posteriori*, using the vocabulary of the radical counterculture – a cultural tendency that he otherwise sees as completely devoid of critical or revolutionary value and that he describes as an "alienation of the subject," a project as accusation, an absurdity, a "negative polemic," an "absolute semantic void," etc. The fact that he reviles Archizoom and Superstudio does not stop him from borrowing their "negative utopia" to read Piranesi's work and then the work of the early twentieth-century artistic avant-gardes.] (*Superarchitecture* 309–10). Rouillard refers to several articles including 'Le avventure della ragione: naturalismo e città nel secolo dei lumi,' which is included in Manfredo Tafuri, *Progetto e utopia*.

19 Concerning the image, Cristiano Toraldo di Francia writes: 'The avant-garde architect from designer of object becomes creator of images, accentuating that practice of self-finalization of the project, started by Archigram and Hollein at the beginning of the sixties. The interest moves from the instrumental and technical significance of the visual image of a certain object, to the self-significance of the same visual data; or better, to the significance of the image in relation to a specific concept or to a sequence of theoretical assertion' ('Superstudio & Radicals' in *Architecture radicale* 336).

20 The Monumento Continuo is a gridded volumetric structure that has lost any 'architecturability' of its volumetric scaffolding. The Superstudio rebellion is a further step in the avant-garde, far removed from other visionary architectures proposed only ten years earlier by artists/architects such as Yona Friedman and Constant. In these Superstudio drawings there is no possibility of a flexible mobile scaffolding like that proposed by Friedman in his *L'architecture Mobile* (1956). Jean-Luis Cohen comments that, for Friedman, cities: 'must be an intensification of existing cities,' intensified with unpredictable and colourful mobile skeletons. With his utopist *Ville spatiale* Friedman proposed superstructures that aim at more freedom for the users. As Cohen emphasizes, 'His *Paris Spatial* and other projects from that period, variable combinations of sublime technology and picturesque urbanism conveyed with a remarkable graphic virtuosity, expressed a desire for complexity that contrasted sharply with the simplicity of most Utopias of the 1960s ... The result was a depth of urbanism whose stratification appeared to evolve from a democratic process, but which certainly read more as randomness, and which in any case integrated the hypothesis of permanent

change' (7). Superstudio, on the contrary, with the Monumento Continuo insisting on Modern Movement pushes the aspects of the utopianism of the 1960s to the opposite side, that of immobile definitive planning where there is no space for change. The Monumento Continuo is the antithesis of the skeletal megastructures drawn and described by Friedman.

21 'Proposte per una semiologia dell'architettura' was also part of an ongoing discussion on landscape as found in the special issue of the journal *Edilizia moderna* (87–8) edited by Gregotti. Gregotti eventually expanded this research in *Il territorio dell'architettura.*

22 'The notion of landscape here used is one that contains a carefully calculated ambiguity: even though in this issue we shall treat the geographic dimension, this will form only one example of our idea of landscape as aggregation of elements – but nonetheless a particularly significant example and precursor of a possibly new method of discussing the problem of the formal structure of architecture. This method makes no claim to being unitary at an operative level but, on the contrary, aims to specify methods and formal optics at the various levels. Thus, given the dimensional level in question, it will first have to be established to what extent the problems of territorial planning, seen in the light of the special issues of formalization that they involve, have generically re-cast the spatial problem of architecture at all dimensional levels and, specifically, at the geographical level; the second matter that has to be dealt with is the elaboration of special operative instruments for the various dimensional levels, beginning from the aforesaid geographical dimension' (Gregotti, 'Il territorio dell'architettura' 149).

23 In 1968 Menna wrote a reexamination of the avant-garde and the Modern Movement as a condition where uprootedness and involvement are in tension: 'L'avanguardia e il movimento moderno quindi sono rivisti da quest'angolazione e le loro poetiche riproposte sulla base della forza d'urto che esse presentano ancora oggi grazie alla loro determinante componente utopica e alla prospettiva di una società dominata dal fattore estetico: una profezia il cui proprio sviluppo della tecnologia moderna e le previsioni di un possibile prossimo avvento di una società post-industriale sembrano conferire probabilità e vigore.' [The Avant-Garde and the Modern Movement therefore are revisited from this perspective and their poetics are suggested again on the basis of the shock value that they still have today thanks to their determinant utopian component and to the perspective of a society ruled by aesthetics: a prophecy to which the advance of modern technology and the expectations of a immanent advent of a post-industrial society seem to grant probability and vigour.] (*Profezia di una società estetica* 37).

24 The connection that I pose between Superstudio and Antonioni can also be defined as a time of 'mal-être' as analyzed by Bernard Stiegler in *La technique et le temps 3.*

25 I cannot here expand on the different scales considered by Superstudio. Superstudio would experiment with this single design in small, medium and large scales, an indifference of scale prophetically discussed by Andrea Branzi in one of his editorial 'Radical Notes' of *Casabella,* and later re-elaborated by Rem Khoolaas in *S, M, L, XL.* Superstudio's catalogue of *Istogrammi* objects, orthogonal and white with black grids, became a series of furniture designed for Zanotta that is still on the market. 'We prepared a catalogue of three-dimensional, non-continuous diagrams, a catalogue of architectural histograms with reference to a grid interchangeable into different areas or scales for the construction of a serene and immobile Nature in which finally to recognize yourself. From the catalogue of histograms many objects have since been effortlessly generated: furniture, environments, architecture' (Superstudio, 'Histogram' 114). The same implacable logic of the grid was applied to a series of houses for the catalogue of villas. 'To project a villa is an inexistent problem: modern architecture has already solved all relative problems, and on the other hand, has demonstrated its social and functional absurdity. However, it remains for young architects, one of the few occasions for actually projecting architecture (at least in Italy). Thus, refusing to consider the personal problems of the clients and trying to think solely of a serene life and a happy construction seen in the light of the small piece of the larger construction that is "the system of architecture" we have compiled a *Catalogue of Villas.* This includes four series: "Suburban Villas," "Villas by the Sea," "Villas in the Mountains," "Great Italian Villas."' (Superstudio, 'The Single Design' 110).

26 Roberts writes: 'If we reconsider Smithson's work of this period in terms of the discourse of hyperspace, we find that it is full of formal, temporal, and optical motifs long associated with hyperspatial puzzles. These include an appeal to simultaneity and stillness, a rejection of perspectival representation, the use of mirrors or shadows as indicators, and the construction of ill- or a-logical structures' (53).

27 Ambasz schematizes three main attitudes: conformist, reformist, and contestation. Among the designers invited were: Gae Aulenti, Ettore Sottsass, Joe Colombo, Alberto Rosselli, Marco Zanuso, Richard Sapper, Mario Bellini, Gaetano Pesce, Ugo La Pietra, Archizoom, Superstudio, Gruppo Sturm, Enzo Mari, Giannantonio Mari, and Gruppo 9999.

28 The film *Supersurface* reminds us of the questions addressed by Jonathan Crary in *Techniques of the Observer*: for example, 'In what ways is subjectivity

becoming a precarious condition of interface between rationalized systems of exchange and networks of information?' (2).

29 Several architects were asked to design an 'environment' for the MOMA exhibition. Superstudio presented as a conceptual model, 'Life; Supersurface.' They were given, Sander Woertman writes, 'a space of 8 x 8 meters that they were allowed to provide with a "programme." With the help of mirrors that covered the walls and a white floor covered with a black grid, Superstudio created an endless "supersurface." In each corner of the wall of mirrors stood a box with wires. Due to the reflection, this 'plug' seemed to extend across a supersurface in a regular grid. No furniture, cabinets or any other objects were presented in the space' ('Distant Winking' 152).

30 The voice-over says: 'Una signora di nostra conoscenza è diventata isterica a sentire tutta questa storia e ha detto detto: figuratevi se ho voglia di fare a meno del mio aspirapolvere e del tosa-erba, e del ferro da stiro, e della lavatrice, e del frigo, e del vaso coi fiori, dei libri, dei bijoux, della bambola e dei vestiti! Pardonissima signora! Si porti pure tutto quello che vuole, anzi s'attrezzi un'isola felice con tutta la sua mercanzia.' [A lady of our acquaintance became hysterical on hearing all this story and said: I certainly have no intention of doing without my vacuum-cleaner and the mowing machine, and the electric iron and the washing machine and the refrigerator, and the vase full of flowers, the books, my costume jewellery, doll, and clothes! Whatever you say madam! Just take whatever you like, or rather equip a happy island for yourself with all your goods] ('Vita' 49; 'Life' 182).

31 My translation; this text is not included in the English version of the script.

32 The most complete and critical analysis of radical architecture's jungle to date is without doubt, Rouillard's *Superarchitecture: le futur de l'archtecture 1950–1970* (2004).

33 Menna clearly defines this debate, in which he was involved, with documentation from various symposia and publications; see 'A Design for New Behaviors.'

WORKS CITED

Ambasz, Emilio, ed. *Italy, The New Domestic Landscape: Achievements and Problems of Italian Design.* Exhibition catalogue. New York: Museum of Modern Art, 1972.

Architecture radicale. Exhibition catalogue. Orléans: HYX, 2001.

Bardeschi, Marco Dezzi. 'Leonardo Savioli: una metodologia di progettazione.' *Marcatré* 26–9 (1966): 36–72.

Barilli, Renato, and Angelo Guglielmi, eds. *Gruppo 63: critica e teoria.* Turin: Feltrinelli, 2003.

Barabski, Zygmunt G., and Robert Lumley, eds. *Culture and Conflict in Postwar Italy: Essays on Mass and Popular Culture.* New York: St. Martin's Press, 1990.

Benjamin, Walter. *The Arcades Project.* Trans. Howard Eiland and Kevin McLaughlin. Prepared on the basis of the German volume edited by Rolf Tiedmann. Cambridge: Belknap Press of Harvard University Press, 1999.

Borradori, Dario. 'Nozione di progettualità.' *Marcatré* 37–40 (1968): 122–4.

Branzi, Andrea. 'Introduzione.' Paola Navarone and Bruno Orlandoni, *Architettura radicale.* 7–15.

– 'Radical Notes.' *Casabella* 379 (1973): 12.

Brunette, Peter. *The Films of Michelangelo Antonioni.* Cambridge: Cambridge University Press, 1998.

Bruno, Giuliana. *Atlas of Emotion: Journeys in Art, Architecture, and Film.* New York: Verso, 2002.

The Changing of the Avant-garde: Visionary Architectural Drawings from the Howard Gilman Collection. Catalogue for exhibition organized by Terence Riley. New York: Museum of Modern Art, 2002.

Cohen, Jean-Louis. 'In the Shade of Planned Cities.' In Sabine Lebesque and Helene Fentener van Vlissingen, eds. *Yona Friedman: Structures Serving the Unpredictable.* Rotterdam: NAi Publishers, 1999.

Colomina, Beatriz. 'Enclosed by Images: The Eameses' Multimedia Architecture.' *Grey Room* 2 (Winter 2001): 5–29.

Crary, Jonathan. *Techniques of the Observer: On Vision and Modernity in the Nineteenth Century.* Cambridge, Mass.: MIT Press, 1990.

Eco, Umberto. *Appunti per una semiologia delle comunicazioni visive.* Firenze: Bompiani, 1967.

– *Opera Aperta.* 1962. Milan: Bompiani, 1988.

– 'Proposte per una semiologia dell'architettura.' *Marcatré* 34/35/36 (1967): 58–76.

Gregotti, Vittorio. 'Il territorio dell'architettura.' *Edilizia moderna* 87–88 (1966): 1–146.

– *Il territorio dell'architettura.* Milan: Feltrinelli, 1966.

Jencks, Charles. 'The Supersensualists.' *Casabella* 6 (1971): 345–8.

Koolhaas, Rem. *S, M, L, XL.* New York: Monacelli Press, 1995.

Lang, Peter. 'Suicidal Desires.' In Lang and Menking, eds. *Superstudio: Life without Objects.* 31–51.

Lang, Peter, and William Menking, eds. *Superstudio: Life without Objects.* Milan: Skira, 2003.

Lavin, Sylvia, Helene Furján, and Penelope Dean, eds. *Crib Sheets: Notes on the Contemporary Architectural Conversation.* New York: Monacelli Press, 2005.

Menna, Filberto. 'A Design for New Behaviors.' In Ambasz, ed. *Italy, The New Domestic Landscape.* 405–14.

– *Profezia di una società estetica: saggio sull'avanguardia artistica e sul movimento dell'architettura moderna.* 1968. Enlarged and revised by Barbara Cirillo. Milan: Modo, 2001.

Natalini, Adolfo, ed. *Superstudio: Storie con figure 1966–1982.* Milan: Electa, 1982.

Navarone, Paola, and Bruno Orlandoni. *Architettura radicale.* Documenti di Casabella. Segrate: G. Milani, 1974.

Pagliarani, Elio. 'Per una definizione dell'avanguardia.' In Renato Barilli and Angelo Guglielmi, eds. *Gruppo 63: critica e teoria.* 2nd ed. Turin: Feltrinelli, 2003. 312–17.

Perloff, Marjorie. *The Futurist Moment: Avant-garde, Avant guerre, and the Language of Rupture.* Chicago: University of Chicago Press, 1986.

Pettena, Gianni, ed. *Radicals, architettura e design 1960–75 / Radicals, Design and Architecture 1960–75.* Trans. Stefania Coppi et al. Exhibition catalogue. Florence: Il Ventilabro, 1996.

– *Superstudio, 1966–1982: storie, figure, architettura.* Exhibition catalogue. Florence: Electa Firenze, 1982.

Rinaldi, Marco. *La casa elettrica e il caleidoscopio: temi e stile dell'allestimento in Italia dal razionalismo alla neoavanguardia.* Rome: Bagatto Libri, 2003.

Roberts, Jennifer L. *Mirror-Travels: Robert Smithson and History.* New Haven: Yale University Press, 2004.

Rouillard, Dominique. *Superarchitecture: Le futur de l'architecture 1950–1970.* Paris: Éditions de la Villette, 2004.

Savioli, Leonardo. *Ipotesi di spazio.* Florence: G. & G. Editrice, 1972.

Savioli, Leonardo, and Adolfo Natalini. 'Spazio di coinvolgimento.' *Casabella* 326 (1968): 32–46.

Scott, Felicity D. 'Involuntary Prisoners of Architecture.' *October* 106 (2003): 75–101.

– 'Italian Design and the New Political Landscape.' In Micheal Sorkin, ed. *Analyzing Ambasz.* New York: Monacelli Press, 2004. 109–56.

Sparke, Penny. '"A Home for Everybody?" Design, Ideology, and the Culture of the Home in Italy, 1945–1972.' In Baranski and Lumley, eds. *Culture and Conflict in Postwar Italy.* 225–41.

Stiegler, Bernard. *La technique et le temps 3: le temps du cinéma et la question du mal-être.* Paris: Galileé, 2001.

Superstudio. 'Design d'evasione e d'invenzione.' *Domus* 476 (1969): 28–33. English translation. 'Invention Design and Evasion Design.' In Jean Ockman, ed. *Architecture Culture 1943–1968: A Documentary Anthology.* New York: Rizzoli, 1993. 438–441.

– 'Histogram.' In Lang and Menking, eds. *Superstudio: Life without Objects.* 114–15.
– 'Monumento Continuo.' In Lang and Menking, eds. *Superstudio: Life without Objects.* 122–47.
– 'The Single Design: Histograms, Villas, Monuments.' In Lang and Menking, eds. *Superstudio: Life without Objects.* 110–13
– 'Viaggio nelle regioni della ragione.' *Domus* 479 (1969): 38–43.
– 'Vita (o dell'immagine pubblica dell'architettura veramente moderna: Supersuperficie (un modello alternative di vita sulla terra).' In Adolfo Natalini, ed. *Storie con figure 1966–73.* Florence: Galleria Vera Biondi, 1979. 45–53. English translation. 'Life: Supersurface, An Alternative Model of Life on Earth.' In Lang and Menking, eds. *Superstudio: Life without Objects.* 180–83.
Tafuri, Manfredo. *Progetto e utopia: architettura e sviluppo capitalistico.* Bari: Laterza, 1973. English translation: *Architecture and Utopia: Design and Capitalist Development.* Trans. Barbara Luigi La Penta. Cambridge, Mass.: MIT Press, 1976.
– *Storia dell'architettura italiana: 1944–1985.* Turin: Einaudi, 1982. English translation. *History of Italian Architecture, 1944–1985.* Trans. Jessica Levine. Cambridge, Mass.: MIT Press, 1989.
Tredicesima triennale di Milano: il tempo libero. Milan: La Triennale, 1964.
UFO. 'Effimero Urbanistico. Scala 1/1, gli U.F.O.' *Marcatré* 37/38/39/40 (1968): 198–209.
– 'GLI UFO. URBOEFFIMERI AVVENIMENTI 1:1.' *Marcatré* 41/42 (1968): 52–91.
Weber, Samuel. 'Double Take: Acting and Writing in Genet's "The Strange Word Urb."' In *Theatricality as Medium.* New York: Fordham University Press, 2004. 295–312.
Wigley, Mark. 'Post-Operative History.' *Any* 25/26 (2000): 47–53.
Woertman, Sander. 'The Distant Winking of a Star, or the Horror of the Real.' *Exit Utopia: Architectural Provocation 1956–1976.* Munich: Prestel Verlag, 2005.

Contributors

Laura Chiesa	SUNY Buffalo
Paolo Chirumbolo	Louisiana State University
Silvia Contarini	Université Paris X – Nanterre
Monica Jansen	Universiteit Antwerpen
Mario Moroni	SUNY Binghamton
Florian Mussgnug	University College London
Francesco Muzzioli	Università di Roma 'La Sapienza'
John Picchione	York University
Lucia Re	University of California Los Angeles
Luca Somigli	University of Toronto
Paolo Somigli	Università di Bolzano
Rebecca West	University of Chicago